CW01467806

The History of the Papal States, from Their Origin to the Present Day, Volume I

John Miley D.D.

BIBLIOLIFE

THE HISTORY OF THE PAPAL STATES,

FROM THEIR

ORIGIN TO THE PRESENT DAY.

BY

THE REV. JOHN MILEY, D.D.

AUTHOR OF

"ROME UNDER PAGANISM AND THE POPES."

IN THREE VOLUMES.

VOL. I.

LONDON:

T. C. NEWBY, 30, WELBECK STREET,

CAVENDISH SQUARE.

1850.

CONTENTS OF VOLUME I.

INTRODUCTION.

§ 1. TERRITORY OF THE PAPAL STATES.

§ 2. DISTRICT OF RIETI AND TERNI.

§ 3. GENERAL VIEW OF THE ROMAN PROVINCE.

§ 6. THE SABINE, LATIN, AND ETRUSCAN LANDS.

§ 7. THE PONTINE MARSHES.

§ 8. Valley of the Sacco.

§ 9. VALLEY OF THE ANIO.

§ 10. CAMPAGNA DI ROMA.

§ 11. ROME.

THE HISTORY OF THE PAPAL STATES.

BOOK I.

The Papal Sovereignty.

BOOK II.

History of the Papal City.

INDEX.

B

C

D

G

H

R

T.

PREFACE.

In the volumes now placed before the public, the reader will find the attempt for the first time made to give a history of the Papal States,—to do that which hitherto has been left altogether undone. Such is the author's apology—his sole, and he hopes, it may be regarded as his sufficient apology, for the three volumes now issued from the press.

Histories of the Roman Catholic Church, there are, of all sorts, in every dialect and in every form; and though the same cannot be said of the History of the Popes, (there being, as yet, no work that properly deserves that name), nevertheless, the series of Papal biography may be regarded as complete, and works of rare merit, produced within the present century to illustrate the lives and times of those amongst the Pontiffs who make the greatest figure in history, have, on that subject, also, left but comparatively little to be desired. A history, however, of that region of Central Italy,—of that realm over which the Popes have swayed the sceptre for more than a thousand years, one may search for in vain. In no language, dead or living, in no shape,—whether of a consecutive narrative or as a digest of materials,—under no title, is any such work to be met with.

From the importance and rare attractions of the subject, it may well be matter of surprise, it is true, that such a theme should have been so long overlooked or so utterly neglected; nevertheless, let the question be put to the most eminent Bibliopolists of London, Paris, Vienna, Rome,—their answer will be—there is no such book as a History of the Papal States. Make the round of the great libraries, from the British Museum to the Vatican, the answer will be still the same.

It is not, therefore, as an improvement on any pre-existing work that these volumes are, with great respect and diffidence, and with a most oppressive sense of their faults and defects, presented to the public. Had the subject been pre-occupied in any form, it is all but certain this work should never have appeared. But, as it is, it meddles with no prescriptive title; it does not aspire to oust any one already in possession, or to supersede any other book, through assumption of superior excellence. The theme on which he has ventured to dilate, the author found not only untenanted, but unclaimed. Like a waif, or a *bonum direlictum*, to use the Roman phrase, it was found thrown by and unheeded beside the great thoroughfare of letters: the circumstances adverted to a little further on, attracted his attention to it, and prompted him to pick it up, conceiving that such neglect was not the fate it merited.

His pretensions, as to what he has been able to effect, are of the humblest character. Like one who has been the first to attempt the reclamation of a vast and teeming solitude, to gather its wandering tribes and marshal them according to the principles of social order and polity, his aim has been rather to clear the ground for future enterprise than to bring it at once to the highest state of culture. He was conscious he possessed no magic-wand that, on a sudden, could metamorphose a howling wilderness into a paradise; but he has done a good deal in the way of those preliminaries, without which, the genius even of a Michael Angelo could not proceed with a supestructure. The foundations of the history he has excavated, thoroughly: he flatters himself, he has made some approximation to the proper plan. That, (beginning in the Catacombs and closing with the Earl Mount-Edgcumbe's pamphlet), he has searched up, collected, sifted, and reduced to something like order and appropriate grouping, an immense mass of solid, authentic materials, he has no shadow of doubt whatever.

But when it is asserted, that, up to A.D. 1850, there was no such book as a History of the Papal States; is it affirmed or sought to be insinuated, that the annals of that singular realm have been allowed to remain in a condition analagous to that, in which it is the wont of the general run of tourists to inform their readers they found the *Campagna di Roma* and the Pontine Marshes, when they posted through them at a rapid pace? So far is this from being the case, that it is, we feel persuaded, to the minute and laborious attention of which the history of this most wonderful section, even of Italy, has been made the object, that the strange and startling deficiency alluded to, is, in a great degree, to be attributed. The Papal States' annals so far from being neglected, have been cultivated in the greatest detail, and the result has been such an abundant harvest of books, that no one library could contain the volumes. The longest life would be too short to peruse them all. In short, no other region of the world is so rich as the Papal States, in *local* histories. "In these states," says Sismondi, "no ancient city is to be found that has not had three or four historians at least, very frequently more; and the more voluminous he is, and the more the historian enters into details, the higher rises the interest of his book over those of his fellows. The Biographical History of the Pontifical States, contains, in a thick quarto volume, *the names only* of the local historians of seventy-one cities, still existing in the States of the Church, and of sixteen which have perished. MANY CENTURIES OF ASSIDUOUS READING," he adds, "WOULD NOT GET THROUGH THEM ALL."*

Thus do we find the immemorial destiny of Italy—both socially and politically considered,—most faithfully and significantly mirrored forth in

* Histoire des Repub. Ital. t. ii. p. 385. The title of the work alluded to by Sismondi, is Bibliographica Storica delle Città e luoghi dell' Stato Pontificio. Roma, 1792, 1 vol. 4to.

its history. It abhors amalgamation. Its parts instinctively repel each other: they will brook no unity that threatens to swallow up their separate identity. The centres of light in Italy are innumerable. Each city is a sun in itself; it has its own system, and forms a little universe *in se.* Each village of Central Italy possesses a perfect Iliad of memories of its own, of which it is so proud and in its admiration of which it is so thoroughly self-satisfied, that it has but little desire to exchange all this for the chance ray or patch of the general sunshine that might fall to the lot of its comparative obscurity in the grouping of a general history. Indeed, a general civil history of Italy, except during the epoch of Roman centralization, is hardly possible. What, after all, is Sismondi's work, or Botta's, but a congeries of entirely distinct histories, with but little in common beyond the uniformity of style and being bound up in the same collection of volumes, under the same title? On the other hand, what else have we in the works of Titus Livius, of Tacitus, or Florus, but histories of Roman domination, in which Italy and the world are the accessories of a single city? But to whatever cause we are to assign it, the fact is as we have stated;—fertile as are the Papal States, even to superabundance, in *local* histories; as a realm, as an aggregate of provinces united under the same sceptre, they are to this day unrepresented in history.

The present writer was not a little surprised and

disappointed, on perceiving, for the first time, this singular *lacune* in the world of letters. Happening to be at Rome in the year 1833, for the recovery of his health, he occupied his leisure with some studies and researches as to the contrasts and reciprocal relations of Rome under Paganism and under the Popes: in the course of these studies he became sensible of the deficiency referred to; and although the idea of attempting to supply it did not for a moment so much as cross his mind, and was never seriously thought of by him until a very recent period, nevertheless, such odds and ends of leisure, as the active duties of a missionary career in Ireland left within his reach, were from that time to the present so assiduously devoted in investigating the sources of what he ever regarded as a branch of the human annals as momentous as it is extraordinary, that when he was prompted by recent events in Rome to actually set foot, in the way of composition, on the untrodden region, he found that his materials—in the form of notes, and extracts, and sketches—had so accumulated for the entire cycle of two thousand years, that the chief difficulty to be contended with in the attempt to execute his task, was, not to discover materials for his book, but to compress those he had ready at hand into something of a reasonable compass. And, notwithstanding all his efforts, the two slim octavos which, in his inexperience, he had pictured to his imagination as the utmost his book was to extend to, have swelled into three,—the two last of which transgress a little the standard allowance of pages. When it is, however, considered that the immense lapse of eighteen centuries was to be embraced, and that the whole subject from the origin of the history to the present day should be, and has been, one way or another, brought within the three volumes, the slight trespass as to dimensions may, it is hoped, be leniently dealt with.

As for the authorities from whence the narrative is derived, copious and numerous as are the local histories, there were many other sources to be resorted to. The Papal biographies, (mostly by contemporary writers, and, with the exception of a *lacune* in the tenth century, forming an uninterrupted series from the Apostolic age to the seventeenth century,) have not only been consulted, but have been laid under contribution very largely, particularly for the Carlovingian epoch,—a period for which they are fortunately rather more graphic and comprehensive than for any preceding one, since they are not to say the richest but almost the only source. Another field of research, indispensable as it is immense, was found in the Ecclesiastical Annals, carried down to the twelfth century by Baronius, and, by his successive continuators, to the eighteenth. When to these we add the works of Muratori,—his Annals of Italy, his Dissertations, his Antiquities, above all his majestic collection of the *Rerum Italicarum Scriptores*, the works of Sigonius and the Thesaurus of Grævius; though, for what may be termed the rudimental and mediæval epochs, we have the chief sources of the history, we have not by any means embraced them all. For the history of the Papal city, for instance—which of necessity must occupy the centre foreground of the canvass in the *tableaux* of nearly every one of the successive cycles, into which the entire history divides itself,—a great deal of the materials must be sought after in various other quarters. Thus, the curious guide or description of the Eternal City, in A. D. 800, which we give *in extenso*, is not to be met with in any of the works already mentioned. It was first brought to light by Mabillon, and is to be found only in his works. Indeed, as might easily be anticipated, the writers on the City of Rome, from the ancient Itineraries down to the late Professor Nibbi, form of themselves a goodly catalogue. Then the erudite disquisitions as to the origin, the limits, and the character of the Papal Sovereignty, from Cardinal Orsis's Dissertations to the very admirable work, Pouvoir du Pape, &c. form another important branch. For the Codex Carolinus, and the diplomas of all the dynasties, from the Carlovingians to the House of Hapsburgh, the exceedingly scarce collection of the Abbate Cenni must be resorted to. In addition, there are several pieces appertaining to the subject in Duchesne, in the *Rerum Germanicarum Scrip-*

tores, and even in the old English monastic writers: and, though in some instances, these have been transferred to his collection by Muratori, such is not the case with many others, and with certain important fragments in the *Acta Sanctorum* of the Bollandists. Besides these, there are some documents which may be called incidental, such as the Homilies and Epistles of St. Gregory and several of the suc ceeding Popes; the letters of Petrarch and Dante's poem. Moreover, we are carried no farther by these authorities, than the confines of modern times, or to the close of the fifteenth century,—where we have to look out for a new corps of guides, as the old ones drop off from us, one by one.

The researches made by Ranke in the Viennese and Venetian Archives, and in those of the princely families at Rome, have brought to light some highly interesting records for this history, from the opening of the sixteenth, to a late period in the eighteenth, century. Besides these, rich gleanings are still left, which it is to be hoped will not be overlooked by the Chevalier Artaud de Mentor, in his anxiously looked-for history of the Popes. It has been in our power unfortunately to add but little—only four MSS. in all—to these hitherto unpublished sources. The first consists of extracts from a Vatican Codex, containing a family history of the Counts of Tusculum. It has enabled us to shed some additional rays of light on the murk of the tenth century. The second is a MS. from the Archives of Monte Casino—it is a terse and ably written report on the "lapse of Ferrara,"—drawn up by one who played a leading part in a transaction, highly interesting in itself, and of the greatest importance within the sphere of this history. It will be found in the fourth Appendix to this volume. The third MS. is a very curious and minute survey of the boundaries of Romagna, or Romaniola, as it was more commonly called. It is also from the same Archives of Monte Casino, and is given *in extenso* in the same Appendix. Both these hitherto unpublished documents are in the Italian language, as is also the Vatican Codex to which we have referred. The fourth MS. is in English and of a much more modern date. It is the diary of a personage who was resident at Rome, from the Autumn of 1828 to the Summer of 1832; we have quoted it largely for the reign of Gregory XVI., and regret greatly that our limits did not permit us to make a much more extensive use of it.

Except in the sources thus briefly indicated, it will be vain to seek materials for the genuine history of the Papal States. In no one modern work, nor in all the modern works appertaining to Italian history put together, are we able to find the substance of even the most meagre epitome of the history of which we treat.

To say nothing of the other grounds of disqualification established against him in the third volume of this work, Sismondi, for instance, cannot supply it,—because the Papal sovereignty has already passed through at least three centuries of development—according to Gibbon's theory, it has passed through four centuries—at the point of departure for Sismondi.—The third volume of this history starts from the same point with Sismondi's History of the Italian Republics. Of course the same objection tells with still greater force against Ranke's work, which opens at a date four or five hundred years lower down than Sismondi's. Moreover, anything beyond an incidental reference to the subject of the Papal States' history was justly regarded as alien to their object by both these very accomplished, but far from unprejudiced, writers. The same is to be said—the *intensity* of prejudice alone excepted—of both Giannone and Botta. The two concluding chapters of the History of the Decline and Fall of the Roman Empire are devoted to this subject; it is also frequently introduced in the earlier chapters, and always with Gibbon's characteristic mastery of erudition, as well as perversity of genius. Nevertheless, if, with Gibbon, Giannone, Botta, Sismondi, Ranke, we combine the historians who in the present age have so splendidly illustrated the lives and times of some of the most renowned of the Pontiffs—such as Voight, Hock, Hurter, De Falloux, Artaud, and others, we shall still be at a loss for the civil history of the Pontifical States. Thus, the second volume of this work begins with the memorable year 800, it closes with another memorable year 1122; it runs to 648 pages, replete with matter.—Now, we venture to assert that all that can be found in all the works enumerated, will not, for the same period, (with reference to the Papal States' history), make up a chapter, or in fact, more than a few paragraphs; and that in almost every sentence of these few paragraphs, some important error may be pointed out. For instance, in Voight's most able and admirable History of Hildebrand and his Age, the matter appertaining to our subject does not quite fill two loosely-printed octavo pages. Out of Hurter's still more able and celebrated history of Innocent III., in three volumes, there are only two chapters relating to our subject, but these are excellent. Yet any one who will compare these chapters—able as they are—with the original sources from which they are derived, will be convinced that the time devoted to secondary sources—where it is not only possible but easy to resort to the fountain-head, may be considered as time almost worse than misspent,—we mean, of course, where there is question, not of perusing, but of throwing any new light on history.

An idea sufficiently clear and comprehensive—with respect to the author's mode of viewing his subject, may be conveyed in a very few words, on each of its two great constituent features, *viz.*, the theatre of the events, and the drama which these events compose.

And first, as to the theatre of the events: we have not hesitated to lay great stress on the description of it, in its entire extent, and in great detail. We have endeavoured, in short, to place it in every light that we thought could help the reader to feel himself perfectly at home in the territory, and to carry with him, throughout, a conception as vivid and truthful as possible, of the scenery and other accessory circumstances of peculiarity, in the midst of which the historic actions and occurrences take place.

We are thoroughly sensible that 185 pages of introductory matter, instead of being an inducement to readers to enter on the perusal of the volumes, may prove an insuperable barrier for many; and yet we felt convinced, from maturely weighing the subject, that it was due not only to the history, but to those who take any interest in it, not to curtail that introduction by a single section.

For, if it be at all a legitimate object of history,—as it most undoubtedly is a lofty and important object,—in some sort to reproduce the successive generations, events, and revolutions of which it treats, and cause them once more, with as much as possible of life-like circumstance, to pass before the imagination of the reader, how is this effect to be obtained, if the *dramatis personæ* are introduced on any sort of platform, no matter how common-place, without heeding in the least whether the scenery harmonize, or be at variance, with the characters that play their parts? If the imagery appropriate to the age, the climate, manners, costume,—in a word, to whatever belongs to the outward aspect of things in the midst of which the scene is laid, be deemed indispensable to the drama in its lowest, and but too often, most demoralizing state, are these accessories to be slighted when there is question, not of the paltry and ephemeral creations of human fancy, but of that drama for which the whole world is but a stage, and of which the great Creator and Disposer of events is Himself the Author?

But be this as it may in other cases, in the one of which there is question at present, the omission of the scenery peculiar to the drama of the history would not be the mere forfeiture of an embellishment, but the lopping off of an attribute essentially belonging to the subject, and deprived of which it cannot be thoroughly comprehended. The territory under consideration is *monumental*, throughout its entire extent, and in every part. It is, in itself, and independently of every other, an immense, most luminous, and most curiously-noted historical document. Nothing can be more just, as applied to the entire, than what Chateaubriand has so beautifully said of a part of it—" Le voyageur trouvera pour société, une terre qui nourrira ses reflections, et qui occupera son cœur. Car la pierre qu' il foulera au pied lui parlera, et la poussiere qui le vent élévera sous ses pas renfermera quelque grandeur humaine."

A reflection that was expressed in another form by the Abbé Barthélemy, when he said, that "in Rome the stones were more learned than the men of other countries."

No other region of the whole world resembles this region of Central Italy. It has been the common scene for two acts of the human drama, the grandest in themselves, the most sharply hostile and contrasted in spirit, object, origin; and yet, as indissolubly united, and as reciprocally essential in bringing out the meaning the Supreme Author intended to convey to us through them, as are the two hostile members of the same antithesis. The history, which we have before us, stands alone in this, that it has a background of two thousand years, and any view of it, no matter how elaborate in other respects, that fails to bring out clearly that perspective to the mind's eye, is as far as a Chinese landscape painting from being a delineation truthfully reflecting the scene it attempts to depict. Now, whoever may think fit to encounter the task of reading the introductory sections, will have a sufficiently pellucid view of the whole background of the Papal States' history, and in recompense of his toil—though he may have never travelled beyond the frontiers of the parish in which he was born,—will be able to form a more comprehensive, distinct, and truthful conception of the real aspect and condition of this most famous region of Italy than a great many who have not only travelled through it, but who afterwards published books to enlighten (as they fancied) the world respecting it. We speak thus confidently on this part of the work, because it is taken, to a great extent, from the report of a personal survey made by the Count de Tournon, when he was Prefect of Rome and its province, under Napoleon.

At the same time, we are far from insisting that, before the introduction has been read, the narrative itself cannot well or advantageously be entered on. We know, on the contrary, that for vast numbers such a perusal would be, perhaps, a waste of time, their previous acquaintance with the classic history of Rome, and with the other topics treated of in the introduction, precluding the necessity for any such perusal. But, as every class was to be consulted for, and the aim of making the work complete in itself rather than in any relative sense, was to be kept in view, the course adopted was thought to be the most suitable. While many without loss may pass the introduction and begin at once with the history, some may find a great advantage in passing through the former as a vestibule to the latter. Others, in fine, may prefer to look first through the body of the work, and then revert to those descriptive sections.

It is not alone as a great centre of the historic plot and the capital of the realm that Rome demands the most prominent place. The rise, the vicissitudes of the Papal City itself, are so to speak, the vertebræ of this history. On this account it has been one of the chief objects to investigate the records of the city, and not separately or beforehand, as in the case of the territory at large, but concomitantly with the current of events, to trace it from its origin among the ruins of its Pagan predecessor, through all its after vicissitudes; and these we are bold to say, were far more chequered and memorable than any book previously written on the subject would lead its readers to imagine.

Thus of the primitive city of the Popes (of which not one-tenth so many vestiges survive at present as of the Pagan city), the complete account and description will be found in the first volume of the work—while from the generality of works written on Rome, one could hardly collect that any such city had ever existed. The city of Hadrian I. and the other Popes of the Carlovingian epoch, lay as completely interred in the dusty records from which we have endeavoured to excavate it, as did Herculaneum under the lava, or Pompeii beneath the ashes, of Vesuvius, for many an age.

From the scenery, we pass to the drama itself, and of this it is sufficient to observe,—that, disengaging ourselves, at the outset, from a labyrinth of what we can only regard as technical litigation, with reference to the precise instant at which the

Popes became temporal sovereigns, we trace the tide of this dominion at once to its fountain-head; and in viewing it in its after development, we have endeavoured to throw ourselves into the centre of each of the great epochs or cycles into which its career, on being fully considered, is found to divide itself; and then, by grouping the figures and transactions round that centre, endeavour thus to bring the reader acquainted not only with the annals of this realm from century to century, or from cycle to cycle, but also to picture each epoch as to its own characteristic identity, without losing sight of the unity and harmonious relations pervading the entire plot, and combining all the separate cycles like so many acts of the same drama.

In several instances an entire epoch will be found to group itself around one dominant figure, as in the instance of St. Gregory the Great, of Leo III., of Hildebrand; but to this there are many and various exceptions. Thus, the epoch from Gregory the Great to Hadrian I., that is during the Lombard devastations to the opening of the Carlovingian æra, there is no central figure: it was a cycle of anarchy, and in its history there is consequently but little appearance of order. Again, in the Carlovingian epoch, it is the general aspect of things rather than any stirring action or dominant character that attracts our notice; because that was an epoch of singular tranquillity and happiness.

The felicity of the States and of Italy in general, during this Carlovingian period, is treated of at some length, and in much greater detail than in any other work we are aware of; the materials for the scenes being derived from the old monastic chronicles, richly tinted as they are with the hues of that period, in which were penned the statements, from which the later compilers of the 11th and 12th centuries derived them.

This Carlovingian period has been usually left so much in the shade, that the author has not hesitated to bring it thus prominently into the light. In no other way can a correct idea be formed of the convulsions out of which emerged the modern nations. For it is not accurate to say, that they arose from the break-up of the world of the Pagan Cæsars. Between that catastrophe and another, perhaps, still more terrific, there is intercalated another empire complete in itself—an empire which, as if for "an hour," gathers up again, and combines the elements of the Romanze and Barbaric nations in a majestic and singularly picturesque form of society, and one altogether unique. The autumnal lustre of the first empire, under the Antonines, did not surpass the lustre of that second empire, during its more rapid decline.

The concussions and scenes of terror, universal and unparalleled, in which that second Roman Empire, or Barbarico-Romanze world, was brought to the ground, dismembered, shattered,—and one may even add, broken to atoms,—comes next; and being in itself a most perfect chaos, admits of but little grouping or system. This terrific revolution plunges us into the weltering brutality and wildest confusion of the tenth century—*par excellence*, the "dark," the "iron" age. And here it is, and nowhere else, we are to look for the travail —an awful one—out of which emerged the modern nations; and from this point also the history of the Papal sovereignty is presented to us under a totally new and singular aspect. During this century, the Popes are much oftener slaves than sovereigns. They pass, by the most sudden and hideous reverses, at the beck of some tyrant, from the throne to the dungeon, there to be sometimes strangled or starved, but invariably tortured.

The Tusculum tyrants, and the Cenci, or Crescensii, are the dominant figures in this age, which they fill and render for ever infamous by their atrocities. Their tower of strength, and the great theatre of their cruelties and oppressive exactions on pilgrims, is the Fort of Sant' Angelo; but every high place among the Seven Hills, and all the strongest of the ruins of Rome are crowned with war towers, and every tower is a fortress of strong-handed robbers. A "reign of terror" was at that time the normal condition of Rome and its States, as well as of all the countries of the West without exception.

The bestowal of the Empire on the Germans, in the person of Otho the Great, by Pope John XII., is the opening of a new epoch, and in some degree prepares the way for Hildebrand.

As the appearance on the scene of this extraordinary personage is the opening of a new era, not only for the Papal States, the Papacy, and the Catholic Church, but for the civilized world at large, we have not hesitated to enter thoroughly into the investigation of his policy and character. The Papal system being singularly personified in Hildebrand, there seems to be a general impression with its opponents that to have it condemned, all that is necessary is to secure a verdict against this single but extraordinary representative of the whole dynasty. We have not shrunk from this issue; and the more fairly to test it—it is from one who seems to us to have more completely mastered the subject, as to research, than any other Protestant writer, and to be second to none in enforcing his views by a rhetoric the most versatile and dazzling,—it is from Sir James Stephen, we have taken the case as stated, *versus* Gregory VII., whilst we have left his vindication to what is said in letters allowed to contain the most hidden workings of his soul, and to his own immortal deeds, as recorded by his enemies. The new order of things originated by Hildebrand, so far as the Papacy itself is concerned, is generally allowed to have been carried to its culminating point in the Pontificate of Innocent III., a highly important one for our history.

Previously, however, to this Pontificate in the

civil history of Italy, and in the aspect of affairs in that region of it, with which we are more immediately concerned, a change of the most startling character takes place. A train of events stirring and memorable begins and is played out through the first act—the Pope and the German Kaisar, Alexander III. and Frederic Barbarossa, being by turns the dominant figures in the scenes: we allude, of course, to the desperate protracted and chequered struggles, out of which the Italian Republics take their rise. Contrary to the generally received impression, that Sismondi has made this epoch his own, we have ventured to suggest some reasons to shew that, as yet, the true history of the Italian Republics remains to be written. So far as one Pope is concerned, and the only English one that ever reigned, we have proved from Sismondi's treatment of an event of vital importance to the history of the Papal States, that he cannot be relied on as a trustworthy historian. On this epoch of Italian liberty, greatness, and prosperity, we have dilated to some extent; but, in apology for having done so, we can refer to its close connection with the subject in hand, and the paramount interest with which it is so justly regarded.

With the fourteenth century, a new and totally different era begins. The tiara so often seen to preponderate during a long series of ages is, with a few and not important exceptions, almost totally withdrawn from the canvas for a term of one hundred and fifty years. This entire period is full of reverses, feuds, disorders, and catastrophes of every kind. It is the epoch in which multifarious tyrannies usurp the place of liberty; in which internecine factions pave the way for petty despots; for "free companies;" Condotteri; universal anarchy; indescribable misery; degeneracy of the Italian character; and demoralization, shameless, profound, and except amongst the humble classes, all but universal. To this period may be literally applied the words of Tacitus, when in sketching a corresponding cycle of the Pagan era, he says that it was, *opimum casibus, atrox prœliis, discors seditionibus, ipsâ etiam pace sævum.*

A new and remarkable epoch is dated from the accession of Nicholas V. The modern city of Rome is founded amongst the ruins of the primitive and mediæval cities of the Popes; the States acquire a unity of organisation in which they continue to progress, rising,—*pari passu,* with the new and wonderful city, their capital, and privileged to a singular degree with the enjoyment of peace and prosperity, during a succession of three hundred and fifty years. Then comes the great social earthquake which not only shook all Europe to its lowest foundations, but was severely felt in parts of Africa and Asia,—and this, the French Revolution, gives rise to the series of events with which we are ourselves immediately connected.

In conformity with our general rule of devoting the greatest amount of care and space to the regions of the history that have been hitherto most neglected we have assigned to the transactions of the present century, and particularly to the late pontificate, what might under other circumstances appear to be more than their due proportion of the two hundred and fifty pages to which we found ourselves restricted after closing the epoch of Nicholas V. The chapter on the Carbonari, though derived from already accessible sources, will probably be new to many.

Having stated the motive that chiefly prompted him to attempt the composition of this history, the sources from which his materials are derived, and having given the foregoing very general outline of the manner in which he has treated the subject, the author feels every prop of confidence by which he has been hitherto sustained, give way, when he comes to consider the mere style and manner of composition in which he has executed his work. Nevertheless, of the many and singular disadvantages under which he laboured in this regard, only one shall be obtruded on the attention of his readers. It is this: at the outset, he found himself in this dilemma, either to commit to the flames the notes from which these volumes have been written, or to complete the task of composition, within six months.

The author being one of those drawn most deeply into the hideous vortex of misery, during the Irish famine of 1849, in the hope of rescuing some few at least of the myriads who were perishing, the composition of his work was interrupted, but, unfortunately, the printing of the first volume was not stopped so soon as it should have been. It was after two months of that species of occupation—the most harassing that can be well conceived to the feelings and mental faculties—that the second volume was commenced on the 15th of August, 1849; and until the postscript of the third was written on the 15th of January, 1850, the author's pastime consisted, exclusively, in the transition from the process of arranging his notes in something like a rude narrative to that very entertaining process of correcting the press.

Any literary work undertaken amid such difficulties, and carried on, despite of such adverse circumstances, could not at its conclusion be free from faults, and clear from error. The author cannot flatter himself that under the most favourable circumstances—with full time at his own disposal—with a year for every month that he has given to the composition of these volumes, and without having at the same moment the printer pressing him for copy and for corrected proofs, he should yet be able to give to the world a history of the Papal States to which just objections might not be urged, and a severe criticism not fittingly applied. No one can be more conscious than the author himself of the greatness of the labour, and the weakness of the workman; both but rendered more apparent by the impediments that served to aggravate the one, and to embarrass the other. The author was well aware from the first moment he sat down to write, what a struggle he had to make, what obstacles were in his way, what disadvantages were to be encountered and what difficulties to be overcome; and yet he persevered, because feeling that such a history as this ought to be written, he hoped he might at its conclusion be able to appeal to the candid and judicious, and that they would remember (whatever were its errors and defects), that the scene selected for his enterprise was, though a teeming, a hitherto untrodden region; that in preparing his materials, great labour and widely extended research must have been expended, and that the cast given to such materials was, in the main, correct.

The author has endeavoured to win for his toil such an admission as this. With its attainment all confidence in his performance ends—except, perhaps, that of being permitted to congratulate himself on having struck off the whole subject, he may say, at a heat,—immense as that subject is, and embracing as it does, either directly or indirectly, a period of three thousand years.

On the importance of the subject or its varied attractions to the lovers of history, it would be superfluous to dwell. No matter what may be a man's religious creed or his views on politics, who is there that is led into the paths of history in the hope of finding in its experience and its lessons a clue to disentangle the present or penetrate into the mysterious obscurity of the future, that can slight a history which constitutes the centre and *primum mobile* of a system, with regard to which the historian of modern England has written in the following terms?

"There is not," says Mr. Macaulay, "and there never was, on this earth a work of human policy so well deserving of examination as the Roman Catholic Church. The history of that Church joins together the two great ages of human civilization. No other institution is left standing which carries the mind back to the times when the smoke of sacrifice rose from the Pantheon, and when camel-leopards and tigers bounded in the Flavian amphitheatres. The proudest royal houses are but of yesterday, when compared with the line of Roman Pontiffs. That line we trace back in an unbroken series, from the Pope who crowned Napoleon in the nineteenth century, to the Pope who crowned Pepin in the eighth; and far beyond the time of Pepin the august dynasty extends till it is lost in the twilight of fable. The Republic of Venice came next in antiquity; but the Republic of Venice was modern when compared with the Papacy, and the Republic of Venice is gone, and the Papacy remains. The Papacy remains, not in decay—not a mere antique, but full of life and youthful vigour. The Catholic Church is still sending forth to the farthest ends of the world missionaries as zealous as those who landed in Kent with Augustus, and still confronting hostile kings with the same spirit with which she confronted Attila. The number of her children is greater than in any former age. Her acquisitions in the New World have more than compensated her for what she had lost in the old. Her spiritual ascendancy extends over the vast countries which lie between the Missouri and Cape Horn—countries which, a century hence, may not improbably contain a population as large as that which now inhabits Europe. The members of her communion are not less than a hundred and fifty millions, and it will be difficult to shew that all the other Christian sects united amount to a hundred and twenty millions. Nor do we see any sign that the term of her long dominion is approaching. She saw the commencement of all the governments, and of all the ecclesiastical establishments that now exist in the world, and we feel no assurance that she is not destined to see the end of them all. She was great and respected before the Saxon had set foot on Britain, before the French had passed the Rhine, when Grecian eloquence still flourished in Antioch, when idols were still worshipped in the Temple of Mecca; and she may still exist in undiminished vigour, when some traveller from New Zealand shall, in the midst of a vast solitude, take his stand on a broken arch of London Bridge, to sketch the ruins of St. Paul's."

Napoleon gave his estimate of the weight of the

Papacy in the European system, at a time when the Papacy had been brought as low as could be in mere human resources, by saying to M. Cacault his ambassador, when sending him to Rome, "Treat with the Pope as if he had two hundred thousand troops;" and the same ambassador writing to Talleyrand in 1802, does not hesitate to estimate the Papal forces at "five hundred thousand;" because, by that time, affairs at Rome were in better train than on his first arrival.* Talleyrand himself was of opinion that Rome would never cease to be a great centre of affairs—*que Rome sera toujours un centre d'affaires très-important.*†

Ere long it may become more evident even than it is at the present moment, that, if Europe is to be plunged into anarchy, in which the struggle is to be decided, not between rival forms of Government or rival parties, but as to whether Christianity or heathenism revived, is for the time to come to regulate the destinies of the hitherto civilized world, it will have so happened, because the history of the Pontifical States, in its decisively sympathetic connexion with the maintenance of the Christian state of society, was not appreciated by our leading statesmen as it deserved to be. What is passing in the instance of Pius IX; what occurred so late as the opening of the century which as yet has more than half its course to run, in the conflict

* Vid. Artaud's Pie VII. t. i. p. 355. Paris, 1837.

† Ib. p. 352.

between Napoleon and Pius VII, must be enough to convince the least reflecting that those fibres which vibrate most keenly in the hearts of all civilized nations, and which determine the course of the greatest and most complicated movements in politics, will, if traced with dispassionate care, be found to have, remotely at least, their common centre in that otherwise, perhaps, insignificant realm.

Again, if there be question of the class of historical readers, who are accustomed to follow the march of humanity, as the curious and the idle are attracted to a military review, or to some dramatic representation, how they are effectually to compass their object, if they evade the subject of which we are speaking, it is not very easy to see.

In the first place, not more strictly related are shadow and body, than are the two realms which in turn have wielded the sceptre on the banks of the Tiber. The power supposed to have been founded by Saint Peter, and that which was founded by Romulus cannot be comprehended, unless when studied in contrast, as acting and re-acting, the one on the other. Morally, prophetically, and most signally in an historical light, their dramatic connection is manifest. Moreover, the Papal-States-history is the only isthmus, if we may use such a phrase, by which it is possible to try back one's way from the social world of the present, into the world of ancient Pagan society. The roots of the one strike deep into the mass of ruins to which it saw its persecuting rival reduced.

Again, if he pass into the mediæval from the ancient world, how is the reader who neglects the Papal States' history, to form a correct idea of the social and international relations of Europe, during an era in which, whether rightly or wrongly, the fact was this, that the king of the realm in question was as decidedly at the head of the confederated States called Christendom, as is the American President at the head of the United States of North America at the present day. The drama of Hamlet, with the part of Hamlet omitted, is not a more glaring absurdity than a history of mediæval Europe, which has not the sovereign of these States, in its middle, beginning, and end.

"The history of Italy," says a modern writer, "from the restoration of the Roman empire to the fall of Napoleon, offers the advantage of a complete drama, which we are enabled to embrace in a single glance. The history of its literature from the earliest revival of civilization in the middle ages, down to the age of Leo X. can be fairly considered as the history of the progress of the human mind, in all the Christian world. The seeds of civil and religious liberty were first developed on Italian soil: all branches of industry and commerce, of letters and arts; had reached their meridian splendour in that country, two long centuries, ere a faint twilight began to break through the darkness that reigned on the other side of the Alps."*

No matter in which of these various lights the reader may consider the history of Italy—whether as to arts, or letters, or political revolutions, the potentates who are crowned with the tiara are still to be seen, in the foreground of the picture.

In fine, it is no exaggeration to say, that since history first dawned upon those regions on either bank of the Tiber, some thirty centuries ago, down to the present hour,—in which we behold the figures half shaped, and terrible in their obscurity, arising from under that hand omnipotent, which presides over the loom of the world's destinies—the unity of the drama thereon enacted, has never for a moment been interrupted, nor has it ever ceased to be the centre-piece of the web. For who can deny that Rome, during that immense lapse of ages, has been the grand central point where the sympathies and the belief of the nations have met?—Whether in religious communion, or in religious hostility, in truth or in error, is just the same for the present view of the subject.

Thus it is that the annals of this realm of the Pontiffs, may be said to be the centre-piece of universal history, connecting all its eras and departments into a compacted and symmetrical unity.

Again, if we restrict our views to the histories of

* Mariotti, Italy Past and Present, vol. i. p. 33.

particular nations; it will be difficult to point out that one amongst them, from Sicily to Ireland, and from Poland and Hungary to France and England, with which the same subject will not be found to be bound up in the most important and varied relations, while as for Italy, those States of the Church are not less central to it, in an historical, than they are in a geographical, light. So much a matter of notoriety, indeed, is this, that it were superfluous to dwell upon it, or set about proving such a point in detail. In short, to tell how this realm began, what else is it but to set forth what was the fate of Italy under the Roman, the Byzantine, and the Barbarian; to describe how it fared with it under the invasions of the Goths, under the nefarious and most degrading tyranny of the degenerate Greeks; when the victim of the brutal fury of the Lombard; when the object of liberation and sway for the Frank? In ancient and in mediæval—still more than even in modern times, their fortunes, for weal and for woe, are perpetually and indissolubly wedded together:—nay the pettiest state, or republic, of all those into which Italy has been broken up—whether it be Venice or Naples, Genoa or Pisa, Montferrat or Florence, Lucca, or Siena, or Milan, or San Marino, is it not so identified with the Papal States, by the transactions which make up its annals, that both seem to be united and knit to each other, as intimately and vitally as are the members of the body united under the head?

But, besides these attractions of the Papal States History, arising, so to speak, out of its foreign relations, has it none of its own —none arising from the intrinsic character of the subject itself?

To set this question at rest, it should be enough to observe that these states have, for their capital, Rome—that, in their centre, is that battlefield, whereon the conflict between Paganism and the Cross, after being desperately waged for centuries, was finally decided. There, is the focus towards which all histories converge; where all ages and nations are so brought together that they may be studied and contrasted at the same time. It should be sufficient to say that the events, which form its groups, come out upon a background of two or three thousand years,—thereby acquiring a character of antique elevation and significancy, which no other history can lay claim to.

In this respect, also those regions are singular, that they have beheld one majestic and polished language, which had grown up, flourished, and also fallen and rotted, like the lord of the forest, give rise to another language, if not so majestic, most certainly more luxuriant and flexible, and hardly less racy, or productive in fruitage.

In its scenery, in its soil, in its monuments, its arts, its architecture, in the attitudes and characteristic relations, (we are speaking throughout in an historical sense) of the various races of men who inhabit it,—what other region of the wide world is there, that can claim to be superior, nay equal to this? "Quare non ab re eam Deus," says a mediæval writer, "orbis terrarûm reginam fore, in eâque et terrenæ et cælestis, hoc est, Ecclesiæ, domicilium in æternum esse voluit."*

But as the object of our first chapter will be to unfold the map of these states, and allow the reader with his own eyes to go round the land and walk through it,—noting in a geographical, antiquarian, artistic, and economic point of view, its provinces, valleys, rivers, lakes, cities, towns, castles, ruins, factories, farms, its mephitic wildernesses and its Eden-like scenery, with such other objects as form its most remarkable features—for the present, in order to remove the doubts of those who may be still of impression that to have been neglected to the present day, was the lot which this history merited, it will be enough to refer them to what has been said and sung in praise of those very regions, by such writers as Cato, Columella,† Virgil,‡ and Varro the learned, in their works concerning agriculture amongst the Romans, and their country life.§

In no words of our own could we better express what we wish to say in concluding, than it is stated in the following passage:

"A history like ours divests of the fetters of an-

* Gabriel Barrius, de Laudibus Italiæ. † L. iii. c. 8.
‡ Georg. l. ii. v. 139 et seq. § L. i. c. 2. & c. 7.

nalistic form, and connects by an internal unity for the relation of civil history or wars, the events of larger periods; and it claims a right to every episode which may be necessary to a deeper, a minuter knowledge, and a clearer view of the subject."

The Roman History by Niebuhr. Introd. Vol. II. Smitz' Transl.

32, *Upper Belgrave Place, London,*
January 18*th,*
Diè Cathedræ S. Petri,
A.D. 1850.

INTRODUCTION.

THE PAPAL STATES.

THEIR SCENERY AND ANCIENT INHABITANTS.

To nothing, perhaps, more aptly than to one of those famous palimpsests of the Vatican—an ancient time-worn manuscript, in which fragments of a Cicero, a Juvenal, or a Sallust are found half buried and obliterated beneath a commentary on the Psalms, or a treatise on some of the mysteries of the Christian religion by Saint Augustine, or some other Father of the Church—can one compare those regions of central Italy which are, and which have been for now close on eleven hundred years, included within the boundaries of the Papal dominions.

From the Panaro and the estuaries of the Po, in one direction, to the mountains of Terracina and the torrent of the Tronto, in another; from the Neapolitan to the Tuscan border, and from sea to sea, this territory is but one vast palimpsest,—crowded over, and crossed, and interlined, and noted with the hand-writing of time—that is, with the memorials of thirty centuries which have registered, on the most prominent and imperishable features of those countries, the events in which they abounded—inscribing them not alone in monuments of art, and in the impressions they have left on society, as, in languages, in laws, in customs, but even on the external aspect of the scenery—on the mountain, the lake, the economy of agricultural life: on the highway, the plain, the hill, the river. Nay, it is every day established by the researches of the spade and the plough, whether in excavating the bowels of the earth, or in tilling its surface, that hardly is there a morsel of their soil to which these regions may not be indebted for some miracle of art: for medals, pictured vases, arms, inscriptions: in short, for all kinds of memorials of the past through all its epochs, up to the remotest antiquity.

How is it ascertained for instance that the Siculians, the first most probably to inhabit those regions, were obliged to give way to the Umbri; or that they, after a career of conquest— after ages of warfare with the Sabines, with the Illyrians—were, in their turn, five hundred years it is calculated before Rome was thought of, repulsed, defeated, and brought under the dominion of the Etrurians, another people who have attained on these same regions, to an eminent degree in civilization, in the ornamental as well as in the industrial arts, before they are doomed to suffer the same barbarities at the hands of the ancient Romans, which the Romans themselves had to endure at the hands of the barbarians of more modern ages? Of these revolutions there can be no more doubt than there can be of the existence and impartiality of the very earth itself, on which they are inscribed in a dialect the most imperishable, and the most eloquent; but had our only dependence been on documentary or written memorials, what should we have known of them? Nothing, we may answer, or almost next to nothing.

"It is truly marvellous," says a modern traveller speaking of the Etruscans, "how little the page of history has recorded of this ancient people—far more ancient and more civilized than the Romans themselves, who seemed to have toiled in the destruction of every trace and relic of their predecessors, proving Rome to have been not the friend but the foe—not the promoter but the destroyer of civilization and art. But there—that is under the soil of the Roman Campagna—there, deep beneath the soil of many centuries, that have witnessed the rise and fall of dynasties and empires, are those sepulchres beyond counting where the bones and the ashes of those by-gone generations slept, to witness to the present age, the existence of a people and of a civilization that have lived and died in ages more ancient than the records of history."*

Again, as for the Umbri, the predecessors of the Etruscans in that sort of ascendancy over the petty nations of Latium and the other parts, which passed to the Romans from the latter people, it is to the territory upon which they stamped, in their own name, the impress of conquest, and to their cities,

* A Pilgrimage to Rome by the Rev. Hobart Seymour, M.A. p. 128. London, 1849.

many of them still existing, such as the "warlike Todi," near the Tiber, Gubbio and Nocera at the base of the Apennine, Pesaro and Rimini beyond it: to Nequino on the Nera "strongly placed," to Mevania "begirt with noble walls," to Interamna—now Terni—to Sarsina, Sentino and several others, that we must have recourse for the muniments and the vouchers which attest that there is nothing of exaggeration in the power and advancement in arts, which are attributed to this nation for many a century—for a thousand years perhaps, before the annals of Italy begin, for us, to be committed to writing. In Pliny the elder's time, it was a thing notorious, that in the overthrow which wrested from the Umbri the headship of central Italy, and transferred it to the Etruscans as we have already observed, they were deprived by the conquerors of no less than three hundred towns.*

Still more emphatic and full, we may almost add importunate, becomes this language of monuments, in proportion as we get involved in the revolutions and wars which so abound in the elder ages of Rome. What with cities in ruin, or such as are utterly cancelled from the scenes where they whilome flourished, and were filled with a turbid or a brilliant existence: what with the battle-fields, with the mountain defiles, with the highways, bearing the names of consuls and censors; what with such names as the Tiber, the Cremera, the lakes Vadi-

* H. N. L. 3. cap. 14.

mon and Regillus, the Allia; what with the Cimini, the Lepini and the Alban ranges, with their Etruscan and Pelasgic cities and scenes of conflict; may not the entire of Latium in its widest extent, together with the lands of the Hernicans, of the Æqui, the Sabines, the Marsi, and the Etruscans, through all their branches, be regarded as one immense inscription, intended to preserve in eternal remembrance the comparative refinement of these several nations—their valour, their enthusiasm for national liberty, and also the relentless and ferocious injustice by which that people, who were the Goths and Vandals of those by-gone centuries, first robbed them of their independence with the strong hand of aggression, and next, in a vast number of instances, exterminated themselves and their cities from the face of the earth? Thus did the Romans sow the whirlwind which was to scatter their own blood-steeped and atrocious glories, like the chaff or the dust which is caught up from the threshing floor in summer-time, and scattered in anger by the tempest to the four regions of heaven.

"Would it not seem," as has been observed by a writer already quoted, "as if the past upon these regions was a succession of waves of barbarism and of civilization, alternating as a deluge of ruin or as a tide of blessing over the land; and new tribes, new manners, new languages, seem borne upon the surface, quietly assuming the places, and forgetting the existence of those that are past."*

* Pilgrimage, &c. p. 132.

When the Romans first started on their career of invasion, the entire territory comprised within the Papal dominions was broken up into a vast number of petty independencies, composed throughout, and not less so on the Adriatic side of the Apennines than on the Romeward side, of a people, if not civilized to the highest degree, at least so to a degree far superior to that of their conquerors. "Civilization was there," says the same writer, "and then the barbarism of the Romans came in as a flood, and destroyed it for ages, till century after century had gone by, and then the cycle of civilization came round again, and settled in the same regions in the towns of the empire. And then, again, the barbarism of Goths and Vandals, and the children of the frozen North, overran and wasted its fair fields till centuries rolled over it; and then, again, a third cycle of civilization may be said to have visited it." Yes, the arena of the greatest events for thirty centuries and upwards, these regions have been the abode of no empire, kingdom, city, one might almost add, the station or encampment of no army, but what has left some memorial, which continues to speak to the eye, and to the memory to the present hour. Amidst these scenes, if one might say it, the past is more present to you than the present itself—its interests, its forms of thought and of life, importune your attention more than do the current events of the moment. It is by an exertion, which but few are either capable of, or care to make, that, ordinarily speaking, we revert to the long departed epochs of human history; but here, so irresistible and incessantly recurring are the attractions for memory, that it is not without effort a mind inoculated with history can cling to the anchorage of every day plodding existence.

Now, it is in the midst of all this—and not nearer to the Empire, upon the ruins of which it is built, and which is as significantly contrasted with it in ten thousand forms and aspects, as the Flavian Amphitheatre contrasts with St. Peter's, or the Palatine Hill with the Vatican, than it is to the relics of those ancient Italian nations who have survived their oppressors—that this singular realm, the history of which we have undertaken to write, rises up and presents itself to our view: there, it rises up majestically before us, in the foreground of that vista which reaches back to the remotest antiquity. Separate this history from those of the Pagan Empire and city of Rome, and you have but one member of the antithesis. You make of it a Chinese picture—a landscape without perspective. You strip it, not alone of its greatest charm, but of its meaning, if you shut out the recollections of the three thousand years aforesaid;—we mean only as these recollections are registered in the monuments, the scenery, and the institutions which are everywhere and in all manner of ways in contact, and interwoven with this temporal sovereignty of the Popes.

Such a retrospect is also one of the conditions, and by no means the least important one, for solving the problem so often and so vividly agitated in past ages, as well as at present, *videlicet,* whether a return to the ancient Roman type in government and in customs be for the glory and the advantage, even in a sublunary light, of the several distinct nations now dwelling within the peninsula; or whether it be a thing possible, even admitting it to be not unadvisable, to combine such an aggregation of discord, as to race, recollections, interests, dispositions, dialects, into the organized unity of one homogeneous form of government—whether of a monarchy or a republic.

Moreover, in addition to this, which should have been of itself sufficient to impose it as an obligation on one treating of the Papal States' history, not to leave the reader without the opportunity, should it suit his fancy to use it, of familiarizing his mind with the general import of this palimpsest, or multifariously over-written document, which we have thus discovered the superficies of the Papal territory to be—there is another very characteristic feature of the Papal dominion which would have made it imperative to describe its general aspect, as it really is. There is hardly a traveller averse to the Popes, or to their pretensions as temporal sovereigns of these States; hardly a writer who descants on the subject but quotes the territory as his text, to demonstrate that Popes are not fit to be temporal princes.—Unless by an acquaintance with the genuine reading of the text, that is, with the actual, *bona fide,* aspect of the

States, as to their scenery, their resources, and the appliances and improvements to which they are turned, how shall the candid mind be able to hold the balance with an impartial hand, or ward off the dupery which by bigots and factionists in their various degrees is so largely practised on multitudes, who have the simplicity to rely on their truth or their honour; or who have not the means at hand to unmask the imposture?

By this latter consideration, it is, that we have been influenced in forming the plan of the following introductory pages. In the first place, we propose, to pass rapidly over the Transapennine provinces, the teeming and Eden-like regions adorned and tilled like a garden, as they extend between the mountains and the Adriatic shore, from the Neapolitan border, at the Tronto river, to the borders of Modena, and the *terra firma* of Venice: and, in the next place, to deal more with details in the description of the Cisapennine provinces, where are found, on the Campagna and the Pontine Marshes, the text of impeachment—the desolation and the neglect which are said to demonstrate the misrule of the Pontiffs. In this debate we shall offer or rely upon no testimony of our own. None shall we adduce but such, as being given by one distinguished for mastery of the subject, and who by office, as a point of honour, and from personal interest, having been opposed to the Papal sovereignty, must on all hands be admitted to be as a witness above suspicion.

The witness we allude to is the Count de Tournon,

a peer of France, a man most highly accomplished as a scientific agriculturist, and as a scholar; and who, in fine, was prefect, or lord-lieutenant of Rome, and the subordinate province, during the entire period of its being usurped by Napoleon, from the year 1810 to the year 1814. In composing his work, entitled Statistical Studies on Rome, and the western part of the Roman States, not content with the resources of every sort, of which he had the complete command in his official capacity, he personally inspected the entire province in every part, and in the most minute and careful detail. In nothing have we departed from his description of what he witnessed and tested, except in the trivial particular of transposing one section, that on the basin of Rieti, for a reason of mere convenience, which will be stated hereafter.

But first, let us take a cursory view of the Papal territory, as to its more prominent outlines, and then descend to details — commencing with the north-eastern or Adriatic provinces, on which we shall have to touch but slightly.

In their course, pretty nearly from west to east, beginning high up in the mountains of Pistoia, and near the source of the river Panaro — thence running on by Pietra-Mala, between Tuscany and Bologna, looking out over the rich and populous Romagna, as they proceed above Forli and Cesena, on through Urbino, along the border of the Marches to the Neapolitan frontier, which they form nearly throughout, from one sea to the other—the Apennines divide the Papal dominions into two moieties of very nearly equal extent, but of very emphatically contrasted character—contrasted not alone as to the aspect of nature in both, but even as to their climate, and above all, as to the temper, the genius, and the tendencies of their inhabitants.

"In scenery," says Vieusseau,* "they differ widely: the north is for the greater part a fertile plain, watered by abundant rivers, divided into well cultivated fields and gardens, full of towns and villages, inhabited by a numerous and industrious population. The landscape is luxuriant but monotonous." It is only to the country from the boundary between Forli and Cesena, to the northern frontier, that this last observation applies. From Cesena, on through Urbino and the Marches, the country is picturesque as well as rich, in the highest degree.

"In the south, on the contrary," he continues, that is, on the Roman side of the Apennines, "the landscape varies every twenty miles. There are to be seen delightful valleys surrounded by stupendous crags—torrents fearfully swelled at one time of the year, and rolling their foamy waters with the noise of thunder, and at other seasons reduced to scanty rivulets, bubbling over the pebbles of their rocky beds—wide uncultivated plains, strewed with ruins of former greatness, inhabited by wild buffaloes and wilder men; and in the midst of these, the

* Italy and the Italians in the 19th century.

proudest city in the world lifting its melancholy head. Farther inland are seen ruinous castles and towns, perched upon almost inaccessible peaks, among beautiful forests of chesnut-trees, and wild solitary glens."

"It is in the same region and on all the south of the Apennines, we find the true classic ground of Italy, the land of the arts, of antiquities, of the grandest recollections of history. It is there we find the most brilliant scenes depicted by romantic travellers are realities; the glowing azure of the sky, the dark blue sea, the purple tinged mountains,—the lemon groves and orangeries and olive groves,—man lawless and impassioned. The eye often recognizes there, the landscapes of Salvator Rosa, and the originals of the queenly forms which live on the canvass of Raphael. Thence it was that Cimerosa, Paisiello, and Pergolesi derived their inspiration. The Coliseum and St. Peter's are there. The north, in modern ages, has given the best soldiers; the south, the keenest politicians. In painting, the masters of the south excel in the genius of composition and boldness of design, those of the north in the delicacy and warmth of tints and the softness of outlines: the architecture of the north is convenient and finished, that of the south characterized by colossal dimensions and imposing aspect."

But, before we enter on any detailed description of the provinces on either side of the mountains, let us cast a glance in passing, at the general appearance of the mountains themselves.

The Apennines of the Papal States are the centre links of the chain which begins at the Maritime Alps in Liguria, and does not terminate but with the peninsula. They send out their branches in many directions. These towards the Adriatic, however, especially in Chesena and the March of Ancona, are only deserving the appellation of hills. In Urbino, they are of a more mountainous character; but, in the direction of Rome, they assume a much loftier bearing—pushing forward their proud and precipitous ridges to the course of the Tiber, and the very verge of the Roman Campagna. Over the latter, their furthest promontories, especially in the vicinage of Palestrina and Tivoli, are distinguished by an elevation and contour which rank them amongst the most formidable in aspect, as they are, far away, the most famous of all the mountains of Italy.

The Apennine scenery is thus depicted by Addison. He travelled in the year 1699 and 1700.

"The fatigue of our crossing the Apennines," he says, "and of our whole journey from Loretto to Rome was very agreeably relieved by the variety of scenes we passed through. For not to mention the rude prospect of rocks rising one above another, of the gutters deep worn in the sides of them by torrents of rain and snow water, or the long channels of sand winding about their bottoms, that are sometimes filled with so many rivers, we saw in six days travelling the several seasons of the year in their beauty and perfection. We were sometimes shivering on the top of a bleak mountain, and a little while after basking in the warm valley, covered with violets and almond trees in blossom, the bees already swarming over them, though but in the month of February. Sometimes our road led us through groves of olives or by gardens of oranges, or into several hollow apartments among the rocks, that look like so many natural greenhouses, as being always shaded with a variety of trees and shrubs that never lose their verdure."*

At length we are arrived in the provinces, or legations, as they are called, between the Apennines thus described, and the upper or Adriatic sea. It is agreed amongst all archæologists—and the ancient name of the countries bears testimony to the fact—that the regions along those shores, so far as at that far distant antiquity they had been cleared of the primæval forests, or reclaimed from the morass, were, if not originally, at least from a period long anterior to history, possessed by the Umbri, beginning from a point of the coast near Ancona, and running on to the marshes, which expanded far and wide at that period, on every side of the present banks of the Po. They are said to have expelled the Illyrian tribes, who had stationed themselves on various points of the coast, and to have built Ariminum, and some other cities. But their sway over those tracts was put an end to by the Etruscans. After subjugating the Umbri, as has been already observed, and

* Vol. ii. p. 56. London, 1721.

crossing the mountains, this enterprising and highly civilized people, so long possessed the provinces of Bologna, Ferrara, Ravenna, and the Romagna, at large, that the cities they founded, in some instances, exist as yet: the immense works by which they effected the drainage of the swamps and the improvement of the arable soil are still to be traced; and the earth itself is not only covered with these vestiges —canals, cities, temples—but in its bosom it is found to contain the vouchers of their arts and their enterprise; such as their coins, their pictured vases, their arms, and other similar objects, especially the famous inscriptions, which as yet, unfortunately, remain uninterpreted.*

"They drained," says Michali, "by immense canals the country round the mouths of the Po, and by the foss called Filistine, which drains the interior, carried away the waste waters to the great river at Brondolo, thus reclaiming the marshes between the lagunes of Venice, and the lake of Comacchio."†

Beyond doubt, they held all the Adriatic coast, formerly held by the Umbri. Cupra of the mountains, and that also of the shore, close to the modern Ripatronsone, both took their names from a deity regarded as propitious to the Etrurians.‡ These towns, as well as Adria of Picenum, built a little inland on an eminence, with its port at the mouth of

* Both Michali and Niebuhr agree in the particulars above-stated, and in those which follow.

† Vol. i. p. 115 ‡ Strabo, L. 5, &c. ib.

the Matrino, at present the Piomba, were colonies of the ancient Adria beyond the Po, which certainly owes its origin to them and not to Diomede, as the Greeks would have it.

They founded Felsina, where stands Bologna at present. It was one of the twelve Etruscan capitals to the north of the Apennine. But as the Etruscans had expelled or subjugated the Umbri, who had previously dispossessed the Illyrians, they were, in their turn, exterminated or oppressed by the Boii, or Senones—a nation of Gauls, from whom the capital, Felsina, took the name of Boionia or Bononia: thenceforward the whole province as far as the Rubicon, became a portion of Cisalpine Gaul. Of another of the Etruscan capitals, called Melpo, not a vestige was spared by these last-mentioned and most ferocious invaders. It is a curious coincidence, that this catastrophe happened on the very same day that the Etruscan city of Veii fell into the hands of the Romans, and was by them made the victim of similarly barbarous treatment.

This latter people, in process of time, deprived the Senones of their conquest: they sent colonies, or rather permanent garrisons of veteran legionaries to the several cities—Bononia, Ariminum, Ravenna, Pisaurum. But during the dreadful civil commotions between Marius and Sylla, these cities and the whole province were ruined. They were restored under the empire, most of them by Augustus, who made Ravenna one of the great naval stations.

Ravenna from the remotest antiquity, if we can credit the description given of it by Strabo, very strikingly resembled in many respects what Venice was in after times. He says, it was situated in the midst of lagunes, and constructed on piles of wood. The communication, as in modern Venice, was by canals, which were spanned by several bridges. He adds that it was remarkable for the salubrity of its climate, as the lagunes were regularly purified by the ebb and flow of the tide. By some antiquarians, it is said, that certain Thessalian adventurers founded it. Others say it was of Pelasgic origin.

Bononia also arose to great magnificence, and Ariminum, the present Rimini, was regarded as the key of Italy on the eastern coast. Great importance was attached to this place by Cæsar; who, as one of the triumvirs, garrisoned it with a colony. Indeed in every direction, those fertile provinces were thickly strewed with flourishing cities and towns, under the Cæsars, as is still the case under the Popes. We turn next to Picenum.

The Sabines, when driven to extremity by the never-ending aggressions which they suffered from the Umbri, and by force of a religious custom, which prevailed among that primitive and inoffensive people, detached a colony, which led by a wood-pecker—picus—that perched on their banner as they crossed the Apennine, established itself in those fertile coasts of the Adriatic, which took the name of Picenum, in pursuance of these events.* As people, rude, and given to agriculture, hunting, and a pastoral life, they left the sea-board of the country—most admirably circumstanced as it is for commercial enterprise—to a variety of adventurers, from the opposite coast of Illyricum, from Umbria, Etruria, and from Greek cities of the south. "No country," says Michali, "is more beautifully diversified than this by nature, with smiling hills and fruitful valleys, and wide-spreading fertile plains. It teems with abundance from the river Esi, at one extremity, to the Tronto, at the other. Ascoli, seated a little inland, at the confluence of the Tronto and Castellano, and fortified alike by art and nature, became the capital of the Picentine nation. To them also belonged the city of Firmo, which had a harbour at the place now called Castello. In short, so prosperous did this region become, on account of its extreme fertility, and the activity and enterprise of its people, that though crushed beneath the weight of Roman invasion, in the year of the city 485, it long continued to be the most populous, and perhaps the richest province of central Italy."† As for Ascoli itself, in the midst of rocks, and woods, and waters, its situation cannot be surpassed in beauty;

* See Michali, vol i. p. 219, who quotes the authorities from Strabo and Pliny. Ib. p. 220. Paulus Warnefrid. l. 2. cap. 19. de Gestis Longob.

† Michali, ubi supra, v. 1. p. 220.

and along the upper valley of the Tronto, the horizon is confined by lofty serrated peaks of the Apennines, running backwards towards the mountains of the Sibyl, which perhaps combines the mounts Severus and Tetricus of Virgil. Shapeless brick walls and broken arches, on an eminence within the city, seem to belong to the Roman period.

It is not alone in modern and in mediæval times that these borders of the Adriatic have been the arena of warlike achievements. What memories arise at the bare name of the Rubicon? The very moment you cross the frontier at Castel-Franco, near the Panaro, you find yourself on the battle-field where Mark Antony was defeated by Hirtius and Octavian,—the ancient name of the place was Forum Gallorum. A bloody victory was won by Sylla near Faenza, over the adherents of Corbo. It was on the plains round Ariminum, that the Goths were so often reviewed, and the captive Cæsars so often derided by Alaric; and, again, it was on the banks of the Metaurus, which falls into the Adriatic at Fano, that Asdrubal, on his march to the assistance of Hannibal, was defeated and slain in a desperate battle, in which the consuls, Livius Salinator and Claudius Nero commanded the Romans.

As for the scenery, let one or two extracts suffice; the first is from Ranke's History of the Popes.

"The writers of the 16th century," says Ranke, "cannot find words sufficient to extol its fertility. What beautiful plains did it exhibit round Bologna all through Romagna! What loveliness combined with fertility down the slopes of the Apennines!" "We travelled," say the Venetian ambassadors of 1522, "from Macerata to Tolentino through the most beautiful fields; through hills and plains covered with corn: there was nothing else to be seen growing for a space of thirty miles; not a foot of uncultivated land was discoverable; it seemed impossible to gather in, not to speak of consuming, such an abundance of corn. Romagna yielded yearly forty thousand stara more corn than was sufficient for its own consumption—after supplying the mountain districts of Urbino, Tuscany, and Bologna, thirty-five thousand stara more were at times exported by sea. In the year 1589, the exports of corn from the states of the Church are estimated at the annual value of five hundred thousand scudi."

The other description is from an old local history in Grævius, of the obscure little town of Recanati. There are similar ones to be found of nearly all the other towns and cities. The description given below represents the place as it was two centuries since, and is translated from the excellent Latin of Joannes Franciscus Angelita, a native of the city whose history he has written.

"The ridge on which the city rests as you come from Rome, looks rugged and all but inaccessible. On passing through it, however, towards the Adriatic coast, you find it nearly on a level with the plain. By reason of this elevation, it is salubrious in an eminent degree, and commands the most charming and varied prospects. On one hand the mountains, the sea of Adria on the other, and in the interval, a landscape enchanting to look upon. A country of hill and dale, with sparkling rivers meandering through meadows, woodlands, vineyards, corn-fields, and gardens—all this interspersed with towns, cities, villas, and the ruins of past ages, and sometimes a view of the Sclavonic mountains, far away beyond the deep blue waters seen through the pellucid atmosphere of morning. For the most part, the boundaries of its territory are formed by the two rivers Potentia and Moscio, but in some places these streams have been diverted with incredible labour from their original beds, either for the purpose of draining marshy grounds, or to form a more commodious harbour on the sea-shore, or for purposes of irrigation. Not that the territory is trusting to these two rivers only, it has, besides, a great many rivulets, whose waters never fail, and fountains in great number, most salubrious and refreshing, the solace and delight of their cattle in summer time. Throughout its entire length and breadth, the soil is teeming with fertility (*fertilissimus*), singularly well suited for agriculture, and totally free from marshes, except here and there in a few spots of insignificant extent along the shores of the neighbouring sea. For wheat, and every species of grain, in short, and for meadow and pasturage, the level parts cannot be better; the valleys and hills are thick set with the olive and the vine. The country is renowned for fruit of every species, and of the best flavour, in particular for that kind of figs called *Cori.* Melons and legumes are produced in great abundance. Of noxious animals there are hardly any. Wolves, very, very rarely seen; and the hounds of Recanati being of the very best breed, there is little chance for foxes; but as for domestic animals and poultry, no where do they abound more or thrive better. As for fish, both in sea and river, so plenty are they that the inhabitants, after helping themselves, have abundance to sell to their neighbours The same is to be said with regard to their agricultural produce.

" In the domain of the town there are but few villages, but the cottages of the peasantry are seen thickly scattered in every direction through the fields and vineyards. There is need for additional labourers who come down from the Apennines in vintage and harvest time. There is no deficiency of wood, either for fuel or other uses. Of old, the heights and other favourable positions were crowned with castles. Many an achievement and tragic tale connected with them still live in the traditions of the people; their names are preserved, but, with one or two exceptions, they now only serve as ruins to impart a picturesque effect to the scenery."*

Besides the cities of Urbino, Pesaro, Gubbio,

* Joan. Franc. Angelitæ Urbis Recineti Origines et Historia, apud Græv. &c. tom ix. par. 11. p. 8.

Sinigaglia, Fosombrone, San' Leo, Cagli, and *Urbania*, (so called from Urban VIII. who raised this place, previously known as Castel Durante, to the rank of city), there were in the Duchy of Urbino a good many towns, most of them with strong castles in them, and all situated, as Muratori says, in a country which though hilly is pleasant and delicious.*

Through this beauteous region passes one of the great highways of antiquity, the branch of the *Via Flaminia*, by which Alaric led his Goths to the sack of Rome, and which before and ever since his time, has been a great thoroughfare for armies.

This pass of Furlo, formed with great labour by the Romans, who called it Petra Pertusa, leads through a striking defile of the Apennine; and Gubbio, representing the obscure town of Iguvium, is celebrated for possessing the inscribed Eugubian tablets of bronze, which as yet no antiquarian has been able to read and interpret.

On the western side of the mountains, the beauty of the scenery compensates for the want of remarkable historical monuments. Città di Castello, not far from the source of the Tiber, is Pliny's Tifernum Tiberinum; and near it must be the site of his secluded Tuscan villa, which he has so delightfully described.

The Tiber we leave to the left, and along the rough mountain frontier of Tuscany, arrive at the lake of Perugia, which seems placed like an immense

* "In paese delizioso ed ameno, benche montuoso."—*Annali D'Italia,* an. 1626. ver. fin.

and beautiful mirror to reflect back the charms of one of the most enchanting, as it is one of the most memorable scenes in the world. Here it was, that sanguinary engagement took place in which the Carthaginian general ensnared, overthrew, and all but annihilated one of the proudest hosts the Romans had ever sent forth. On both sides they contended like giants:—"and such was their mutual animosity," says Livy, "so intent were they upon the battle, that the earthquake which overthrew in great part many of the cities of Italy, which turned the course of rapid streams, poured back the sea upon the rivers, and tore down the very mountains, was not felt by one of the combatants."*

But tearing ourselves away from the memories and the fascinating charms of these regions, where wood and lake, the hills studded with cities and villages, the valleys teeming with the blessings of corn, and oil, and wine, unite to form a landscape the most enchanting, we hasten through the valley of the Caina, and merely salute, in passing, the brave and famous city of Perugia—the home of valour and a sanctuary of the arts—as it reposes majestically on the summit of the mountain. Assisi, so abounding in claims and attractions for the pilgrim, whether in religion or in art, Hispellum also, and Foligno, though places of great renown and interest, we leave behind us. Speeding still onward towards the south, through scenery every moment varying, but everywhere characterised by beauty and abun-

* L. 22. cap. 12.

dance,—its hills and mountains crowned with beacons of the past, in towers and fortresses in ruin, and in villages and little cities, the origins of which are lost in the night of ages. The vale of the Clitumnus, in which we have at length arrived, has been in every age the theme of poets. It is the sojourn of an everlasting spring. The fountain which Virgil celebrated in his verses, and which was worshipped as something partaking of divinity in Pagan times, is still seen to burst forth on a sudden as a copious river, from beneath the rocky hill, which was shaded by a grove of cypresses in the days of Pliny.

"The chill waters," says a modern traveller, "still form a full and wide stream, the moment they come from the cliff; and the cream-coloured cattle browse on the rich meadows that form the banks immediately beyond, but the decorated temple, which from a beautiful rock, now overlooks the little valley, cannot be that primæval shrine whose religious simplicity Pliny describes.* Bevagna is Mevania, the birthplace of Propertius; and Spoleto, celebrated under the name of Spoletium, for its repulse of Hannibal, stands on a picturesque hill, separated by a dell from the higher Apennines, and exhibits an honorary arch of Drusus, the portico of a temple and a Roman gate. A beautifully wooded ascent of the Apennines carries us across into the valley of the Nar or Nera."†

* Ubi supra, L. 8. Ep. 8.

† Italy and the Italian Islands, by Wm. Spalding, Esq. vol. i. p. 283. Edinburgh, 1841.

Here we meet the Count de Tournon. We join in his excursion through this district, because it partakes throughout of the same character of cultivation and scenery, as the regions we have only just quitted, and because, beginning at Radicofani, the circuit of the territory immediately round Rome, and concluding with the valley of the Anio, which brings us out on the Campagna, within sight of the Seven Hills, we shall find ourselves in a position the most favour able for gathering up and adjusting the distinct and life-like impressions, the result and the reward of our wanderings, that they may keep us company, entertaining and instructing us as we advance through the Papal cycle of our history.*

THE DISTRICT OF RIETI AND TERNI DESCRIBED.

In order to study the basin of Rieti, the best point of observation is from the eminence overlooking the city from the south, and on which is built a convent of Capucins, in the midst of a wood of evergreen oaks; the view enjoyed from thence, takes in not only the rich and beauteous

* The title of de Tournon's work is as follows:—Etudes statistiques sur Rome et la partie occidentale des états Romains: contenant une description topographique et des recherches sur la population, l'agriculture, les manufactures, le commerce, le gouvernement, les établissemens publics; et une notice sur les travaux éxécutes par l'administration Français, par le Comte de Tournon pair de France, grand officier de la legion d'honneur, associé ordinaire de la société centrale d'agriculture, Préfet de Rome de 1810 a 1814. Paris. 1831.

plain itself, but also the admirable frame in which nature has enclosed it. To the east, Mount Terminillo, one of the highest of central Italy, lifts itself on a series of vast elevations, the first clad with vines and olives, the next with the evergreen oak: still higher are naked crags; and in fine its peaks, seven thousand feet above the level of the sea, are shrowded in those snows which hardly yield to the hottest summers. Along the flank of this range, there is a mountain gorge, the celebrated pass of Antrodoco, leading through Bondeno into the interior of the Neapolitan provinces by Cività Ducale and Aquila. Towards the north the Sierra subsides, curves to the westward, and ending abruptly, lays open to view the valley of the Nera. The eye in continuing the circuit by the west, views other mountains still more lofty, more arid, and more broken into ravines. They complete the circle which encompasses the plain. The villages of Grecia and Contigliano, both seated on mountain-crests, are seen perching upon their abrupt acclivities. Towards the south-west, one can follow to a great distance the *Via Valeria* onward towards Rome, and through a second valley, watered by the Turano, the view can penetrate into the deep glens of the mountains, and climb from stage to stage up to their loftiest summits.

Such is the frame, more admirable still is the picture itself, for it presents the spectacle of riches and prosperity carried to the highest degree. Under a forest of mulberries, maple-trees, and elms, connected together by garlands of the vine, the soil is constantly covered with abundant crops in the greatest variety: wheat, maize, beans, flax, hemp, woad or pestel, and vegetables experience the care of the industrious husbandman by turns; so that one would say it was an immense garden, disposed not less to delight the beholder, than to enrich by its teeming plenty. Two beautiful rivers, which unite at a league distance above the city, intersect the brilliant verdure of the plain, with the azure line of their waters: in fine, the foreground of this rich picture is occupied by the belfries, churches and numerous edifices of Rieti.

This plain is in part a conquest of human skill and industry. Formerly a lake occupied the greater part of it. According to Pliny, the waters of this lake contained calcareous substances in great quantity: for he says, that pieces of wood cast into the Velino were speedily covered with a "cortex of stone." The drainage was first effected in the year of Rome 480, by M. Curius Dentatus, who opened a canal of emission, and the valley thus drained, to use the expression of Cicero, "became like another Vale of Tempé." Virgil calls these fields: "Rosea rura Velini." Both the horses and asses of those parts were in great esteem with the ancients. Varro tells us this, and mentions the high prices the asses of Rieti used to bring in Rome, in his own times.

In quitting this charming city, you traverse the plain in the direction from south to north, under an arcade of mulberries trelliced with vines, through the stems of which thickly planted over the fields of maize and pastel, the country villas are seen in all directions, reminding one of the very richest districts of Lombardy. The Turano and the Velino reunite in the centre of this plain, and form a fine river, over which you pass by a sorry wooden bridge. Beyond, the road approaches the foot of the western mountains, and a footpath up the side of a high hill conducts to Aspra and Cantalupo. Eastward the plain is terminated at the foot of the Apennine, whose first ranges serve for a base to the villages of Castel Franco, Appuleggia, Poggio-Bustone, and Labbro, situated at different lines of elevation, and overhung by Mount Terminillo. It is probably in this region that Trebula Mutusca was situated, which Virgil designates by the epithet of *Olivifera* (the olive-bearing), and Assia famous for its mineral baths.

In following the right bank of the Velino, in still approaching the mountains, you arrive at a marsh fed by the waters which descend from the Apennine, and which connects itself with the two lakes called Lungo and Ripa-sottile. These are separated from another large mountain-lake called Pie-di-Lugo by a rocky promontory rising abruptly from the waters, and having its base covered with the poor dwellings of a village of the same name as the lake. On its ridges and summit are the decaying walls and ruinous towers of a town which must have been considerable in mediæval times, as it numbered 1370 families during the 14th century: but in 1600, it was reduced to 120 families, from the influence of *malaria*, and its population has not increased, since it has at present only 600 inhabitants.

The lake of Piè-di-Lugo has not the vast extent of Bolsena or of Bracciano (lakes to be hereafter described), nor the mysterious charm of the lakes of Vico, Albano, or Nemi, whose waters, shut up in the depths of extinct volcanoes, reflect only the shadows of tufted and sombre forests, but it combines in itself all the distinctive beauties of these various reservoirs; and enormous masses of rock, battlemented with ancient fortresses now in ruins, mountains which lift their heads to the region of the snows, wooded slopes, plains displaying the highest culture, and numerous dispersed villages contribute to impart to it a character which belongs not to any of the others.

The Velino flows at a little distance to the west of the lake, and by a navigable branch is connected both with it and with a chain of little lakes, very deep, not far from the route between Rieti and Terni, which winds along the foot of the mountain, in describing long curves to keep the level ground. At this point the two mountain chains close in upon each other, and leave but a narrow gorge. This was the pass which the Constitutional troops of Naples (under Pepé) strove to defend against the Austrians, in 1820. The Velino and the waters of Piè-di-Lugo were but little tinged with the blood which was shed on the occasion.

This river flows with brimming banks through

lines of noble trees, overshadowing the canal, which has been traced for it by the hand of man. Its gentle current increases in speed and rushes at length along its rocky bed with fearful rapidity, until it reaches the brink : it is rather heard then, than seen to precipitate itself through whirlpools of clouds and vapour into the gulf beneath.

At this point a new horizon reveals itself. — A beauteous valley at an immense depth below displays its fields and gardens irrigated by the Nera, the amphitheatre of mountains by which it is sheltered, and in the distance the plain of Terni. It is on a rocky eminence jutting somewhat over the abyss that one must take his stand, and that not without emotion, in order fully to enjoy this sublime and enchanting prospect. Thence descending by a path, rendered perilous from the slippery nature of the rocks and of the turf, ever humid from the spray of the cascade, and formed of the softest verdure, you at length arrive at a little pavilion named *La Specola*, erected in 1781 by order of Pius VI. and there obtain the finest view of those renowned falls of the Velino, in the description of which the poets both of modern and of ancient times have exhausted their grandest images. Not, however, distinguished by the original character of the cascades of the Anio, bursting upon the view as it were from the heart of a city, and in the midst of the monuments of art, or by the charm of mystery which envelopes the subterranean cataracts of the grotto of Neptune, in the same place;

but the mass of its waters, the immense height from which it is precipitated, the richness of the prospects, the variety of points of view, the luxuriant vegetation, give to the cascades of the Marmora, or of Terni, the advantage over the finest waterfalls of the Alps or of the Pyrenees.

The Nera, which in winding through the beauteous vale of Terni already noticed, receives the waters of the Velino below the falls, has its fountains in the mountains of Visso and of Norcia, in the duchy of Spoleto, and after opening for itself a passage between Monte Somma and Monte Leone, it comes to water the charming valley in which are built the villages of Ferentillo, Monte Franco, Arrone, and Collestato: swelled by the Velino, it traverses the gorge of Papigno, and debouches into the magnificent plain of Terni. The road follows the sinuosities of the mountain, and reveals in succession to the view of the traveller, the vast plain of Terni, Terni itself, the mountain circle which surrounds it; the cities of Cesi, San-Gemino, Aqua-Sparta, Amelia, and twenty other villages crowded on their acclivities: canals from the Nera disperse fertility through the plain, which is diversified with groves of mulberries, the olive, the vine, and the most varied cultivation.

The city of Terni, a bishop's see, is situated in the centre of a country remarkable for fertility, and of an aspect the most charming: it occupies the site of the ancient Interamna, an Umbrian city, so called from being placed between two branches of the Nera, and which received a colony in the year of Rome 436, after the power of the Etruscans and Umbrians as independent nations had been completely broken. At present, Terni is one of the handsomest cities of the Papal States, and is the sojourn of several families of distinction.

The *Via Flaminia* crosses the Nera at Terni, and after passing over the mountain of Somma, by which the basin of the Nera is separated from that of the Clitumnus, proceeds to Florence through Spoleti, Perugia, and Arezzo; and into the marches by two branches, one through Tolentino and Macerata to Ancona; the other, through the celebrated pass of Furlo, or of *Saxa Incisa* as the ancients called it, [from its having been cut through the heart of rocky mountains by order of Vespasian,] leads the traveller through the Duchy of Urbino, and down the course of the Metaurus to Fano, as has been before described. In the direction of Rome it traverses an admirable plain thickly strewed with villas, shaded with trees, adorned with the most varied culture, and commanded by a chain of hills on which the villages of Collescipoli and Stroncone are seen to pile up their dwellings in a fashion the most picturesque amongst the rocky ledges and terraces along their sides. From the midst of this plain another road branches off through a savage ravine, at the entrance of which the poor village of Vacone seems placed as a sentinel on guard. This road passes in the direction of

Rome, through the mountain region of Cantalupo, a country which we shall have to visit hereafter in surveying the basin of the Tiber.

At the western entrance of the plain, the mountain chain laps in upon itself and shuts the horizon: on its crest the sombre towers of Narni are seen to lift their ruined battlements; and the road in its zig-zag career down an inclined plane of rapid descent, conducts to the gates of this city, which perched in a situation one of the most singular even for those countries, with its ancient castle, its walls, its belfries, the habitations rising in stages one above another on the mountain side, presents a most imposing aspect: but, you enter its streets and the delusion vanishes.

Narni occupies the site of the ancient *Narnia* or *Nequinum*, a city of great strength in the times of the Siculi and the Umbrians, and the key of the valley of the Nera. The latter people after having driven out the Siculi at the epoch of the Trojan war, spread themselves through the upper valley of the Tiber as far as the Arno; but repulsed by the Etruscans they withdrew between the Tiber and the Nera, and remained strangers to the earlier wars of the Romans; but the two pitched battles lost by the Etruscans under the walls of Sutri, and the passage of the Cimino having borne down the power of the latter people, the Umbrians at length found themselves in contact with the conquerors, and hastened to the assistance of their neighbours. It was too late: the last dykes had yielded; and the battle of the lake Vadimon, lost in the year of the city 444 by the two confederated nations, delivered Umbria to the Romans, who crossing the Tiber, and occupying Ocricolum, laid siege to Nequinum, which at length succumbed in the year of Rome 452. This laid open the entrance to Umbria and Picenum. Thus was Nequinum the last bulwark of Eastern Italy, as we shall see that Vulsinii was one of the passes through which the all-conquering people directed their legions on the north. Nequinum gave birth to Nerva.

From the heights of Narni, the view extends over the magnificent basin of which the southern bound is occupied by Terni, and which is watered by the Nera. The bed of this river under Narni is wide, and bordered with trees, but after a little, the hills which shelter it on the right, approach the range on which the city is seated, the two masses leaving but a narrow gorge between them. It was at the entrance of this ravine the *Via Flaminia* crossing the Nera by a bridge erected by Augustus, and repaired by Nerva, conducted through a wild scene of rocky precipices and forests of the ilex. The landscape, hitherto so smiling and so fertile, becomes barren and savage on a sudden: the surface broken into deep defiles and caverns is overhung with woods: no sign of a human habitation or of culture cheers this desert, and the apprehensions inspired by the aspect of the place, are not lessened as one approaches a bridge thrown over a rocky chasm, which bears the name of Ponte Sanguinaro, from the blood often shed there by the hands of the banditti. But after two hours through a region worthy the pencil of Salvator Rosa, the forests cease, the hill sides become less abrupt, cultivation and the dwellings of man reappear once more, and the gay village delle Vigne is seen amidst the foliage of its gardens. Through the trees the eye begins to get glimpses of the tops of the Cimino range and of Soracte; in fine, at the extremity of a long succession of hills gently sloping towards the west you descry Otricoli perched above the Tiber, as it pursues its course between Tuscany and the Sabine country on to Rome. Thus are we at length arrived in that region of the States which as it is the theatre of the chief actions and events in the history of the Papal States, is deserving of attention still more studious and detailed than the provinces already noticed.

GENERAL VIEW OF THE PATRIMONY OF ST. PETER.

As to its geological character, this portion of the Pontifical States included between the Neapolitan and Tuscan frontiers, the Apennine and the sea, is divided into two regions pretty nearly equal, of which one appertains to the compact calcareous stratum, the other to the volcanic formation. The limit between these two geological provinces, is traced at first by the Tiber to the height of Correse, and afterwards by a line which runs along the base of the Sabine Mountains, passing below Palombara,

Tivoli, and Palestrina; afterwards trending westward it touches the Lepini chain of mountains at its northern extremity, and thence goes direct for the sea, which it reaches near Astura. All to the eastward of this line is calcareous, except the environs of Valmontone, of Ferentino, (in the Val di Sacco) and of Vico-Varo, as all to the westward is a volcanic soil, —Mount Soracte, the calcareous formations along the coast, and the schistous group of La Tolfa excepted. In fine, the southern region of the Val di Sacco is formed of argillaceous sandy hills.

The calcareous or limestone rock is found in all degrees of hardness, from the marble of Cori and Cattanello, to the spongy deposits which float on the *Lago dei Tartari* on the Campagna under Tivoli. The volcanic soil in its turn presents innumerable varieties of products, from the prismatic basalt of Bolsena and the lava of the quarries of *Capo di Bove*, to the pumice stone.

The mountains of the limestone formation are in their forms bold, sharp, and angular in outline, their summits battlemented, declivities rugged, scorched, frequently protruding the dark grey rock in naked grimness. The volcanic mountains much less elevated, affect a rounded form, their slopes prolong themselves, and their culminating line is softly undulating. On the limestone soil the vegetation is frequently impoverished, and the oak and the olive alone amongst the greater plants are found to prosper: on the contrary, the earth of a volcanic character is covered as if spontaneously with vigorous vegetation in the greatest variety, and the oak of every species, white, red, and green, the chesnut, the elm, the beech, there attain to proportions which are truly gigantic.

Taking this territory in its entire extent, the mountainous parts are pretty equal to the parts which are not so; and within its limits there is every variety of climate, from the declivities of Terracina, covered with the palm, the cactus, and the orange, to the summit of Terminillo, from the northern aspect of which the snow never disappears. It abounds in mineral and medicinal springs.

As for metallic substances, they are found in a variety of places. The Sabine mountains contain mines of copper pyrites, which have been worked, and which have no doubt acquired the name of Monte dell' Oro, for a mountain near Salissano. Near *La Tolfa*, is a lead mine, which yielded 60 *per cent* of that metal. Brown oxide of iron is found in abundance near Monte Leone, and the mines when worked yielded 40 *per cent.* Another mine of the same description at Guercino, on the Campagna, yields 35 *per cent.* Finally, between Civita Vecchia and the alum works, is another iron mine—a very rich one—" Une mine très riche."

If trees, isolated, or in smaller clumps, are rarely met with in the *malaria* districts, the forests in those regions, are on the other hand, of very great extent: the greatest masses of wood are to be met with from

Lake Bòlsena to the Tiber, on the mountains of Cimino, from Soriano to *La Tolfa*, along the seaboard, from the Pescia to the Marta, from the Avone to the Tiber, from that river to Terracina, and on the Arthemisian Mountains, from Albano to Valmontone: on the Lepini chain, from Monte Fortino to Vallecorsa, and on the Apennines through the whole length of the States.

The timber most commonly met with in those forest tracts, are the various species of the oak—the white, or *racemosa*, the red, called *robur*, the green or *ilex*. This species in a rich soil, as in the environs of Arricia, attains to prodigious dimensions. The species of oak called *Suber*, succeeds particularly well in the more southern provinces, as may be seen in the forest of Casanuova, near Piperno. The elm, the beech, the ash, grow spontaneously in the wastes, and to an immense size. Amongst the coniferous trees are found the pine, called *Maritima*, and that called *Silvestris*. Many of the limestone mountains of Sabina, are clad with this kind, and the species called *pinea*, is the finest ornament of the sea coast to the south of Ostia, their trunks as erect as columns, supporting with elegance the capital of its spreading branches, which from a distance, look like a prairie suspended in mid air.

These forests, along the shore, abound in wild boars; still greater is the abundance of hares and rabbits; but the deer, the harts, and wild goats, formerly abounding there, are now extinct. The wolves drawn thither by the flocks, which are wintered on the neighbouring plains, find an asylum in these forests, where multiplying in numbers, they become such a scourge, that high rewards are given by the farmers for their destruction, and they take Modenese huntsmen into pay for that purpose, as the latter are very adroit in taking them by traps and snares. Porcupines, badgers, and hedgehogs, are numerous on the Campagna, which abounds in all sorts of game, such as grey and red partridge, woodcocks, and quails, which in spring-time arrive in clouds not to be numbered. They precipitate themselves, especially along the beach, between Terracina and Cape Circe, and are taken in heaps in immense nets, hung upon the trees which line the shore; but as they come quite lean, from their long flight from Africa, they have to be fattened before they are fit subjects for the cook. Wood pigeons also furnish a very abundant aliment in the autumnal months; for, in certain gorges of the Sabine Mountains, they take them by thousands.

Fish, such as the "thori," the sturgeon, mullet, turbot, sole, whiting, red-mullet, are common in the waters which ripple on the Roman coast, and the rivers and lakes abound in trout, carp, tench, pike, and eels, of a size very remarkable.

Amongst the insects which have attained to an historical notoriety in those regions, the locust holds the foremost place, the means for destroying them and preventing their most destructive ravages, having as history tells us, formed many a time and oft the subject of debate for the Senate, and of charge to the Consuls, from the earliest times of the republic. We shall also find the Pontiffs endeavouring to deal with them in the middle ages. The locusts and the French simultaneously occupied the States from 1809 to 1812.

In the time of the ancient Romans, this territory was traversed in all directions by the celebrated highways, by some of which the city was connected with the most distant provinces. The principal of them continue in use to the present day : in many parts the pavement of the Appian road is the same that was laid down by order of the Censor whose name it bears, more than two thousand years since.

On the left or Roman bank of the Tiber, there started no less than fifteen of these great roads, directly from the city gates.

The *Flaminian*, issuing from a gate of the same name, pretty nearly coinciding with the modern Porto del Popolo, passed over the Milvian bridge, by the foot of Soracte through Otricoli, Narni, Spoleti and Fano. Beyond Rimini it was called the *Æmilian*, as far as Aquileia.

At the Milvian bridge, now the Ponte Molle, the *Via Cassia* branched off from the Flaminian, and passed by Veii, Sutri, Bolsena, to Florence and Lucca.

Again, the *Via Cassa*, arrived at the station called *ad Sextum*, threw off a branch, which taking the name of the *Via Clodia*, led to Cosa, on the present Etruscan frontier. It passed to the west of Lake Bracciano. At Veii, this road in its turn threw off two branches, one running into Umbria, whilst the other to arrive at Vulsinii, traversed the mountain chain of the Cimino.

The *Via Salara ;* which, like the gate from which it issued, owed its name to its having been the way of transit for the salt, with which the ancient Sabines used to supply the mountain countries at the early period, when the salt works in the forest of Mæsia, a part of the Campagna, on the sea shore still belonged to them. This road passed through Fidenæ, Ereto, Cures, Rieti, in the direction of a line drawn across the peninsula. Another road which issued from nearly the same point—the ancient Porta Collina, was called the *Via Nomentana,* because it led to the city of Nomentum.

The *Via Tiburtina,* after it passed through Tibur (now called Tivoli) went by the name of the *Valerian* way, from Marcus *Valerius* Maximus, who had it made in the year of Rome, 453. The main trunk passed in the direction of Arsoli, but it threw off a branch called the *Via Sublacensis,* leading to an ancient town on the site of which Subiaco has arisen.

There was the *Via Prænestina,* to Prænestæ, and the *Via Labicana,* to Anagni. Both are still used.

From the Cælimontana gate there were three roads —the *Via Campana,* of no great length, the road to Tusculum, and a road leading to ancient Alba, or rather to the temple of Jupiter Latiaris, on the Alban Mount. Its pavement winding up the woody steeps of Monte Cave, to the Convent of the Passionists built on the ruins of the ancient temple, are marked to the present day with the letters V. N. *i. e. Via Numinis*, the Road of Jove.

Issuing from the *Porta Capena*, now the *Latin* Gate (closed up), a road which crossed the hills of Tusculum, in an oblique direction, joined the *Via Prænestina*, and the *Via Labicana*, at Anagni, and from thence under the name of the *Via Latina*, pursuing the course of the Val di Sacco, passed on through Ferentino, Frosinone, Fregellæ, (the modern and mediæval *Ponte Corvo*.)

The *Via Appia*, called the *Regina Viarum*, or queen of highways, led from the *Porta Capena* to Brundusium. It is still in a great part the high road from Rome to Naples, as far as Capua. According to Scamozzi, it was bordered with footpaths paved with a kind of rude mosaic, of divers coloured stones. The *Via Ardeatina* and the *Via Laurentana*, passed from the south side of the city to the sea shore, through the Campagna, then thickly studded with villas.

The *Via Ostiensis* connected ancient Rome with its sea-port, in issuing from the Ostian Gate, now called the Lavernale.

On the right bank or *Trans-Tevere* side, the city had only five gates. From the *Porta Portuensis*, on the river side, a road led to the New Port constructed by Trajan; and as this was an immensely crowded thoroughfare, it was twice the usual width of the other highways, and so divided in the middle as to prevent collision between the two great currents of life and bustle, the one towards the Port, the other from the Port to the Capital.

From the *Porta Janiculensis*, opening from the highest ridge of the Janiculum, where stood the old Acropolis, and in the remotest times perhaps, a city founded by Saturn, the *Via Vitellia*, extended to the sea shore. Between the Janiculum and the Vatican the *Via Triumphalis* extended—it was like an avenue—leading to the Triumphal gate and bridge.

The *Via Aurelia*, so called from the name of the private citizen who commenced it, had one terminus at the Pons Ælinus, at the foot of the Janiculum, and the other at Arles, on the Rhone, to which it was extended by Æmilius Scaurus. It passed along the shore of the Tyrrhenian sea by Lorium, Pyrgos, Pola *Centum Cellæ* (now Civita Vecchia), &c.

Besides these great highways, which had Rome for their centre, thence extending like rays to the most distant provinces, the territory of which we are treating, was traversed by a great number of subsidiary roads, such as the *Antiatina*, from Rome to Antium, the *Asinaria* leading into the *Campagna*, the *Casperia*, a branch of the *Via Salara*, leading to the city of Casperia, near Aspra, the *Cimina*, which branching from the *Via Cassia*, near Sutri, wound through the mountains of Cimino, in the direction of the Roncilione of the present day: the *Lavinensis* from the *Via Laurentana* to Lavinium, the *Setina*, from the *Via Appia* to Setia, the *Tiberina*, branching from the *Via Flaminia*, ran up the right bank of the Tiber, the *Via Trajana* led from the *Via Lavicana* to Segni.

The bridges are still nearly the same as in ancient times, and will have to be spoken of at a future stage of this history. Of the aqueducts the same is to be said.

BASIN OF THE LAKE BOLSENA.

In filling up the picture of this portion of the Pontifical States thus sketched in ruder outline, we propose to follow in the footsteps of Count de Tournon, Prefect of Rome, as has been already said, from the year 1810 to the year 1814, and who has left in his work the most incontestable proof that he cultivated the opportunities which his official position enabled him to command, to the utmost advantage.

He commences his survey at the northern extremity, where the Siena road crosses the frontier from Tuscany into the Papal States, approaching his subject with the following very solid and natural reflexion: "In times long gone by, this country had for inhabitants, Pelasgians, Siculi, Umbrians, Oscans, Etruscans, Latins, Sabines: the Equi, the Marsi, the Hernicians, and the Volsci: it was afterwards for five hundred years the arena of a bloody struggle between these ancient nations, and the robber town of Romulus, which ultimately vanquished and subjugated them one by one; and since their disappearance, engulfed in the abyss of Roman power, this part of the world has not ceased to be that point upon which has been concentrated the attention of all nations. In fine, this noble Roman land is made to produce its impressions on us from our most tender years, and is associated with the recollections of our earliest studies, so that for such as are devoted to history, to the natural sciences, or to political economy, a detailed description of it cannot but be fraught with interest."*

At the foot of the grim summits of Radicofani, you cross in coming from Tuscany, the valley of the Paglia, and enter the Pontifical States, at Ponte-Centino. Crossing the Paglia, by the Ponte Gregoriano, a little farther on you mount a steep ascent, and enter the little mountain city of Aquapendente, the first city of the States on the route from Siena. Its ancient name was Aquila. Its picturesque position is its only claim to attention: it was the birth-place of Jerome Fabricius, renowned as a professor of anatomy at Padua, to whom a statue was voted by the Republic of Venice, in the year 1603.

Beyond the city commences an elevated plain, partly cultivated and partly wooded, having to the

* L. i. p. 2.

north the volcanic peaks of Radicofani and Santa-Fiora, and to the east the mountains of Umbria. At the extremity of the plateau, towards the south, the eye is struck with the graceful aspect of a village recently built, it looks down upon the lake of Bolsena, which is concealed from view as you advance by a line of eminences interspersed with detached habitations, and in the background of the picture, a vast plain extends, which is crowned by the summits of the Cimino.

If this landscape has a character of grandeur which predisposes the mind for serious impressions, on the other hand the history of the village of San'-Lorenzo-Nuovo, gives rise to an agreeable emotion. Pius VI. caused it to be built not many years since, to receive the inhabitants of San' Lorenzo Vecchio, as they used to suffer terribly from the summer fevers, their former dwelling being situated at the bottom of an unhealthy valley. The Pope bore the whole expense of erecting the new town. " At one's first entrance into a country," observes M. de Tournon, " it is delightful to meet such an affecting proof of the beneficence of the Sovereign. What arch of triumph raised at the entrance of the States of the Church, could avail so much for the glory of Pius VI., as the little village of San' Lorenzo Nuovo ?"

A rapid descent through the remains of a forest brings you to the ruins of the abandoned village, the houses of which, dispersed in decay along the route of the traveller, seem destined to demonstrate to him how fatal is the influence of the *malaria,* and to justify by the action of this invincible power, that vast spectacle of depopulation and inactivity which he is about to behold.

The foot of this descent is bathed by the waters of Lake Bolsena (Vulsiniensis lacus) a vast reservoir of seventy square miles in extent. Its borders, partly elevated into hills, and partly level, are either wooded or covered with carefully cultivated fields and gardens. A great number of villages are scattered along its shores, and two inhabited islands arise from the bosom of its waters, one of them is called *Isola Bisentina,* the other *Isola Martana.* It was in the former the unfortunate Amalasonta, Queen of the Goths, and only child of the great Theodoric, was imprisoned by her second husband Theodatus in the year 535. Thus hardly have we set foot upon it, when we begin to learn by terrible examples how wild have been the sports of fortune on this Roman soil!

The shores of this vast sheet of water, clad as they are with forests interspersed with villages, surrounded with olive groves and vineyards, present a scene at once imposing and beautiful; but the pleasure arising from the prospect of scenery so charming is checked by the reflection, that those who inhabit it are decimated by the autumnal fevers; for these regions which look so enchanting to the view, are unwholesome to an extreme degree. Its waters are discharged by a single outlet on the south-west margin, and from the river Marta, which falls into the sea at Corneto after a course of thirteen leagues anda half.

After following for some time the margin of the lake you come to Bolsena, the ancient Vulsinii, one of the twelve principal cities of Etruria, and perhaps the most important of them all. This ancient metropolis was seated in a strong position on the summit of an eminence ending in an abrupt precipice towards the lake, as well as on two other sides, and accessible only on one side of its enclosure. It was not till the year of the city 445, that Vulsinii saw the Roman armies beneath its walls. It bought them off on that occasion by a subsidy imposed by the Consul Decius: thirteen years after, the Consul Postumius levied from it another subsidy in corn, garments, and 500,000lbs of brass. To such a height of prosperity had it attained, that the Romans when they finally took and plundered it in the year of the city 488, discovered in it amongst its other treasures no less than 2000 statues. Jealous of its splendour, as they were of that of Veii, they destroyed it; and of so much former grandeur, some vestiges of a temple, and a few ruinous arches of an aqueduct are all that now remain.

From the borders of the lake, the road traverses a forest tract of the white and green oak, presenting, on account of the accidents of the ground, broken into fell and glen, a constant variety of scenery, and all stamped with a character of savage beauty.

They point out a place in this forest where it is believed the Etruscan city of Ferentinum stood in ancient times.

The town of Montefiascone, the ancient Phliscon-Mons, is built on the summit of a volcanic eminence of a conical form. It occupies the centre of the basin of Lake Bolsena, and its cathedral, surmounted by a dome, being seated on the culminating point of the hill, gives effect to its lofty situation. From this point, as from a watch-tower, the eye can range over the ancient Etruscan territory to a vast extent.

To the north, in the foreground of this diorama, are seen extending down the slopes to the lake side, those vineyards whose vintage is so renowned. To the right of the lake, which is seen in its full extent, the beautiful forests arise which shade the heights of Bolsena and Bagnorea, ascending as if step by step until they become identified with the mountains of Orvieto (Oropitum), of Todi, and of Amelia: in the middle distance the horizon is closed by the extinct volcanoes of Radicofani and Santa Fiora. Nearer hand to the westward, the villages of Marta and Capo di Monte, of Valentano and Gradoli are descried upon the gracefully winding borders of the lake; and still more to the west, the plains of Canino, of Montalto, Toscanella, and Corneto, stretch away to seaward farther than the ken can reach. To the south the beautiful chain of the Cimino clad with forests towers above Viterbo: in fine, between this city, so distinguished for its numerous spires, belfrics and tower-defended ramparts, and Montefiascone, the high road can be traced like a furrow of dust across a plain, sun-burnt and unshaded by a single tree. This plain is a specimen perfect in its way of the malaria regions so frequent in this part of the States. A soil covered here and there with thickets, broken into ravines, denuded of trees, thinly scattered at intervals with grey and dark reddish masses of volcanic rock, which look like compacted cinders; corn fields of the most cheerful verdure, tracts of pasturage which during the showery season are carpeted with the most luxuriant vegetation, display their charms in a framework the most sombre and desolate. But the fields seem to have been cultivated by invisible hands, for the eye can discern neither farm-house nor cottage; the ear is not saluted by the barking of the watch-dog, or the crowing of the cock—a lugubrious stillness reigns on every side; and far away, from distance to distance, you see a few habitations which fear seems to huddle close together at the very top of some craggy eminence—it is from these piles of houses, the peasants descend to their daily toil upon the *malaria-plain*.

To the east of Montefiascone, and behind the forests which intervene between it and the Tuscan frontier, there extends an elevated plain, clayey, cold, covered with oak woods, and inclined towards the Tiber. The chief place in this district is Bagnorea, *Balneo-regium* in ancient times, a little episcopal city, of only 2,700 inhabitants. In the same direction is found the confluence of the Paglia and the Tiber, a point, at which the latter turns brusquely from east north-east to a south-easterly direction. To the south of Bagnorea, are situated the villages of San-Michele, Celleno, Civitella, d'Agliano and Graffignano. To the north of the same city, at a distance of two leagues, is seated the city of Orvieto, on the Paglia: its cathedral is one of the most curious monuments of mediæval art. We now descend from Montefiascone to follow the river Marta, the only outlet of the lake Bolsena, in its course along the Tuscan frontier towards the sea.

On its banks is a little village of the same name; the ancients called it Lartes, and a little further on is Capo di Monte, another village of an aspect highly picturesque, as it is seated on a promontory which looks out over the beauteous lake. The Prince Stanislaus Poniatowski has there a château, commanding a variety of charming views. The ancient Bisentum stood somewhere hereabout, probably opposite the islet of the same name. From Capo di Monte to Valentano, runs a chain of hills, on whose sides the vine, the olive, and various sorts of corn crops, display a careful cultivation. The ancient name of the latter village was Verentum. All about this district is thickly peopled; within a rather narrow circuit you count the four large villages of Pianzano, Gradoli, Grotte San-Lorenzo, and Latera.

The hillsand the wholesome regions both terminate at Valentano, and with them what the French call *la petite culture.* Towards the west, commences a volcanic plain, arid and stoney, of a monotonous aspect. The first inhabited place you meet is *Ischia,* of some 1600 inhabitants: further on is Farnese, which gave its name to the family of Paul III. At some distance beyond it, are the famous ruins of Castro, and beneath them rest those of the ancient city of Statonia. Thus do the ruins of two widely separated epochs strew this devouring soil.

In these plains was seated the city of Sudertum, on a branch of the *Via Claudia:* you find there at present the large villages of Pianiano, Celleze, and the town of Canino, sheltered under a chain of hills called Monte dell' Oro. It is well built, and differs in this respect from the surrounding villages. It is from this fief of the Apostolic Camera, or Papal Exchequer, that Lucien Buonaparte derived the title of Prince de Canino. Various ruins of baths and the ancient city of Vetulonia, renowned in ages past, have been brought to light by the excavations set on foot by Lucien, in this neighbourhood, as also of Vulsia, a city of the Etruscans, over which Tiberius Coruncanius, had a triumph in the year of Rome, 473. The bridge over the Fiora is of the Etruscan epoch, displaying great boldness of design. This river, which the ancients called Arminia or Armenta, descending from the mountains of Santa-Fiora, on which is seen an ancient residence of the

Sforza family, after a course of eight or ten leagues flows across the frontier, into the States, under the Tuscan city of Petigliano. Around Canino the air is bad: and the wide pasture tracts are but thinly scattered here and there with patches of cultivation.

From Canino the country is gently inclined in the direction of the sea, and is cut through without being watered by the Fiora. Beyond its deeply furrowed bed the *malaria plains of Tuscany* expand their vast undulations, in every respect resembling the *Maremma* of the Papal States; the same depopulation; the same risk from residing during summer, and withal the same system of treatment of the soil. "So true is it," continues de Tournon, "that like causes in both countries are followed by the same effects. The vigilant administration of Tuscany, the industrial activity of its people, their abundance of capital have been productive of no advantage for those malaria regions, over those of the Pontifical States. Is not this," he asks, "a *prima facie* demonstration, how unjustly it is that travellers, who are in raptures with Tuscany, see nothing on the Roman side of the boundary, but proofs of the maladministration of the Popes and the sloth of their subjects? But when has the tourist been known to turn aside into the *Maremma* of Grosetto, and of Volterra (in Tuscany), while the similarly situated regions of the Papal States are viewed from the carriage windows on both sides of the great thoroughfares from Naples, from Civita Vecchia and Tuscany to Rome."

The Pescia, which flows from the Tuscan *Maremma*, forms for two leagues or so the boundary line: beyond it in the distance is seen the Etruscan headland of Monte-Ercole, or Argentario, close to which is the little port of Orbitello, the object of frequent wars during the fifteenth and sixteenth centuries.

The ancient posting station, *ad Novas*, on the *Via Aurelia*, is on the Fiora, as is also the city of Montalto, thirteen or fourteen leagues further on. It is built on the ruins of the ancient *Forum Aurelii*, and is the centre of the great estates which belong to the Apostolic exchequer, lands which are let at very moderate rents. The surrounding plains are of surprising fertility. Immense corn crops of the richest green are surrounded by grass lands of a not less luxuriant verdure, on which are seen at pasture, herds of cattle and flocks of sheep, which look as if they could not be numbered; and in every direction the landscape is animated with a multitude engaged in all kinds of country work. Such are the scenes of spring-time and winter, but with the advent of the summer heats what a change comes over all this. The dusty and crumbling soil looks as if a conflagration had swept over it: all vegetation has ceased, the flocks have regained the mountains: and the population has vanished. Thus to judge correctly of those regions, the traveller should judge of them under the varying influence of the seasons. Nothing can be more favourable than these countries for the winter feeding of sheep.

When visited by M. de Tournon, one farmer, Sig. Adorno, had a flock of merinos, numbering 5000, the breed of those which had been imported by Pius VI. from Spain.

Extending parallel to the sea coast is a succession of shallow lakes, Catignolo, Arquato, Furiano, Gracciera, Burano, and del Vescovo, which contribute not a little to the malaria, and are bordered by low woods of oak, beech, elm, and pine trees, in which are fattened a vast number of hogs. The entire coast, to Terracina, is for the most part covered with woods of this description.

The cities of Regis Villa, Quintianum, and Martanum, all on the *Via Aurelia*, were seated in ancient ages near where the river Marta discharges itself into the sea, but hardly a trace of them is to be discovered. Not far distant is Corneto, built on a volcanic acclivity; its lofty ramparts, its towers and numerous belfries, impart to it a picturesque effect, and from its dwellings the eye can range over the rich circumjacent plain, and the vast expanse of the Tyrrhenian deep, from the promontory of Hercules to Civita Vecchia. Like Montalto it varies in its population with the seasons: in winter its streets are filled with 3300 inhabitants; they are deserted during the summer. This town is the centre of an agricultural commerce as little known to the generality of travellers as it is curious, and on a scale which may be safely termed immense. Wheat, oats, beans, and hemp, are raised in great abundance; its flocks and herds resemble those of the patriarchs in numbers, and the ex-president of the Roman province when he inspected this portion of it, was struck with the easy circumstances amounting to wealth, which reigned universally among the inhabitants.* The ancient Tarquinians also cultivated a great quantity of hemp, and during the second Punic war, they were obliged to supply sails for the fleets. During the healthy season, Corneto is a scene of gay life and activity: all the proprietors have returned to their houses: the peasantry of the mountains have come in hundreds, marching under their *Caporali* and to the sound of music, and are dispersed over the fields at their various tasks, imparting to the otherwise beautiful landscape, the charm of life and activity; but let him who would treasure impressions so agreeable amongst his recollections of travel, beware how he returns to the same scenes during the heats! Death alone is then awake and abroad.

This was the territory of the Tarquinians, one of the principal nations of the Etrusci, and still abounds in monuments and remains which attest the high condition of art and civilization amongst this ancient people. There rose one of the twelve metropolis's of the Etruscans, Tarquinii, built by Pelasgians, the birth-place of Tarquinius Priscus, and the powerful ally of Tarquin the Proud. It entered with fury into the conflict with Rome, devastated the Roman Campagna, put its Roman captives to the sword: its priests advanced to the charge, wielding not

* "Une grande aisance règne parmi les habitans."—Tom. 1. p. 20

swords but serpents above their heads. But in vain; Tarquinii succumbed in the year of the city 365, that is, seven years after the conquest of Veii: and, although this city had attained to great splendour, not a trace of it, above ground at least, is left. Many fragments of its edifices and its arts were brought to light by Cardinal Garampi, about the year 1780, by excavating in a field which went by the name of *Tarquinia!* This place, now a league distant from the shore, was formerly washed by the sea: so singular and impressive are the lessons which Time has inscribed in his transit over the regions which we have now under our view.

On the mouth of the little river Mignone (Minium fl.), to the south of Corneto, once flourished the city Graviscæ, a Roman colony, established in the year 571, and also the towns or posting stations of Rapinium and Algae: after three leagues across a desert you arrive at Civita Vecchia; but this place appertains to the basin of the Tiber, at which we are not arrived as yet.

Not far from the road which runs from Civita Vecchia to Viterbo, and after you pass the thermal springs called *Aquæ Apollinares*, there comes in view the pretty little town of Monte-Romano seated upon the highest of a number of woody eminences, erected by way of experiment on the estates in this quarter, of the hospital of the Santo Spirito at Rome. This little colony conducted with prudence, has succeeded to perfection.

Its inhabitants continue to reside in it the year

round: they are extremely prosperous, and when the ex-president, the Count de Tournon, visited the place, it reminded him, he says, of the most beautiful villages of France and Germany. Its horizon is bounded on the south-east by the wooded slopes of the Cimino, and in its neighbourhood the cities of Axia and Blera existed in long departed centuries: it is probable that the village of Bieda occupies the site of the latter place. To the northward the plain seems boundless. It is profoundly rent by ravines, in which some water seems rather to stagnate than to flow, so sluggish is the current.

The route traverses this sombre plain, leaving on the right the populous town of Vetralla, agreeably situated on the northern acclivities of the Cimino, and occupying the site of an ancient city or posting station of the *Via Cassia.* Thence forward to Viterbo, the road is through a hilly country, planted with the olive and the vine: but we turn aside from it for a passing glance at Toscanella, the ancient *Tuscania,* seated on the Marta, and in the midst of a beautiful and fertile country. We shall find it performing no ignoble part on occasion of the invasion of Charles VIII. but it is now exclusively devoted to the arts of peace—to raising herds of horses and oxen, and flocks of sheep.

The country between this place and Viterbo, at three leagues distance is slightly inclined from north to south, and by aid of the many streams descending from the Cimino, the rice cultivation is flourishing and extensive, which is but little conducive to the health of the inhabitants.

On approaching Viterbo one is agreeably impressed with the new aspect of the scenery. Cultivation becomes varied, and wears the appearance of care and intelligence: vineyards, gardens, and olive groves, are thickly interspersed with stately villas and country houses, and above these plantations and trees so refreshing to the sight after the naked monotony of the plains, the city lifts itself with its crown of high towers, the belfries and cupolas of its sixty churches, their dark mass coming out upon the misty hues of the Cimino mountains, which close the horizon in the distance. It is supposed to have been built by Didier, the last of the Lombard kings, on the site of Fanum Voltumnæ, a temple and city of great renown, before the ancient Etruscan nations fell under the yoke of the Romans. We shall meet with Viterbo more than once in pursuing the annals of the Papal States. In its vicinage, which presents the richest and most charming scenery, some excavations have brought to light the ruins of an ancient city,— thought to be those of Voltumnæ or of Ferentinum. On an isolated mass of rock, between the hills and the entrance of the plain in going towards Rome, is perched a castle of irregular architecture but imposing aspect, belonging to the Albani family: the town of Soriano is crowded round its base, and from its terraces the prospects are fine and extensive, commanding on one hand the acclivities of the Cimino, covered with the most brilliant vegetation, and on the other a cultivated plain, extending to the Tiber: beyond the banks of this famous river, the horizon is closed by the Umbrian and Sabine mountains. Somewhere in this plain was that lake Vadimon, empurpled in the year of the city 444, by the gore shed in a bloody and decisive battle in which the Umbrians and Etrusci were defeated. It was the scene of another sanguinary struggle, likewise favourable to the Romans, when the Etrusci but half subdued were roused by the Senones and Boians, when they invaded central Italy, to appeal once more to arms. In vain has this lake, which received the life-blood of the last champions of the independence of the Italian nations, been sought for: so completely has it been dried up that even its situation is unknown. According to Pliny the younger, its sulphureous waters were covered with little floating islands, overgrown with aquatic plants. The city of Castellum Amerinum which flourished in this country in bygone ages has disappeared and left not a trace behind. Its scanty population is at present confined to the three villages of Bomarzo, formerly Polimartium, Mugnano, and Sipicciano, and in returning towards the north-west you pass by the spot where stood the ancient Etruscan city of Trossulum, taken in the year of Rome 429, by the Consul Carvilius. The privilege of supplying the nine valets of the Roman senator called *fedeli del Campidoglio* belongs to Vitorchiano, one of the many villages of this district.

It was the reward of the courage and fidelity with which they resisted the attack of the Viterbians in 1267. Before entering the basin of the Tiber, let us survey that of the Lake Bolsena, in one rapid and comprehensive glance from a commanding point on the side of Mount Cimino with Viterbo embowered in its groves and gardens at our feet. It comprehends the entire of central Etruria, the country of a people full of energy, well governed, a land of civilization and of valour. It was this plain, now-a-days so monotonous, and well nigh a desert, which was looked down on with so much proud exultation by Quintius Fabius as he stood on the summit of the Cimino, attained through so many battles, and saluted it with the title of "Etruria the opulent,"—"Opulentæ Æturiæ arva."

BASIN OF THE TIBER, WESTERN SECTION, OR RIGHT BANK.

The basin of Lake Bolsena is separated from that of the Tiber by the Cimino range of mountains, the northern and eastern acclivities of which we have already surveyed. These were the enchanted heights, whose dense gloomy forests had the same power to impress with terror the Roman soldiers of the earlier times of the Republic, which was exercised by the Hercynian Forests, over the minds of the legionaries in the times of the Emperors. But the soil, to which was assigned by the superstition of those distant ages, the magic faculty, as if of nailing to it the foot which rashly dared to invade its sanctity, at the present day presents no terrors, and gives rise only to the emotions which spring from the view of scenery, in which field and forest are mingled in most enchanting disorder. The beholder is constantly taken by surprise, by the ever-varying points of view which open upon him—all beautiful and indicating the volcanic characters of those regions, by the florid richness of their foliage and vegetation.

It is through the glades and brilliant foliage of these forests, so charming in themselves, and so renowned in classic story, that Latium, the Sabine country, the hills of Algidus, and ancient Alba, are first discovered in the distance, with, in a word, the entire extent of that arena, on which was played out the bloody game of five centuries of battle, in which the headship of Italy, and the consequent empire of the world were won by Rome. "The first view," says M. de Tournon, "which we obtain of a region, which is invested with such a charm for the imagination from earliest youth; the first revelation of the land, for which Æneas and Turnus contended, which Numa governed by his laws, and Cicero by his eloquence; whereon the Cæsars struggled for a falling throne, and the holy Pontiffs founded the imperishable empire of religion, all this has the power to inspire and agitate the soul with inexplicable emotion."*

* Lib. i. p. 34.

That part of Etruria which we have hitherto surveyed, is but little known to the history of the classic ages. For those ancient times the Romans are unfortunately our only guides, and they seldom deigned to notice foreign nations, except to register their defeats; so that hardly do they record the cities they destroyed, and the tribes they uprooted, once they had won the passes of the Ciminò, in their march to more distant conquests. But in the countries to the south of this range, they had to fight for the territory inch by inch; each village cost them a campaign; one city alone ten years of siege. It is here then in reality the domain of history begins, and the interest increases with every step, as we approach that centre from which proceeded so many calamities, and which radiated such an effulgence of military glory.

The deep shadows of the forests, which overhang the *Via Cassia,* as it winds down the mountain's side, are reflected in the deep bosom of the lake called Ciminus Lacus by the ancients, and now known as the Lago di Vico, and which is one of the reservoirs so numerous in those regions, in which the most cool and limpid element has taken the place of the seas of lava which used to burst in by-gone ages from the craters of the long extinct volcanoes; and memories of this reign of terror impart a double charm to the sylvan scenery now so tranquil and so attractive, beneath which such scenes of red-hot ruin and devastation lie interred. But still, it would look as if this region was under some fearful doom: for after being allowed to rest and recover from the effects of volcanic fury, the fury of the ancient Roman for conquest began in forms not less terrible to wreak itself upon it. The ancient city of Vicus Elbii once flourished on the borders of this lake—it has disappeared: a town called Vico arose in distant times upon its ruins—Vico also has vanished—no trace of it is anywhere to be found. Thus it is that on this land of ancient fame, the cities disappear by generations, as doth the human kind in other places.

The lake is circular in form; originally, there was no vent for its waters but where they found their way over the brim of the ancient crater, and frequent and destructive inundations were the result; but a grand-nephew of Paul III. a duke of Castro and Roncilione caused a tunnel or *emissorio* to be formed, by which the superfluous waters might discharge themselves into a neighbouring valley, and the level of the lake be thus constantly secured. "Neither can Switzerland, the Vosges, or the Pyrenees," says Tournon, "present a fresher valley, one more animated or distinguished for industrial activity, than the glen through which the waters of this *emissorio* are precipitated over a succession of cascades; one time they flow under a leafy vault formed by the spreading trees, another time they tumble over rocks, or under the wheels of the paper mills, the forges, and other factories; offering to the painter a variety of the most picturesque effects, and to the traveller a picture of industry which comes upon him by surprise in this region of Italy." Hard by is Roncilione, a handsome and prosperous town of 3350 inhabitants, reposing with its turreted walls and the cupolas of its churches upon a bed of lava. The country is highly cultivated and planted to perfection, through which the Via Cassia still continues to tend Romeward down these pleasant slopes. From the line where the hills subside, a champagne country well watered with the mountain rivulets, unfolds its meadows and fields of richest verdure artificially irrigated by these streams; and these delights of nature, blending her most graceful charms with the cheering scenes of industry and plenty, continue to escort the traveller as he passes along through Capriola (a pretty town of the Farnese, where they had a princely castle, quite a sanctuary of the arts), and the fields of remarkable fertility and interspersed with majestic trees, which are cultivated by the husbandmen who inhabit the surrounding villages of Canepino, Valerano, Carbognano and Fabricana. But beyond Vignanello where the Ruspigliosi have a castle on the last swells of the hill country, these scenes of rural cheerfulness and prosperity are left behind—cultivation becomes rare and seems to languish; the woody tracts increase in extent, and the silence and gloomy solitude of the landscape once more announces that the reign of the *malaria* has commenced. The villages of Bassano, Bassanello, Galese and Corchiano are in this unhealthy plain, and at its extremity runs the Tiber with the ancient *Hortanum*, now called Orta, seated upon an eminence above its course. At Orta the *Via Ameria*, a branch of the *Cassia* passes over the Tiber, and lower down is the mouth of the Nera, a point from which the Tiber becomes navigable to the sea. All this country belonged to the Falisci in ancient times. They were very powerful in the confederacy of the Etruscàn nations.

The views are fine and diversified as you descend by the right bank of the Tiber, the valley of the Nera opening a vista into the Umbrian mountains over successive terraces of cultivated hills : on their summits are built Otricoli, Magliano, Calvi, which look out over the abrupt and rugged hills of Sabinia, whilst the long and graceful curves of the Tiber are winding in the foreground through a fertile valley waving with flourishing crops of wheat and Indian corn. To the north, the horizon is bounded by the Cimino, to the east, by the Sabine mountains, on whose sides the villages in great number seem to sparkle like pearls in the sun, while their last undulations spread away to the south and west without a bound. In the distance, Allano, and the mountain verdant with foliage which towers above it, and on the Campagna, Rome proudly reposing amidst its solitude.

The territory of the Falisci was separated by Mount Soracte from that of the Capenates, and Capena, the metropolis of this latter nation, which offered as stout and protracted a resistance to the Romans as Veii itself, was built between that mountain and the Tiber, probably on the spot where at present stands the town of Civitella : near to Soracte was the temple of the goddess Feronia, for which a less reverence was not felt by the Latins than by the Etruscans themselves. The tract on the opposite side of the river was the theatre of the earliest exploits of the Romans: there flourished Eretum, Nomentum, Cenina, Cameria, and Cures, in fine, the country of Tatius and Numa, and metropolis of the Sabine nation. Thus from Soracte's ridge the territories which were conquered by the first victories of the Romans, and those which were nobly defended against all their efforts for four centuries may be surveyed at the same moment. Those two regions whose fate presents a contrast so surprising are separated only by the Tiber.

The villages of Sant' Oreste at the foot of Soracte, to the south, Rignano, Civitella, San-Paolo, Nazzano, Torrita Filacciano, Ponzano, Calcata, and Stabbia, all villages, are within view upon the level country by which we are journeying towards Rome. A branch of the road which crosses over the Ponte-Felice from the Sabine side, passes on to the capital through Marlupo and Castelnuovo di Porto. Nearer the Tiber are situated the villages of Fiano, a duchy of the Ottoboni, Riano and Frassinetto, in ancient times a villa of Livia, called *ad Gallinas,* because a white hen let fall from the talons of an eagle in its flight, at that place alighted on the bosom of the empress.

We pass by Civita Castellana, of which we shall have much to say hereafter, observing merely that it has probably succeeded Fescenia, an ancient city of the Falisci of great strength. In following one of the picturesque valleys by which Civita Castellana is surrounded, after crossing a rocky tract overshadowed by enormous trees, you reach a bushy plain. Suddenly the ramparts of a city quite complete, the gates perfect, the walls rising from amidst the trees reveal themselves to view. You hasten to pass under those arches so lofty and large as to promise a great city; but beyond them is nothing but a desert space, strewed with some fragments of marble, and masses of brick, amongst which a few sheep are quietly feeding on the patches of scanty herbage. In vain you search for vestiges of the dwellings which those ramparts once protected, and which, if they still existed, so perfect and uninjured are they, they could protect as yet. Even the habitations of an after period, erected here after those of the first city had disappeared, have left not a trace behind. One solitary monument survives, amidst a scene which so impressively demonstrates how evanescent are the works of mortals.—" A poor shepherd informed us," says De Tournon, "that this little temple, displaying the elegance of the revival in its style, was *Santa Maria di Faleri*; thus," he adds, has the patronage of the Virgin preserved the memory of this ancient city."*

Falerii, like Fescenia, was founded by the Oscans, a people who preceded the Umbrians in this part of Italy: this gives a date anterior to the siege of Troy: yet these walls, and the sculpture on the archivalt of one of the gates, like the tombs of Tarquinii, are proofs of a high degree of art. The Falisci, who are honoured by Virgil with the epithet of "just," *(æquos Faliscos)*, took part in the struggles of the Etruscan confederates against the Romans; and their city was taken by Furius Camillus in the year of the city 369, two years after the fall of Veii: a lot which was probably shared by Fescenia, which would seem to have been one of its dependencies. The Falerii could not tamely succumb to the yoke of the invaders: they rose in arms more than once, and under the wrath of their oppressors the last vestige of their homes and altars disappeared.

In pursuing our route from Civita Castellana, over a bushy flat much broken into abrupt ravines and hollows, the village of Castel-Sant'-Elia, the *Suppontonia* of the ancients, is seen picturesquely seated on an eminence. The road next passes through the little city of Nepi built upon a salient promontory, with precipitous valleys on three sides—a position very usual for the towns and villages all through these parts. Its ancient walls, its elevated

* L. 1. p. 43.

towers, an aqueduct in ruins, which leave the waters that have altogether ceased to flow above its arches, to drip down the ivy and other climbing plants which seem in pity to mantle their decay, are indications at once of present misery and by-gone grandeur. The ancient Nepete was, in fact, an important city. It played an important part in the Etruscan confederation ; but the fall of Sutrium, its metropolis, seemed to drag Nepi after it, for five years after that disaster, it succumbed in the year of Rome 369, to the fortune of the conquerors. The importance of Nepete, in a military point of view, induced the Romans to establish there a colony, that is to say, a garrison of veteran warriors to overawe the surrounding country, and hold the mountaineers of the Cimino in check. A revolt drew down on the colony the anger of its parent, the insurgents were made to pass under the yoke by the consul Valerius. Probably from that time the ancient city sunk to ruin, but under the name of Nepi, a new one rose to considerable importance during the middle ages in its stead. It had attached to it the title of a duchy, and we shall find it playing a part in the feudal wars of the Roman Barons.

Although not one of the twelve metropolises, few cities of Etruria were more important than Sutrium, already mentioned. It submitted voluntarily to the Romans after Veii and Falerii were taken ; but an Etruscan army descending from the heights of the Cimino, surprised the conquerors in their recent acquisition and retook it. The Romans, being joined by reinforcements which were encamped in the neighbourhood, once more recovered their prize: so that thrice in the same day this hapless city changed its masters. It was strongly fortified by the Romans, and with Nepi became the chief bulwark of their territory against the incursions of Etrusci from the neighbouring mountains. These, in effect, delivered battle to the invaders beneath its walls, in the year of Rome 441. Defeated but not vanquished, they two years afterwards selected the same field of battle; and Sutrium for the second time saw them routed. The Ciminian forest, like that of Tasso, was robbed of the enchantment which had so effectually defended this last barrier of Etruscan independence for seventy years and upwards: soon after this victory, in the year of the city 445, the Roman armies for the first time crossed these formidable heights. The Sutri of the middle ages, as we shall see hereafter, becomes the scene of some of the most stirring events in the history of the Papal States. The honour of being the birthplace of Rolando is awarded to it by the poets who preceded Ariosto in his theme. An amphitheatre, excavated in the volcanic rock, is all that remains of its ancient grandeur, while it is only the defeats of its citizens that have been recorded by the historians of their oppressors.

Seated on the rising undulations of the Cimino, a little to the north of Sutri, we see the towns of Viano,

Capranica (where we shall hereafter meet with Petrarca in sore distress), Barberano, and lower down in a delicious valley is Bassano di Sutri, where the Justiniani possess a castle of imposing architecture, and adorned within with some of the finest productions of Domenichino's pencil. Beautifully wooded hills, valleys cultivated with care, and handsome houses surrounded by plantations and gardens, admonish us as we advance towards the south that we have entered again the healthy region ; and the fair village of Oriolo, where the Altieri have a castle, surrounded by parks and ornamental grounds, is descried in the midst of a rich and cheerful looking landscape. It occupies the site of the ancient Vicus Aurelii, and at a little distance stood Forum Claudii on the highway, from which it took its name.

At a little distance from Oriolo, close to which are mines of sulphur, the conical hill called *Monte Virginio* marks where the last undulations of the Cimino range subside into the Campagna. It is completely covered with enormous trees that look as if they had flourished there for centuries. From its summit, which juts like a promontory above the plain, which, at first slightly undulating and broken into dells, is seen to stretch away clad in brilliant verdure, and apparently as smooth and level as the sea with which it is confounded in the far off horizon. Through it the Tiber winds its course, while the ridge of Monte Mario conceals from the view that object which of all others the eye of the traveller is most eager to behold. Towards the east, the lake Bracciano appears surrounded by smiling scenery; its vast mirror reflecting the villages, castles, and noble forests which ornament its borders. All that level country extending to the Tiber and the sea, belonged to the Cerites and the Sutrians: that to the east of Monte Virginio belonged to Veii while it stood. Here again, as in the basin of Balsena, the *petite culture*, the careful garden-like cultivation, and the *aria buona*, or good air, cease together; and with the solitude of the Campagna, the *aria sospetta*, and then the *aria cattiva* begin their reign. In the wholesome hill country all is life, movement, and prosperity: crop succeeds to crop without intermission on the soil, which is embellished by a multitude of trees: the dwellings of the husbandmen, scattered over the gentle rising grounds, are half embowered in foliage amidst the happy scene of cultivation: but on the plain, the air of solitude, the nudity of the soil, the huddling together of the habitations in unsightly villages, illustrate the truth for the second time, that the mode of cultivation is contingent upon the sanitary state of the localities. A style of tillage diversified, and the result of thorough intelligence is pursued with active and persevering industry wherever the inhabitants can reside without risk of their lives amongst the scenes of their labours; when they are exiled from them by the pestilential air—an enemy which no courage can defy, at least a second time—they are driven to the alternative of tillage on a great scale, and then allowing the lands to run into grass for an uncertain interval. It is the concluding remark of the ex-Préfet, that this observation should be present to the mind with such as are not fain to be misled by prejudice in judging of this portion of the Papal States. Some hermits have found an appropriate abode under the forest trees of Mount Virginio, and look for nothing from that world which is at their feet, but a morsel of bread and to be forgotten.

Manziana, a village not surpassed in charms by any in France or Germany, is the centre of a most enchanting landscape: indeed, on every side the borders of the lake are extremely beautiful. The castle of Bracciano of a most imposing aspect, as it rears its vast bulk, crowned with parapets and towers, from a rocky promontory well nigh surrounded by the waters of the lake, was erected by the Orsini in mediæval times, where stood, it is probable, the Capitol or Acropolis of Sabate, or Arcenum, an ancient city of the Cerites. We shall meet with it in the baronial wars, and on other occasions also. The lake, which went by the name of the *Sabatinus lacus* amongst the ancients, is two and twenty miles in circuit: its waters are deep and abound in fish, especially eels, which are greatly prized. Overshadowed by the lofty forests which rise upon its northern margin, we discover Vicarello, a hamlet built upon the ruins of a pleasure villa of Lucius Varo; and here, also, it is that we come for the first time in this direction upon some traces of those monuments which bear the stamp of Roman grandeur. The torrent which causes the Janiculan hill to re-echo with its fall, is borne from this lake by five and thirty miles of arches. This stupendous work, first executed by order of Augustus, more than 1800 years since, will meet us again in the progress of our history. Another aqueduct was supplied from the *Alsiatinus lacus*, now lake Martignano, which like the *Papirianus lacus*, now Straccia Cappa, lies to the east of Bracciano, and between those two former lakes, once flourished the city of Larthenianum, which has totally disappeared for ages. Anguillara now reduced to 650 inhabitants, was in the middle ages another stronghold of the Orsini, whom we so often meet with around those lakes, as we shall meet with their rivals, the Colonnas, by and by, amongst the hills of Tusculum and Palestrina. At Baccano, still nearer to Rome, there was another lake, but Pope Alexander VII. had it drained, in the hope of improving the salubrity of the surrounding country. In vain, however, the corn fields are flourishing, and the verdure of the pastures most luxuriant upon the volcanic soil improved by the irrigation, as in the instance of the *emissorio* of the lake de Vico before described; but it is with difficulty some few families attached to the posting station at Baccano make good their ground against the deadly influence which claims this terrible region for its own. Even the situation of the ancient city of *Baccanæ*, which stood somewhere hereabouts, is no longer accurately known.

For the rest, the route from Baccano onwards is over the beds of lava, which poured destruction from the surrounding craters in times long anterior to those in which history attended the inroads of the Roman freebooters upon those plains. The soil is partly covered with wood and partly barren; some patches are enclosed with palisades as pasturage; and now and then you pass a cultivated spot by the way side. A farm-house, solitary and grimly seated on some eminence amidst the desert, excites you to speculate as to whether it is the homestead of the peaceful tiller of the ground, or the stronghold of a bandit chief. There are about it none of the graceful and cheering appendages of a farm-house in other countries: it has towers and strong walls with loops for shot or arrows; one might mistake it for a fortress, or be forced to the conclusion that here men cultivate the soil with arms in their hands; and, as frontiers are guarded in other places, the harvests are here within sight of the capital to be defended. In the course of our history we shall discover that this is not fiction but reality: we shall become impressed with the truth that it is not exclusively on account even of the *malaria* that the Campagna of Rome has assumed its present aspect. Here, where Veii flourished, and was the prize for which two people so long and so fiercely contended, the trace of the plough is scarcely to be seen. The once fertile fields are usurped by thickets, and no one seems disposed to disturb their reign. Few are the passengers upon these ancient highways: and these come to wonder at the solitude from regions little known to the conquering people who so proudly lorded it upon these scenes: no symptom of industrial activity, or of commerce with the interior is any where to be discerned. The soul is oppressed by the sad stillness around, disquieted by the spectacle of desolation; and it is not without some anxiety one inquires how one is to exist in the centre of such a desert.

At half a league to the east of La Storta, the city of Veii once occupied the summit of a hill, abruptly separated from the plain by two deep glens, through which there flow two rivulets that unite under the promontory from which the Veians, secure in their impregnable position, used to look out upon the pleasant valley of the Cremera, more especially after it had become renowned by their defeat and slaughter of the three hundred Fabii with their 5000 clients or retainers. For a term of 350 years of almost uninterrupted war, this people maintained the cause of freedom against their haughty and unprincipled aggressors. They often carried the war to the very gates of Rome, and encamped more than once on the ridge of the Janiculum. Their fall drew after it that of Central Italy, which lay open to the invaders by the conquest of Etruria, to which the Veians had acted as a vanguard for so many centuries. Delighted with the healthy and secure position of their conquest, the Romans, those at least of the populace, were eager to forsake the Seven Hills, and deposit their penates within a fortress which they had proved could not be taken except by stratagem. We have elsewhere described how the plebeians were diverted from this secession which must have proved fatal to Rome, and have changed the after destinies of the world. Occupied by the fugitives who escaped from the sword of Brennus at the battle of the Allia, just opposite the valley of the Cremera beyond the Tiber, the ruined city served for a while as a place of refuge to its destroyers. But after the retreat of the Gauls allowed the fugitive Romans once more to congregate around the Capitol, it would seem to have been again abandoned to solitude and to ruin. The Empress Livia revived it by establishing a colony which would seem from the monuments it has left to have flourished there for a long time. But this second Veii disappeared in its turn: and the site where two generations of cities, so to speak, had existed for such a long series of ages, at length became a matter of doubt! The place of Veii is at present partly occupied by a farm-house which was a fortress in the middle ages. At a little distance stood the ancient city of *Aremutiæ*, but its exact position is no longer known. Some think it stood where the village of Formello stands at present.

In following the valley of the Cremera, the first post

obtained on the left bank of the Tiber by the Romans, we come at the same moment to the ancient *Via Flaminia* and the banks of the Tiber, at a posting station called *Saxa Rubra,* where of old the Veians had a fortress, and which in after ages became immortalized by the victory won by Constantine, as the champion of the cross, over Maxentius the cruel Pagan Emperor. Corn fields and verdant pastures now occupy the plain. It is here we come upon the *Prati di Quinzio,* pointed out as the farm from which *Quintus Cincinnatus* was summoned by the ambassadors of the Senate to abandon his plough and assume with the dictatorship the command of the Roman armies.

Before descending the last hill on the *Via Cassia,* towards the Milvian bridge, the postillions are wont to point to a ruin by the way-side as the sepulchre of Nero. It is, however, as a very legible inscription informs us, not the tomb of Nero, but one erected to "C. VIBIUS MARIANUS." But in defiance of the warning to the contrary inscribed on marble, the fancy still clings to the tradition that it is none other than the hateful matricide and the murderer of the Princes of the Apostles who has his tomb in such a desert.

From this point the Eternal City is no longer a vision or a mystery: it is distinct before the view. The Monte Mario, crowned with cypress trees, and the pine forests of the Borghese Villa and of Villa Ludovisi form the imposing vista through which you see it: its towers, belfries, obelisks, and cupolas innumerable fill the interval, and towering in massy grandeur above them all is seen the "wondrous Dome," from which the cross of Jesus Christ looks out in benign triumph over the city of the Cæsars.

As yet, however, we must not set foot in Rome, but turn to survey what remains of the valley of the Tiber. This we shall do more rapidly than hitherto, and in less detail, in order not too much to fatigue the patience of the reader; at the same time that we feel convinced that next to a personal inspection of the scenery, nothing can so effectually assist the reader to derive advantage and entertainment from the history, as to be thoroughly familiarized by description with the theatre of the deeds and transactions to be narrated.

At the foot of Monte Mario, to the south-west, a deep glen called the *Val d' Inferno* reveals itself. It was through it the avenue called the *Via triumphalis*, passed in the direction of the triumphal bridge and the Campus Martius. Having passed along through the villas, gardens, and vineyards, interspersed with convents and churches, you forsake the ridge of the Janiculum, enter on the *Via Aurelia*, and at no great distance find yourself once more amidst the pestilential air and concomitant desolation of the Campagna. Its aspect here, however, is different from what we witnessed in the north. The ravines by which it is broken are less abrupt and profound; the cultivated tracts are more frequent and extensive: it is only the steeps and precipices that are abandoned to the forest: the volcanic soil, in fine, is covered with a more luxuriant herbage. The little river Arone winds through this country to the sea. Beyond a bridge which is thrown over it you see the farm-house—it occupies the place of the ancient city of *Buxetum*, and Castel Guido is built on the site of the ancient *Bebiana*, as some will have it, or according to others on the site of *Lorium*, the place where the Emperor Antoninus Pius was either brought up, or breathed his last. To the north were situated the city of *Artena* on the Arone, and that of *Caneia* on the Claudian way. Polidoro occupies the place of the ancient *Pales*, which was near the Roman station, called *ad Turres*. Not far off is the village of Ceri, and near to it is another village called *Cer Vetri*, constructed on the ruins of the Etruscan city of *Cere Vetus*, or Agylla, which was one of the twelve metropolises of the Etrusci. Its citadel was raised upon a volcanic eminence, rocky, isolated on all sides, and pierced with several grottos. Before Rome was founded this city groaned under the tyranny of Mazencius, but it expelled him and became the ally of Æneas against the Latins. In more recent times the Cerites entered into alliance with the Romans, and seem to have had but little share in the efforts of the Etrusci to resist their inroads, they however, opened a retreat to Tarquin when he was dethroned. They also received the Vestals within their walls when Rome was burned by the Gauls; and the alliance was renewed at the instance of Furius Camillus, in gratitude for this generous act. The Romans were also bound to them by religion: their *ceremonies* having for the most part been a boon from Cere; but with the Romans every consideration was subordinate to the ambition which coveted to absorb the whole world in itself: in the year of Rome 400, the refuge of the Vestals was doomed, and in the lapse of ages entirely disappeared. The Cereites were devoted to sea-faring, and had a little port called Pyrgos on the adjoining coast. Hard by this city the mineral waters called *Aquæ Ceretanæ* took their rise. In treating of the industrial resources of the States during the Papal epoch, we shall have to revisit these scenes again. In this neighbourhood, concealed by an immense forest, are the alum works, and some of the great farms, the management of which is as singular as one would expect to meet in a romance. Not far off is Civita Vecchia, with its double mole, which Trajan erected to break the impetus of the waves: its citadel and Pharos are the erections of Michael Angelo. From this the eye runs on by the chain of watch-towers which guard the solitary shore as far as the promontory of Hercules, and the Tuscan frontier, the region of Montalto and Corneto which we have already traversed. To the south, the shore is also studded at intervals with towers, each held by a few invalided soldiers, who in any emergency can communicate by signals along the whole sea-board with great rapidity. Santa-Marinella, Santa-Severa,

Palo, Macarese, are modern villages, occupying the sites of the ancient Etruscan cities of Pyrgos, Alsium, Castrum Novum, Punicum, and Fregenæ: still further along the coast are Fumicino and Ostia, merely marking the place where the two vast emporiums of the Old and New Port extended when the haughty city of the Consuls and the Emperors was in the zenith of its glory. These were the resorts so beloved by all "who had ships upon the sea," as St. John has described. They saw arrive the immense rafts which bore the obelisks of Egypt, the fleets which were laden deep with the spoils, the plenty, and the luxuries of the world. Both were taken and plundered by the Vandals under Genseric: they were again taken and sacked by Totila, who endeavoured to rase them to their foundations, as was his wont with all cities and all walled places which could afford a refuge to his enemies the Greeks. But we hasten away from these scenes of desolation, as our history will require us again to revisit them. In reascending the Tiber, we come to the forest of Mesia, close to which were the salt-works of Veii, on a space between that river and the Arone. Ancus Martius in making himself master of this place, was the first to carry the frontier of the embryo empire to the sea: in winning the mouths of these two rivers, he opened one of the great gates which led the Romans to the dominion of the world.

VALLEY OF THE TIBER.—EASTERN OR ROMAN SIDE.

Through Etruria, both central and southern, we have travelled, visiting in succession the cantons of the Vulsinians, the Tarquinii, the Falisci, those of Capena, of Sutrium, of Veii, and of Cere: we are now in the ancient land of Saturn, where vestiges of the Rutuli, the Volsci, of the nations of Alba and of Sabinia will meet us at every step. These two confederations were separated by the Tiber, from where it received the waters of the Anio to the sea, and the country of the Sabines was intercalated like an acute angle between the two nations. It was on some abrupt and rugged eminences, defended by marshes and by the Tiber, not far from the point where the confines of three nations converged, that a band of desperate and outlawed men established their city, or to speak more properly, their camp, with Romulus for their chieftain or king. If the choice of this position did not arise from accident, great was the foresight which suggested it; for no place could be better adapted for defence and for making rapid strides in aggrandisement at the expense of its neighbours. Latium was naturally the first object of the ambition of the Romans, and while in Etruria we have everywhere met with the traces of a glorious resistance, maintained for upwards of four centuries, we are now entering on scenes, when cities and nations fell victims speedily, and without much struggle, to that want which goaded on the upstart city to create a territory for itself. We are on the soil which served as a theatre for those poetic exploits with which the Romans were fain to adorn the cradle of their grandeur; and viewed in that double light that Latium, which was entitled *Antiquissimum*, most ancient, inspires the most lively interest.

We issue forth by the Ostian gate, through which Totila entered when he destroyed the imperial city: the solitary and sombre mass of St. Paul's resembles a monument of the desert. This basilica, and the great tillage tracts between it and the sea we have left behind; we have reached the tower of Paterno, on the sea-shore to the south of Ostia. Here stood Laurentum, which the aborigines founded after the expulsion of the Siculi, and where reigned the good king Latinus, the father of Lavinia. Even after the foundation of Rome, Laurentum continued to prosper by means of commerce at sea, and the Romans as its allies made stipulations in its favour in their first treaty with Carthage. This, however, did not save it from being blotted out from the list of cities: no trace whatever of it is left. Nigh hand, in after ages, in the sunny epoch of the Antonines arose the splendid villa which Pliny the younger loved so much. He called it *Laurentina*. A little further inland Hortensius had a villa: and those of Scipio and of Lælius were not far off. In the same neighbourhood, seated upon the low hills running parallel to the shore, were situated the cities of Ficana and Tellena, conquered by Ancus Martius in the year of the city 117. Their inhabitants were forced to come and settle on Mount Aventine. In the same region stood Palitorium and Lavinium, founded by Æneas. It was here that Tatius, who shared the throne with Romulus, was slain by an assassin's hand. This did not interrupt its friendly relations with Rome: but its turn came, and like all those other cities, it was absorbed or crushed by the all-conquering people: the little hamlet of Pratica now occupies its site. From a castle belonging to the Prince Borghese you can view the country of the Laurentines and Rutuli to a great distance, towards the north is the lake Turnus and the place where the temple of the mysterious Anna Perenna once stood.

Beyond Pratica we enter an extensive wood, sacred of old to Æneas, under the designation of Jupiter-Indigetes; and crossing the Numicus, now called the Fiume Torto, by which the territories of the Laurentines and the Rutuli were divided, we arrive at Ardea. This metropolis of the Rutuli had attained to a high degree of splendour long before the Trojans arrived in Italy, as was attested by the numerous paintings by which its dwellings were adorned, and by its temple of Juno, celebrated in all antiquity. Fortified by art and nature, it repulsed the attacks of Tarquin who was besieging it at the moment the Romans had risen to chase him from the throne. It became the ally of the young republic, and sent into Spain a colony to found the city of Saguntum. It was itself in process of time reduced to receive a colony, and ultimately amidst the splendours of its ancient rival it utterly disappears!—In traversing those regions the cemetery of so many cities and long buried nations, how frequently and with what pathos do the beautiful lines of Tasso force themselves upon the memory:—

> "Giace l' alta Cartago: appena i segni
> Dell' alte sue ruine il lido serba:
> Muojono le città, muojono i regni
> Copre i fasti, e le pompe, arena ed erba."

The *Via Severia* led along the sea-shore from Ostia to Ardea, and had branches to Lavinium and Antium. From these ancient realms, long reduced to solitude, and now partitioned between forests, tillage farms, and pastures, all of vast extent, we hasten with pleasure into the hill country around the Mons Latiaris, which formed the dominion of ancient Alba. These majestic trees, casting widely their refreshing shade, this puissant vegetation, these scenes of a cultivation as varied as it is characterized by skill and industry, how delightful and refreshing to the wayfarer fatigued and depressed by the solitude and the monotony of the plain! Here, as on the Cimino, agriculture receives its laws from the sanitary state of the scenes in which it is pursued. Absence of population and wide extended pastures mark the dominion of the malaria on the plain: with the first stages of the hills above which

Monte Cave lifts its wooded head, we are welcomed by smiling scenes of diversified and skilful industry.

On one of these terraced hills rests the ancient city of Aricia, buried under its own ruins. It was founded by Hippolytus, and saw fall, Aruns, the son of Porsenna, in leading an assault against its walls. Its temple of Diana was a place of periodical meeting for the Latin Confederates. Another temple of this goddess of the chase, once occupied the platform on the mountain side where the town of Nemi, a famous retreat of the Frangipani, Savelli and Colonna, in the middle ages, now stands above the lake, called by the ancients "Diana's mirror."

As Homer had placed his fabulous deities upon mount Ida during the wars of Troy, so did Virgil select the Alban mount for Jupiter and Juno to view the combats of the Rutuli and the Trojans: a better selection there could not be, both on account of the great height and admirable position of this mountain. The noble forest trees which adorned it to its very summit, (the great sanctuary of the Latin nations) and cast their massy shadows into the deep blue waters sleeping in the deep craters, which before the memory of man used to pour out oceans of molten lava from its sides, bestowed upon it a charm of mystery, which suited it admirably for the poet's purpose. Close behind it rose Mount Ariano, and Mount Algidus a little farther off, beyond the lofty arena overlooked by this amphitheatre of mountains, whereon it is said by tradition that Hannibal pitched his tents, before rushing down across the Campagna against Rome. Nearer and to the left of Algidus, were the rounded hills of Tusculum, and over the summits of both the arid and battlemented ridges of the Apennine were distinctly visible, with the cities and fortresses on their craggy summits,—from Prenestæ inhabited by the Equians, to the ridges of Mounts Gennaro and Lucretelis, far away in the land of the Sabines. Along the foot of these mountains, the territories of the Gabii and of Tusculum extended over the plain, now naked and a desert, where a few unsightly granaries now occupy the places of once puissant cities. Towards the north, the meanderings of the Anio and the Tiber are distinctly seen: those conical hills in the interval between them mark the region where formerly stood the cities of Cures, Fidenæ and Nomentum; at the horizon is Soracte commanding the ancient dominions of the Falisci and the Capenates, and on the amphitheatre of hills which swell by degrees into the summits of the far distant Cimino, extends the country where the brave nations of Veii, of Sutrium, and Cere arose into civilization and prosperity, flourished, and were invaded; fell gloriously struggling for liberty, and disappeared beneath the ruins of those countries many and many a long century ago. In the same direction, and at the centre, where long lines of aqueducts and highways converge, is seated the city of the Pontiffs, its domes, palaces, and towers, interspersed with ruins, and girdled with gardens and vine-clad hills. Towards the west all the elevations subside into the vast level which melts away into the azure line of the Tyrrhenean waves. From Pyrgos, the Pyreus of the Ceretes, to Antium, the entire coast is distinctly seen, and the Tiber traced in a double line of silvery light which seems to enclose the delta, the Isola Sacra, where branching into two channels it flows into the sea: much nearer and reposing on the sunny acclivities of the mountain on which we too are seated, the cities of Frascati, of Marino, Albano, Genzano: the villages of Castel Gandolfo, Rocca di Papa, Monte Compatri, Nemi Aricia, shew themselves amidst sylvan scenes and fields, and vineyards teeming with abundance; while the two deep blue lakes of Albano and of Nemi seem placed where they are to reflect such admirable scenery.

On the terraced side of this very mountain, and overhanging that deep mirror of the lake which is at our feet, it was that ancient Alba flourished and sent out its colonies all over Latium long before Rome was heard of. Livy has depicted in vivid colours the scene of its destruction in the year of the city 104. Its inhabitants were dragged or driven away captive with their flocks and other substance: the place where it stood was long a subject of dispute: it is most probable that the little convent of Pallazzuola is built amongst its ruins. The modern city of Albano has arisen on the pleasant ground once occupied by the villas of Pompey, of Claudius, and of the Emperor Domitian. Bovilla, once the metropolis of a free people, and afterwards a posting station on the *Via Appia* lower down in the direction of Rome, was witness of the affray between Clodius and Milo, as of many another bloody scene; more to the right, on the hill side is Marino, near the shady valley and the fountain, where the Latin Cantons used to celebrate the festival of the goddess Ferentina with games as well as with idolatrous rites. We pass by Tusculum, founded by Telegon, son of Ulysses and of Circe, by Colonna, where the city of Labicum stood in ancient times, and where Julius Cæsar had a villa. More into the plain a farm-house marks the site of the ancient Gabii. To the north-west of this city was Collatia, which in submitting to Tarquinius Priscus accepted a most ignominious capitulation preserved by Livy. It is also associated with the story of Lucretia. When its proud destroyer was in her palmy days, it had disappeared, and was replaced by the pleasure grounds of some rich citizen. Those proudest monuments of Roman grandeur, the aqueducts, extend their gapped and time-worn arches in several lines across these parts of the Campagna.

To the right of Colonna, on the range of woody hills which form the boundary between the basin of the Tiber and the Val di Sacco, the village of Lugnano is seated on the spot where stood the ancient city of Longianum. In the same region was Pedum a city of the Latins, conquered first by Marcus Coriolanus, and afterwards by Furius Camillus; also the Roman colony of Vitellia, which the Equians took and plundered: the village of Zagarolo of 3000 inhabitants, which gives to the Ruspigliosi Pallavicini family a ducal title, now occupies the plain; and suspended, so to speak, upon the mountain side, the city which has succeeded to the ancient Prenestæ, with the Pelasgic citadel upon the mountain summit above it, is seen under the most picturesque and striking aspect. According to Virgil, Prenestæ was founded by Ceculus five or six hundred years before Rome, and for a long time stood in the first rank of the Latin Confederates. Alternately the ally and the enemy of Rome, it was taken by Cincinnatus, and probably reduced to the state of a colony. It was taken by Pyrrhus, who viewed from its citadel that great object of his ambition which was destined to be disappointed. A pitched battle was fought between Marius and Sylla under its walls, during the civil wars, and Marius after being defeated sought refuge within its walls, but soon after fell along with the city into the hands of the victor, who, in cold blood, caused 12,000 of its citizens to be put to death. We shall repeatedly meet with Palestrina during the middle ages.

The mountain range, which commences here, and runs on by Tivoli, the ancient Tusculum, into the country of the ancient Sabines, as compared with those of the Cimino and Alba so often spoken of, presents the most striking contrasts. Instead of the gentle declivities and graceful waving outline of the latter, the mountains over Palestrina are precipitous, grim and rocky. They are for the most part denuded of vegetation and of trees; but on their skirts the olive prospers, and higher up, the clefts and rocky precipices are garlanded with stunted trees, underwood, and plants and flowers, which diffuse an aromatic perfume. Among these craggy heights were situated in ancient times, the cities of Æzula and Empulum, brought under the yoke of Rome, in the year of the city 398: Bola, Corbio, which Coriolanus wrested from the Equi, which this brave people recovered, and which the Volscians ultimately destroyed. Here also was the city of Scaptia. At present, the only inhabited places between this and Tivoli worth notice, are Poli, a duchy of the ancient family of the Conti, and the Castle della Catena, which is the property of the Sforza of the present day. Tivoli, which belongs to the valley of the Anio, we leave to our right for the present. Where the hills on which it is seated sink into the Campagna, a vast scene of ruins overgrown with lichens intertwined with roses, and interspersed with vineyards, and corn-fields, overshadowed by the cypress and the pine, the fig-tree and the ilex, indicate where extended in the heyday of imperial Rome, that scene of architectural magnificence in which Adrian erected the counterpart, so to speak, of those edifices which in his progresses through the various provinces of the Roman world, had most excited his admiration. But this paradise which the Emperor of a world so laboured to adorn with every miracle of art, and to fill with every delight of nature, has been nothing for a long lapse of ages but a pestilential solitude. Beyond it, hard by the Ponte Lucano, which spans the Anio, the ancient tomb of the Plautian family still subsists. It is a round tower, constructed with great elegance and solidity, and like all other structures of the same kind in those parts was converted into a fortress in the feudal ages. The bridge was one of the many, destroyed by Totila and repaired by Narses at the close of the Gothic wars.

From the Ponte Lucano, the Sabine territory begins. On a rounded hill top to the right, the mediæval town and castle of Monticelli, usurps the place of the ancient city of Cænina. Acron, who was its king, fell under the sword of Romulus, and gave occasion to the first triumphal pomp that ever mounted the Capitol. A little to the west, was Corniculum, which Tarquin the Elder subdued. This was the birthplace of Servius Tullius. More northward, on another rounded hill—the ancient Mons Patulus—is seated Sant' Angelo and its feudal castle now in ruins, and close under the lofty Mount Gennaro, the highest of this lower range of the Apennine, the populous town of Palombara occupies the place of the ancient Cameria, another of Tarquin the Elder's conquests. All these cities were overthrown during the first epoch of Rome's existence, and apparently with much facility; so much more feeble than that of the Etrusci, their neighbours beyond the river, was the resistance which was offered by the Sabines to their invaders. The blending of hill and dale, makes this region most agreeable, and in the heart of it was placed the ancient metropolis of the nation. By Virgil the citizens of Cures are called *Prisci Quirites*. Its exact site is no longer known: but probably it was where the poor village *Correse* stands at the present day. The picturesque and highly diversified character of the surrounding country adds greatly to the pleasing effect of the towns and villages, Monte Flavio, Scandriglia, Nerola, (the ancient Suna), Monte Leone, Poggio Nativo, Poggio Majone, which (as is indicated by their names) are all seated upon hills. Their happy valleys are watered by the Correse, called Himella by the ancients, and the Farfa. *Fabaris* was the ancient name. In these same pleasant countries, once rose the cities of Trebula, Suffenatis, of Casperia and Forulum; but where they were situated no one can tell.

The *Via Salara* forsakes the course of the Tiber, to penetrate into these mountains, and gradually winds its way to the culminating point between the Tiber valley, and that of the Velino. Here too was situated the Abbey of Farfa, so celebrated in mediæval history, of which we shall have much to say. Not far from this monastery is Poggio Mirteto, in an enchanting country, as also the villages of Monpeo, Salissano, Monte Nero, all on hills, and Cantalupo on the mountain side over the road to Terni. Perched above it still higher is Aspra, surrounded by a cincture of olive groves, in a position to which it is with difficulty a goat can climb. Calvi is another of the mountain villages, in these rocky and savage regions. From these scenes, where we shall have to witness a battle in 1799, we hasten to descend through a succession of olive grounds, vineyards, and richly cultivated fields, into the beauteous regions, where the ancient Ocriculum looked around upon a charming country which belonged to the Umbrians, until they were subjugated by the Romans in the year of the city 446. Like so many other cities, especially in Etruria and the south of Italy, Ocriculum fell a victim to the destructive cruelty of Sylla during the civil wars. Near it on our return down the Tiber, we see the handsome town of Magliano, the villages of Colle-Vecchio, of Forano and Gavignano, in the midst of cultivated fields: we traverse the immense prairies beyond Correse along the Tiber, thus re-entering those scenes where at every step we are reminded of the fatal effects of conquest. "Each of those hills," observes De Tournon, "was crowned by a city of which in many instances the very names have perished." Nomentum, a conquest of the elder Tarquin, has been for ages but a souvenir; like the city of Eretum, its neighbour, it had the honour to be named by Virgil in the review of the nations leagued against Æneas.

It is probable that the villages of *Mentana* and Monte Rotondo occupy their sites, as it is likely that Marcigliano does that of the ancient Crustumerium, quoted in the Æneid as famous for the manufacturing of arms, and the second place which fell before the Roman arms; the inhabitants were forced to migrate to the Seven Hills. A brook flows unheeded from these mountains into the adjoining Tiber; it was called the Allia, and on its banks in the year of Rome 363, the blood of the Romans swelled its current as they were slaughtered by the swift swords of Brennus and his followers, who then marched on the city, and, with the exception of the Capitol, burned it to the ground. A farm-house called Castel Giubileo, marks the spot where Fidenæ once stood. This city was first taken by Romulus—it was but a few miles from the Salarian Gate—it threw off the yoke by a successful insurrection. In the year 90 it was taken a second time: a second time the men of Fidenæ rose, chased the Romans, and opened an asylum for all who were foes of Rome. In the year 329 the victorious Romans razed it to the ground. Some vestiges of its citadel can be still discovered. Ficulea was a city to the eastward on the *Via Nomentana*, but its site is not known: it was blotted out in the blood of its people more than five and twenty centuries ago.

Near Fidenæ, Phaon, one of Nero's freedmen, had a country-house, where it is the opinion of many that that monster put an end to his horrible existence, and a little farther on is the Ponte Salara, another of the bridges broken down by Totila, and repaired by Narses. It is about here, as is thought by many, that Hannibal had his camp, when by the admirable courage and conduct of the Senate, he was compelled to draw off his forces—a scene which is most brilliantly described by Livy.

The mass of volcanic mountains rising above and around the ancient Alba, and from whose highest summit that of Monte Cave, the ancient Mons Latiaris, our vision has been ranging over this famous scenery, is marked by many features in which between them and the Cimini mountains there is a strong resemblance. Both formed of volcanic matter, the craters still yawning upon their sides from which the lava torrents were poured over the adjacent regions; these mountains are equal in their fertility, equally rich in vegetation, in aspects equally graceful and imposing, but a charm peculiar to the ranges of Alba and Algidus, is found in the prospects which they command over the Campagna, over Rome itself, the sea, the Apennines,—over all that theatre of events, in fine, so marvellously grouped with the reminiscences of thirty centuries.

If we turn our footsteps from these glorious regions, the retreats of all in nature that is best calculated to strengthen and nerve the frame of man, and to fill his mind with noble and beauteous images, in order to survey the marshes which are proverbially the domain of pestilence, it shall be only with a passing glance. The efforts made for their drainage will enter into our subject at a much later period. This rapid detour will bring us over the wild range of the Lepini mountains into the lovely valley of the Sacco. That surveyed, and with but a rapid glance, once more we cross an offshoot of the Apennines, and accompanying the "headlong Anio" in its course, conclude with the cascades of this river at Tivoli, the complete circuit of the Pontifical States.

BASIN OF THE PONTINE MARSHES.

This basin is bounded on the north by the Alban Mountains, with their subsidiary ranges of Algidus and the Mons Arthemisius: to the east by the Lepini mountains; to the south by the Neapolitan frontier and the sea; and on the west by the seashore. It consists of an immense level tract encased on the south and west by the two limestone mountain ranges, but connected with the volcanic mountains on the north by an inclined plane, which forms a region diversified with hill and dale, most highly cultivated, and teeming with activity and abundance.

This basin, which from the Mons Arthemisius to Terracina, and from Porto d'Anzo to the mountains of Cori, is about forty miles by twenty, is traversed in its extreme length by the ancient Appian road, except that from Genzano to the plain, the modern route has diverged from the straight line which the ancient one pursued, in order to obtain a level by winding skilfully round the hills. The foreground of the picture as seen from the elevated points of this winding descent is made up of vineyards varied in aspect and displaying the perfection of cultivation and arrangement; beyond this are vast tracts of forest and pasturage upon the flat country, terminated by the sea in the distance. The two headlands of Astura and of Antium, the mountain of Circe, and the isles of Ponza, dot the shore at divers distances, and to the southward, a light haze is brooding over the locality where the Pontine marshes extend. This territory was in ancient centuries inhabited by the Volsci of Antium, neighbours of the Rutuli, and by other Volscian nations, the implacable, and, for a long time, the indomitable enemies of Rome. Under our eyes is the ensanguined field, on which were won and lost a thousand bloody battles in defence of freedom.

At a little distance to the westward of our route is Civita-Lavinia, built on the site of the ancient Lanuvium, a city said to be founded by Diomede, and which was in after times one of the strongholds of the Rutuli. Frequently engaged in war with the Romans, it at length became their ally; but having entered the last Latin and Volscian league, it shared in the overthrow of this last effort for the independence of the Latin nations, and experienced the wrath of the victors in the year of Rome, 417. There was at Lanuvium a celebrated temple of Juno, and the Emperor Antoninus Pius was born there. Fragments of the ancient walls, built of volcanic masses of rock, are still to be traced around the precipitous sides of the eminence on which the ancient city stood. Its modern successor, the village of Civita-Lavinia is frequently visited by the malaria fever in summer-time, but withal, the cultivation round about is perfect.

Our route is sometimes through oak forests, above whose tops the mediæval castle of San Gennaro is seen to lift its time-worn turrets; sometimes through charming vineyards, till coming to the southern descent of the Mons Arthemisius, we see the city of Velletri at our feet, with the entire Pontine plain stretching out before us to the far distant headland of ancient Anxur, and from the Lepini mountains to the sea. This point of view is admirable, and the vineyards which form its foreground are not its least charming feature, by reason of the perfection of culture and management which they exhibit.

Velletri is built upon a current of lava, detached from the mountain, and in a position the most felicitous; the verdant acclivities of Mons Arthemisius, protect it from the chilling blasts of the north, and the edifices of the city cover the southern slope of an eminence, which is crowned by a beautiful palace, the bishop's residence. The prospect from its windows ranges over all the country of the Volsci, in one direction, while in another, to the eastward, through the opening of a large valley, which separates the Alban mountains from the Lepini, the distant Apennine can be seen rising in form of an amphitheatre above, where Palestrina is seated. The contrast between the volcanic range, with rounded tops and gracefully undulating outline, and the abrupt and rugged aspect of the Apennine and Lepini, or limestone, ranges, the brilliant verdure of the plain, the proximity of the sea, impress upon this scenery a character altogether different from what is presented in the basins already traversed.

The city of Velletri, generally speaking, is badly constructed; its streets are rugged, tortuous and confined, and its dwellings huddled too closely together on the mountain sides; but the episcopal palace, an hospital, some churches, and the palace Lancelloti are worthy of attention. This latter edifice, built by Martin Lunghi, is chiefly remarkable for a grand marble staircase, not less elegant in design than it is bold in execution. The beauty for which they were so renowned, has departed from the gardens of this palace, with the fortune of its former lords: the palace of the Lancelloti princes, is now only an indifferent hotel. In former times, the traveller of taste was sure not to pass through Velletri without inspecting the admirable museum, which the erudite Cardinal Borgia, who died in 1802, had collected—consisting of a numerous series of Egyptian, Indian, and American antiquities, in bronze, basalt, and granite, &c.; of bas-reliefs in terra-cotta, which evinced how far were the warlike Volscians from being backward in the arts; and, in fine, of a rich collection of the coinage called the as, of medals, inscriptions, vases and pictures, of the early masters,—it is long however since it has been dispersed.

Velitræ, of which Velletri occupies the site, was a city of the Volsci, and fell a victim by times to Roman conquest. It burst its fetters after some time only to have them more firmly rivetted again by Furius Camillus, who, in the year of the city, 396, and in the eightieth of his age, at the same time closed his life and his brilliant career as a warrior with this achievement. As a colony, Velitræ continued to be a place of some importance; it gave birth to Augustus, whose family belonged either to the city or its neighbourhood. The overthrow of the empire drew after it that of nearly all the Latin cities, nor was Velitræ exempted any more than the rest from the strokes of the barbarians. The new city which sprung up under the Pontiffs from its ruins was erected at an early period into a bishop's see, and being united with the see of Ostia ranks first among the Suburbicarian dioceses. On occasion of the war of 1744, between the Austrians and Don Carlos of Naples, we shall have to return to this city and its environs again. Its present inhabitants are about 10,000.

Through a region of vineyards, pulse gardens, and olive grounds, the descent down the mountain side is rapid from Velletri to the malaria plain,—naked, parched, and monotonous—alternately rising and subsiding like the long rolling billows of an ocean: but as you come near Cisterna everything sinks into an uninterrupted flat, over which the view can expatiate without a bound. The burgh of Cisterna, a melancholy looking place and the last aggregate of habitations to be met with in the direction of the marshes, is built on the site of the ancient Tres-Tabernæ, the place where, according to the Acts of the Apostles, St. Paul was met by the Christians when on his way to Rome. It is ravaged by the malaria fever every year.

Here it is that the modern road rejoins the ancient *Via Appia*, which went in a straight line across the plain; but its pavement lies buried in these parts far beneath the present surface. To the south of Cisterna, the soil is flat, argillaceous, and usually covered with water, a bed of limestone rock preventing all absorption. Immense pasture-tracts extend westward to the forests, and again in the opposite direction towards the mountains; further on in front, another forest fills the interval between these mountains and the road. At present the entire of this territory forms but a single farm, belonging to the Dukes of Sermonetta, a title of the illustrious and once puissant house of the Gaetani. Herds of oxen beyond number, hogs and buffaloes pasture on these solitudes, beyond which commence the marshes of the Tepia, the advanced post of the Pontine marshes; and triste and monotonous as it is, this landscape is not without a certain air of grandeur which leaves a not disagreeable impression on the memory.

We turn from the Pontine marshes for the present, to visit the western regions of the basin; and traversing the wooded plain between Cisterna and the shore, we come, first, to where was situated Corioli, a powerful city of the Volsci, and the taking of which, in U. C. 260, acquired the surname of Coriolanus for Caius Martius; and next to Satricum, belonging to the same people, taken by the same Coriolanus, retaken by the Volscians; a second time taken by the Romans, a second time wrested from their grasp, and, finally, after so many vicissitudes, stormed by Papirius, and burned to the ground. A third city was Palusca, which after it had been captured and long in possession of the Romans, was taken from them by Coriolanus, who, to be revenged of his ungrateful fellow countrymen, placed his sword at the service of their rivals: a fourth was Longula; and a fifth, immediately on the shore was Aphrodisium, which possessed a temple of Venus, common to all the nations of the Volsci; so that in an archæological point of view, no country can more abound in interest; but at present it is a perfect desert. The two farms of Campo Morto and Conca divide between them a territory, on which a once great and warlike people flourished, and two crazy tenements, the abode in summer of a few wretched herdsmen and farm servants wasted with fever, are the only representatives of five cities, which were swarming in ancient times with a vigorous population. Thus at every turn we see exemplified the terrible effects of climate, for it is not fertility that is wanting at the present day to these beauteous plains, where wheat crops, the finest that can be, alternate with pasturage the most luxuriant and abundant, and where Indian corn and rice rotate with beans and barley.

Beyond the Campo Morto farm, we enter a forest which covers the entire interval to the shore with the exception of a narrow zone of cultivated ground running immediately along the margin of the sea into which projects the head-land, where is seated the city of Porto d' Anzo, in place of the ancient Antium.

This city, celebrated in antiquity, was founded soon after the Trojan war, and according to the tradition, by a son of Circe and Ulysses. Its happy position in the midst of a fertile country caused it to prosper in commerce, long before Rome was founded; posterior to this great event, we find Antium making a great figure in the affairs of the

Latin League, sometimes as the enemy, and sometimes as the ally of the conquering city. It is one of the maritime towns for which Rome in her earliest treaty with Carthage, stipulates the freedom of navigation, immediately after the expulsion of the Kings. At a later period we meet with Antium contending against the aggressions of the Republic, in the confederacy of the Latin States. Coriolanus finds an enthusiastic reception and ardent avengers of his quarrel within its walls; there also he meets his death. In the long run, U. C. 417, the fate of so many other cities falls to the lot of Antium: compelled to bow before the fortune of Rome, the bronze prows of its numerous galleys are borne in triumph to the Forum, where they served to adorn the tribune or platform, in the assembly place of the Populus, which was from that circumstance called the *rostrum*. The place was repeopled time after time by colonies from Rome, through a desire to preserve a naval station of importance; and Nero, who was born there, accorded to Antium a special protection, and caused a harbour of a circular shape to be formed there, which he had surrounded by edifices of different kinds. The temple of Fortune at Antium was one of the most remarkable of its monuments ;* we shall have in mediæval and modern times to return to this city, or rather to Porto d'Anzo its successor, again.

* Horace. L. 1. Carmin. Car. 30.

About half-a-league to the south-east along shore, we come to the little town of Nettuno, a name derived from a temple of the Sea-god at Cæno-Portus, a city which occupied the promontory in former ages. The inhabitants, about 1200 in number, are an industrious seafaring people, who suffer little or nothing from the neighbourhood of the malaria. Their Greek descent is attested in a striking manner by the elegant and very picturesque costume of the females.

To the south of Nettuno, the forest continues to extend along the shore, and at three miles is interrupted only for a moment by the promontory of Astura defended by a tower which is built on the ruins of the house inhabited by Cicero immediately before he sailed for his Formian villa near Gaeta, where he was overtaken and beheaded by his pursuers. Astura, which bore the same name in antiquity, was fortified by the Frangipani in mediæval times. It was to their castle here that Conradin fled for refuge after being defeated by Charles of Anjou at Tagliacozzo; but, with Frederic of Austria, his cousin, he was delivered into the hands of his more fortunate rival, who soon after put him to death.

The forest still continues beyond Astura, the only encroachment on its dominion being a chain of lakes, called *Saturæ Pallus* in classic times, which are separated only by a narrow tongue of land from the sea. The first and most extensive of them is the Lago di Fogliano, in which are lost the waters of the Conca, formerly the Lanuvius, or Astura. It has an outlet to the sea, and the rent of its fishery brings a profit of 24,000 francs, or £960 per annum to the Gaetani family, to whom it belongs. In proportion to their extent, the other lakes, de' Monaci, del Caprolace, and di Paolo, are equally productive, and constantly assist in supplying the fish-market of Rome. On these shores, now so solitary, deserted, and infected with the miasm of deadly pestilence, the voluptuous Lu̇cullus had planted one of his sumptuous country retreats of luxury. A military station or depôt called Claustra Romana was established here; but now-a-days, the primæval woods of America do not present an aspect more savage and solitary than the borders of these lagunes. The vegetation with which nature amidst these wild and sequestered haunts sets forth her charms, is of the most luxuriant and brilliant description; the oak, the beech tree, the elm, and the pine, in their most colossal proportions seem to contest the headship of the forest, while an underwood, of infinite variety as to the shrubs and climbing plants which form it, is cast up around their trunks by the teeming exuberance of the soil. Scarcely can the adventurous explorer force his way a few paces through these thickets over the decaying trunks which have fallen beneath the weight of centuries, but at the risk of losing the narrow track of the horses used occasionally to carry the fish that is taken along the shore. The wolf and the wild boar dispute these solitudes with the herds of cattle and immense droves of horses, and swine, which multiply in their retreats, and wander at large in a perfect state of nature; but amidst a landscape where the sun seems by its intense brilliancy and heat to impart a superabounding life and gorgeousness of complexion and hue to every object, the only representatives of humanity to be met with are a few herdsmen, pallid, emaciated to the last degree, clad in skins as they stripped them from the goat or the wild animals of the chase, and armed with a lance as they ride in silence across the prairie, or sit motionless, as the enchanted knight-errants of romance, under the shadow of some forest tree. The reed covered hut of a pyramidal form, which is his habitation, you might mistake for a Hottentot kraal, as it comes upon the view in some opening glade of the woodlands; while the multitude and variety of tropical plants which meet the eye on every side assist not a little the delusion, and serve to transport the thoughts of the beholder far away from Europe. Beyond the Lago di Fogliano, the forests are cut through by an enormous excavation attributed to Pope Martin V. Such is its great depth that the tops of the tallest forest trees which grow on the bottom of it cannot be seen without ascending the mound on either side. When treating of the measures adopted by Pius VI for the reclamation of the marshes, we shall have to speak of this work in greater detail.

After having traversed this savage region for six leagues distance, to count from the Fogliano farm, we arrive at the foot of the mountain of Circe, an enormous calcareous mass, a good many miles in circuit. It rises perpendicularly between the immense plain of the marshes and the sea. All appearances would indicate that there was a time, when it was on all sides surrounded by the waves—forming under the appellation of Ææa, a part of the same archipelago with Ischia, Procida, Vandoneta, Ponza, Zanona, Palmarola, and other isles along the Tyrrhenian shore; and the traditions collected by Homer, Pliny, Theophrastus, and Strabo, confirm this opinion.

This mountain or promontory, for here the land juts far into the sea, is well deserving of the traveller's attention; whether it delights him, with Homer to trace the footsteps of Ulysses, or to indulge in researches of natural history and archæology. Both as to its form and composition, the mountain, now called Monte Circello, is very curious, seeing that alabaster, limestone rock like that of the Apennines, and marble are the elements of which it is formed; and that the vast cavernous openings in its sides permit of your scrutinizing its interior in all directions. One of these caverns, called, la grotto della maga, is lofty, of great depth and extent, and according to M. le Baron de Prony, it communicates by side passages and galleries with all parts of the mountain. Another cavern to seaward, is open to the waves and in rough weather often forms a harbour of refuge for the fishing craft along the coast. It is not less interesting for the botanist, by reason of the variety and number of tropical plants and flowers which adorn its acclivities and sunny recesses; while for the antiquarian it has on its highest pinnacle, the ruins of an ancient acropolis or citadel, with lower down, on the site of the ancient Volscian city of Circe, the ruins of a temple of the Sun, together with other vestiges of the bygone grandeur of the place; for after the poetic fables of Homer have melted away, a city rises here before the steady gaze of history; the Romans take it: aided by Coriolanus the Volscian citizens expel the invaders; but they return, and under their domination, this hill city, like its neighbours of the adjacent plain, is doomed to lapse into decay and oblivion, and finally to disappear. At present, the only inhabited place on the mountain is the little village of San Felice, of about 800 inhabitants. There is also a castle belonging to Prince Stanislaus Poniatowski, and the customary watch-towers, in this part as along all the rest of it, from the Fiora on the Tuscan border to Epitafio near Fondi, defend and watch the sea-board of the States.

From the summit of this foreland, towering high above the sea and the marshes, the eye can trace the Roman coast to the north-west by the azure line of the waters, the promontories and the large curves of its gulfs, until all these features become confounded in the vagueness of the far distant horizon; the chain of lakes, Astura, Antium, the guard-towers, set like sparkling beads along the water's edge; more to eastward, the successive stages of the amphitheatre formed by the Monte Arthemisio are seen rising in succession, the zone of vineyards above that of the corn-fields, that of the forests above both; and Civita Lavinia, Genzano, and Velletri glittering in the midst of foliage and verdure; to the east, the Lepini mountains seem to rest their rugged and battlemented summits against the sky—their highest cliffs being surmounted by Cori, Norma, Sermonetta, Sezza, and other villages, which are hardly to be distinguished from the crags upon which they are built. Monte Cacume crowns this range as if with a lofty pyramid, and on a less distant line of view, the whitish cliffs of ancient Anxur support the ruins of King Theodoric's palace and the town of Terracina. The centre of this landscape, set as it were in the frame-work of the coast and the mountains, is filled by a plain covered with spreading forests. In the very heart of that region a slight haze is seen to rest over an extensive space—it is the shroud spread out over the field of death; in a word, there are the Pontine marshes. But towards the south, the prospect is still more grand; the gulf of Fondi, as if excavated from the very recesses of the Apennine; the promontory of Gaeta, surmounted by the tomb of Plancus, called Roland's tower, near to which Cicero was slain; the cape of Mondragone hiding Naples, but leaving open to view the double summit of Vesuvius, from which is ascending a wavy column of smoke or vapour; and, in the foreground between us and that shore, so rich, so pellucid in its outline, so fascinating in the reminiscences connected with it, the dark blue ocean, above which the isles of Ponza and the Archipelago of the gulf of Naples exalt their grey cliffs, and their summits tinted with volcanic colouring.

The air is salubrious at San Felice, on account of its elevation and its vicinity to the sea, but at the foot of the rock we are in the region of pestilence once more; and so it continues until traversing a chain of sand-hills or downs, extending for a great many miles along the shore, we at length arrive at Terracina, distant about sixty-eight miles from Rome, and built on the steep acclivity of the mountain chain, which forms the frontier between the States and the kingdom of Naples.

What recollections are conjured up by the sight of this ancient city, placed on the border between the ancient Volscians and Arunci, flourishing long ere Rome was thought of, subjugated by this young republic in the year of the city 338, and becoming in after times the key of Southern Italy: embellished in succession by Appius Claudius, by Augustus, Trajan, Antoninus, Theodoric, Leo X; and which Pius VI strained every nerve to restore to its ancient prosperity. Galba, who was born here, had a villa in the neighbourhood. The streets of the old town are narrow, dirty, and hardly accessible, except for foot passengers. In the environs, which are of an extremely fertile nature, both cotton and indigo succeed, and even the sugar-cane in sheltered situations; artichokes, peas, beans, and the like, come to maturity in mid-winter, to furnish dainties for the tables of the Romans: the citron, in fine, the orange-tree, and the palm, attain to no ordinary dimensions upon this singularly favoured soil. Moreover, Terracina is the natural outlet for the produce of the Pontine regions, and yet, so fatal are the effects of climate in counteracting these advantages, that it would look as if this profuseness of nature had no other object but to supply flowers to strew upon the graves of the constantly decimated population.

A little beyond the last houses of the lower or new town, built by Pope Pius VI, the rocky promontory was cut through by Appius Claudius, to open a passage for the great highway which bears his name, and by which we travel at the present day. Beyond this pass, called Pisco Montano, the road is terraced along the steep and lacerated side of the mountain above the sea, until you come to the marshy plains of Fondi, where a post called Epitafio marks the boundary line between the Papal States and Naples.

Returning to Terracina, we take the road opened

by Pius VI, in a straight line Romeward across the marshes, while that of Appius Claudius described a curve by the mountain-foot, in order to keep on a more solid foundation. Both roads meet again under the rock Feronia, a salient point of the mountains coming out bluffly on the low ground, and from the base of which flows a fountain, still retaining its ancient name—that of a fabulous nymph, supposed to preside over the fruits of the earth, and to whom, according to Denys of Halicarnassus, a colony of Lacedemonians, coming to those shores in the time of Lycurgus, erected a temple, surrounding both that and the fountain with a sacred grove; and so the place would appear to have stood when Virgil saw it.* It was customary with the superstitious wayfarer, to make his ablutions at this fountain as he passed; but for Horace and his fellow tourists, it is likely this act was prompted not so much by devotion as by a feeling of pleasure and convenience.† From this point to the foot of the Mons Arthemisius, near Lanuvium, the ancient Via Appia ran in a perfectly straight line, a distance of nearly forty miles.

An excellent position is this same rock of Feronia from which to take a general view of the marshes, and to form an idea of the system adopted for draining them. The soil in the foreground is car-

* Viridi gaudens Feronia luco.

† Ora manusque tuâ lavimus, Feronia, lymphâ.—
Horat. Sat. V.

peted with the most brilliant verdure, and watered by the torrent of the Amazene, which descends from the valleys of the Lepini range. Further off is the canal del' Uffente (or of the Ufens), which has its fountain head in the mountains about Sezza, and between these two water-courses, and also beyond the Uffente, as far as the view can extend, there expands a perfectly horizontal plain, producing the most luxuriant grass, on which innumerable herds of cattle, dispersed in every direction, are seen at pasture. A little towards the west, the Via Appia, marked by four ranges of trees, traces an apparently interminable straight line, and alongside of it the great drainage canal, called the Linea Pia from Pius VI who constructed it, is seen sparkling through the foliage. Not far from the rock all these waters are seen uniting at Ponte Maggiore, and flowing rapidly towards the sea, through the canal called Portatore di Badino, while the Linea Pia is put by another canal in communication with the port of Terracina. The stations for post-horses, the only structures in these immense prairies, exhibit their whitened and massive walls, at regular intervals along the route, which cuts the marshes into two nearly equal parts. The excellent construction of this road (also the work of Pius VI.) formed of a bed of gravel, the verdant foliage of the double range of trees, the beauty of Linea Pia-canal which borders it, the luxuriant vegetation with which the soil is teeming in every direction, the variety of the prospects along the Lepini, their highest summits crowned with villages; all combine to render the crossing of the marshes an excursion as agreeable as it is replete with interest. The original causeway, first constructed by the Censor Claudius in the early times of the Republic, repaired by Augustus, Nerva, Trajan, and Theodoric the Goth, having been submerged during the middle ages, was restored to its present admirable condition by Pius VI, who also restored the ancient bridges of Ponte Maggiore, della Ninfa, and of For-Appio, besides building many new ones. The posting establishments also are the works of this Pope, as are the immense granaries at Ponte-Maggiore, at Mesa, at Bocca-di-Fiume, For-Appio, and Tor-tre-Ponti; but already, even when de Tournon saw them, the immense buildings at Mesa, the ancient *Mutatio ad Medias*, destined to be a great centre for the exportation of the produce of the marshes, and the Church and Capuchin Convent at For-Appio, were fast falling to decay. In the rest of the plain few and far separated are cabins thatched with reeds, in which the emaciated herdsmen rest their fever-worn limbs; even the haggard features and diseased appearance of the postillions, who sweep you at full gallop along this smooth and spacious avenue, evince, in an appalling manner, how implacably hostile to health and life for man, at least, that same country has become, which contained no less than three-and-twenty cities in ancient times,* one of which, Suessa Pometia, the metropolis of the Volscians, for a long time set the proud King Tarquin at defiance, and which, when it fell, enriched the victorious city with its spoils.† The soil has not, however, degenerated from its ancient fertility. On all sides are unfolded vast tracts of pasturage, whose luxuriant verdure defies alike the winter frosts and the parching heats of summer, and where herbage abundant and sappy is never wanting. Interspersed with these prairie tracts, are seen others under wheat of the finest quality and Indian-corn little less extended.

On every side, and in every light in which it can be viewed, there is a smile upon the face of the scenery; but, alas, it is a smile that only allures to death! Hence it is the Pontine marshes are a desert. Into the probable causes of this startling difference between the modern and the ancient state of the atmosphere we shall inquire here-

* Aliud miraculum a Circæis Palus Pomptina est, quem locum xxiii. urbium fuisse Mucianus ter Consul prodidit. *Plinius,* H. N. l. 3, c. 9. Thus 1800 years ago, the 23 cities were no more.

† With the treasure thus procured, Tarquin commenced to build the Capitol, less, we opine, from devotion to Jupiter, than with the design of curbing the Romans, just as Louis Philippe fortified Paris, with somewhat similar success.

after; but now our route is across the mountains. We travel by an ancient road in wretched order, which winds round the heights that, like an amphitheatre, overlook the plain, and which, before the reconstruction of the Via Appia, was on this side of the Lepini, the only communication between Rome and the South. It mounts through the rugged and savage gorges along the banks of the rapid Amazene. In these precipitous and lonely haunts was situated (when de Tournon travelled), the little city of Sonnino peopled by from two to three thousand inhabitants. It was called Sunnina in the classic epoch, and stood on the border, between the Aurunci and the Volscians: in the reign of Pius VII we shall have to revisit Sonnino again.

The plain extending between the Amazene and the mountain foot, cultivated with much care and intelligence, is incessantly menaced by the river, notwithstanding that lofty dykes on either hand restrain its waters, which not only rush down with violence, but carrying with them from the mountains a variety of fragments, such as rocks, trees, and the like, are moreover liable to become swollen to a terrible degree, and as if upon a sudden. It is in the midst of this mountain wilderness, we come in sight of the ancient Trappist monastery of Fossa-Nuova—its massy time-worn walls, looped and castellated like a fortress, reminding you of similar retreats of holy recluses among the Lebanon. The rocks and the forests which surround it, form a lively and striking contrast with the luxuriant and smiling imagery of the sea-shore, and of the Pontine regions. Here it was, no doubt, that Metabo, when fleeing from the pursuit of the Privernites, his revolted people, attached his daughter Camilla, still an infant, to his javelin, and so cast it safely to the opposite bank of the Amazene, which was flooded at the time. It is pleasant with the accompaniment of the torrent's harmonious sound to recite the charming verses in which this poetic fable is told by Virgil. The frequency of the names both of daughter and father amongst the people of Piperno is a curious instance of the anchorage by which tradition will hold firmly by the occurrences or impressions of the most distant ages.

This latter city is situated on a long ridge of hills, planted with olives, at no great distance from Fossa-Nuova. Here the scene is changed. No longer boundless plains and the immense horizon presented by the marshes; the valley, very circumscribed in extent, is hemmed in by a precinct of lofty mountains, their successive stages covered with olive grounds and woods as they ascend from the carefully cultivated plain. Behold us once more escaped from the malaria districts: surrounded on all sides by works of industry, directed by skill and intelligence in the cultivation of the country, which is divided into a great number of small properties, while the surrounding eminences are embellished with little towns, such as Maenza and Rocca-Gorga, appearing from among the woods upon the mountain sides, and Rocca-Secca on the pinnacle of a cliff several hundred feet in height. Yet in this sort of eyrie, soaring enough for the ambition of an eagle, they shew you a fresco by the pencil of Domenichino of surpassing beauty.

Privernum, of which Piperno occupies the place, was a city of the Volscians, of which, previous to the foundation of Rome, we know nothing but what Virgil tells us. In the war for independence, Privernum took a distinguished part, defending itself with obstinate valour until taken by Caius Marcius, who on this occasion obtained the honours of a triumph. The vanquished city seized an opportunity to throw off the yoke, and avenged itself by ravaging the Roman colonies established in Norba at Setia. Caius Plancus retook it in the year of Rome 425, and commemorated this event by a medal. It was on this occasion that the senators of Privernum, conducted into the presence of the Senate at Rome, and interrogated as to the chastisement their fellow-citizens ought to be subjected to in consequence of their revolt, replied so nobly:— "that which they deserve who judge themselves worthy of liberty: however, only give us an equitable peace, and it shall be permanent; one on unjust conditions shall be but transitory." The attention of Sejanus was attracted to Privernum.

He built in its environs a beauteous villa, to the ruins of which the arts stood indebted for a fine statue of the Emperor, or rather the monster, Tiberius. We shall find Pope Gregory VII sojourning here for some days in the year 1073. The modern town is badly built, but occupies an agreeable situation. Some will have it, that Privernum was on the plain, but with little probability; high positions with strong natural defences, such as abrupt cliffs, or very steep ascents, having been uniformly selected by the people of remote antiquity for their towns.

To the east of Piperno, the plain, of a gravelly soil and tilled usually by buffaloes, is laid out in vineyards and corn-fields. At its extremity, the road commences to climb the mountain side through a line of trees which flourish among the rocks; the Amazene is foaming in the ravine below. After the road has turned the crest of the mountain, you discover Prossedi, a village of 1000 souls, placed on the ridge between the two basins of the Val di Sacco and the Pontine. These wild regions, mountainous, wooded, and interspersed with villages like San-Lorenzo, San-Stefano, and Vallecorsa, which swarm with a fierce and hardy race, have been from age to age, the favourite resort of the brigands who infest the two great thoroughfares to Southern Italy. Beyond Prossedi the route descends into the valley.

The mountains to the north-east are well worthy of

a visit. They form a confused assemblage of clumps, craggy summits, and deep ravines, every where invested, except where the naked rocks protrude, with various sorts of trees and thickets, amongst which the herbalist discovers a quantity of aromatic plants. The mountains called Schiena d' Asino, Capreo and Cacume, the three loftiest pinnacles of this group, look down upon these solitudes, formidable on account of the banditti who find harbour among their caves and forests. But for the solitary town of Carpineto, the vast region would look as if it had never been inhabited; but in ancient times the fortresses of Ulubra, of Ecetra, and Verrugo, all belonging to the Volscians, were placed upon the vantage positions round about, and afforded refuge to their armies when broken and routed on the plain or in the passes. Verrugo was destroyed by the Romans U. C. 343.

Sezza, a city of from five to six thousand inhabitants, is situated at the extremity of this plateau in a most romantic situation, surrounded by beautiful plantations of the olive and the vine, and at an immense elevation above the Pontine region, which it commands in every direction. It occupies the site of Setia or Setinum of the ancients, a powerful Volscian city subjugated and reduced by the Romans U. C. 371 to the condition of a colony. The Privernites took and sacked it in one of their revolts against the Romans. Its wines have been celebrated by Martial and by Juvenal, though at the present day they are middling enough. Some vestiges of a temple of Saturn are the only relics of antiquity at Sezza.

At a little distance to the south, a rock named Monte delle Muse lifts its head. It was from this commanding spot that the Pontiff, Sixtus V, took a view of the marshes with a view to their drainage, and in effect, for the study of their northern regions it is as favourably situated, as is the rock of Feronia for the study of those to the south. The streams called la Cavata, la Cavatella and la Ninfa, are seen to rise at the mountain foot beneath, to meander through the plain, and flow into the canals which were opened by Pius VI to receive them. They unite their waters in the Linea Pia canal which acts as the great artery of the marshes. More to the west, the Tepia, the most northerly of these currents, is seen to empty itself into the canal named Fiume Sisto, which forms the cincture of the marshes, of which the entrance is marked by the edifices of Tor-tre-Ponti and For-Appio—the station of Forum Appi mentioned by Horace in his tour to Brundusium.

The ancient route to Naples passed at the foot of the mountain; but one can better observe the country in following the path which runs along a rocky ledge from Sezza to Cori, sometimes overhanging the plain, and sometimes wheeling round the gorges which penetrate far into the interior of the range. In winding onward the town of Sermonetta of 2000 inhabitants, is seen as it were embedded between two enormous peaks of a dark yellowish hue: this was the formidable position occupied by Sulmo, a city of the Volscians, which after having shared in the vicissitudes of its neighbours in those parts was utterly subverted by Sylla. Two leagues further on, the town of Norma, peopled with 1500 inhabitants, is built on the brink of a precipice 400 French metres high. It was a colony of Alba, its people took part in the confederacy formed by no less than nine-and-twenty cities and nations in the wood of Ferentinum for the restoration of Tarquin. Its position, apparently so unassailable, could not save it. In the year of Rome 262, it was brought under the yoke, received a colony and became the bulwark of that part of the Roman frontier against the Volsci. The Privernites ravaged it at the same time as Setia. At a later period, Sylla razed it to the ground on account of its attachment to Marius. The ruins of the citadel still survive—of the Cyclopian style of masonry, and entered by three gates. Beneath this range of heights, formerly bristling with garrisons, there was another tier of Volscian cities, such as Mucanitis, Artena, taken by the Romans, 338 U. C., Ninfa, built on the borders of a little lake, and replaced by a modern town; besides several others, the very names of which have perished—making in all three-and-twenty Pontine cities, the existence of which is established by every species of historical proof.

When one witnesses the toil and difficulty with which the inhabitants of these eyries are obliged day after day to descend to their laborious task upon the plain, and of course to reascend at eventide again, one easily comprehends why they so much prefer to agriculture the rearing and pasturage of cattle; much of the labour and loss of time just alluded to being thus got rid of. And this is a reflection which is frequently forced upon one in traversing those districts, and others similarly circumstanced throughout the States.

On a pinnacle immensely higher still than Norma, is seated the village of Basciano of 1600 inhabitants, the birth-place of Aldus Manutius, father of a race of illustrious scholars, and founder of a press from which issued the most correct and elegant editions of the Latin and Greek writers that have ever appeared. This chain, after running from Fossa-Nuova, from south to north, turns here at right angles towards the east, and at the summit of this angle, 430 mètres high, is seated Cori, on the site of the ancient Cora founded by Pelasgians, or according to another opinion by the Trojan Dardanus, and enumerated amongst the Latin cities.

Strong by position, Cora maintained itself for a long time against Rome, and did not yield till all Latium was subdued. Its citadel is still surrounded by walls similar to those we meet with at Palestrina,

Circe, and Norma : but its most remarkable remains of antiquity are three columns of the temple of Castor and Pollux, and the temple of Hercules, built in the reign of Claudius, a perfect model of the Greek Doric order: four columns form its façade, and two others are placed laterally in the prolongation of the wall of the Cella. This temple, like that of the Sibyl at Tivoli, derives its beauty still less from the perfection of its architecture than of its position on an isolated rock. The inhabitants of Cori, about 4500, are nearly all occupied in husbandry.

The prospect enjoyed from this city has a charm peculiar to itself: it extends not only over the Pontine, the sea, and the Mons Arthemisius, but penetrates to the Apennines, over Palestrina, through an opening between the Lepini and another chain called the Ariani mountains. Nothing more graceful can be imagined than the undulating curves of the volcanic masses, caparisoned with the vast forests of Fajola, when contrasted with the grisly rocks of the Apennine, its arid flanks, and summits gapped and pointed in the most abrupt and broken fashion.

Beyond the promontory on which Cori is seated, the Lepini mountains lose that roughness and savageness, characteristic of their western aspect, and on the woody stages of this declivity, are situated Roccamassimi and Monte Fortino, a town of about 2500 souls. It occupies the place of Ortona, an ancient city of the Latins, repeatedly taken and retaken by the Æquians and the Romans; but the key of the valley is more to the north ; the fortress called Arx Carventana. From the year of the city 344, the struggle for it between the Romans, the Æqui, and the Volscians was incessant, and it repeatedly changed masters. So important was it, that the Senate on two occasions made the risk in which it was placed a pretext for suspending the discussion of the Agrarian law, it being necessary to forget everything, in order to save that bulwark of the republic. In the bottom of the valley, the poor village of Ginlano, situated near the crater of a volcano now filled with stagnant water, sees its inhabitants, summer after summer, mowed down by fever. Passing this village, and still following the wooded valley, we arrive at the basin of the Sacco.

In closing the description of this basin, de Tournon renews the expression of his surprise at the feebleness of the struggle maintained by the cities and nations of this part of Latium, as well as by those situated along the left bank of the Tiber, in comparison with that by which the Etruscan confederates on the other side of the Tiber were enabled for centuries, after Suessa-Pomatia, Circe, Antium, Anxur, Corioli, and, in short, all the Latin and Sabine cities without exception had fallen, so successfully to repulse all the efforts of the Romans. But, if we mistake not, the solution of this so widely different fate of two countries so contiguous, is to be looked for, not in any superiority in courage or in civil institutions, or in military skill, as de Tournon seems disposed to opine, on the part of the Etruscans, especially over the Volscian nations, as in the profound and consummate strategic foresight with which that astonishing people, the Romans, projected and carried out their plans of conquest. In the then state of tactics, and of military engineering, the Tiber, deep, broad, rapid, and without any bridges, except those of the city, left the Romans perfectly secure against attack from the side of Etruria; not so from the various Latin tribes. There was, in their direction, no such barrier as the Tiber; and, in fact, we find them repeatedly and from every direction extending their forays to the very gates of Rome; it is therefore evident enough, that the course adopted by the Romans was that which at once grew out of the necessity of the case itself, and was the dictate of that unerring tact and foresight, for which, as conquerors, they stand unrivalled in the annals of the human race. While engaged with their Latin enemies, the Tiber alone sufficed to keep the Etrurians from falling on their flank or rear; but never until Latium was subdued could they without obvious risk direct their undivided energies to subjugate the nations beyond the Tiber. This river it was, and the admirable position of Rome with regard to it, that alone made all the difference.*

* Nearly all the remarkable scenes and cities described in the foregoing section will be found mentioned in the seventh book of Virgil.

VALLEY OF THE SACCO.

The Valley of the Sacco extends from Lugnano, where this river has its sources, to Ceprano, where it mingles its waters with the Liris—a distance of about forty miles. After the monotonous levels of the marshes, and the vast solitudes through which the Tiber winds its course, the contrast which its scenery, full of variety and of the most exhilarating character, presents is most agreeable. Two noble mountain ranges, the Lepini and the Apennines, so close in upon the valley, remarkable for its fertility and the luxuriance of its vegetation, that, as far as Frosinone, it is seldom more than a league or two across: at every step, a new point of view presents itself; as the opposing mountains seem alternately to recede or to approach each other, their acclivities on one hand abrupt and clad with forests, on the other more gently sloping and variegated with the most luxuriant crops of corn, with the vine and the olive; the summits and the hill sides in both instances being crowned with cities and villages, very beautiful to behold, and full of a happy people. It is a region where Nature has arrayed herself in her most noble and impressive charms, such, in a word, as Poussin has represented in his landscapes.

The entrance of this delightful valley is situated between the eastern masses of Mount Algidus and the Mountains of Palestrina, and is very confined until you come to Valmontone, a handsome town seated on a volcanic eminence, adorned with some fine buildings, and amongst the rest with a castle of imposing aspect, belonging to the Doria Pamfili family. Beyond Valmontone the valley widens; and, on the hills, which rise upon the interval between the Lepini on the west and the Apennines on the east, as you advance, a numerous population is collected in the towns of Capranica, of Genezzano,—celebrated as a place of pilgrimage,—of Olivano, the ancient Olibanum of the Æqui, and the city of Paliano, the capital of a principality belonging to the Colonna from time immemorial, and, from the time that Palestrina was taken and destroyed, the chief seat and stronghold of their power. Mark Antony Colonna had it surrounded with a triple wall, defended by eighty pieces of cannon of various sizes. The palace or baronial castle is irregular in style, but vast and noble. Of old, its halls were filled with arms and with trophies, displaying on all sides, and in every form, the feudal grandeur of its masters; but of all this glory, little now remains except the frescoes representing the exploits of Mark Antony Colonna, who commanded the galleys of the Pope at Lepanto, and in various other actions against the Turks.

From the donjon of this castle, the views are beautiful as they are varied; a line of planted hills beneath; towards the east, the Apennines lifting their scorched and craggy summits, crowned with, or beaming on their rocky sides, profoundly indented and broken, the villages del Piglio, and del Serrone, called Surro in ancient times: towards the north, a gorge of the mountains with the village of Rojate, on one side, and that of Olivano, on the other, extends in the direction of the Anio, and more to westward, rises the rocca, or acropolis of Palestrina, with its ancient Pelasgic walls. Through the vista between it and Mount Algidus, the Campagna is seen stretching away in the direction of Rome, the Lepini mountains close the horizon and bound the valley, towards the south.

Here, as we journey along the ancient Latin way, and through a pleasant country of hill and dale—distinguished for fertility and excellent management of the soil—we enter the confines of the ancient Hernicans, a warlike people who made the Romans pay dearly for the conquest of their savage rocks, and whose descendants exhibit at the present day in their lofty stature, and in the boldness and vigour of their bearing, a very striking contrast with the diminutive size and feeble constitution of the actual inhabitants of Latium. Anagni, the first city of this country, with a population of near 6000, occupies the summit of one of the first stages of the Apennines, to the east, and is surrounded with vineyards, olive-grounds, and gardens. It is a bishop's see, and the residence of a great many noble families, of whom the most ancient are distinguished by the title of the "twelve stars of Anagni." The illustrious family of Caetani, to which belonged the famous Pontiff, Boniface VIII; and the puissant house of Conti, which from 1198 to 1254 gave to the Church three Popes, *viz.* Innocent III, Gregory IX, and Alexander IV; and Innocent XIII, in the eighteenth century, were at the head of this constellation. It was a boast of the Hernicans that this, their metropolis, was one of the cities built by Saturn. Virgil gives it the epithet of the "rich"—dives Anagnia*—it offered a protracted and gallant resistance to the Romans, who, when at length they became masters of it in the year of the city 448, avenged themselves upon its inhabitants with extreme severity. It had revived in the age of Strabo, who calls it the "illustrious." In the middle ages, it was the key of the valley of the Sacco, at that period the only military communication between Rome and the south of Italy. The transactions of our history will bring us to Anagni, on more than one occasion.

The view which it commands is fine, extending along the valley to the heights of Frosinone; but the country round it, though fertile in a high degree, is any thing but wholesome; hence, the solitary air, the absence of trees, and of dispersed dwellings, the characteristic features of the malaria regions reappear again. Those who cultivate the soil have to journey forth to the scene of their labours every day, and with evening to return to the city, where alone

* L. vii.

in the troublous times this valley had so often witnessed, they could calculate on safety. "Sad result of the wars," observes de Tournon, "which ravaged those countries during so many ages, as to make it a second nature for the husbandman to trust himself, only behind the ramparts of a town."*

On the opposite side of the valley to Anagni, is seated the city of Segni, on a height where the chain of the Lepini begins. Its situation is highly picturesque, and occupies the site of the ancient Signia, a city which stood where the confines of the Latins, the Hernicans, and the Volscians met. Judging from its ruins, it must have been a very important place. Its walls of irregular polygons, and of four miles in circuit, are entered by seven gates: the architecture of two of them, the *Porta Saracinesca* and the *Porta in Lucina*, are in the most massive Cyclopian style. It was colonised by Tarquin the Proud, and long remained the chief bulwark of the Roman frontier on that side against the Hernicans and the Volsci. It remained firm in its allegiance, during the Samnite wars, and the wars of Hannibal.

Beyond Anagni, the valley reveals itself in all its beauty: its breadth is more than a league, the variety of its cultivated fields, its hills clad with vines, wedded to the elm, the contrast of the heights, wooded on one hand, naked and savage looking on the other, combine all the charms of a scene of riches and prosperity, with features of the grandest

* L. 1. ch. 5. p. 145.

character, in this landscape. To the left, on a jutting rock is seen the village of Fumone, resembling the eyrie of a bird of prey, rather than a dwelling of men. Here it was that Pope St. Celestine V, after his abdication, passed the evening of his days. A little further on, a promontory of the mountain, coming out boldly on the plain, is occupied by the town of Ferentino. At a glance, you see how well suited it was for the use to which it was turned by the Hernicans, who made it one of the chief fortresses of their country. Every object hereabout is eloquent of the long departed grandeur of this ancient people: their history is inscribed on walls which have survived the ravages of thirty ages. On the Cyclopian structures which formed the primitive defences of the place, another wall in that elaborate style of masonry, called the *opus reticulatum*, was erected by the Romans: to this, the barbarians, in after ages, superadded towers, built from the debris of ancient structures and monuments, in their customary rude and tumultuary style. These precipices tapestried with shrubs and creeping tendrils; these successive labours of the Pelasgian, the Roman, and the Goth, now harmonizing under the tints of beauty, which the hand of time has shed upon them; those edifices sacred to religion, which lift their heads in serene security above these memorials of so many fierce and bootless struggles, exhibit Christianity as alone able to inherit and appropriate all the labour and acquisition of the past; and dispose the mind to reflections of the most elevated and salutary description.

Ferentinum, after having taken part in all the wars against Rome, was taken in the year of the city 344, by the Volscians, but the Romans obliged them to restore it to the Hernicans, with whom they happened at that juncture to be at peace. Somewhat better than a century afterwards, the Ferentines made submission, and were admitted to the *jus Latii*, or freedom of Rome, with permission to preserve their ancient municipal institutions. At present, the population is close on 7000, and are mostly occupied in the cultivation of the surrounding regions.

At the gate of Ferentino, and on the Latin way, there is a monument sculptured in the rock, and adorned with pilasters and an entablature, in a good style. Its centre forms a tabular slab on which is engraved the testament of one *Aulus Quintilius*, a magistrate of the city, who, in the second century of the Christian era, made a bequest to his fellow citizens of certain lands, of which the produce was to be distributed amongst them. Not far from this interesting memorial, there is a small lake of sulphurated water.

The groups of hills which, from Palestrina to Ferentino, intervene between the valley and the Apennines, subside at this point, from which the two opposite mountain chains, diverging more widely from each other, have between them a plain of above two leagues in width, inclining somewhat from east to west, as far as the banks of the Sacco, which flows in this part of its course, close under the skirts of the Lepini range. The soil is deep, and very fertile, as the luxuriant fields of Indian corn, wheat, flax, tobacco, and vines, which extend in every direction, agreeably attest; while the acclivities, on the eastern side of the valley, are highly suited for the olive, that covers them almost to the mountain tops. To westward, the Lepini rise abruptly in a succession of steeps all covered with forests, which do not, however, shut out from view the mountain towns of Morolo, Supino (of about 3000 inhabitants), and Patrica, that seem to recline beneath their shade. The road crosses the little river Cossa, descending from the Apennines, and brings you to the gates of Frosinone, a city of 6000 inhabitants, on a hill in the centre of the valley, which continues to widen more and more, and throw open a more expanded horizon to the view. Its environs are most agreeable; and an ancient castle, with its donjons and battlemented walls, towering high above the other edifices of the town, impart to it a picturesque and imposing aspect.

Though in the midst of Hernican cities, the ancient Frusinum belonged to the Volsci; but few traces of its existence are to be found in history. From its terraces, the greater part of the valley of the Sacco can be surveyed, the view extending along by slopes of the Lepini to Valmonte and Palestrina, to the north; and eastward, to Ferentino, Alatri, and Veroli, occupying successive ledges or stages of the Apennines; to the south, the horizon is closed by vine-clad hills interspersed with trees; while a gorge of the Lepini, to the west, lays open the very interior regions of that mountain chain to view, on as far as Prossedi, following the road which leads to Terracina by Piperno. In fine, the beauty of the cultivated fields and plantations, together with the luxuriant character of the vegetation entitle these regions to be ranked amongst the most fertile and smiling of the Papal States.

At every step you advance, a number of fair and prosperous looking villages, mostly seated upon round and not very elevated hills waving with luxuriant crops of various kinds, and clad with vineyards and gardens, salute the view; to the left of the route, Torrice and Ripi with 3000 inhabitants; to the right, l'Arnara and Pofi; beyond the Sacco, Ceccano, peopled with 4650 souls, and another town called Castro. Country houses are seen in all directions, peeping from amongst the leafy trees: the atmosphere is salubrious, and hence activity and life on all sides characterise this charming country, which was traversed by the *Via Latina*, in ancient times. The soil becomes level and gently inclined towards the Sacco, to the west, and towards the Liris, to the south-east; and at their junction is seated the village of Salvaterra, the ancient name of which was Fabraterria, the first city of the Samnites. A league higher up the Liris, is Ceprano, a frontier town of 2500 inhabitants, in a situation quite delightful. The Liris rising in the Abruzzi, and passing by Sora and Isola-di-Sora, where it forms a cascade, flows through Ceprano; and assuming the name of Garigliano after it receives the waters of the Sacco, pursues its course to where it falls into the Gulf of Gaeta, beyond Trajetto.

The valleys of the Sacco and of the Liris have been witnesses of the most memorable events. Defended by the warlike Hernicans and the indomitable bravery of the Samnites during the fourth and fifth centuries of the city, they were watered with torrents of Roman gore. It was through these valleys, that is, along the Latin way, that both Pyrrhus and Hannibal marched on Rome, as did Belisarius and Totila, in later times; in the middle ages, the Appian road through the marshes being broken up, it became the great thoroughfare for armies between the mid-regions of Italy and the south: both Charles of Anjou, and Charles VIII, led their forces by this route to the conquest of Naples. We shall meet with more than enough of other warlike expeditions passing and repassing by it, in modern times; so that sumptuous and diversified as are the blessings strewed over these scenes by the lavish hand of nature, their inhabitants, through the ambition and perversity of man, have been made to taste their full share of distress and suffering, from age to age.

Leaving Ceprano in a north-west direction, the

road is gradually mounting through an amphitheatre of hills, sandy, and planted with flax, corn, and red clover. Vines sustained by elm-trees are flourishing on the most precipitous of the acclivities, and oak woods adorn the summits of the hills: on all sides the brilliant verdure which robes a soil, in itself impoverished, bears witness to the industry and skill of those who are occupied in its cultivation. But alas! their cabins, scattered here and there through the fields, evince how miserably their labours are rewarded; for abodes more miserable there cannot be. They are composed of a few branches thatched with straw. This state of things is the result of over population, which enables the landowners to exact such an exorbitant portion of the produce as condemns the over-tasked cottiers to hopeless penury, in the midst of the smiling abundance created by their toil. Thus, in the same province, we see illustrated the evil effects of two opposite systems, those of concentrating and subdividing, when carried to excess. The village of Strangolagalli is in the centre of this little-farm district, which extends from the Liris to the Apennines, in which direction is the city of Banco seated on a lofty dome-like mountain, commanding a bird's-eye view of the battle fields, on which the Hernici and the Samnites so long and so gloriously defended the independence of Southern Italy against the aggressions of the Romans. The valley of the Garigliano is seen from this point of view in all its grandeur, allowing the ken to penetrate to a great depth, and in several directions between the intervals of the mountains, which rise in these parts in isolated majesty, instead of being formed into unbroken chains and masses, as in the north and west of the valley. On one of the loftiest of these cones is situated the ancient and far-famed monastery of Monte Casino, a sojourn of peace in the midst of scenes of violence and disorder, an asylum for the vanquished of all parties; an institution, in fine, to which all who feel grateful for the blessings of civilization and learning must hold themselves indebted. The cities of San Germano and Venafro are seated in these valleys, which open as if to make way, the one for the Garigliano, the other for the Vulturno, and for the high roads which lead to Naples, in one direction, and in the other, to Benevento.

Opposite to Bauco, but in a less elevated situation, is the city of Monte San Giovanni; both these places are for the most part employed in manufacturing cloth of a coarse description. Alatri and Veroli are two other mountain towns of this same region; the latter, was a place of importance in the times of the ancient Hernicans, who boasted of its being, like Anagni and Alatri, built by Saturn. It fell at the same time with Ferentinum, that is, in the year of Rome 447, and its conquest secured for Q. Marcius Tremulus the unusual honour of an equestrian statue in the Forum. Content with their own laws, the

Verulians refused to follow the example of Ferentinum, in accepting the freedom of the city. Its inhabitants amount at present to 7000, mostly occupied in agricultural pursuits.

To the south-east of Veroli, and on the plain, is situated the *Casa Maria*, a Trappist monastery; but towards the north, a narrow path conducts you through mountain gorges of the wildest and most savage aspect, until you find yourself upon a narrow platform hemmed in on all sides by enormous rocks, naked, deeply chasmed, and, on one side, overhanging an abyss, through which foams a raging torrent. Hardly, could you assign a place so terrible as a prison for the worst of criminals, yet it is the spot the sons of St. Bruno have voluntarily selected for their abode. The graceful arcades and long galleries of the cloisters are seen combined with the projecting crags and fantastic minarets of the impending precipices, with which the numerous belfries and spires of the church, a magnificent structure, seem to contend for the highest place. The effect produced by a spectacle such as this is profound and edifying in the highest degree; for ardent and disinterested indeed must have been the piety, which laboured to bring around the sanctuary all that is most costly and elaborate, in a spot so savage and so completely sequestered from the world.

The torrent, which has its origin in those wild ravines, continues to rush and tumble tumultuously over a succession of cascades, until it passes beneath the walls of Collepardo, which is built upon the margin of a precipice, and not far from Collepardo you come to Veroli—a city of more than 8000 inhabitants, chiefly engaged in the cloth manufactory, which is in a flourishing state amongst them. The city is built upon a steep ascent, and after climbing rather than traversing its streets, you arrive at a vast open space upon the mountain top, enclosed by a Cyclopian wall, with the cathedral of the bishop of Veroli rising from the culminating point of its centre, in a most admirable and commanding situation.

These ring-walls of the ancient acropolis of the adjacent city, seem to the eye as new and uninjured as if built but yesterday, although no doubt, they have borne their share of the shocks and accidents of the three thousand years they have seen pass away; yet they are formed of irregular blocks of stone, held in position merely by their weight and skilful arrangement, and without mortar or cement of any sort whatever. In elevation and in compass as well as in perfect preservation, they surpass the walls of a similar kind at Palestrina, Circeii, Segni, or Ferentino.

In comparing these ancient structures of the Val di Sacco, with those of Falerii already noticed, we see distinctly registered the first stage of progress or transition of Italian masonry. In the first stage, the brute material is taken up and made use of in its rude original form, as we see exemplified in these primeval limestone walls of the Val di Sacco regions; in the second stage, illustrated in the walls of Falerii, constructed of volcanic tufo, we meet with the earliest intervention of the chisel and the square, making their first essays on an easily sculptured substance; a third epoch, is that in which the Etruscans begin to take their materials from the quarry, and to make use of cement in uniting the huge regularly squared and chiselled blocks; the last is the Roman epoch, in which the massive blocks of the ancients are set aside, for others of a more manageable size, and a mortar is introduced so excellent as to hold the smallest fragments combined in masses, as imperishable as any marble or granite-rock.

As for the neighbouring town of Alatri, under the name of Alatrium, it was in ancient times one of the chief cities of the Etrusci. In alliance with the Verulans, after long resisting the Roman arms, it at length fell under their power in the year of the city 450, received a colony, and was in the sequel reduced to utter ruin.

The Apennine towers high above this ancient place, and, on a terrace of the amphitheatre which it forms, is seated Guercino, a little town of herdsmen and shepherds, embowered in the overhanging woods: beyond it vast and grassy plains extend (as on the summits of the Pyrenees), connecting the valley which we have been traversing with that of the Anio into which we are now about to enter.

VALLEY OF THE ANIO.

This valley extends from the mountains of the Filetino in the high Apennines to the point where the Anio reaches the Campagna di Roma, below the city of Tivoli, and is bounded by two rocky chains of mountains; the Anio, flowing through its centre, is swelled as it sweeps along its rapid course by the streams, and, at some seasons, by the torrents which come rushing from their rocky sides.

These arid mountain walls, pressing in upon the view of the traveller, and leaving but a narrow space between them, now shut out that vast range of horizon which he enjoyed amidst the immense expanses presented by the basin of the Tiber, and the mountain amphitheatres which surround the Pontine marshes and the Val di Sacco with such an air of grandeur; but for these he is compensated by a charm of another character. Here it is that he beholds the ennobling spectacle of human art and industry in conflict with the disadvantages of soil and situation, nor will the recollection of the courageous people, who, through four hundred years of struggle, upheld the cause of liberty among those barren crags, permit him to traverse those scenes without emotion.

Rising in the high Apennine, the Anio (called

also the Aniene and Teverone) is already a considerable stream before it crosses the borders of the Pontifical States. Its course is thence through a gorge of the mountains, narrow and profound, the elevated regions on either side of it forming immense tracts of pasturage, where innumerable flocks of sheep find refuge when driven from the Campagna and other low plains by the torrid heats of summer. Filetino, a shepherd village placed in the midst of these vast prairies, is the first collection of habitations one meets with after leaving Guercino and Alatri. The farming of the pastures, the produce of the flocks, and the spinning of the wool are sources of profit which appear in the easy circumstances that are so obvious in the appearance of every thing about these kind-hearted mountaineers. In the centre of their territory ascends a lofty mountain, to which they give the expressive name of *Crepa-Cuore*, or the heart-break. In the abrupt, profound, and sterile valleys, which open in all directions towards the course of the Anio and the Val di Sacco, you get a view of Vallepietra, d'Affile, Ponza, and Trevi, swarming with a population, poor, but sober and robust, who hire their services to the farmers of the lowlands after the tillage of their own little farms and gardens is finished; and thus forsake the bracing and salubrious air of their native mountains to confront the insidious destroyer who lays waste the teeming harvest fields of the Agro Romano during summer. Between the prairies and those mountain villages the interval is clad with noble forests: but their timber goes to waste for want of roads to transport it to a market.

In pursuing its course across rocky masses, the Anio comes to where formerly the *Simbruinian Pool*, as it was called, received its waters, and it was from this point the Anio Novum-aqueduct commenced. Its canal was on a level considerably higher than any of the other aqueducts, by which the tributes of the most remote, and of the coolest streams and fountains were carried over valleys and through the bowels of mountain chains, to minister to the pleasures of the all-conquering and haughty people. Hard by the *Simbruina Stagna* stood one of Nero's villas called *Sublaqueum*; but for ages past the only habitation that has replaced it in those wild solitudes is the monastery which has arisen over the mountain cave, in which St. Benedict took refuge from the allurements of the world, while yet in the first bloom of youth. The cliffs which overhang this edifice, vast and irregular in its style, as if ready to descend and crush it with their weight, which they say is sustained by the cincture of the saint: the enormous substructures of the monastery; its outworks, its numerous terraces and galleries sustained against the mountain sides by arches, and the deep abyss beneath, through which the torrent of the Anio is heard to rage and thunder, combine to render the entire scene one of the most singular and attractive. Any thing but devotional enthusiasm must have shrunk, however, from attempting to construct a vast and highly adorned establishment in the face of difficulties and dangers, enough to deter the most audacious genius. But all such obstacles disappeared before devout and grateful attachment to the memory of the saintly youth, who conceived and matured amidst those solitudes, so savage and inaccessible, those plans which made the order which he founded the forlorn hope, not only of religion but of letters, during the horrors and the darkness, in which the inroads of the barbarians involved the Roman world. Around the altar which stands in the little cave—once the cell of the holy youth, and the cradle of the mighty institution which he founded, the descendants of the ancient Marsi, of the Sabines, the Pelignians, and the warlike Hernicans assemble to adore the God of Christianity, and to kiss the feet of the effigy which reminds them of the saint, who passed twelve years in penitent austerities, hard by the spot where Nero used to wallow in every species of debauchery. In the chapels and round the cloisters, are many pictures in the earliest and purest style of the revival of the arts. Here too was established the first printing press ever known in Italy.

To relieve the monotony of the style, we introduce here the description which Maceroni gives of the city and environs of Subiaco, which is hardly more than two Italian miles below the convent.

About midway between them stands Santa Scholastica, another monastery of the Benedictines, which possesses a famous library, and a full-length portrait of Charles Edward, marked on the breast with a pistol bullet, which was fired at it by an English traveller in descending the grand staircase, to shew his feeling for the Pretender.

"From Tivoli, the road to Subiaco is most beautiful and interesting. About six miles from Tivoli, we came to an ancient Roman castle, which I take to be the most perfect piece of antiquity of the kind in existence. I have never met with any account of it in any books of travels or antiquities. The main building is quadrangular, each side of about one hundred yards extent. At the four angles are round towers, of much larger diameter than those of the middle ages. The windows, both in the side walls, which I will call '*curtains*,' and in the towers, are large and adorned with cornices and pediments, in the best style of Ionic architecture. The deep rocky bed of the river Teverone, encompasses a large portion of the castle, from which there is a massive stone stair, down to the water, and a bridge over it. I will leave to the future traveller in these parts, the task of further describing the castle, and go on to Subiaco, where we arrived, by short stages, in three days. A straight, broad, and beautiful Macadamized road, upwards of a mile in length, leads by a gradual ascent into the town, at the entrance of which is a very handsome gate, or rather triumphal arch, built in commemoration of some Pope (I forget which) who honoured this town with a sojourn of several weeks. I have little to say of the town, except that, although most of the streets are narrow, there are some good squares; the houses are well constructed, and extremely clean, both inside and out. We took up our abode at the house of a gentleman to whom my uncle had given me a letter of introduction, and this kind man, appeared to think it the most important duty of his life to devise means for our comfort and amusement. He provided an antiquary to perambulate with Greenough. To me he introduced a noted sportsman, guided by whom I was presented to numerous companies of hares, partridges, and quails. I also enjoyed the society of several men of very superior intellect and education, who joined me in my shooting walk. After ten days spent at Subiaco, in one round of delightful exercise, instructive intercourse, and convivial good cheer, we started for the central mountains. On the road we dined at a convent perched upon the brink of a vast ravine, with the river foaming at the bottom. I was much struck with the beauty of the arabesques which covered the white walls, but not so as to mask or mar the clean simplicity of the apartments. I must not forget to mention, that at Subiaco I was very much surprised to see the walls of the rooms of the simplest houses painted in arabesque, generally on a white ground, in the style of the *Logge* of Raffaelle at the Vatican. Even a little wine shop, in which I several times smoked a cigar, was most beautifully decorated with arabesques, quite à la Raffaelle.

"The face of this part of the country is most beautifully cultivated. Vineyards, olive-woods, fig-orchards, corn-fields, maize, and pulse gardens, covered every inch of ground; rocks, precipices, foaming torrents, mountain peaks above the clouds; the road winding round the sides of—but all this has been said over and over again, by thousands of travellers. Only one thing concerning the picturesque, which so prevails in Italian scenery, I will add, as I have not seen it ever remarked upon. It is the admirable admixture of various coloured vegetation, especially of trees, which gives such striking variety and beauty to an Italian prospect. Besides the difference of *colour*, the *shape*, and general appearance of the trees are beautifully various. The monstrous one-shaped woods of chesnuts, oaks, and firs, are continually relieved by the tall bright poplar; the gigantic pine, with its flat, broad, cauliflower top; the towering cypress, of sombre hue, contrasting with the brightness of the yellow walnut, bright vine, and pea-green plane-tree. The white and blue olive, contrasted with the bright or golden wheat or maize beneath it. In fine, all the shapes and colours of ground and trees, of rocks and mountains, offer the most relieving contrasts, in which picturesque harmony consists. But pray, gentle reader, look at the view from Richmond Hill, or any other hill of celebrated prospect, in this country of England. What a pity that our anxious eyes never discern any other trees, than elm, elm, elm—with here and there, horse-chesnuts, horse-chesnuts; all our public parks, elm, all our roads elm, in every hedgerow, elm, or else horse-chesnuts, horse-chesnuts! Hence the monotony; often have I thought what a great pity it is, that over the entire face of this fine country, such comparatively worthless trees as elms and horse-chesnuts should be exclusively planted. Why not oaks and walnuts. Of the importance of the former, I need not speak; of the latter, both the timber and the fruit are very valuable.

"From the summit of a range of table-land, at length we had a clear view of both the seas of one side and the other of the Peninsula. Other mountain rocky ranges were far above us, but it was superfluous to climb them. I only, being much intent upon the subject of boulders, of which I had but recently obtained a clear idea, discovered that in the deep ravines and roaring torrents, which intersect this country, such specimens of boulders might be found, in all the various stages of their formation, as might suggest to a Doctor Silliman, or a Professor Buckland, a rational explanation of the phenomenon."

From the castle of Subiaco, which was built in mediæval times on the mountain promontory that formed the Acropolis of the ancient city of Sublaqueum, the view can penetrate through the ravine into parts of the savage regions, which the Equians and Marsi long defended against the Romans. *Monte Porcaro*, of which the ancient name was *Mons Præclarus*, and Monte Carbonaro, are the highest of the mountain ranges towards the east, on which at an immense height, is perched the village of Cervara, on the very summit of a mass of crags; and the miserable towns of Roiate, called by ancients *ad Rojas*, and Affile are seen on the range to westward, on the same heights which were once occupied by the city of Trebia long since extinct.

Not far below the city, the stream of the Anio is much increased by the accession of several torrents from the mountains, and after escaping from the narrow glen, which has hitherto confined its course, seems to disport itself in graceful meanderings through a little plain, divided between luxuriant crops of corn, maize and flax, and shaded with the mulberry and the vine; but immediately below this verdant zone, two enormous rocky masses rise abruptly, to an immense height, their sides rent and torn by ravines, and their craggy summits disposed in forms of the most fantastic appearance and variety. Through those grim and rocky vistas, as if rent right through the mountains, to the right and left, as you pass along, the eye catches glimses of other mountains beyond, and other craggy steeps, as arid, as much lacerated by ravines, which seem to bristle along the horizon, and pierce the brilliant azure of the sky with their sharp and broken summits. Upon such craggy pinnacles it is, that the villages of Rocca-Canterano, of Rocca-di-Mezzo, of Austa, in ancient times, Augusta, of Cervara, Marano, and Civitella, are perched in situations so singular, and apparently so perilous, from their enormous perpendicular elevation, as literally to impress the beholder, if not with terror, most certainly with amazement. In such situations it is, on mountain cliffs the most inaccessible, that the hut of the Equian peasant and husbandman is still secured as if from some daring enemy : so indelible are the impressions left by the terror of pursuit, or the passion for independence, which first drove the ancient inhabitants to those eagle-like eyries for refuge and security. Each day it costs the husbandman two hours of toil to descend to the scene of his labours on the plain, and two to return when wearied with his toilsome day ; still will he not settle in the valley, so sad and terrible are the memories they inherit from their sires of what used to happen when the ancient Sabines, the Hernicans, the Romans, the Visigoths, the Herulians, the Greeks under Belisarius, the Saracens, the Lombard and Frankish Dukes of Benevento and Spoleti—when, in fine, the feudal bands of Colonna and Orsini, disputed the passages of the Anio, and swept with fire and sword whatever could be slain or ravaged along its banks. Melancholy and incurable result of twenty ages of hostilities!

This austerity of the landscape is somewhat mitigated as you descend the valley along the *Via Sublacensis*, a road opened by Nero, and the villages of Anticoli, of Corradino, of Roviano, Scarpa and Arsoli, occupy positions more propitious, and announce by the look of their habitations a greater degree of comfort. At this point the Anio which ran from south to north turns at a right angle towards the west and meets the *Via Valeria*, which, coming from Tivoli, passes in the direction of the Abruzzi through the villages of Riofreddo and of Vallinfreda, situated on the frontier of the States. The city of Carseoli, one of the strongholds of the Marsi, destroyed during the social war, was situated in these mountains, as was also Carentia and Alba Fuccensis, where Syphax, Perseus and his son Alexander were confined, and which saw the last of the kings of Macedonia starved to death.

Although the valley after the deviation above noticed becomes altogether changed in character, some instances are still met with of steep rocky eminences serving as sites for villages, among which Sambuci and Saracinesca are remarkable for the picturesque appearance they present; but at each step the mountains subside, and their acclivities, retreating from the valley more and more, display themselves in cheerful amphitheatres broken by valleys which send their purling brooks to swell the Anio. In this region of the valley, we come to where the villages of Cantalupo and Bardella have replaced the Laminæ and Mandela of the ancients.

In one of these valleys is found the village of Licenza: the traveller might pass it by without wasting even a momentary glance on a group of dwellings so mean and insignificant; yet they cover the ruins of the villa where Horace dwelt. The mountain by which it was sheltered was the *Lucretilis* of his charmingly polished and witty verses; this valley was his *Ustica,* that rivulet was his *Digentia,* but the fountain which owned the sweet poetic name of *Blandusia* has disappeared. Perhaps, by some earthquake its sources were dried up or diverted to some other outlet. Not even a fragment of the sanctuary of the most refined of Pagan voluptuaries, the favourite of the epicurean Mæcenas, has survived; and even the charms which inspired his poetic genius have so faded from the scenery, that great have been the discrepancies of opinion amongst the learned, who would determine the precise locality of Horace's Sabine farm by the descriptions which he has left us of it in his writings.*

At no great distance beyond this vale of Horace

* Nevertheless, the words of Horace are still applicable to this debate about his estate—*adhuc sub judice lis est.*

the road leaves the border of the Anio to mount a sort of promontory round the base of which the river rushes through a narrow channel, and on which is built the convent of San-Cosimato, over which St. Benedict for some time presided. Further on, upon a cliff rising in a perpendicular line from the Anio, you come to the town of Vicovaro commanded by an enormous castle of the Orsini formerly lords of all this country, which has passed into the ancient house of Cenci Bolognetti, to which belonged the hapless Beatrice Cenci, more agreeable to know through the pathos of Guido's art than through the horrors of her tragic history.

This town of about 1200 inhabitants, is built on the site of the ancient Varia, or Valeria, a Roman station—(a garrison camp)—and vestiges of extensive outworks are still to be seen around the place; it has a fine church in which is a chapel, very quaint and elegant as a specimen of the *cinque cento* revival of the arts. It was built about the year 1450 by the Orsini family. Vicovaro was the birth place of Marc Antonio Coccio, an historian celebrated in the fifteenth century. From this point of view the horizon is abruptly bounded by the mountains of Arsoli towards the east; but to westward the hills assume the form of a vast and graceful circus covered on their lower slopes by fields of various sorts of grain and other crops, while the next stages are occupied by the vine, the olive, and the evergreen oak. The gentle acclivities, studded here and there with villages, enliven the natural charms of the prospect and bear witness to the salubrity of the air.

The Equi and the Sabines were separated by the Anio in this part of its course, as above Arsoli it formed the boundary between the Equi and the Marsians.

The mountain villages of Rocca Giovine, built on the site of Fanum Vacunæ, dedicated to Victory, a favourite goddess with the Romans, and of San Polo, come in view on one hand as we proceed, and on the other, Siciliano, Guadagnolo, Castel Madama, and the ruins of Sant Angelo, destroyed long since as being a retreat where the brigands were ever certain of sympathy and refuge.

The *Via Valeria*, on which we are journeying, the work of M. Valerius Maximus, constructed in the year of Rome 453, crossed the Anio by a bridge which is now in ruins, and traversing the territories both of the Marsi and Pelignians, crossed the frontier of the Abruzzi where Tagliacozzo stands at the present day. After a little, Monte Gennaro, the ancient Mount Catyllus, to the north, and the mountains Ripoli and Affliano, to the south, approach and are separated only by a narrow dell, in which was the point of junction for the various streams, that were to be conducted from the distant springs and rivers of the mountains, on those aqueducts which form the proudest monuments of the grandeur of the Romans. Here at the place called *Ponte-degli-Arci*, the four greater aqueducts united; that is, the *Anio Vetus*, supplied by the Anio; the *Aqua Marcia*, supplied from a fountain at the foot of Mount Elias over Arsoli: the *Anio Novum*, also from the Anio, but from a higher point of its stream; and finally, the *Aqua Claudia*, like the other two from the neighbourhood of Subiaco; and here was guaged and regulated the volume of the cool and limpid element, which was to hasten along the interminable succession of triumphal arches, for the refreshment and luxury of the Queenly City. Their ruins, now overgrown with ivy and garlanded with shrubs and flowers, are a study for the painters, who annually resort to those regions in quest of scenery. The beauty and effect of the landscape is heightened by two valleys, the one in the direction of Castel-Madama, the other of San Gregorio, and both leading into that savage mountain tract, where probably once flourished the city of Sassula, for a long time a bulwark of the Equian land, but which, in the year of the city 398, fell into the hands of the Romans, and was afterwards so completely swept away, that its exact situation has been long a problem. Monte Guadagnolo commands this region, and serves as a base for a fortified village close to which is a monastery, named Mentorella, of very striking and picturesque appearance.

The valley as we approach to Tivoli is luxuriant,

and adorned with varied charms, but the city itself is not seen to such advantage, as from the subjacent plain beyond ; for it is placed on an eminence so commanding with regard to the Campagna, that the vast expanse of the latter can be surveyed in its fullest extent from the promenades of Tivoli, with Rome majestically reposing in its centre, and the ocean, towards Ostia and Porto d'Anzo, marking where it touches the distant horizon with a zone of azure light. This great elevation of the upper course of the Anio, several hundred feet even at this point above the Campagna, it is, that gives rise to the far-famed cascades of Tivoli. Any attempt to describe them will enter more appropriately into the account of the magnificent works which were executed during the reign of Gregory XVI, in order to save the town from the dreadful ravages to which it was constantly exposed, and from which it had repeatedly suffered during the inundations, to which, as a mountain river, the Anio is very liable. These works, which chiefly consist in a double, lofty, Gothic-formed tunnel, by which the floods are carried through the bowels of a high and rocky mountain, have been crowned with the most complete success.

Tibur (the ancient name of this city),* was founded by the Siculi, received a Theban colony at an after period, and merited the epithet of *Super-*

* The Greek writers call it *τα Τιϐουρα*.

bum so early as the epoch of Æneas. It afterwards sustained protracted wars against the Romans, who saw the Tiburtines on more than one occasion encamp beneath their walls. Though vanquished, they again flew to arms when opportunity occurred; but, after the fall of Empulum and Sassula, about the year of Rome 400, they sued for the alliance of the conquerors, who, by the capture of these two cities, had completely turned their position, till then most difficult to attack. Then it was that Tibur became the favourite retreat of the voluptuous Romans, attracted thither by the coolness of its streams, the charms of its scenery, and the prospects it commanded; and amongst those who had sumptuous villas there, we distinguish Cassius, Brutus, Augustus, Mæcenas, Horace, Catullus, Vopiscus and Varus. A vast tract, where its declivities subside into the Campagna, was covered with the gardens and architectural wonders of the entire Roman world, which the Emperor Hadrian caused to be represented there, though upon a diminished scale. The odes of Horace bear eloquent testimony to the raptures with which its scenery had inspired him.

The invasion of the barbarians changed these scenes of splendour and dalliance into scenes of massacre and destruction. Totila, infuriated against the hapless Tibur, exterminated its inhabitants and razed it to the ground. The new city which sprung up under the name of Tivoli upon those ruins, we shall have occasion to visit more than once during our progress through the middle ages, and also, indeed, in modern times. The temples of Vesta and of the Sibyl, the ruins of the temple of Hercules, the tomb of the Tossi, that of the Plautia family beside the Ponte Lucano, the villa of Mæcenas, of which the vast galleries are still entire, and which instead of the verses of Horace re-echo at present with the hammer and the file; in fine, the vestiges of the country houses of Cassius, Brutus, Vopiscus, Horace, shew how important was this city in the classic ages. But none of these ancient villas, it is probable, could be compared to the magnificent structure erected in the year 1550 by the Cardinal Hippolyto d'Este, but which, with its curiously terraced gardens, has long been sinking to decay.

The ancient Via Tibertina, descending the steep in a straight line from the city gate, passed the Anio by the Ponte Lucano, and so proceeded to Rome through some of the most lonely tracts of the Campagna.

CAMPAGNA DI ROMA.

There is every reason to conjecture that this immense plain surrounded by a semicircle of mountains, beginning at Terracina and ending near Civita Vecchia, was, in ages long prior to the historic period, a portion of the sea; and, that it was in the same or some subsequent epoch the theatre of tremendous volcanic eruptions, the still existing craters of no less than ten extinct volcanos, besides innumerable other vestiges of a similar nature, leave no room whatever for doubt. That it was first taken possession of by emigrants, or adventurous explorers, or fugitives who came thither by sea, is the statement commonly received by the ancients, as we learn from Denys of Halicarnassus, from Cato, Varro, Pliny, and Virgil; but with some ingenious moderns, who seem to have profoundly considered the subject, the notion is in greater favour, that the plains in proportion as the waters retreated from them were taken possession of by the Aborigines descending from the mountains and high lands in the neighbourhood—especially from along the banks of the Anio which originally disembogued itself, they imagine, somewhere close under Tivoli, without, of course, at all mingling its waters as at present with those of the Tiber. The latter river fell into the gulf somewhere in Sabinia. In the very name of the country itself, and of the tribes —the Sicani, Siculi, and others, who are known to have first possessed it, they are fain to discover additional proofs of their theory. Contemporary with the tribes just mentioned, were the Equi, the Hernicans, the Volsci and the Sabines.

The earliest erected shrines or temples of those regions appear to have been dedicated to the fabulous goddess of the chase, Diana, which shews that hunting, in the vast primeval forests with which they found it covered, was the favourite pursuit of those who were the first to explore or inhabit it. In the mountains round Alba Longa, *viz.* at Aricia, near Genzano, near Algidum, near Tusculum, there were temples to Diana. But the clearing away of the primeval forests to make way for the plough proceeded in process of time to such an extent, that, here and there, were woods preserved as sacred. There was one, for instance, dedicated to fabulous deities called Picus and Faunus, between Ostia and Ardea; one of Diana, near Nemi and Aricia, besides the wood of Feronia near Anxur, with the fountain of the same name; the wood of Ferentino near Marino, in which were held the famous gatherings of the confederated Latins: the wood of Diana near Algidum, of Juno Sospita or Pronuba near Lanuvium—now Civita Lavinia—of the nymph Egeria, near Aricia—another dedicated to the same near Rome, a favourite retreat of Numa; one of the Tibertine Sibyl; one of Feronia near Monte Soracte, one of Diana near Ferentinum, one of Mercury near the tomb of Cœcilia Metella, one of Tiburtus near Tivoli, near the Quintilliola, another of Herilus, son of Feronia, on the Ostian way; another near Alba of the Bona-Dea or Fauna; another of Anna-Perenna, near Pratica: one of Jupiter Indigetes, or of Æneas on the banks of the Numicus; near Crustumerium, one of Mars; and near Rome, but at a comparatively modern period, a grove of the Muses.

So populous, in a word, did the former forest-scenery become in after ages, that, within the semi-circle of mountains, forming the headlands, harbours, and magnificently abrupt and towering coast of the primeval gulf of the Campagna, so to speak, there flourished at one and the same time very close on a hundred cities: ninety-seven are counted.

It next, after the appearance of Romulus, became the grand arena of battles: of no less than sixty-nine of them, from the foundation of Rome up to the period with which our history opens; not to speak of an infinity of subsidiary fighting, in the shape of sieges, forays, skirmishing of detached parties, insurrections, civil commotions and the like.

Having thus made the circuit of the Pontifical States, from Epitafio and Terracina to Castel-Franco and the Po, from the Fiora on one coast, to the Tronto on the other; and having traversed them in their fullest extent and in every direction, from the two seas and the mountains up to the walls of the city, minutely inspecting the various regions, their

* This refers to a period previous to the assassination of Count Rossi; and what Rome is to become in the hands of the faction who inaugurated their reign of terror by that act, is still in the womb of the future.

cities, their scenery, their resources, the productions of their soil, the present and the past condition of their inhabitants, the ruins and other memorials of ancient ages by which they are so marvellously distinguished; and having glanced at the most memorable recollections attaching to the scenes and localities through which we have journeyed, we come at length, to turn our regards for an instant—an instant only—on Rome, their capital, in order that when starting forward on the career of its later history, we may carry with us a distinct idea of its present position and appearance, as connected with the past.

Although seated in the centre of the vast solitude of the Campagna, the immediate environs of this city are singularly beautiful, fertile, and diversified: being adorned and set off to the highest pitch, as well by the refinements of art, as by the most brilliant and varied gifts of nature.* Without pausing, however, to admire, at least for the present, this florid zone of vineyards, orchards, orangeries, groves in which flourish the palm and the aloe tree, the platanus, the myrtle, the fig, the citron, the acacia, and the pine; and gardens brilliant with the rarest flowers, the entire interspersed with stately villas, fountains, basilicas, monasteries, and many a memorial of departed grandeur, we pass at once

* See Hobhouse. Historical Illustrations of the fourth Canto, &c., p. 46-48. Maceroni's Memoirs, Vol. 1, p. 50-51. De Tournon, Etudes Statistique sur Rome, L. 1, ch. 3, p. 61.

within the precinct, which is fenced by walls exhibiting the scars and the decay of twenty centuries. They are garrisoned by the grandest recollections: and if all that is most dear to the arts and to civilization be not disregarded, they ought for the future to be dispensed from the assaults of war. Studded here and there with broken inscriptions and divers monumental fragments; garlanded with wild flowers, with grass, parasitical herbs, and precarious shrubs, they resemble, not so much the bulwarks of a fortress, as the precinct of some holy place,—a fence to guard the ashes of martyr, and saint, and hero, from being scattered or confounded with ignoble clay.

The region thus encompassed, is, in part, occupied by a city, singularly beautiful, and magnificently seated, for the most part, upon the Campus Martius, and on the Vatican fields beyond the Tiber; the rest,—far the greater portion,—is "a marble wilderness,"—scattered with—

"—the chief relics of almighty Rome."

Of this latter district of the vast enclosure, the stillness is seldom interrupted, except by some melancholy sound—at night by

"—from out the Cæsars' palace,
The owl's long cry,—"

the howl of the watch-dog, or, haply, by some catches of psalmody from monks, in chanting their nocturnal prayer. The vine-dresser's song by day may sound less drearily; yet is that also a solemn chant, and harmonizes not inaptly with the tolling of the "Angelus," at noon, and the "Ave Maria" bell, at evening. A mean osteria, perhaps, by the way-side, with wild shepherds and herdsmen of the Campagna refreshing their animals at a pool or a fountain, or regaling themselves with a flask or a siesta in the cypress shade; a cassino, or a monastery, here and there among the solitudes, with barricaded doors and casements, a gardener's hut, or a hermit's cell, patched into the sanctuary of a temple, or the alcove of a bath, a theatre, or a banquet hall:—these, the only symptoms of animation to be met with, do not relieve but rather enhance by the contrast of so much meanness with so much of fallen grandeur, the indescribable desolation of the scenery. The very ruins of palace, amphitheatre, and triumphal arch, have the look as if they would exalt themselves still higher in sullen haughtiness, to scathe with their glances of unutterable scorn and indignation those vile intruders upon the cemetery of heroism and empire which they seem to guard.

To this central position among the Seven Hills—to the "imperial mount"—the Palatine, once a volcano's edge—now "matted and massed with ruins,"—the debris which passions wilder than the volcano's rage have left behind them, and at the junction point of so many of the surrounding petty states it was, that, five-and-twenty centuries ago, a blood-stained outlaw fled for refuge. Surrounded by a band of followers as guilty and as desperate as himself, and like him, too, compelled to seek the fastnesses of this border district, in order to escape from the pursuit of justice, his eagle glance ranged keenly through the region, at that period a solitude partitioned between pasturage for kine and flocks, and forest scenery, in order to select the post from which to hurl down his gage of defiance to all the surrounding nations, and prospectively to declare a war of aggression and of conquest, against the entire of the then known world, with the best effect. And well did the outlaw make his selection and choose his ground; for Romulus, who laid the first stone of Rome, with befitting auguries, and in his own brother's gore, is strictly entitled to be regarded not alone as the founder of the city, but also of that defiant and aggressive policy by which Rome at length succeeded in crushing the independence of all the surrounding nations, and in usurping and concentrating within herself all resources and means for monopolizing the influence, wealth, enjoyments, and dominion of Italy, in the first place, and of the entire earth, after the Italian nations had been subdued.

On all sides of the robber town, or rather of the permanent encampment of this brigand, and of the kings and consuls who succeeded him, we have met, in the course of our peregrinations through the States, with vestiges of its aggressive genius, fierce, merciless, persevering, and irresistible as Fate itself.

The Campagna especially, we saw inundated with the blood of those who fell for liberty, during ages as many as afterwards it continued to drink in the martyrs' blood: Rome of the kings and consuls as fiercely persecuting freedom, as Rome of the Emperors persecuted Christianity, at an after period. Nation after nation, we have seen stript of independence, and city after city, like Veii and Alba, and Vulsinii, with a thousand others, we have seen extirpated and blotted out, that by their subjugation, their spoils, their tribute, and ultimately by their utter extinction, the robber-camp might be enriched, recruit its forces, and monopolize every species of resource which was to pave the way for it to universal empire and domination.* The acquisition of Sabinia, of the various Latin and Etruscan territories: of Campania, Samnium, Umbria, Picenum, or even of all Italy, from the Alps to the bounds of Sicily, so far from satiating the ravening hunger of Rome for war and conquest, only seemed to stimulate the appetite for havoc and usurpation, with which, monster-like, this power rushes over every boundary by land and sea, to invade, to massacre and subjugate the nations. So long as a single one of

* Egressis urbem Albanis, *Romanus passim publica privataque omnia tecta adæquat Solo,* unâque horâ quadringentorum annorum opus quibus Alba steterat, excidio et ruinis dedit. ROMA INTERIM CRESCIT ALBÆ RUINIS. *Livy,* l. i. 29.

In these few brilliant strokes, the gist of Rome's history, so far as it records her conquests, is placed in the most vivid light.

them, from Caledonia to Egypt, and from Mauritania to the remotest east, remains erect, the two-edged falchion of Romulus's city is never sheathed,—never! except in the hearts or the bowels of those who presume to defend their liberty.

"It was," says Schlegel, "as if the iron-footed god of war, Gradivus, so highly revered from of old by the people of Romulus, actually bestrode the globe, and at every step struck out new torrents of blood; or as if the dark Pluto had emerged from the abyss of eternal night, escorted by all the vengeful spirits of the lower world, by all the furies of passion and insatiable cupidity, by the blood-thirsty demons of murder, to establish his visible empire, and erect his throne for ever on the earth. There can be no doubt that, if the Roman history were divested of its accustomed rhetoric, of all the patriotic maxims and trite sayings of politicians, and were presented with strict and minute accuracy in all its living reality, every humane mind would be deeply shocked at such a picture, and penetrated with profound horror and disgust."*

Then it is, that The City, the concentration of a boundless empire, becomes itself so unbounded in extent, in magnificence, in riches, in adornments, in the multitudes of her king-like inhabitants and the variety and unbridled excesses of their enjoyments, that all the figures and highest flights of

* Schlegel, Phil. of Hist. vol. i. p. 337.

rhetoric in modern and ancient times, have been overstrained in the abortive effort to describe it. From Gaul, Britain, Illyricum, Dacia, Greece: from Egypt, and from Spain, from the remotest shores of Africa, and the recesses of Asia and the far distant East, the great highways, nineteen in number, which tend to this precinct like radii, to a centre, from every point of the horizon, are thronged with the plunder, with the captives, the regalia, the tributes, and even with the vanquished deities, of every tribe, and tongue, and people. The jaws of the monster which the Prophet beheld, in inspired vision, devours them all; and, in return, inebriates the nations with the chalice of her abominations, through the establishment of a refined, a highly brilliant, and complicated system of civilization, intrinsically, and in ten thousand forms and complications, interwoven by traditions, by arts, manners, literature, and laws, with an idolatrous and most abominable religion, of which The City was herself the supreme and only presiding deity.*

This Rome was in its prime, in the very zenith of its glory and of its power, when the original founder of the principality, upon the history of which we are about to enter, came on to assault and overthrow its dominion. Holding commission for

* The proofs of all this we adduced in a former work, "Rome under Paganism and the Popes:" see also, F. Schlegel's Phil. of Hist. Roherbacher, &c. The subject shall be fully examined in the concluding chapter of this History.

that purpose from the Crucified, from the "Lion of the tribe of Judah," who had sent him to emancipate "all nations," and free "every creature" from the thraldom by which they had been for so many ages and so miserably oppressed, the prince of the Apostles, St. Peter, with his colleague St. Paul, selected this head-quarters and chief stronghold of the mystery of iniquity, as the grand point of attack. Both were crushed in the attempt, upon the same day, and apparently with ease. They were got rid of with contempt, as were their successors after them, for three centuries; but nevertheless, from the moment the Roman power was struck by the "sword" which they wielded, that is by the "word of God," its doom was sealed; it struggled with more than Titanic force, and put forth the whole weight of the world's power, repeatedly; age after age, and with every circumstance of terror, it bared its red arm, not only to repulse this new foe of its empire, which wielded none but hitherto unheard of and invisible weapons, but utterly to crush and exterminate every vestige of it from society, and even from the memories of men. In this conflict, the cities and the provinces are drenched with blood: but the Christians seem to multiply under the sword. From the gore of the martyrs new harvests of believers are seen to spring up and flourish. The idols are seen to totter, and with them the Roman power. The temples begin to be deserted for the catacombs. Paganism is on the wane, and the Crucified is rapidly and visibly winning the victory. As he predicted, he is "drawing all things to himself." Even the supremacy of the state and of paganism, both personified in the Emperor, are vanquished. It is as the champion of the cross, and wearing at the same time the purple and the imperial laurel of Augustus, the victorious Constantine ascends the Capitol. There upon that "hill of triumphs," and as the symbol of divinity and of conquest to which he stands indebted for his victory, he plants the emblem of that gibbet, on which, by order of a Roman magistrate, the God of the Christians had suffered an ignominious and cruel death.

But although the emperor, and with him the greater part of the Roman world have declared for Christianity, at Rome, the majority in the senate, in the schools, in the tribunals, the baths, the circus, the forum, and the amphitheatres are still so ferociously opposed to it, and so infatuated in favour of idolatry, that even the mighty hero and conqueror, the imperial Constantine himself, though wielding despotic power, can neither soothe their fanatical execration of the religion of the cross, nor bear up against the incessant insults and derision, from which even the imperial dignity could not secure him, for having embraced it. In consequence of these affronts, it is, that, at length, he is constrained to withdraw from where Romulus first founded the seat and sanctuary of pagan domination, and to build his throne upon a new basis, in one of the most distant provinces. Thus does Providence prepare the scene for the display of its tardy but most terrible judgments. Discomfited in the empire at large, it is to Rome that paganism retreats, there to gather up its dispersed and broken forces for a last and most desperate effort. There, entrenched behind the sanctuaries, the trophies, the fascinating associations, and the stirring memories of a thousand years of victory, and of a progress the most brilliant and astonishing, in arts, and laws, and letters, as well as in arms, and in all that appertains to the material well-being of society, and the most epicurean enjoyment of existence—there, with the most fierce and mischievous passions of our perverted nature rallying with enthusiasm around it, the antiquated monster holds its ground, resisting alike all the labours for its conversion, all the denunciations and entreaties of the successors of St. Peter, as well as the terrific and repeated warnings it receives from heaven; until, at length, having as if wearied the longanimity of the Almighty, and overflowed the measure of its enormities, He beckons to the barbarian nations of the north and east. At His call, they obey; they precipitate themselves on the culprit city. Their vanguard is led by Alaric. But, in their fiery ardour, they are pressing on each other's steps. After the Goth, the Vandal, and the Moor, the Hun, the Herulian, with other unnameable hordes, each surpassing the other in ferocity, and in a sort of inspired fury, to wreak vengeance on everything belonging to the guilty city, to exterminate and destroy its people, its palaces, temples, trophies, down to its very walls and their foundations, all "make haste to come." Not the sword alone, but fire, famine, and repeated plagues, lay waste her palaces, her streets, and all her multifarious resorts of pleasure. This precinct, which superabounded in the debaucheries of the whole earth, is converted into a monster grave. These multitudes, so brutish and infuriated, which rushing from the wilderness and the forest, fall upon her with the rage and the appetites of wild beasts when falling on their quarry, to use the language applied to the subject by an inspired writer, "devour her flesh, and strip her naked, and make her desolate." Genseric takes with him what Alaric left behind. The city of Romulus, which grew and waxed mighty, and unparalleled in magnificence and riches, and treasures, and all sorts of spoils—the plunder of the whole world, is now in her turn plundered, sacked, reduced to beggary, and overwhelmed with ruin. Her temples are wrecked, her idols shattered to pieces, or carried off as pillage: the shrines are stripped: the palaces, the thermæ, the theatres, the offices of administration, the magazines and bazaars of all that was most costly and exquisite in the appliances of luxury, the resorts of amusement and indulgence are gutted and ransacked; and their occupants are subjected to tortures as exquisite as had been inflicted on the martyrs, to drag from them the discovery of some imaginary treasure. The arches of triumph, and the other trophies, pillars, obelisks, equestrian statues, are, for the most part, laid level with the earth.

As it was with the crimes and delinquencies of Rome, so was it with her chastisement—it is spun out through a long succession of generations, and nations almost as numerous as those which she had injured and oppressed, are seen to take a part in inflicting it. The provinces, for the acquisition of which she had saturated the three great continents with blood and tears, she saw wrested from her one by one—she saw the Goth and the Vandal with their colleagues in the work of retribution and of ruin, lay waste her environs, up to the Pomarium, with fire and sword—burning her villas, trampling her gardens of delight—cutting off her aqueducts, profaning the temples of her gods, and even the tombs of her heroes; and allowing nothing which belonged to her pagan renown, to remain erect, that could by barbaric fury be laid prostrate and disfigured.* Whatever remained erect, after these tempests of Gothic and Vandalic rage and havoc, was in great part subverted in the intestine wars, waged with still more destructive fury, and in the very heart of the city, between Anthemius and Ricimir.† Next

* See Rome under Paganism, &c. vol. ii. p. 166-169.—Gibbon, vol. iv. ch. 36.

† See Rome, ubi supr. p. 169. Gibbon, ib. p. 376. Of this

comes the conflict between Odoacer and Theodoric, one of the most protracted and atrocious that ever desolated Italy.

The former, who, though of Greek extraction, was bred up in the camp of Attila, having gathered round his banner a motley army of the various bands, or free companies of barbarians, Herulians, Turchilingi, as Muratori calls them, Rugians, and Huns, with a multitude of other savage hordes; and having constrained the last of the Roman Emperors, who was significantly called ROMULUS AUGUSTUS, to abdicate, assumed the sceptre, but only under the title of king, and ceased not, with the props and partners of his fortune, to roam through the length and breadth of the lovely but hapless peninsula, filling it every where with scenes of horror and rapacity, until his reign, or to speak more correctly, his invasion and ravages of seventeen disastrous years, were put an end to by the counter-invasion of Theodoric, the king of the east Goths.*

The struggle over the prostrate and bleeding spoil that took place between these two ferocious rivals was sanguinary as it was destructive and obstinate. After several pitched battles, campaigns of devastation, sieges in which the few remaining cities

transaction, Pope Galesius writes: "Nuper Anthemii et Ricimeris civili furore (Roma) subversa est." In Epist. ad Andromach. apud Baron. ad an. 496. n. 42.

* Rome under Paganism, &c. Vol. ii. p. 178-179. See also Muratori Annali d'Italia, an. 476-489.

were well nigh depopulated by the horrors of war and famine, King Odoacer was at length reduced to the last extremity. He offered to surrender his claims and titles on certain favourable conditions, and Theodoric joyfully responded to his advances. The rival invaders met and cordially embraced each other under the gates of Ravenna; but, amidst the hilarity and confidence of the banquet which followed, the Ostrogoth found an opportunity to plunge a dagger into the heart of his unsuspecting guest.* The crown thus acquired, after it had been worn by Theodoric for three and thirty years, devolved upon Athalaric, the son of his only child, the beautiful and ill-fated Amalasontha. This princess, who is said to have been distinguished for prudence, love of justice, and a magnanimity quite heroical, not less than for her personal beauty, had no sooner evinced a disposition to have the young king instructed in the arts and accomplishments of civilised life, than she was rudely menaced for the attempt by the leading nobility of the Ostrogoths, who forthwith deprived her of the tutelage of her son. The study of letters, they told her, was inimical to the martial

* "In fatti, dopo aver fatto buona ciera e carezze per alquanti giorni ad Odoacre, invitatolo un di a pranzo coi suoi cortigiani nel palazzo di Lauro, gli fece levar la vita, e se vogliam credere all' anonimo Valesiano, lo stesso Teodorico di sua mano l'uccisse, con aggiùngere, che nel medesimo giorno tutti quei, che si poterano trovare del di lui seguito furono d'ordine d'esso Teodorico tagliati a pezzi."—*Murat. Ann. d'Ital.* Ann. 493. Tom. 3. par. 1. p. 373. Roma, 1786.

spirit; it engendered meanness and timidity. They added it was not a pedant but a warrior-king they wanted, a hero inured from boyhood in thought and action to the reckless liberty of a soldier. The great Theodoric who had made so many nations tremble, concluded these remonstrants, and who had achieved so many conquests, knew not how to read or write his own name, and never permitted his Goths to go to school, observing on that subject, that spear and falchion were never wielded vigorously by those who had been accustomed to tremble at a rod.* The result of this remonstrance was, that Athalaric, already prone to youthful excesses, did not long survive his Gothic mode of education; and the Queen Amalasontha, who had continually kept up a friendly intercourse with the Emperor of the east, having been barbarously murdered by Theodate, a Gothic duke to whom she had given along with her hand a partnership in the throne, her death afforded the excuse long desired by Justinian, for attempting the re-conquest of Italy. In the war which ensued, and in which we shall find Totila and Belisarius opposed to each other, the one as king of the Ostrogoths, the other as general of the Greeks, no less than fifteen millions of human beings are calculated to have perished.

* The gold plate with which Theodoric used to impress the initials of his name, instead of writing them, on state papers, is perhaps one of the first approaches to the art of printing. The bricks and tiles in ancient Roman buildings are stamped, and so are the loaves of bread found in Pompeii.

The fate which was meted to Alba and innumerable other cities by Rome was meted to Rome herself with interest, before this struggle was brought to a close. It will be for the history on which we are entering to tell the sequel. But it is not alone during the period of its decline and fall, that the history of the Popes is interwoven with the fortunes of that portentous power, which we have been thus tracing rapidly but correctly through the stages of its development and vicissitudes, from the moment of its foundation to that of its overthrow and final destruction. As often as revolution shall be seen to lift its head against the sway of the Pontiffs, so often shall we be startled at discovering the phantom of this power, vanquished through the virtue and grace of the cross, reappearing again. Whoever will thoughtfully consider the various attempts, whether in modern or mediæval times, to pluck the sceptre of Rome from the hand in which it was placed by the same Being who confided the keys to St. Peter, cannot fail to be struck with the singular resemblance they bear to each other. These attempts will in every instance be found, if not to spring from, at least to be characterized by what we must consider a delirium of memory. They occasion the most incongruous jumble of history, and instigate people to rave in a language which should have been spoken to the generations, from whom we of the Christian modern world are dissevered by an abyss of some thousands of years, in order to have a shadow of meaning. Another, and a far more hideous effect of this frenzy is—it not only raves about the Scipios, Horatius Cocles, the Catos and Scevola, in a cigar shop, or a caffè, but it arms every ferocious assassin with the dagger of Brutus. This spectre of the Pagan Past seems at intervals to return to haunt and torment its destroyers; and, if impotent against that institution, which is defended by the ægis of the Almighty himself, still it would seem to be but too successful in its endeavours to pervert the understandings and the hearts of such Christians, as guard not against, but rather court its seductions. In a word, revolution at Rome, from the days of Innocent I to those of Pius IX, has ever worn a certain semblance of a reactionary attempt to restore that order of things, on the destruction and the ruins of which, the Prince of the Apostles and his successors have founded the Christian Religion.

These introductory observations could hardly have been curtailed, but at the risk of withholding from the reader the data for forming his opinion correctly, and solidly, with reference to that hitherto untrodden region of the world's history, the threshold of which we have at length attained. We shall bring them to a conclusion, by quoting the following passage from Frederic Von Schlegel's Philosophy of History—in which he is treating of this very relation, to which we have been alluding, between the Rome of the Cæsars and the Rome of the Popes—and then hasten to proceed with our narrative.

"In this period of the world," says Schlegel, "in this decisive crisis, between ancient and modern times, in this great central point of history, stood two powers opposed to each other: on one hand we behold the Roman emperors, the earthly gods and absolute masters of the world, in all the pomp and splendour of ancient paganism; standing, as it were, on the very summit and verge of the old world, now tottering to its ruin—and, on the other hand, we trace the obscure rise of an almost imperceptible point of light, from which the whole modern world was to spring, and whose further progress, and full development, through all succeeding ages, constitute the true purport of *modern history*."*

* Philosophy of History, Robertson's Trans. vol. i. p. 358.

"On ne trouve ici, ni traités, ni combats, ni intrigues, ni usurpations; en remontant, on arrive toujours à une donation. Pepin, Charlemagne, Louis, Lothaire, Henri, Othon, la Comtesse Mathilde, formèrent cet état temporel des papes, si précieux pour la Christianisme. Mais la force des choses l'avait commencé ; et cette opération cachée est un des spectacles les plus curieux de l'histoire."

De Maistre, *Du Pape,* Liv. 2. chap. 6. p. 245.

THE PAPAL STATES.

BOOK I.

CHAPTER I.

The perplexity in which Sir Walter Raleigh is said to have found himself, when preparing to write the history of the world, was not greater than that which would seem to have beset the steps of as many as have hitherto approached the history of the Papal sovereignty: they seem utterly at a loss from what precise epoch to date its beginning.

The discrepancy between them is not as to days, or months, or years; it amounts to several centuries —in one instance to eight, in another to seven; for, while on the one hand such writers as Nicolas Alamanni,* Græevius,† Thomassin,‡ De Maistre,§ Orsi,|| Giannone,¶ Cenni,** with several others of

* De Lateranensibus Parietinis, Dissert. (Romæ, 1755), pp. 71, 95, 107, &c.

† Thesaurus Antiquit. et Histor. Italiæ, t. 8.

‡ Ancienne et nouvelle Discipline, t. 3. l. 1. c. 27. n. 8. & ch. 29. n. 1.

§ Du Pape, l. 2. ch. 6. p. 249—257.

|| Dell' Origine de Dominio, &c. cap. 1—8.

¶ Storia del Regno di Napoli, &c.

** Monumenta Dom. Pontif, t. 1. p. 12. et seq.

not less note for erudition and genius, will have it, that the origin of this sovereignty is to be discovered in the commotions excited by the Iconoclast heresy, which had their commencement in the year 726; it is, on the other hand, insinuated by Gibbon that the Popes were not possessed of the kingly prerogative (strictly speaking) until the time of Martin V, whose pontificate begins in 1417, and ends in 1431;* and by Ranke, when treating of the Papal States, it is roundly asserted that Julius II, who was elected in 1503, and who died in 1513, "must be regarded as their founder."† We have a host of the highest names, such as Bossuet, De Marca,‡ Natalis Alexander,§ Lebeau,|| Bernardi, Velly,¶ Magnin,** in favour of the view that the sovereign power of the Popes is to be traced to the liberality of Charlemagne and Pepin; this is denied by Muratori, who, for whatever concerns Italian history or antiquity, is a host in himself.

He contends that their only valid title is to be found in the prescription of ages; and he moreover contends that their sway over the States was not

* Hist. of the Decl. and Fall, &c. vol. 8. ch. 49.

† Hist. of the Popes, Introd.

‡ Dissertationum de Concordia Sacerdotii et Imperii, seu de libertatibus Eccl. Gallic. l. 8.

§ Dissert. 25. in Hist. Eccl Sæcul. iv. art. 3. pr. 1.

|| Hist. du Bas Empire, t. 13. l. 63. n. 54 and 64. n. 1. &c.

¶ Hist. de France.

** Vid. Pouvoir du Pape, &c. Paris, 1843.

supreme, at least until comparatively modern times, but only subordinate, first to the Byzantine, then to the Carlovingian, and, finally, to the German Cæsars.* As for Protestant writers, such as the Centuriators of Magdeburgh,† Basnage,‡ Mosheim,§ Sismondi,‖ Hegewisch,¶ Hallam,** Bowden,†† (indeed the exceptions to the general opinion are exceedingly few), their statement is, that, for their secular power, the Popes were exclusively indebted to their own bad ambition, and to their intrigues in the eighth century; but here again, as to the precise epoch from which to date the origin of that power, there reigns the greatest discord and inconstancy of opinion. We have found Gibbon, for instance, bringing it so low down as the fifteenth century, in the reign of Martin V, and against that, again, we shall find him speaking of St. Gregory the Great, who reigned from the year 595 to 604, as if, even in his times, the Papal sovereignty had

* Muratori never loses sight of this theory, either in his Rerum Italicarum Scriptores, in his Antiquities, or in his Annals of Italy. He also wrote expressly on the subject, and was ably and triumphantly refuted by Fontanini. Moreri, in his Dictionary, gives a list of the writings on both sides.

† Ab an. 725—731.

‡ Hist. de l'Eglise, t. 1. p. 260. t. 2. p. 1347.

§ Instit. Hist. Eccl. Sæcul. viii. par. 2. c. 2. §. 6. and c. 3. §. 11.

‖ Hist. des Repub. Ital. t. 2. p. 146.

¶ Hist. de Charlemagne, p. 56, &c.

** Europe in the Middle Ages, vol. 2. p. 11.

†† History of Gregory VII.

been already established. The theories on this subject are, in short, as conflicting as they are numerous, and each of them is upheld by an imposing array of learning, and by a host of authorities, distinguished alike for their acumen as jurists, and for their profound antiquarian researches.

Into this conflict of theories as to the precise instant, and the precise formality by which the Popes became temporal sovereigns, in the technical sense of the jurists—of the writers who have treated the subject in the spirit of a lawsuit, and not in the spirit of history—it is not our purpose to enter.

Instead of getting entangled in this labyrinth of litigation as to a formula and a title, it is for history rather to search out the primitive facts, and so to arrange them with their graphic circumstances as to make it, not a wearying and perplexing task to the reader, but a pastime, to trace how this singular power increases from obscurity and a state of proscription, until it becomes, by steady and progressive development, the subject of so many debates. It is not at Bingen or at Basle, or where the mighty river thunders through the rocky fastnesses of Schafhausen, nor yet where with resistless impetus it charges, so to speak, right through the vast opposing mass of waters of the lake Bregentz, that the origin of the Rhine is to be sought for; neither is it there, we are to fix the origin of the temporal sovereignty of the Popes, where that power has already become the occasion of the most gigantic enterprises and revolutions, such as the repeated passage of armies across the Alps, pitched battles and sieges, upon which hangs the fate of dynasties and nations; and the throwing out into the sublime attitude of the first Christian empire, the unwieldy Barbarian West, to which (previously to the events growing out of this temporal sovereignty of the Popes), no other status belonged but that of a *province*, subordinate to the vile and degenerate emperors of the Greeks. As in the case of the river, we have to seek in the high solitudes of the Alps for the fountain head, not alone of its waters, but of the power by which they are sustained in the majesty and force of their immense career, so is it alone in those lofty devotional sentiments with which the privileges conferred on St. Peter occasioned him to be looked up to and venerated, in a singular manner, by the Christians of those primitive ages, that we shall find at once the genuine spring head of the temporal sovereignty of the Popes, and that self-sustaining vitality, which apparently exempts it from the common destiny, by which it has seen, through the vicissitudes of one thousand years, so many realms and dynasties involved in destruction around it.

Some will have it, that, then began this sovereignty when the inhabitants of Rome and its duchy, as well as those of the Exarchate of Ravenna and the Pentapolis, placed themselves by a spontaneous impulse under the sway of the Popes: but by what were the people prompted to take this course, apparently so strange and difficult to account for? They were prompted to it by their devotion and love for the Prince of the Apostles. The fact is not only recorded in the written muniments of the age, it is stamped on the territory itself in the name—"the Patrimony of St. Peter," which it bears to the present day. It is contended by others that the source of the temporal sovereignty is to be found in the donation of Pepin—but by what motive was Pepin impelled to make the donation? under what influence is it that this ambitious barbarian, on two several occasions, risks the loss of his dearly prized, because newly acquired crown, by marching his armies across the Alps to engage in conflict with an entire warlike nation in arms? In his tent pitched on the field of battle he proclaimed it, that no earthly consideration could have induced him to embark in the enterprise—"Nothing but the love of St. Peter"—"Nisi pro amore Sancti Petri."* He retained not one cantred of the land: not a single city or castle of all his conquests: the keys of them all, with the act of donation signed by himself, by the princes his sons, and by all the nobility of the Franks, was borne to Rome by his Ambassadors, and reverently deposited by his command on the tomb of St. Peter. When Charlemagne came to make good the victories of his sire, and not only to

* Anastasius, Bib. in Vit. Steph. II.

ratify but to enlarge the donation, such was his reverence for the Prince of the Apostles, that he would not ascend even the steps which lead to St. Peter's, but upon bended knees.* He renews the donation of Pepin: it is still to the "Blessed Peter" the cities and territories are given.† When it came to the turn of Ludovicus Pius, as emperor, to renew these acts of his sire and grandsire, he states expressly in his diploma, that the States are guaranteed to St. Peter, and to the Popes *as his vicars.*‡

Examine the Fasti and the annals of this most singular of realms, from first to last; inspect, consider them in every sense—in the charters and diplomas of the Emperors, no matter to what race they belong: in the ordonnances of the Popes, whether promulgating laws for the Government of the States, or protesting against their dismemberment or invasion. Whether it is Pope Stephen II who calls to King Pepin for assistance, to rescue the States; or Pius VII, who launches an excommunication against the Emperor Napoleon for usurping them, it is still the Prince of the Apostles,

* Ibid. in vit. Hadrian I.

† Ubi concessit easdem civitates et territoria BEATO PETRO, etc. Anast. Bibl. in vit. Hadriani.

‡ This diploma or charter may be seen in Baronius, ad. Ann. 816, in Pagi ann. 816, and in Cenni Monumenta Dom. Pontif. Its authenticity can be no longer disputed. We shall have to refer to it again, when fixing the boundaries of the States as constituted by Charlemagne.

who everywhere appears as the true and only Sovereign of the States. It is to St. Peter, the Normans of Naples and Sicily pay homage for those fiefs of the Apostolic See. The Popes are only his vicars—such they constantly and uniformly professed themselves—holding the States in trust for him, and administering them as faithful stewards for the benefit and interests of the See of St. Peter. Throughout the enormous archives of this history, you will find nothing—not a particle of evidence—to contravene this assertion, but you will find innumerable proofs to sustain it; a great many of them, we shall have to notice as we proceed. As for the merits, that is to say, whether this view of St. Peter's privileges be scriptural, and theologically well founded or otherwise, we pause not to inquire; what concerns our history are the facts; and these, instead of sending us headlong into the throng of the litigants, whom we have left engaged in the effort to decide the question by Notaries' Latin in the eighth century, have led us up to the catacombs themselves, as to the true spring-head of this sovereign power.

We find on diligently searching after the hidden roots and fibres from which it grew, that it was planted as early, as to its germ at least, as the "mustard seed" itself; for none of his successors in the palmiest days of the Papacy ever pretended to such an extent of power in temporals, as was exercised *de facto* over the Christendom of his time by

St. Peter:—"as many as were possessors of lands or houses (says the Scripture), sold them, and brought the prices of the things that were sold, and laid them down at the Apostles' feet."* This economy was established at Rome from the first, for it was not confined to Jerusalem, but as we collect from various passages of the Apostolic writings, was established as the uniform and obligatory discipline of all the dispersed churches.†

We find it practised by the Christian communities established in Asia.‡ St. Paul, in exhorting the Christians of Corinth to be zealous and active in its fulfilment, points to the example of the "churches of Galatia."§ Those of Macedonia, notwithstanding their "very deep poverty," begged of the Apostle, "with much entreaty," to have their share in this "ministry (of charity) that is done towards the saints," in contributing to their support.

The principle of this economy, which shews that it applied universally, is thus laid down by St. Paul in his second Epistle to the Christians of Corinth.‖ In urging them to make the contributions generously he says: "I mean not that others should be eased and you burthened, but (that all should be regulated) by an equality. In this present time, let your abundance supply their want, that

* Acts iv. 34—37. † See 1 Cor. xiv. 1—4.
‡ Acts xi. 29 § 2 Cor. viii. i. 1—16, and ix. 1—15.
‖ 2 Cor. viii. 13.

their abundance also, (in your day of need) supply your want, that there may be an equality," that is, a reciprocity; and from the earliest Christian writers, it is plain, that as the discipline was not of a local character, but applied with equal force, whereever the Church was extended, so neither was it of a merely transitory nature, but permanent. Thus, two sorts of offerings are mentioned in the Apostolic Canons as in use, when this very ancient code of discipline was committed to writing; the one of corn, grapes, oil, and similar matters, such as incense, which were made at the altar; the other of milk, legumes, animals and other similar objects which were brought to the bishop's place of abode, to be by him distributed in conformity with the established order.* St. Justin Martyr and Tertullian speak of quests or collections made regularly every Sunday, just as we find St. Paul enjoining the Christians to do, in his day; and this practice was one of the chief features, which impressed the Pagans with admiration of the new, and so much persecuted religion.†

Far from being weakened by time, this tendency of the Primitive Church became more and more confirmed and excited as the persecutions increased. Everything conspired, during those seasons of tribulation and danger, to detach the faithful from

* 1 Canon Apost. 3, 4, 5.

† S. Justin. *Apologia* 1 (alias 2), ver. fin.—Tertul. Apol. cap. 39.

mere earthly enterprizes and enjoyments, and to prompt them to such investment of their earthly treasures as is so frequently and impressively enjoined in the Gospel; and these influences produced their effect with much greater force and uniformity at Rome than in any other part of the Church.*

It could be easily proved from the "Acts of the Martyrs," that during the three first centuries the wealth of the Christians in Rome was completely at the disposal of the successors of St. Peter; and hence we find that the Prince of the Apostles, and the earlier Popes, for centuries before they emerged from the catacombs, were possessed of the sources of very great temporal influence. "But as for the Roman Church," says Sigonius, "instituted as it had been by St. Peter, and consecrated by his blood with that of the Apostle St. Paul, as it was of all churches the chief in jurisdiction and dignity, so was it pre-eminent in riches—for it abounded in massive plate, sacred vessels, and ornaments of every kind; and in estates the most fertile, and in rich possessions, dispersed through almost every region of Africa and Europe."

Very great even before that event, the property

* See Fleury, *Hist. Eccl.* t. ii. l. 7. n 39. Alban Butler. 10th. August. St. Ambros. de Officiis. l. 2. cap. 28. Prudentius, *in Hymn. 2. de Coronâ.* Bingham *origines et antiquit. &c.* t. ii. l. 5, c. 4. Thomassin, *Ancienne et nouvelle discipline,* t. iii. l. 1. ch. 1, 2, 3, 12.

of the see of St. Peter, was vastly augmented by the munificence of the Christian Emperors, after the conversion of Constantine the Great, and by the offerings and bequests of opulent converts, and more especially of the patricians, who were at that period enormously wealthy, and greatly under the influence of the imperial example. The catalogue of the donations of Constantine alone, as they are recorded by Anastasius, in his Lives of the Popes,* is truly astonishing; nor have the severest critics been able to take exception to the account. The items extend over several folio pages; suffice it to say, that, not including the cost of the workmanship, which was exquisite, the value of the gold and silver ornaments, amounts, for one single Basilica, that of the Lateran, to no less a sum than £68,000 of our money. He also settled on the same church estated property, worth more than £10,000 a year, besides a yearly tribute of 150 pounds weight of frankincense for the altar.

When it is recollected that the property of the pagan establishment, which Constantine had at his command, was well nigh unbounded, and what enormous heaps of treasure used to be squandered by his predecessors, in donatives to the legions, and in the shows of the amphitheatres and the circus, the mind will be less indisposed to give to these statements the credence which they certainly merit.

* In Vit. S. Sylvest.

We learn from the Epistles of St. Gregory the Great, that in his time the Roman Church was possessed of *Patrimonies* of great extent and value, not only in several districts of Italy, but also in Dalmatia, Sicily, Sardinia, Corsica, in Egypt, Gaul—both ultra and Cisalpine—in Africa, and in many other provinces.* Of these *Patrimonies*, some were estates, the rents of which were paid to the Roman Church, others were seigneuries, strictly speaking; sometimes embracing cities and entire provinces, and in which the Pope, by his officers, exercised all the rights of a temporal lord or sovereign.†

From authentic muniments, we learn, that previous to the close of the seventh century, the districts or cantons of the Cottian Alps, including the city of Genoa, and the sea coast, called the *riviera*, as far as the frontier of Gaul, belonged to the Popes, and we find the Lombards, by whom those provinces had been invaded, *restoring* them towards the year 708, as an ancient property of the Roman Church, to Pope John VII. "King Aripert," says Venerable Bede, "restored to the Apostolic See several *seigneuries* and patrimonies of the Cottian Alps, which had from ancient times belonged to the said see, but which had for a long time been usurped by the

* *S. Greg. Vita per Johan. Diac.* l. 2. cap. 53-54, etc. *Fleury, Hist. Eccl.* t. viii. l. 35. n. 15 & 45.

† S. Greg. Epist. l. 1. Epist. 44 & 75. l. 9. Epist. 9, 14, 99, 100. Thomassin Ancienne et Nouvelle Disciplini, t. iii. l. 1. ch. 27. n. 7.

Lombards; and this donation, written in letters of gold, he forwarded to Rome."* The revenue of the Sicilian patrimonies, with those of Magna Græcia, or Calabria, amounted, yearly, to three and a half talents in gold, or about £16,000, according to the most probable estimate.

Sigonius, in his enumeration of the estates, besides those above mentioned, says there were patrimonies in Tuscany, Sabinia, in the Cantons of Abruzzi—both ultra and citra—in Lucania, Calabria, and other places.†

History bears testimony to the spirit in which these vas tpossessions were administered. As long as the persecutions lasted, they were expended in the maintenance of the poor, and of the sick, the widow, the orphan, and the captive; in the solemn interment of the martyrs, in the erection and embellishments of oratories in the crypts and catacombs, in sending out missionaries, in procuring consolation or liberty for the captive confessors, manumissions for slaves, and in sending aid to the most distant provinces of Christ's kingdom, in their

* In Chron. An. 708. Aripertus rex Longobardorum, multas cohortes, et patrimonia Alpium Cottiarum quæ quondam ad jus pertinebant Apostolicæ sedis, sed a Longobardis multo tempore fuerant ablata, restituit juri ejus : et hanc donationem aureis scriptam litteris, Romam direxit.

† Ex quorum omnium vectigalibus, Pontifex cum vetera urbis templa reficiebat atque in Majorem splendorem ornabat, tum frumenta pullicè coemebat, atque in horrea publica ad necessarios usus pauperum congerebat.—*De Regn. Ital.* A. D. 570.

distress. "Moreover, there is extant," says Eusebius, "an epistle of Dionysius, Bishop of Corinth, to the Romans, *superscribed to Soter, that time the bishop there,* out of which it is not amiss here to insert some words, wherein he much commends the usage and custom of the Romans, observed by them even until the time of the persecution (of Diocletian) raised in our own age. He writes thus: "For this hath been your custom even from the beginning (of your conversion to Christianity), to be divers ways beneficial *to all the brethren, and to send relief to most churches throughout every city:* sometimes supplying the wants of such as are in necessity, at others, supplying the wants of those brethren that are condemned to work in the mines. By such charitable munificence, which from the beginning you have been accustomed to transmit to others, being Romans, you retain the custom received from your Roman forefathers. *Which usage your blessed Bishop Soter has not only diligently observed, but greatly improved; being both instrumental, and ready in the conveyance of your bounty designed for the saints, and also comforting with blessed words, (as a tender and affectionate father does his children), those brethren who come as strangers to you.*"*

During the terrible series of disasters, which hum-

* Eccl. Hist. book iv. ch. 23. See also a similar testimony from S. Dionysius of Alexandria, relative to the churches of Syria and Arabia, ap. Euseb. l. vii. c. 5. with the note of Valesius.

bled the empress city to the dust, the Popes became the forlorn hope of the once haughty Senate and of the Roman People. It was customary with them to store up the produce of their immense estates, and, during the seasons of famine which frequently recurred, on account of the imbecility or negligence of government, as well as of the almost constant ravages of war, to dole it out with no niggardly hand, and gratuitously, to the starving multitude.* They attended to the repair of the public edifices, the endowment of institutions, to the maintenance of the churches, of the colleges for missionaries, of the monasteries, and of the hospitals for strangers and the sick. "Every year," says Anastasius, in the Life of Pope Symmachus (A. D. 498), "he sent garments and money throughout Africa and Sardinia to the bishops who had been dragged into exile. He also sent great sums into Liguria, Milan, and divers other provinces, to redeem those who were in captivity, and in dismissing them to return to their homes, he loaded them with gifts." "Et dona multiplicavit, et dimisit."†

* Sigonius, l. 1. "Romani vero terrarum quando victores ac domini," says Sigonius, "post sedem imperii ex urbe remotam, quantum libertatis adepti erant, tantum antiquæ dignitatis amiserant. Post autem urbe sæpius a barbaris capta atque incensa, ut opes infirmiores, sic spiritus humiliores nacti erant. In tantis tamen detrimentis, unâ ipsius pontificis latè ecclesiis omnibus imperantis sede, veterem splendorem nominis tuebatur."

† "Hic fecit cæmeterium jordanorum in melius—omni anno per Africam et Sardiniam ad Episcopos qui in exilio erant retensi

Of Pelagius II (A.D. 577 to 590) the immediate predecessor of St. Gregory the Great, the same writer tells us, that he converted his own dwelling into "a hospital for the poor and the aged."* At a time, too, when hospitality was an apostolic virtue, the hospitalities of the Popes were renowned over the whole world. No matter how lowly the pilgrim, or from what country he came, whoever visited "the threshold of the Apostles" was allowed to want for nothing. The needy palmer was as welcome as the prelate or the crowned head, while the precedency and more sumptuous treatment, due to rank, were religiously conceded to the latter: nor was any one permitted to depart without bringing back with him some token of St. Peter's bounty to his native land.† From the same funds were equipped those expeditions which constantly went forth from Rome to convert and humanize the barbarians; and the residue after these demands had been satisfied, were never spared, when they could purchase the public safety, or promote the public prosperity.

By arts such as these, the rudiments of papal dominion were first established; they were still further consolidated by the sacrifices and patriotic services of the Pontiffs, especially during the pro-

pecunia et vestes ministrabat. Hic captivos per Liguriam et per Mediolanum, et per diversas provincias, pecunia redemit et dona multiplicavit, et dimisit."

* "Hic domum suam fecit pthochiam pauperum et senum."

† Anastasius Bibliothec. in vit. S. Martin. "Et nullum imuninem suis donis S. Petrus rapellit."

tracted agonies and final destruction of the Rome of the Cæsars.

As if the power founded by Romulus and the Cæsars had been designed by Providence to serve as a chrysalis to the temporal influence of the Papacy, the latter begins to appear and advance in development, in proportion as the former crumbles away, or is shattered to pieces by the hosts of invaders. "The public and private indigence," says Gibbon, "was relieved by the ample revenue of the Popes, and the weakness or neglect of the Emperors compelled them to consult, both in peace and war, for the temporal safety of the city."* It was behind the chair of St. Peter that the remnant of the senate and the people sought protection, in the last extremities of their distress.† When the legions were annihilated,

* Observe that it is not by choice, not from "ambition or through intrigue," but through the overbearing pressure of events, the Popes find themselves placed for the first time at the head of affairs. When St. Gregory (afterwards Pope) was nuncio or apocrisarius at Constantinople, Pope Pelagius, his immediate predecessor, directed him to arouse the Emperor Maurice to a sense of the utter misery to which Italy was reduced through the neglect of his government, with a view to obtaining assistance against the Lombards.

† Thus, we read in the life of Pope John VI, Ap. Anast. Bib. that when the whole country from Beneventum to Horta had been swept by the Lombards, devastating all before and around them with fire and sword, he sent priests with treasures into the Lombard camp, and ransomed the captives. "Pontifex misit sacerdotes cum Apostolicis donariis, et universos captivos de eorum manibus redemit."

and their proud walls could no longer protect the Romans, the venerable priest went forth, and turned back the furious Hun ; he moved the ruthless Vandal to compassion, and interposed the Apostolic ægis between the sword of Alaric and the vanquished. The great St. Leo was more than the sovereign of his country, which he SAVED from destruction, more than once. At a later period, it was at the intervention of the Archdeacon Pelagius (Pope Silverius being at the time in exile), that the miserable remnant of the Roman senate and people were not sacrificed to Totila's wrath ; and it was to the exertions of Pope Agapitus, under the tyranny of the Goths, and of Pope John, under that of Narses, they were indebted for their safety. It is not, however, until the pontificate of Pope Gregory the Great, that the pontiff and the prince began to appear conspicuously identified in the same individual : for it was at that period precisely (A. D. 590 to A. D. 604), that Rome and Italy in general had arrived at the crisis of utter abandonment and misery.

"Between the years 566 and 569, all Italy," says Muratori, "was afflicted by a pestilence which well nigh reduced the whole country to a desert. Such was the mortality, that in many districts nearly all the inhabitants were swept away, nor was there any one left to reap the harvests, or gather in the vintage —'nè v' era chi mietesse, ne chi recogliesse l'uve.'" "Every where," says Paul Warnefrid, "was wailing, tears were every where. For as the rumour ran, habitations were left deserted, none who could fly the havoc remaining behind, but only domestic animals. Herds and flocks roamed about without an owner; in villas and towns, (castra) to-day swarming with people, to-morrow no sound was heard to interrupt the death-like silence. Sons fled from the unburied bodies of their parents; and parents forsook their offspring in their agonies. If any one not dead to the former instincts of humanity, consigned his neighbour's body to the earth, his own was sure to remain unburied. On all sides primeval silence seemed to have resumed its reign. In the field no voice was heard, no sound of the shepherd's reed on the hills; the wild beasts no longer molested the flocks, nor had the poultry anything to dread from birds of prey. The corn, the time for the sickle passed, fell from the head from over ripeness; the purple grape bursting with racy juice was left to drop shrivelled from the leafless vine."* With the approach of winter, he continues, the sound of martial instruments was audible both day and night; and it was the impression of many that they could discern the murmur of a distant host as if upon the march. These were but the preludes of the woes which impended over Italy; for Alboin or Albion, king of the Lombards, burst down through the passes of the Julian Alps in the following year; and, at the head of a countless army of rapacious and sanguinary barbarians, swept with irresistible fury

* De Gestis Longobardorum, l. 2, cap. 3.

over the hapless land, to devastate by fire and sword whatever the pestilence had spared. These ruthless hordes, composed of the most fierce and warlike adventurers from a variety of barbaric nations, either Arians in religion, or still addicted to the most savage practices of heathenism, overran the country with such rapidity, that in less than seven years we find them permanently established not only in the rich provinces on which they have impressed their name (that is in Lombardy), but also in Tuscany, Spoleti, and Beneventum; while the garrisons of the Greek emperors, formidable only to the exhausted and heart-broken Italians, beheld from the walls of Ravenna, and a few other fortified places, the dwellings of their subjects in flames, and themselves coupled together like dogs, and dragged away into slavery beyond the sea and the mountains.

The invaders, who spread themselves in every direction without resistance, were to be tracked by the horrors and dreary solitude they left behind. "Behold," says St. Gregory, writing to the Emperor Maurice, "every thing in these parts is given over to the mercy of the barbarians; the cities are destroyed, the fortresses dismantled, the open country, stripped of its inhabitants, is become a wilderness for want of cultivation, and the servants of Christ are the daily victims immolated by the sanguinary superstition of these idolators." Their fanaticism, specially directed against the sanctuaries, the clergy, and whatever else was consecrated to Catholic worship, left St. Gregory to mourn over many a ruined church, and to complain that, in several districts, there was not left a single priest to baptize the newly-born, or absolve the dying from their sins.* But that, perhaps, which gives us the most lively idea of the horrors of this bitter epoch, is the impression, universally prevalent at the time, that fiery coruscations in the heavens, and signs similar to those that ushered in the destruction of Jerusalem, had been beheld by the terrified population, especially in the northern regions of the sky, for some time previous to this terrific invasion of the Lombards.

It was the destiny of Rome to be as pre-eminent in the disasters of Italy, as she had been in its triumphs. To beleaguer, plunder, and make desolate that queen of empire, had been the grand object of ambition, apparently, a kind of monomania with every invader, from Alaric, who found it a boundless aggregation of palaces, baths, theatres, and temples, peopled by the aristocracy of the earth, down to Totila, who left it "a marble wilderness."

The elements themselves conspired to put the last hand to the work of desolation. There is a prophecy attributed to St. Benedict,† which said, that "Rome was not to be *exterminated* by the hands of

* Baron. Ann. 590, p. 13, says, he was obliged to unite parishes, in a great many instances, from want of pastors.

† See Second book of St. Gregory's Dialogues.

barbarians; but that, exhausted by tempests, by whirlwinds of fire, and by earthquakes, it should of itself collapse into a heap of ruins;" and the holy pontiff, in one of his discourses to the people, appeals to the scenes by which they were actually surrounded to prove the truth of this prediction. "The lofty tree," says Gibbon, "was deprived of its leaves and branches, and the sapless trunk was left to wither on the ground. The ministers of command, and the messengers of victory, no longer met on the Appian or Flaminian way; and the hostile approach of the Lombards was often felt and continually feared. The Campagna was reduced to the state of a dreary wilderness; in which the land was barren, the water impure, and the air infectious.* Curiosity and ambition no longer attracted the nations to the capital of the world; but if chance or necessity directed the steps of a wandering stranger, he contemplated with horror the vacancy and solitude of the city, and might be tempted to ask, 'Where is the senate, and where are the people?'"

Such was the condition of the eternal city, when the successors of the fishermen were induced, not by ambition, but through mercy, to take it under their care and protection; and if those regions along the Tiber, which had been the theatre, for so many centuries, of all that was most illustrious and important in human affairs, have not long since reverted to a

* This is no proof that the desolation of the Campagna is a consequence of the misrule of the Popes.

state of aboriginal wildness and solitude, similar to that in which they were when first explored by the shepherd king, Evander, it is to the Popes, as successors of the fisherman, the credit must be attributed. "Like Thebes, or Babylon, or Carthage," says Gibbon, "the name of Rome might have been erased from the earth, if the city had not been animated by a vital principle which again restored her to honour and dominion."

In short, it would not be possible to imagine anything more wretched and utterly hopeless than the condition of Rome at the juncture when St. Gregory was compelled by the voice of heaven, expressed through the united and impassioned entreaties both of the clergy and the people, to abandon the cloister where he had consecrated his life to study, austerity, and prayer, in order to undertake the labours and solicitude of the pontificate, and, along with them, the still more intolerable burthen of watching over the temporal affairs, not of Rome alone, but of Italy. A pestilence, brought on by the stagnant waters which a dreadful inundation of the Tiber had left behind it, was raging at the time of his accession to the chair of St. Peter; and such was the mortality, that, according to the testimony of an eye-witness, an envoy of St. Gregory of Tours, no less than eighty persons fell dead on one occasion, during the procession of the Litanies. "The sword has reached the very soul!" exclaims the afflicted pastor, addressing himself to the miserable remnant of the once lordly and innumerable people, during this visitation; "behold the falchion of Divine chastisement is unsheathed against us, and wide wasting, and so terribly sudden are its strokes, that death, as if impatient of delay, no longer waits till languor and the ravages of disease have prepared the way for him; but, as your eyes, alas! bear witness, springs, as if with a bound, upon his victims. Parents behold their offspring hurried before them to the tomb. The moribund and the decrepid survive the blooming and the ambitious; nor is it merely here and there the people fall: they are struck down in multitudes, and whole houses are made desolate on a sudden."

Shortly after, in a homily to the people on the woes announced in the first chapter of the prophet Joel, beginning, "What the palmer-worm hath left, the locust hath eaten," he says: "Behold, my brethren, in the new disasters which come thickening upon us every day, we are made eye-witnesses of the woes which our ears have heard denounced in the words of prophecy,—Ecce, fratres mei, jam cernimus quod audiebamus. Of a population once innumerable, you see what is left, and even of this wretched handful, numbers are continually swept away by the sudden casualties which fall upon us in quick succession, and by the strange and diversified calamities which each new day brings with it. How many, for instance, retired to repose the other night, full of projects for the morrow, who were buried under the ruins of their own dwellings, ere the dawn revealed to the survivors the extent of devastation caused by that sudden whirlwind, which not only tore up the sturdiest trees by the roots, and blew down houses, but levelled the most massive of our sacred edifices to their foundations ?"

Again, in his Homilies on the Gospels,* when commenting on the words of our Lord in St. Luke, chap. xxi. descriptive of the signs and prodigies by which the day of Judgment is to be preceded, he says, "Erunt signa in sole," &c., "there shall be signs in the sun, and in the moon, and in the stars, and, on the earth, distress of nations, on account of the confusion, and the roaring of the sea and the waves: —of which terrors, brethren, some we have already witnessed, while the rest we dread as imminent. For as to the conflict of nation with nation, and the affliction and distress too heavy for earth to bear, it is not so much in the annals of the past we have to look for all this, as in the miseries occurring around us. How frequently the tidings of cities in great number overthrown by earthquakes arrive to us from distant countries, you are aware; as for pestilence, we suffer from it without respite; signs in the sun, and moon, and stars are not yet visible, it is true, unless indeed we forebode, from this strange alteration in the state of the atmosphere, that they are not far distant."†

* Homilia 1. † Rom. Br. Pars Hiem, p. 156.

But, as if the catalogue of miseries still wanted something to complete it, the seditious violence of foreign mercenaries within the walls is added to the ruthless hostilities with which the Lombards lay waste the environs of the city. "Hostiûm gladiis foris *sine cessatione* confodimur, sed seditione militûm interno periculo gravius urgemur," are the words of one of the Pontiff's letters written to the Greek exarch about this period.

Time brought no alleviation of this distress to St. Gregory or his people. Five years later, we find him breaking off from his series of expositions of Ezekiel, on account of the public dangers and distress which called him to far different occupations. "Let me not be blamed," he says, "if after this lecture, I cease from these expositions, for the public tribulations are hourly increasing, as alas! you are too well aware. The ravages of the sword hem us in on every side, and momentarily threaten us with destruction. Some of our wretched people return with their hands chopped off, to tell us of others who are groaning in captivity, or who have already suffered some cruel species of death. Oh! wonder not if my tongue falter and refuse to proceed further with these sacred expositions, for my very soul is weary of existence." And in the following year, writing to the Patriarch of Alexandria, the afflicted Pontiff says,—"I am unwilling to enter into any description of all we suffer from the swords of the Lombards, who sack and slaughter all before them, lest, in seeking for commiseration, we add to the sorrows of a heart already but too much afflicted."

In preaching the panegyric of the martyrs, Saints Nereius and Achilles, he says: "Behold, how the world, when we love it, eludes our pursuit. These saints, beside whose tomb we are now standing, despised and trampled on its allurements, when all was flourishing and fascinating around them. But now, the world is withering, and yet the love of it is blooming in our hearts: on every side is death, on every side is grief and desolation: from all quarters we are struck with calamities, we are deluged with bitterness, and nevertheless we love to desperation what is our ruin: what flies us, we pursue, we cling with infatuation to fortunes which are falling."*

Again, in 603, he writes to Phocas the emperor: "It is not possible for human language to suggest any adequate idea of what we have had to suffer daily, and without intermission, from the Lombard incursions, during the last five-and-thirty years;" and in the year 604, immediately previous to his death, the following is the picture of Rome and Italy given by the venerable Pontiff, in one of his expositions of Ezekiel, which he had again resumed: "Scenes of misery meet our eyes, and our ears are assailed with the cries of lamentation and suffering,

* Homil. xxviii.

no matter to what side we turn. The country is reduced to a wilderness, strewed with the ruins of towns and cities.—Nullus in agris agricola, pene nullus in uribus habitator remansit,—and it is our doom to see the trifling residue of the population that is still left incessantly subjected to the horrors of mutilation, or slaughtered, or dragged into captivity. As for this city, once the queen of the world, judge ye who are spectators of the immensity and variety of her disasters, how she is crushed and humbled to the earth by incessant shocks of invasion, by the carnage of her citizens, and the dread of dangers incessantly impending over her. All her mighty ones are taken away. What has become of the senate and the Roman people? Of the majestic order of the past, not one trace is left; and after her people have perished, her walls and trophies fall of their own accord, and crumble into dust."*

To imagine, however, that St. Gregory's patriotism was confined to the outpouring of lamentations over the public calamities would be entirely to mis-

* "Ipsam autem quæ aliquando mundi domina videbatur, qualis remanserit, Roma, conspicimus; immensis doloribus multipliciter attrita, desolatione civiûm, impressione hostiûm, frequentiâ minarûm, jam de illâ omnes potentes ablati sunt. Ubi enim senatus, ubi jam populus? Omnis in ea dignitatûm ordo extinctus, et tamen nos ipsos paucos qui remansimus, adhuc quotidie gladii, adhuc quotidie innumeræ tribulationes premunt, *et postquam defecerunt homines, etiam parietes cadunt.*"

construe his history. Notwithstanding the bodily infirmities, of the most tormenting description, which made his life a protracted martyrdom, and the cares and duties of his apostolic office, every day of his fourteen years' pontificate was signalized by exertions the most devoted and effective for saving his country. During that entire period, the administration and the defence, not only of Rome, but of Italy, were thrown altogether upon his shoulders, by the neglect and embarrassments of the Greek emperors: so absorbed in troubles at home, and in struggles against the Avars and Persians, as to be utterly incapable of affording any protection or assistance to their Italian subjects. It is to no purpose that the Pontiff prays for succour against the public enemy. His remonstrances, both by letter, and through his nuncios at Constantinople, are equally ineffectual. Mauritius never interferes, unless to requite the sacrifices of the Pontiff with reproach or invective, or to cross and frustrate his plans for the public safety.

"The misfortunes of Rome," says Gibbon, "involved the Apostolic pastor in the business of peace and war; he sends governors to the towns and cities; issues orders to the generals; relieves the public distress; treats of peace and of the ransom of captives with the enemy." What wonder, if in discharging these offices in conjunction with those of his supreme vicariate over the Church, the dignities of prince and pontiff should seem to be united in his person?*

"To superintend the hierarchy of the Church, and the various orders of the clergy; to provide for the temporal and spiritual necessities of the monasteries and of the poor; and, at the same time, to be ever on the alert against the stratagems of the Lombard foe, and, what is still more harassing and difficult, to frustrate the treachery and plots of the military leaders; the torment and toil of all this will be estimated by you," writes the Pontiff to a holy bishop, "to be great, even as that brotherly affection is, with which we are confident your fraternity regards us."

Several of St. Gregory's epistles to the bishops have for object to arouse their zeal to the defence of their episcopal cities, and, in a word, to the discharge of those duties of the civil magistrate, which were left to total neglect, owing to the misrule and anarchy of the times. They were to look well and

* Mr. Gibbon, with his wonted ingenuity and bad faith, makes St. Gregory doubt "whether power or ambition prompted him to supply the place of his absent sovereign:" whereas no such uncertainty, as to his motives, can be collected from the words which the Pontiff uses: "Ita ut sæpe incertum fiat, utrum pastoris officium an terreni proceris agat;" (lib. i. ep. 25. ad Johan. Episc. Const.), but on the contrary, it is evident, not only from his express declarations, but from the uniform tenor of his life, that he deplored as the heaviest of his many afflictions, the dire necessity that forced him to take the lead in secular transactions, rather than see his country and his people utterly ruined.

with assiduity to the walls, their repairs, their defence, the maintenance of the forts, with men, provisions, and munitions of war.* To a Bishop, whose advanced age and infirmities had rendered him inapt for such offices, the Pontiff assigned a coadjutor in the full vigour of life, that he might look to them. Abandoned every where, or miserably betrayed by the secular rulers, the cause of social security and order was taken up by the Pope, and maintained by him with devotedness and success.

But while he was thus active in warding off invasion, and in providing against external danger, he never ceased to minister to every want, and mitigate the sorrows of his people, with the wisdom and affection of a parent. "The Church of Rome," says Gibbon, "as has been formerly observed, was endowed with ample possessions in Italy, Sicily, and the most distant provinces; and her agents, who were frequently sub-deacons, had acquired a civil and even criminal jurisdiction over their tenants and husbandmen. The successor of St. Peter administered his Patrimony with the temper of a vigilant and moderate landlord; and the epistles of Gregory are filled with salutary instructions to abstain from doubtful and vexatious lawsuits; to preserve the integrity of weights and measures; to grant every reasonable delay, and to reduce the

* See S. Greg. Epistol. l. viii. ep. 18. (alias 20), l. 9. ep. 4 & 6, alias 2 & 5, preface to Com. on Job, et alibi passin, item Orsi. Dissert. de Origine, &c. p. 1.

capitation of the slaves and the glebe. The rent or the produce of these estates was transported to the mouth of the Tiber, at the risk and expense of the Pope; in the use of wealth, he acted like a faithful steward of the Church and the poor, and liberally applied to their wants the inexhaustible resources of abstinence and order. The voluminous accounts of his receipts and disbursements were kept above three hundred years in the Lateran, as a model of Christian economy.

"On the four great festivals, he divided their quarterly allowance to the clergy, to his domestics, to the monasteries, the churches, the places of burial, the almshouses, and the hospitals of Rome, and the rest of the diocese.* On the first day of every month, he distributed to the poor, according to the season, their stated portion of corn, wine, cheese, vegetables, oil, fish, fresh provisions, clothes, and money; and his treasures were continually summoned to satisfy, in his name, the extraordinary demands of indigence and merit.

"The instant distress of the sick and helpless, of strangers and pilgrims, was relieved by the bounty of each day and of every hour; nor would the Pontiff indulge himself in a frugal repast, till he had

* This term is frequently used, particularly when applied to the Roman Pontiffs, to signify a whole province, sometimes, as by the Council of Arles, to signify the entire Church; and, on the other hand, a parish or title is sometimes designated by the same name.

sent the dishes from his own table to some objects deserving of his compassion. The misery of the times had reduced the nobles and matrons of Rome to accept, without a blush, the benevolence of the Church; three thousand virgins received their food and raiment from the hand of their benefactor, and many bishops of Italy escaped from the barbarians to the threshold of the Vatican. *Gregory might justly be styled the father of his country;* and such was the extreme sensibility of his conscience, that, for the death of a beggar who had perished in the streets, he interdicted himself for several days from the exercise of sacerdotal functions."*

"Gregory awakened the emperor (Mauritius)," continues the same historian, "exposed the guilt and incapacity of the exarch and his inferior ministers; complained that the veterans were withdrawn from Rome for the defence of Spoleto; encouraged the Italians to defend their cities and altars, and *condescended*, in the crisis of danger, to name the tribunes, and to direct the operations of the provincial troops."

"If we may credit his own declarations, it would have been easy for Gregory to exterminate the Lombards by their domestic factions, without leaving a king, a duke, or a count, to save that unfortunate nation from the vengeance of their foes. As a

* What a *monster and minister of Antichrist* was this founder of the secular dominion of the Popes!

Christian bishop, he preferred the salutary offices of peace; his mediations appeased the tumult of arms; but he was too conscious of the arts of the Greeks, and the passions of the Lombards, to engage his sacred promise for the observance of the truce. Disappointed in the hope of a general and lasting treaty, *he presumed to save his country without the consent of the emperor or the exarch.*

"The sword of the enemy was suspended over Rome; it was averted by the mild eloquence and seasonable gifts of the Pontiff, who commanded the respect of the heretics and the barbarians. The merits of Gregory were treated by the Byzantine Court with reproach and insult; *but in the attachment of a grateful people, he found the purest reward of a citizen,* AND THE BEST RIGHT OF A SOVEREIGN."

Such is the testimony borne by the most implacable and accomplished enemy of the Popes, as to the *arts*, the "ambition and the intrigues," by which their secular dominion was founded; their right to the sovereignty is pronounced, even by Gibbon, to be "*the best.*"

Nor was it alone during his mortal career, that Rome was indebted to St. Gregory. His works lived after him; but in nothing has he bequeathed such a blessing to his successors as in the example which so many of them have imitated, and which shall be a mirror of every apostolic virtue to them all, until the last of them shall resign his charge into the hands of the "Prince of pastors."

In all his struggles against the cruel and faithless Lombards, he never ceased to regard them with pastoral solicitude.* He kept up a friendly correspondence by letters, embassies, and presents, especially of pious books, with Queen Theodelind, during all the confusion and violence of the wars; and, before his demise, he had the consolation to see the foundation of a more peaceful future established in the conversion of the Lombard king, and of most of his followers, to Catholicity:† while the spiritual conquests effected by him over the Saxons of Britain, and the Goths of Spain, had the inevitable effect of securing that immense influence to his successors, which gradually matured into a political preponderancy, in all the temporal as well as in the ecclesiastical affairs of Christendom.

Never have the destinies of Europe been so completely risked upon the conduct of a single individual, as in the instance of Pope Gregory the Great; never, since the times of the Apostles, have

* "They were a noble race, of pure morals (!), and bold, manly, generous, and even romantic character, presenting the strongest possible contrast to the corrupt and degenerate Romans, whom they held personally in utter contempt, and refused to mingle with on the familiar footing of their predecessors, the Goths. It was, therefore, from the Church, rather than the natives of Rome and Italy, that they derived their civilization, and to the Popes accordingly they paid a free, but a zealous deference," &c.—Lord Lindsay's Sketches of Christian Art, vol. 2. p. 5. Following Gibbon, his Lordship is wrong on the Lombard history.

† Baron. ad. An. p. 38.

such claims been established, as in the person of this Pontiff, upon the admiration and the gratitude of posterity. Under heaven, it is due to this Pontiff, that the last gleam of civilization in the west was not extinguished for ever. By saving Rome from the Lombards, and converting England, he prepared the events which gave birth to modern Europe. When he ascended the chair of St. Peter, nothing but scenes of horrible disorder and violence could his eyes discern through the gloom of barbaric ignorance, which had already settled down, or was fast impending over the Western nations. Scarcely a trace of Christianity, or of Roman civilization, had survived the Saxon conquest in Britain: in France the labours of St. Maur and of so many other Apostolic missionaries, had been subverted, almost irretrievably, under a succession of profane and nefarious tyrants of the Merovingian dynasty: Spain was trampled on by the Goths, who combined the grossest superstitions of paganism with a violent attachment to the Arian heresy: while Germany, Switzerland, the Low Countries, with the immense regions to the north and east, were still involved in the chaotic night of barbarism and idolatry. As for Italy, partially exempted hitherto from similar misfortunes, the ruin of its institutions became so complete under the incessant ravages and barbarous despotism of the Lombards, that a "ferocious ignorance," to use the expression of Muratori, invaded the population. The enmity borne by these tribes to learning and every thing connected with it, was remarkable, even in comparison with that of their fellow savages, who had at former periods invaded the Roman provinces. The seats of education, they everywhere destroyed; the clergy and the monks, the only learned men of the times, they slaughtered without mercy. Monte Casino, the fountain from which knowledge flowed for so many ages over Europe, was reduced to a heap of ruins, and so remained until restored, after a century of desolation, by Pope Gregory II.*

How Europe was ever to be extricated, if Rome also, the only remaining fortress of light and order, had been plunged in the abyss, it is impossible to conceive. Other seat of recuperative principle in the west itself, there was none; and as for the east, there was, from that quarter, no single ray of hope to be looked for. "While the patriarch of Constantinople was a domestic slave under the eye of his master," says Gibbon, "a distant and dangerous station, amidst the barbarians of the West, excited the spirit and freedom of the Popes. Their popular election endeared them to the Romans; the public

* See the entire passage, Dissertazioni, &c. Vol. 1. p. 5. "Allora fu," says Muratori, in speaking of the effects of the Lombard invasion on Italy, "che l'Italia veramente mutò facia. Andarono a terra le belli' arti: le lettere piu non si coltivarono: l'ignoranza stese l'ali dapertutto.

and private indigence was relieved by their ample revenue; and the weakness or neglect of the Greek emperors, compelled them to consult, both in peace and war, the temporal safety of the city. The same character was adopted by the Italian, the Greek, or the Syrian, who ascended the chair of St. Peter, and after the loss of her legions and provinces, the genius and fortunes of the Popes again restored the supremacy of Rome."*

Besides, the simoom of Islamism, which was shortly to sweep over the fast-fading empire of Byzantium, was already brooding in the desert. In thirty years from the death of St. Gregory, Bozra, Damascus, Emessa, Balbec, Tyre, Tripoli, Antioch, and Jerusalem itself, had fallen before the apostles of Mahomed; the successor of Constantine had fled from Asia before the Arab robbers. Instead of bringing aid of any kind to Europe, the Greek emperors never are heard of there for the future, but as meddlers in theology, attempting by *ectheses* and *types*, as they entitled their missives, to dictate what the vicars of Christ were to teach the Church, over which he had placed them; or, much more frequently, in the attitude of suppliants for assistance against the Saracens and Turks, who kept them hemmed in within their capital.†

* Decline and Fall, &c. c. xlix.

† The best vindication of this great Pope from the charge of "intrigue and ambition," brought against him by such writers

Had Rome fallen under Lombard sway (and it must have fallen but for St. Gregory), the hope of Christendom was obviously undone. But with incomparable virtue and magnanimity, he repelled invasion without sullying his Christian meekness; and in saving his country, he preserved the only seminary for the new race of apostles, who, in little less than a century from his demise, had succeeded to an extent which may well be called miraculous, in converting and humanizing the entire West.

as Gibbon (Decline and Fall, vol. viii. c. 45) and Hallam (Europe in the Middle Ages, vol. ii. p. 326), is to be found in his own letters. For the annoyances he had to suffer from the Byzantine Court, see Sigonius de Regno Italiæ, p. 3, an. 595, and Baron. ad An. 595. No one who reads them but must pronounce the charge to be most unfounded and unjust. Even Cave, in his History of Literature, is loud in his praise of St. Gregory. He blames him, however, for having treated the usurper Phocas with respect, and joins in accusing him of a desire to destroy all the writings and monuments of Pagan antiquity. Alban Butler ably refutes the first, and the Abbè Emery the second of these charges.—Christ. de Bacon. t. ii. p. 332, &c.

CHAPTER II.

The Pontiffs who succeeded St. Gregory, so justly surnamed the Great, continued to tread faithfully in his footsteps; and the misconduct of the Byzantine court, and of its ministers in Italy, did not fail to perpetuate the necessity for their attending to the public safety, as he had done. "When invasion was to be warded off," says Thomassin, no flatterer of the secular pretensions of the popes; "when the Lombards were to be propitiated by subsidies, the Pontiffs of this period never spared either their treasures or their personal exertions." However, it was not until Leo the Iconoclast, by his profane and infamous tyranny, destroyed every tie that could attach the Italian provinces to a union by which they gained nothing but disgrace and misery, that the titles and honours of a power, which they had exercised for better than a century previously, began gradually to be given to the Popes.

The impulse by which the Byzantine emperor was driven to such an onslaught upon the religious liberty of his subjects, as involved the empire in anarchy, is attributed to his superstition by the Greek writers Theophanes and Zonoras. The ignorance and prejudices natural to an Isaurian peasant, as well as his subserviency to the Jewish and Mahomedan impostors who surrounded his throne, would render such a view of this despot's conduct sufficiently probable: however, it would appear from the Latin writers generally, and from Anastasius in particular, that Leo, like most of the potentates who have been zealous for Church reformation, was urged, much less by a burning zeal for religion than by the lust of plunder, to declare war not only against the images of the Redeemer and of his saints, but against whatever else belonging to the rich adornments of the temple, that could help to replenish his treasury. But, be this as it may, certain it is, that in the year 725, he issued an edict prohibiting all from manifesting respect for images, whether of the Redeemer or of his saints, ordering the sanctuaries throughout his dominions to be stripped; and, as an example to the rest of the empire, he commanded the great golden crucifix which had been erected by order of Constantine the Great, over the grand entrance of the imperial palace of Constantinople, to be torn down, and broken to pieces. A tumultuary rising of the people, especially in the Greek islands, and an ineffectual attempt to storm Constantinople, and dethrone the Iconoclast, were the immediate consequence of these proceedings, so far as the east was concerned. "But in the west," says Giannone, "and above all, in Italy, not only was the edict not obeyed, but it excited such indignation among the people, that they broke out into open insurrection. Nay more, the exarch, wishing to carry matters with a high hand at Ravenna, gave rise to commotions still more serious and ruinous; for having issued orders that the images of the churches should be destroyed by main force, such a tumult was raised, that the Ravignani formally revolted from the Emperor, and transferred the dominion of their city to Luitprand, the Lombard king."*

Sigonius, by whom these transactions are more fully narrated, enumerates the provinces which rose upon this occasion against a tyranny, which bears a striking resemblance to that so often practised by the Turkish pashas, on the Greek and other Christian nations of the Levant; and in fact, the exarch was nothing less than a pasha, under another name. They were the Roman Duchy, Campania, Ravenna, and the Pentapolis; as we proceed, the precise extent of these several provinces shall be determined. In Campania, Duke Exhilaratus and his son, when endeavouring to stir up the population to an attack on the Pope, were themselves attacked by the Romans and slain.

Charges of treason, of insolence, and of fomenting rebellion, are preferred against Pope Gregory II, for his conduct in this emergency, with much more heat than consistency, (considering that those by whom these charges are preferred are the very same, who glory so much in vindicating that liberty of conscience which the Pope merely defended), and

* This latter statement is incorrect, as we shall have occasion to shew, a little further on

with still less regard for what the genuine history of the transactions requires. Had there been a shadow of foundation for such accusations, it is not in terms like the following, that a writer, so decidedly hostile to the secular pretensions of the Holy See as Giannone, would have spoken of the conduct of St. Gregory II, with regard to the transactions in question.

"There governed the see of Peter in those times," says the historian of Naples, "Pope Gregory, the second of that name. He, although greatly opposed, along with the Roman people, to the designs of Leo, did not cease, nevertheless, to watch over the Greek interests in Italy, with exemplary vigilance; straining every nerve, chiefly from that apprehension of the Lombards which he inherited from his predecessors, lest the authority of the Emperors should be impaired; and notwithstanding the most unworthy treatment which he received at Leo's hands, for all that, overlooking his private wrongs when the public interests were in peril, *he directed all his thoughts to prevent the revolt of the Italians,* and to defend the imperial possessions against the Lombards."*

* That even Mr. Bowden, the Puseyite biographer of St. Gregory VII, has not yet got rid of the prescriptive tendency to misrepresent the history of the Popes, is strikingly evinced by his version of these transactions. According to him, it is the Pope who incites the Italians to rebel, and causes the exarch to be murdered. "The Pope defended himself," he says, "by methods more consonant with the character of a sovereign than with

"God is my witness," writes the Pontiff in his reply to the menacing letters of the Iconoclast emperor, whom he reminds of the faith pledged by him in his coronation oath to the see of St. Peter, and of the orthodox and dutiful tone of his letters of salutation, during the ten preceding years;—"God is my witness, that year after year, I ceased not to commend and extol your majesty to the potentates of the west by every means in my power, even persuading them to receive your laurel-crowned effigies ('laureta tua') with every mark of respect; but when the impieties perpetrated on the image of their Saviour, by your order, were reported amongst them by the Franks, Vandals, Moors and Goths—merchants, and pilgrims of all lands, who, being at that time in Constantinople, were witnesses of what occurred—then it was," pursues the Pontiff, "that *they* in their turn having cast down *thy* images,

that of a Christian prelate. *The Italians, inflamed by his addresses, rose in arms in support of his cause.* At Ravenna the exarch was slain," &c. As is evident from Giannone, already quoted, the facts of the case are reversed in Mr. Bowden's narrative, and this will be more clearly evinced by the sequel. "E quantunque, per aversi egli dovuto aponere agli sforzi di Lione, fosse stato dall' imperadore indegnissimamente trattato, con tutto ciò, post-ponendo le private injurie alla publica causa, *dirizzò tutti i suoi pensieri per impedire la revolta de' popoli d' Italia,* che a lui ubbidivano, e per difendere le terre dell' imperio dall' invasione de' Longobardi." Sigonius says it was with difficulty he evaded the demand of the Italians to have another, instead of the Iconoclast, proclaimed emperor.

trampled them under foot, and cut and hacked *thy* face,"—"tunc, projecta laureata tua, conculaverunt et faciem *tuam* conciderunt."

In expostulating with Leo, in the same letter, on the impolicy of his attempts to usurp the prerogatives of the Apostolic See, and to destroy its influence, the Pope reminds him that he and his predecessors in the chair of St. Peter had ever striven to make their influence subserve the great interests of Christendom, by rendering it a kind of *binding wall* and *common causeway*, or medium of amicable intercourse and reciprocity between the east and west.* So that instead of fomenting disaffection, to inculcate loyalty to the Greek emperors, and, by every means, to prop up their tottering influence, seems to have been, up to this juncture, the chief political tendency of the Popes.

Indignities, however, and unrelenting persecution were the requital of these services. No less than six attempts were made upon the life of the Pontiff by the emissaries of the Isaurian, and defeated by the chivalry of the faithful Romans. The contemporary writers of this Pontiff's life, as we have it in Anastasius, gives the following detailed account of the sixth attempt by one Eutychius, a most sanguinary and nefarious minion of the Byzantine

* "Romæ conciliandæ pacis causâ sedere (Pontifices) tanquam parietem intergerinum septumque medianum Orientis et Occidentis." Ap. Baron. an. 726.

court, despatched with the twofold mission, to pillage the churches at Rome, and murder the Pontiff with the leading men of the city.* "But after some time," says this writer, "Eutychius the patrician, who had been formerly exarch, arrived in Naples, charged with orders from the Emperor to put in execution what neither the exarch Paul, nor the imperial equerries, with the other instruments of mischief, previously sent for the same purpose, had been able to effect. Neither did Providence in this instance permit the designs of the imperial emissary to lie hid. Despite of all his artifice, it soon became evident to every body that his real object was to strip the Christian sanctuaries of their riches, and to destroy and pillage all before him. And when he sent written directions to the Greek authorities at Rome to kill the Pope, and with him the magnates of the city, this most cruel and insane conspiracy having come to light, the very messenger who was the bearer of it would have fallen a victim to the public indignation, were it not for the extraordinary efforts of the holy father to protect him. However, they pronounced anathema against Eutychius himself, and big and little of the Romans bound themselves by oath not to suffer a pontiff so zealous for the faith, and such a defender of the Church to be murdered or

* It is the opinion of Cardinal Scelestrate, adopted by Muratori, in his Rer. Ital. Scriptores, t. iii. p. 2, that the Liber Pontificalis was first digested, the detached biographies and entries having been collected from the archives, at or about this period.

dragged into exile, but rather to lay down their lives with cheerfulness in his defence. Thus foiled in this attempt, the next proceeding of Eutychius was to send bribes to the Lombard chiefs, and messengers to their king, in order to detach them from the Pontiff. But the Lombards, detesting his perfidy, of which they had the clearest evidence, in his own intercepted letters, joined themselves like brothers with the Romans for the defence of the Pope: both parties being emulous to see which should outstrip the other, and suffer death more readily in so glorious a cause."

When the patrician Paul, says Warnefrid, was marching on Rome, to put St. Gregory II to death by order of Leo, the Lombards of Spoleti and of Tuscany drew together at the Salarian bridge, on the Anio, and forced the Greek to retire. He adds that Leo burned the images collected from all parts, but that the Pope spurned his order to act in the same impious manner. Also all the army of Ravenna and Venetia did the same, and only the Pontiff prevented them, would have proclaimed another emperor.* Meantime the fortresses (Castra) of Æmilia, Feronianum, Monte Pellio, Buxeta, Persiceta, Bononia, the Pentapolis, and Auximum, are seized by Luitprand: also Sutrium, but this he again restored to the Romans.†

"But while all parties were thus vieing with

* Et, nisi eos prohibuisset Pontifex, imperatorem super se constituere fuissent aggressi. L. 6-49. † Ib.

each other in devotedness to his person, this venerable father seemed to place greater reliance on the abundant alms which he ceased not, with a liberal hand, to distribute among the poor. Constant in prayer, in fasting, and in public acts of supplication with his clergy, his hopes rested more firmly on these appeals to Heaven than upon any human assistance. Not omitting, at the same time, to express his acknowledgments for such zealous exhibitions of attachment on the part of the faithful, his bland and persuasive eloquence ceased not to move all to works of piety towards the Almighty, to be firm in the faith, and not to fall away from loyalty and affection to the Roman Empire. By arts such as these did he soothe the excitement, and mitigate the calamities occasioned by the insane and violent proceedings of the Iconoclast."*

* Doubtless it was by this simple statement of the conduct pursued by St. Gregory II, in this crisis, that the Centuriators of Magdeburgh, with their numberless imitators, were inspired to brand him with the "tyranny and ferocity of Antichrist." "Nota hic," say they, "Antichristi tyrannidem et ferocitatem," and that a noble author, Lord Lindsay, has been led to pronounce such a judgment as the following on these transactions. "It was a step," he says, "before God and man alike indefensible——at once schismatical (!!) and rebellious" (!!). Sketches, &c., vol. ii. page 6. London, 1847.

Even Sismondi, in writing of these very same occurrences, finds himself bound by the evidence of the facts of the case, to bear the following testimony, so honourable to the Popes:—"le pouvoir croissant des ces Pontifes sur la ville de Rome, était fonde *sur les*

While the Pontiff thus endeavoured to pour oil upon the troubled waters, he ceased not to vindicate the cause of religion with unshaken intrepidity. In answer to the Emperor's threats, that he would cause him to be dragged from Rome to Constantinople, and there treated as had been his martyred predecessor, St. Martin, he answers :—" Would, that it were pleasing to the Almighty to call us to himself, by the same path our predecessor, the blessed Pope Martin, trod ; not that we are anxious to be rid of life: on the contrary, we wish to have it prolonged for the advantage of that people who, with the entire west, turn their eyes upon our humble person, with a confidence far greater than our deserts. *And as for St. Peter, whose image you threaten to cast down, know that he is regarded by all the kingdoms of the west in some sort as a terrestrial deity.** Be certain that if you shall attempt to make experiment of their devotedness, by the perpetration of any such outrage as you mention, they will be prepared, without a doubt, not only to vindicate their own altars, but even to avenge the wrongs which have been inflicted on their brethren of the east.

titres les plus respectables, des vertus et des bien faits." Hist. des Rep. Ital. t. 1. chap. 3. p. 122.

* It says but little for Ranke's honour as an historian, that he makes the Pope assert (in quoting this passage) that it is himself, Pope Gregory, who is venerated as a "God on earth" by the western nations! whereas, in the Pope's letter, it is as we have rendered it in the text! See his Hist. of the Popes, Introd.

However, we fervently implore Almighty God to turn your mind from any such unworthy and insane attempts. The fidelity of these warlike nations to the prince of the Apostles is unbounded, as I have already said: and, we take God to witness, that we are innocent of the blood which they will not fail to shed, if you attempt to violate the image and tomb of the Apostle. Upon your head be the consequences of this sacrilegious experiment."

"Tyrannically you persecute," continues the Pontiff, "and harass us with the arm of the flesh, and with military violence; but we, helpless and destitute as we are of terrestrial legions, invoke the Prince of the celestial hosts, Christ Jesus, seated at the right hand of the Father, that he send on thee a devil, according to that of the Apostle, 'to deliver such an one over to Satan for the destruction of the flesh, that the spirit may be saved.'"

However, the animosity of the Isaurian was alike insensible to denunciations as to entreaties, and unable, with the forces of his own empire, to crush this venerable old man, he at length prevailed upon Luitprand, A. D. 729, the declared enemy of his own dominions in Italy, to lay siege to Rome.

St. Gregory made every exertion to be prepared against the storm which he had long anticipated. He had put the city into the best posture of defence he could; but, in his anxiety to put a stop to the devastation of the country, and the violation of the sacred temples of the Almighty, he determined not to confide in the strength of the walls, or the valour of their defenders, but to present himself as a suppliant before the fierce Lombard invader.

With this view, he issued forth from the gates of the beleaguered town, with an august retinue of the Roman clergy and nobles, and advanced to the Vatican fields, where the enemy had pitched his tents hard by St. Peter's. Being come into the presence of Luitprand, the Pontiff thus addressed him:—

"Were I of impression, O King Luitprand, that the forces by which he carries on this siege belonged to Leo himself, depend upon it, I should never have ventured forth to treat of peace, or of suspension of hostilities. To what purpose would it be, to seek the liberation of consecrated shrines and hallowed sepulchres, from one, who had so recently not hesitated to destroy with fire and sword the images of the saints, and of Christ our Lord himself, and to lay his sacrilegious hand upon the sanctuary. But, having been given to understand that the war, and the conducting of this siege, are placed almost entirely under the direction of a prince, who is said by the voice of fame to unite an ardent piety and a profound veneration towards the saints to his other royal virtues, I have not hesitated to come forth into a hostile camp, in order to admonish King Luitprand of some things in which, as it appears to me, the cause of God is vitally concerned.

"I am satisfied that the King is not ignorant that the Church which he is preparing to assault was consecrated, in their blood, by the princes of the Apostles, St. Peter and St. Paul; thereby rendering the soil which contains their sepulchres most venerable to all the nations of the earth. Art thou, then, O King, who hast given such a weight of treasure to rescue the relics of one confessor from the danger of being treated with insult by barbarian infidels, and hast translated and enshrined them in your own royal city of Pavia, with so much pomp and magnificence, prepared, at the bidding of another, to plunder and profane the most august sepulchres, and the temples themselves of the great apostles?* Is it not more worthy of thee, O King, to persevere in that course which thou hast marked out for thyself, as a benefactor to religion, than to become the follower of another in his impiety? More glorious to imitate many great and good princes in preserving the most august of cities, than be led to destroy it by the example of one, and that one a reprobate! We have all heard of King Attila, so renowned for cruelty; but his history must be still more familiar to your majesty, whose ancestors have obtained dominion of the regions

* The Pontiff alludes to the relics of the great St. Augustine, translated from Sardinia by King Luitprand to Pavia, from which city a portion of them is to be translated (A. D. 1847), to Hippo, in a ship of war given for that purpose by the French king (now an exile! 1849).

that were held for some short time by the Hun. He, in ages past, ravening for blood and slaughter, came rushing with furious speed to burn Rome. Whereupon St. Leo, who was then Pontiff, hastened forward with all speed to meet this king, who was called the 'Scourge of God.' He met him on the banks of the river Po, implored him not to proceed in his design ; and the invader was so overawed with the appearance of the apostles St. Peter and St. Paul, as if looking down upon the conference, that he became docile and obedient to the entreaties of the Pontiff, contrary to all expectation. And, is it to be credited, that Attila, who, far from being a Catholic, was addicted to rites the most opposite to Christianity, and of a nature, I may say, inhuman, was induced to turn back almost at the nod of a Roman Pontiff, and that Luitprand, a king conspicuous, and destined to be renowned with future generations, for his devotedness to the Catholic religion, is relentlessly bent upon the destruction of a city which cannot be consumed without giving to the flames those temples and tombs which have been ever regarded by all nations, far and near, and even by those little removed from barbarism, not only with veneration, but with a species of religious awe the most thrilling ; or that Attila, overawed by the mere apparition of the Apostles, retired, while the sight of their sepulchres, close to which he is standing, has no power to move a Catholic king to pity ?"

Whether it was from secret impulse of religious

emotion or that he was overawed by the venerable air and aspect of the Pontiff, scarce had the latter ceased to speak, when the king prostrated himself before him, and promised to retire with his armies from the Roman territories, without doing further mischief. When urged by the exarch to fulfil his engagement with the emperor, which was, either to seize the Pontiff and send him captive to Constantinople, or to slay him himself, he not only recoiled from such a proposal as impious and detestable, but on the other hand, exerted himself to effect a reconciliation between the exarch and the Pope. Then proceeding to the temple of St. Peter (at that period outside the walls, and hard by the camp), he divested himself of his mantle, diadem, military belt, silver cross, and other royal ornaments: placed them before the most august body of St. Peter; and there, as a suppliant, having devoted them to God and to the said prince of the Apostles, he rose up from his knees and returned home with his armies.*

No: never were charges more unfounded than those of the modern writers, who accuse St. Gregory II of fomenting disaffection amongst the Italian subjects of the Greek empire, and of usurping power by means of rebellion and intrigue. Never was loyalty proof against mere reiterated and

* Hist. de Reg. Ital. Sigon. lib. iii. 20, &c. The sources from which the Pope's address to Luitprand is derived, we are not aware of, but the name of Sigonius is in itself a sufficient voucher that it is sustained by authority.

outrageous acts of tyranny, or signalised by more useful and disinterested services. We have already heard how Ravenna was lost; it was by the wisdom and energy of St. Gregory it was recovered from the Lombards and restored to the Greeks again. In like manner, it was by him that Cuma was recovered; and when a pretender to the purple arose in Tuscany, the wretched Eutychius was forced to supplicate the influence of the Pontiff, whom he had so long laboured to destroy, in order to check the insurrection.

"Unfortunately for the Emperors of Constantinople," says Lebeau, in speaking of the times and transactions of which we are treating, "a virtue the most eminent, united to a prudence the most enlightened, was seated at that time in the chair of St. Peter. During a period of eighty years, there happened a succession of seven Popes, as venerable for the sanctity of their lives as they were formidable to their sovereigns, on account of their profound wisdom as statesmen. The wisdom of Gregory III., of Zachary, of Stephen II., but above all of Adrian I., of genius as solid as it was comprehensive, a Pope truly worthy the age of Charlemagne—what a contrast with the frivolity, the headlong violence of Leo, the Isaurian, and of Constantine Copronymos, his son!"*

In fact, up to the grant of Pepin,—several years

* Hist. du Bas Empire, t. 13, l. 66. n 51.

later than this,—the jurisdiction of the Greek Emperors continued to be recognised at Rome, while as heretofore the burden of the government devolved entirely upon the Popes "Although from what we have seen," says Muratori, "the Greek Emperors still had their ministers in Rome, it would seem that the principal authority of the government was vested in the Pontiffs, who, by the force and majesty of their station, and by that escort of virtues with which their character was surrounded, continued to wield a placid sway over the city and dukedom, defending them with vigour from the Lombard grasp, whenever occasion required it."*

They assumed no high titles, none of the *insignia* with which royalty loves to be surrounded; in letters and public dispatches the title assumed by Gregory II, is *servus servorum Dei*—servant of the servants of God.† Nor was it until every prospect of the often-solicited, long-promised, but never forthcoming aid from Constantinople had utterly

* "Benchè i Greci imperadori tenessero in Roma i loro ministri, pure la principale autorità del governo sembra, che fosse collocata ne' Romani Pontefici, i quali colla forza e maestà del loro grado, e *colla scorta delle loro virtù,* placidamente reggevano quella città e ducato, difendendolo poi vigorosamente nelle occasioni, dall' unghie de' Lombardi."—*An.* 752.

† See his Ep. to Ursus, Duke of the Venetians, ap. Sigonium. Since the times of St. Gregory VII, this title has been reserved to the Popes; previously it was sometimes used by bishops.

vanished, that Pope Stephen, the second in succession from St. Gregory, took the resolution of seeking beyond the Alps for help and protection against these restless and implacable enemies. "He sent letters and legates to the Byzantine Court," says Muratori, "to implore his august sovereign, that, in pursuance of so many promises already made, he would expedite into Italy an army, capable, not only of defending the Roman dukedom against the Lombards, but of expelling them from all their other usurpations."*

But like those of his predecessors, the representations of Pope Stephen were to no purpose. Rome and Italy were abandoned to their fate by the corrupt and imbecile Greeks, until, by the indomitable patriotism and sacrifices of the venerable Pontiff, both had been rescued from the invader's grasp: then it is that the Byzantines enter once more on the scene. The imperial ambassadors appear with gorgeous presents, and with still more gorgeous promises in the camp of Pepin, in order to induce the generous Frank to restore to the empire the territories which his sword had wrested from the Lombards in battle, or, in any case, not to grant the exarchate and Pentapolis to the Popes. It was then that King Pepin made solemn oath, that it was not for any earthly consideration he had so often exposed himself in the field of battle during this war, but solely

* Vid. Muratori, Ann. 753, p. 47.

through love of St. Peter, and for the remission of his sins; asserting, moreover, that for all this world's treasures, he would not revoke what he had once made an offering of to St. Peter.*

It was long since every claim upon the fealty of the Italians had been forfeited by the emperors of the east. To their tyrannical and imbecile rule, they were indebted for the series of disasters consequent upon the Lombard invasion, the bitterest—the most protracted and pernicious in its consequences, of all they had ever suffered. The most rapid review of the misrule of the Byzantines in Italy will remove every shadow of doubt upon this head.

After cutting his way back to Ostia through the ambuscade which the Goths had placed to intercept his retreat, Belisarius had once more returned, taken post in Rome, and the vacant space of the eternal city became again the scene of destructive and furious hostilities; for scarcely had the Greeks thrown up some hasty defences round the ancient circuit of the walls, by blocking up, with every thing they could seize, the gates and the immense ruptures made in the fortifications by the Goths,

* "Asserens et hoc, quod nulla cum thesauri copia suadere valeret, ut quod semel beato Petro obtulit, auferret."—Anastasius, ap. *Baron.* Ann. 755, No. 25.

than Totila, raging like a lion, returned to the charge; resolved to obliterate the disgrace which he had incurred, by leaving a station so renowned without a garrison. This was in the year A.D. 547. He was beaten off by Belisarius, but in 549 he effected his purpose, and the Goths were masters of the ruins, until after the defeat and death of Totila, A.D. 552, when the Greeks, under the command of the eunuch Narses, recovered the place by storm.

A select body of Lombards, obtained by the latter from Alboin their King, and transported across the Adriatic, would seem to have been chiefly instrumental in the final overthrow of Totila, and of the power of the Ostrogoths in Italy. They were sent back laden with spoil and gifts, and Warnefrid adds, that all the time the Lombards were in Pannonia, they assisted the *Roman Republic** against those who attacked it. Under his sway, as representative of Justinian I, the Romans soon had reason to sigh for the less intolerable oppression and rapacity of the Goths. They complained to the Court of Constantinople.† The eunuch became infuriated; and despite of all the entreaties of Pope John III,

* This Roman *Republic* is confessedly not a republic in the modern sense, it means the Greek Empire.—Warnefrid. de gest. Longob. l. 2. cap. 1.

† "I Romani scrissero a Giustino Augusto e a Sofia sua Moglie, rappresentando d' essere si altrattati ed oppressi da *Narsete*, che meglio stavano sotto i Goti, che sotto di lui."—*Murat.* Ann. 567. See also Anastasius, Vit. Johan III. Warnefrid is the primary source, de Gest. Longob.

who followed him as far as Naples, he brought destruction on Italy, by inviting the Lombards to fall upon the unfortunate country, at a time when, as we have already seen, it was exhausted by a fearful pestilence, and by his own oppression and exactions. And, far from even seconding the efforts of St. Gregory the Great and his successors to make head against the devastating hordes, thus introduced into the heart of the country, the minions of the Greek court came with a view "not to serve the interests or mitigate the sufferings of the Italians, but," as Muratori expresses it, "to suck the very blood from their veins." "Non per far del bene ai popoli ma *per ismugnere il loro sangue.*"

Again and again, they plundered the treasures, and stripped even of the sacred vessels the most venerable sanctuaries of the Roman Church; they attempted to traffic in the Apostolic office itself, and laid violent hands, more than once, on Christ's anointed vicars: and when unable, on account of their own impotence, to perpetrate their schemes of avarice, of fanaticism, or of revenge, they never hesitated to league themselves with the public enemy, in order to make war upon those whom they had the effrontery to call their subjects. Yet, with all this, the rule of the Byzantine Cæsars was not cast off by the Italians; it became effete, and was permitted to drop from their hands through very impotence to retain or defend it. The provinces thus abandoned, were driven to take measures for their own defence.* But being unable of themselves to cope with the invaders, and despairing of any help from the east, what other course remained open for them but that which was taken, to invoke the intervention of that warlike monarch, who was not more renowned for his prowess as a warrior, than for his enthusiastic devotion to the see of St. Peter.

And it is quite as unworthy of the probity and candour of Muratori, as it is in keeping with his theories relative to the secular dominion of the Popes, to pretend, that when Pepin made his celebrated "donation," he was generous at the expense of the Greek emperors; because he must have known, that according to the acknowledged principles of the "jus gentium," the provinces won by Pepin from the Lombards, were *his* by right of conquest. "Beyond all controversy," says Grotius, "if we regard the law of nations, what is wrested from us by enemies, cannot be reclaimed by those who were in possession before those enemies came in, but who were ousted by the fortune of war."† Now this was precisely the case of the Greeks. We have seen how they permitted Italy to be ravaged and usurped by the Lombards, and how ineffectual were the repeated entreaties of the Popes for aid to resist

* "Elegendosi i proprii duci, capi, e governatori; e una tal carica in Roma e nel suo ducato fu da quel tempo appresso il Romano Pontefice."—*Orsi, Dissertat. &c.*

† Vide Fontanini, ap. Murat. nn. 755. p. 60. Roman edit.

and dispossess the invaders. Ravenna and the Pentapolis were beyond all question lost to *them*, before ever Pepin had set foot in Italy. So far as the Greek emperors were concerned, these provinces were, to all intents and purposes, "bona derelicta," possessions abandoned by them through impotence or apathy; they had also been placed by the general and spontaneous act of their inhabitants, several years previously, under the secular government of the Popes. So true is this, that in all the original muniments connected with the act of Pepin, he is said, not to have made a gift of the States, but to have *restored* them to the see of St. Peter.

Surely the Greeks had no claim upon the military services of the Frank King! When, therefore, that valiant warrior drove out the tyrannical invaders of those provinces, at the prayer of the aboriginal possessors, what pretension had the Byzantines to step in and claim the hard-earned fruits of victory, or to prevent the Pontiffs from being formally invested, by the victor, with a sovereignty, the duties of which they had proved themselves so eminently qualified to discharge, and to which they had been called by the entreaties of a much injured and misgoverned people.

Long prior to the final expedition of Pepin, we find the King of the Lombards surrendering the entire province of the Ravennate and two parts of Cesena, to Pope Zachary, as by act of *restitution*.*

* Ab eodem rige nimis honorificè susceptus (Zacharias) salutaribus monitis eum allocutus est, obsecrans . . . ut *ablatas* Ravenna-

Before he crosses the Alps to seek aid from King Pepin, it is to *restitution* Pope Stephen makes every effort to incline the ruthless Astolfus by rich presents, by many entreaties, and even with floods of tears; and it is to oblige the Lombard to *restore* to the see of St. Peter the exarchate of Ravenna, with the other cities and territories of which he had deprived it, that Pepin solemnly pledges himself in the general assembly, at Quierzy-sur-oise, of the Frankish clergy and nobles.*

tûm urbes sibi *redonaret*, Qui prædictus rex, post multam duritiam inclinatus est, et duas partes territorii Cesenae Castri ad partem reipublicæ restituit." Anast. Bib. in Vit. Zach.

* Ib. Vita Stephani II.

CHAPTER III.

It is observed by Ranke, in his Introduction to the History of the Popes, that "at certain stages of history, we feel peculiarly disposed, if we may so express it, to investigate the divine plan of the world's government and the forces at work for the education of the human race." And, certainly, in pausing to take a retrospective glance from the point which we have at present arrived at, it is impossible not to be struck with the uniformity with which secular influence continued to be forced upon the Pontiffs, as if by some overruling necessity—a necessity that warps and constrains events the most unpromising to bring about this result. Even Gibbon confesses that the Popes were *compelled* to reign. We find them constantly battling against the tide which bore them into temporal power. They, no doubt, like their contemporaries of every class, were inclined to view the removal of the seat of empire from the "Seven Hills" to the Bosphorus as a most grievous calamity; yet that step was indispensable for their independence, as the supreme pastors of the Church; and according to the language of a very ancient document, was designedly brought about by the intervention of Providence. "Because it was not meet," it observes, "that the emperor of the earth should hold his sway in that place, where the prince of the hierarchy, and the capital of the Christian religion were constituted by heaven's eternal Emperor."

Surely those disasters which *forced* Pope Gregory the Great, as we have seen, into a political importance, from which his successors were never afterwards able to recede, were not of his own choosing. Did St. Gregory II court those outrageous attempts of the Isaurian upon his own life, and upon the religious liberties of the Italians, in consequence of which *he* was forced into the position of an independent temporal prince? Look again to the next stride in power made under Pope Stephen. The Pontiff seems to battle with might and main against the destiny which pushes him perforce towards the throne. First, he strives, by the sacrifice of immense treasures, to buy off the invader; he next implores assistance from Constantinople. Disappointed of all earthly succour, barefooted, and carrying a heavy cross, in imitation of his divine Master, he endeavours by public processions and penitential austerities to propitiate the help of Heaven. He exposes his venerable person to the fury of the raging and perfidious Lombard in Pavia, and humbling his hoary head to the very dust, beseeches Astolfus to spare his people, and to desist from invading and usurping the patrimony of St. Peter, or to speak more correctly, the patrimony of the poor. Nor is it until this last effort proves fruitless, that the aged Pontiff, at the risk of his life from the Lombards, who pursue and hem him in on every side, and in spite of the Alpine storms of mid-winter, hastens (the first Pope that ever crossed the Alps) to supplicate the King of the Franks for assistance. And, when at length the cause of the Church is espoused by Pepin, the Pope will not hear of an appeal to arms, until every effort that could suggest itself in order to adjust matters by negotiation had been resorted to in vain.

"To the letters sent by King Pepin to Astolfus others were united from Pope Stephen himself," says Muratori, "conjuring that prince to spare the shedding of Christian blood; but all was to no purpose; words of menace and of defiance were the only answer that either of them received from the rancorous and exasperated Lombard."*

Astolfus assumed a milder tone, however, after his defeat; "and well for him," says Muratori, "that the merciful Pontiff, although eager for his conversion, had no wish for his ruin. At his instance, the victorious Pepin withdrew his forces again across the Alps; but Astolfus, instead of

* "*Infellonito* Astolfo,"—is the expression of Muratori, a most impassioned admirer and apologist of the Lombard Kings. An. 754.

restoring the estates of the Church, as he had sworn to do, marched against Rome; laying waste its environs, carrying away even the sacred relics of the saints from all the churches without the walls, and harassing the city itself with repeated assaults."* And thus out of another persecution, as cruel and unprovoked as that which gained for St. Gregory II, the Roman dukedom and the original cession by the inhabitants of the Pentapolis and the exarchate, the grant, or rather the *restitution*, of the exarchate and the other provinces was derived by Pope Stephen; for it was after crossing the Alps a second time, and defeating the perfidious Astolfus, that Pepin made the renowned "donation" of those States to St. Peter.

But it is in the last epoch of development, intervening between the grant of Pepin, in 755, and the coronation of Charlemagne, in the year 800, that the hand, which brought about the secular independence of the see of St. Peter, becomes most strikingly manifest.

True it is, that the sceptre of sovereignty was now wielded by the Popes over a diversified and

* "E buono per lui che il misericordioso papa bramava, bensi di lui correzione ma non già la rovina—Astolfo passò al assedio di Roma con dare il guasto ai contorni asportare i corpi dei santi ritrovati, nella chiese fuori della città te tomentare con frequenti assalti la citta medissima."—*Muratori.*

fruitful territory, extending from the right bank of the Po, to the southern boundaries of Latium, besides their estates in Sicily, Istria, Sardinia, the south of France, and the Cottian Alps; but it was evident, nevertheless, that both the integrity of those States, the independence of the Pontiffs as supreme governors of the Church, and even their personal safety, must ever remain in jeopardy, so long as, their Frank protectors far away, they continued to be placed between two such unscrupulous and inveterate enemies as the Greeks, on the Neapolitan, and the Lombards, on their northern borders. Equally evident it was, that to guarantee the perfect freedom of the spiritual kingdom, by guaranteeing the secular independence of its supreme head and ruler, it was not only requisite that an end should be put to the Lombard aggressions, but that the tyrannical pretensions of the Byzantine Court, with regard to the Papal elections, should cease. This will not be questioned by any one who dispassionately considers the miserable vassalage, the plunderings, the persecutions, to which the Holy See had been subjected from the time that the conquests of Belisarius and Narses transferred the dominion of Rome, and the greater part of Italy, from the Goths to the Greek emperors, in the person of Justinian the Elder.

Their treatment of Pope Silverius,—his cruel expulsion from Rome,—his exile and assassination, formed but an appropriate introduction to this tissue of sacrilege and villany; but the greatest, perhaps, because the most enduring hardships, the Holy See had to suffer from the Greek emperors arose out of the perpetuation, on their part, of the abuse of a veto introduced by the Arian Goths, and the pretension to a right of confirmation on the election of each successive Pontiff. Frequent, long-protracted, and always disastrous vacancies of the Apostolic See were the consequence.* Thus, after the death of John III, contemporary with Narses, the first exarch (whom we have seen him following as far as Naples, with a view to avert the calling in of the Lombards), the Holy See remained vacant ten months and three days.† Again, in 605, soon after the demise of St. Gregory the Great, the See is vacant for no less than a year.‡ Again, in 608, there is a vacancy of ten months and many days—"varj giorni." After the death of Pope Honorius, on the 12th of October, 638, "the Holy See," says Muratori, "was a long time vacant; for although the clergy, with the senate and people of Rome, proceeded without delay to the election of a successor, who was Severinus, the consent of the emperor was delayed for a year and seven months."§

It was during this long interregnum that Isaac, the Greek exarch, seized so favourable an opportu-

* Vid. Orsi. Istoria Eccl. l. 43. Num. 27.

† "Dieci mesi e tre giorni." Muratori, Ann. d'Italia.

‡ "Per tutto quest' anno stette vacante la cattedra di San Pietro." Ib.

§ Ib. Ann. 638.

nity to plunder the widowed church. He had an understanding on this subject with Mauritius, the Byzantine envoy or resident at Rome, who on occasion of the garrison becoming clamorous for their pay, (which had been designedly withheld,) informed them, that, as for himself he was without funds, but that, in the treasury of the Lateran, there was a prodigious quantity of money hoarded up by Pope Honorius—money, he said, which ought not to be left idle in the Pope's coffers, while the brave men were in want, on whom devolved the defence and security of the city. Nay, he went so far as to assure them, that various remittances sent by the Emperor for their use had been laid by, amongst the rest, by his Holiness. These ingenious incitements to plunder were not lost on the licentious soldiery: they flew to the Lateran palace, and not being able to effect an entrance into the treasury—the domestics of Severinus, the Pope elect, making resistance—they furiously besieged the place for three days, at the end of which, Mauritius succeeded in obtaining his object. Apprized of this, the exarch hastened to Rome, and under a variety of pretexts, there being no one to resist him, sent into exile the principal of the clergy, and then entered the treasury of the Church, which for eight whole days he continued to ransack and plunder; taking care to send a portion of the booty to his imperial master.*

* The particulars may be seen in the contemporary biography of Pope Severinus, in the collection of Anastasius.

Tired at length of such sacrilegious tyranny, and fearing to leave the election of the great guardian of the deposite of the faith depending on a court devoted to the heresy of the Monothelites—at that time most violently agitating the oriental church—the Roman clergy and people, on the demise of Pope Theodore,* proceeded to the election of a successor, when Martin of Todi was chosen, and consecrated without waiting for the Byzantine placitum. "This Pontiff," says Muratori, "one of the most distinguished for striking qualities and energy of character that ever filled the chair of St. Peter, although aware of the penalties denounced in the *type* or edict of Constantius against all who refused to subscribe to the court-heresy, lost no time in convening a Council of the Italian bishops. On the 5th of October, the same year, they met in the Lateran to the number of one hundred and five, including those of Sicily and Sardinia, and were still sitting when Olympias arrived in Rome. This new exarch had been recently dispatched from Constantinople with orders to enforce submission to the *type* throughout Italy, or, if thwarted in that design, to lay hands on Pope Martin, either by fraud or force. Arrived in Rome, he found that the Pontiff and his Council, far from quailing before the threats of imperial vengeance, had unanimously condemned the Monothelite heresy, with the *ecthesis* of Heraclius, as well as the new creed promulgated by Constantius. For a long time, the fidelity of the

* 13th of May, A.D. 649.

Romans frustrated all the efforts of the exarch against the Pontiff. At length, in the year 652, he sought to effect by the hand of an assassin what he durst not openly attempt, not only from fear of the people, but also of the military who were zealously devoted to the cause of the Pope. Feigning a devotion to receive the blessed eucharist from the Pontiff's own hand, Olympias went to assist at his mass, having at the same time given orders to one of his guards to stab the holy father, when in the act of administering the sacrament to himself! But the Almighty, remarks the ancient writer, did not permit a sacrilege so horrid to be perpetrated; the soldier, to whom the diabolical order had been given, afterwards attesting upon oath that he could not see the Pope, either when he was giving the kiss of peace to the exarch, or when he administered to him the adorable eucharist.*

Olympias having failed in his nefarious attempt, a new exarch, Calliopas, was sent into Italy, with peremptory orders to seize Pope Martin by force. Calliopas arrived in Rome at the head of a large body of troops, June 15th, 653. The Pontiff, though well aware of his designs, sent his clergy to present the salutations due to the representative of his sovereign, not being able to do so in person, on

* "Iniqui Greci! non si può qui non esclamare," says Muratori, (though biased in favour of the Greeks, as opponents of the Papal pretensions to the States), "e di lungo mano più iniqui per quello che reconteremo." This he adds, in reference to the persecution and martyrdom of Pope Martin.—An. 652.

account of a severe and protracted illness. To this deputation the Greek expressed how anxious he was to present his personal homage to the Pontiff, but excused himself from doing so until the next Sunday, on the score of fatigue. Apprehensive, however, that the concourse of the faithful would be, on the Sunday, too great to admit of the execution of his design, he failed in his promise. But, on the Monday following, he sent to complain to the Pope that munitions of war had been provided in the Lateran palace, as if to ward off a violence to which, he assured him, there was not the slightest intention of resorting. This was only a manœuvre to gain information; for, so soon as it was ascertained by his spies that no preparations for defence had been made, he invested the palace with his squadrons in most formidable array. Having got admission to the presence of the Pontiff, who lay stretched on his sick bed before the altar of the Basilica, he produced an imperial mandate to the clergy to proceed to a new election under the pretence that Pope Martin was to be looked upon as deposed, having, he said, been uncanonically intruded into the see. The clergy and domestics were eager to prevent the satellites of the exarch from laying hands on their pastor and father; but he, who abhorred every species of violence, and had rather die ten times over than be the cause of bloodshed, forbade the slightest attempt at resistance. He was, therefore, carried forth amidst the cries of the clergy, who repeatedly exclaimed, "Be he anathema who shall say or believe that

Pope Martin hath abandoned, or shall ever be induced to abandon, one apex or iota of the faith, or that he will not be faithful unto death, in the orthodox belief."

Calliopas had his victim carried on board a small vessel in the Tiber, on the 19th of July, and conveyed in the first instance to Misenum, and from thence to Calabria. After casting anchor at several of the Greek islands during a voyage of three months, they came at length to Naxos in the Archipelago, where there was a delay of several months more. It would be difficult to describe the sufferings of the venerable Pontiff during all this time. Deprived almost of the common necessaries of life, languishing in sickness, and confined in the hold of a miserable vessel, from which he was not permitted to disembark even once, he suffered during the entire time from dysentery, extreme exhaustion, and a seasickness, from which he had scarcely any interval of respite whatever. Both the clergy and laity of the Greek islands, at which the vessel touched during the voyage, were accustomed to flock from all sides, to testify their homage and sympathy; but they were fiercely repulsed by the guards, who denounced as an enemy to the Emperor, whoever was a friend to Pope Martin; at the same time seizing and appropriating to themselves the gifts and presents that were brought for the holy confessor's use. "Such was the condition to which this innocent and patient sufferer was reduced," says the historian, "that one cannot think of it without being excited to indignation, both against the despot who ordered, and the vile minions who executed such outrages upon a Roman Pontiff, so deservedly venerated by the entire Church of God."

From the authentic narrative of the sufferings of Pope Martin,* we collect that he was conveyed from the isle of Naxos to Constantinople, on the 17th of September, A.D. 654. He was immediately cast into a dungeon, and prevented from seeing or conversing with any one for three dreary months. On the 19th of December, he was submitted to an examination by the chancellor or fiscal of the imperial Court, by whom a variety of false accusations were brought against him. Perceiving their object, the intrepid Pontiff conjured the imperial officers to do with him, at once, what he knew they were resolved on effecting, without going through the mockery of a trial; and thereby procure for him a great recompense in heaven. By order of the Emperor, he was then carried in a chair (he not being able to walk, or so much as to stand), into an outer piazza, where there was an immense concourse of people. There, the pallium and other pontifical ornaments and robes were torn off his person by the soldiers, so that the venerable confessor remained almost naked. Then placing a collar of iron round his neck, he was dragged from the palace through the entire city, fastened by a chain to the jailer, or hangman, as if he was a culprit going to execution for some horrible crime. Amidst so many out-

* Labbe, Concilior, tom. iv. p. 67.

rages and sufferings, the venerable martyr never lost his serenity, and the greater part of the multitude wept aloud, and mourned over the spectacle of iniquity which they beheld. Dragged back to his dungeon, he continued to be treated with the greatest barbarity, exposed to every hardship and privation, until, at length, he was summoned, from the place of his exile in the Chersonesus, to receive the immortal recompense of so many trials endured for the faith.*

In the year 663, and during the reign of Pope Vitalian, the Greek Emperor, Constantius, honoured Rome with his presence; and, after tarrying there for twelve days, "took leave of the Pope," says the annalist, "carrying away with him all the bronzes which still decorated that once empress city, even to the lamina of bronze that covered the dome of St. Mary of Martyrs, better known as the Pantheon."†

To the catalogue of outrages which St. Gregory II had to suffer at the hands of Leo the Iconoclast, must be added the confiscation of all the possessions of the Roman Church which were within the grasp of the latter, in Sicily and in Magna Græcia; and also the violent rending of Illyricum from the patriarchate of the west.‡

* See Muratori, Ann. d'Italia, and the original life in Anastasius

† Muratori, Ann. 663.

‡ Between the parent and daughter churches, a certain relationship of subordination and reverence had been recognised from the first. Thus did the see of Antioch, established by St. Peter, preside over the Asiatic churches, while those of Egypt, the Pentapolis, and Libya, were subject to Alexandria, founded by his

Illyricum, which comprehended the two great dioceses of Decia and Macedonia, had always appertained to the patriarchal jurisdiction of the Popes. The bishop of Thessalonica, from the time of Pope Damasus, had acted as their vicar, and without his approbation no bishop could be canonically instituted in any see belonging to the provinces of Dardania and Prævalitana, of Mæsia, the two Decias, composing the first division of Illyricum, or of the second division, which embraced Macedonia, the Old and New Epirus, Achaia, Thessaly, and Crete: he also had the power delegated to him of convening synods of all those countries. The greater causes, however, and appeals, as from all other provinces of the Church, being reserved to the Apostolic See. Attempts had been made as early as the reign of Theodosius the Younger to draw these provinces, or some portions of them, into the newly-instituted patriarchate of Constantinople: but the remonstrances of the holy see, supported by the strong representations of the western Emperor

disciple, St. Mark. In the west, this dignity, conjointly with their supremacy over the universal Church, was enjoyed by the pontiffs of Rome—the parent church of the entire West; *i. e.* of Italy and the surrounding islands, of Gaul, Illyricum, Spain, Africa, Britain, and of Ireland, when converted by missionaries from Pope Celestine, A.D. 430. This division of provinces had been ratified by the great Council of Nice, in its sixth canon. The provinces began to be called patriarchates, from the time of the Council of Chalcedon, by which Pope Leo the Great was addressed as Patriarch of the universal Church. See Döllinger's Church History, translated by Dr. Cox, vol. 2. sec. 4.

Arcadius to his brother, had the desired effect: and it was reserved for Leo the Isaurian, to add this to his other sacrilegious acts of rapine and injustice. In a word, so far as their contemptible resources would allow them, the despots who had enslaved religion in Greece and the East never ceased to carry on a war of annoyance and perfidy against the Apostolic See, until at length the revival of the western empire by Charlemagne, or rather by Pope Leo III, at once put an end to their sacrilegious pretensions, and guaranteed to the successors of St. Peter, the free exercise of their apostolic supremacy.* But it is now time that we resume the onward course of our history.

The truce granted to the cities of Italy, depending on the Greek empire, having expired in the year 749, "the city of Perugia," says Muratori, "was immediately beleagured by Rachis, the Lombard king; he likewise menaced to let loose his fury upon the entire extent of the Pentapolis. These disastrous tidings had no sooner reached the ears of Pope Zachary, who had succeeded to Gregory III, than with a number of prelates and magnates of Rome, he hastened to Perugia, and by moving entreaties so mollified the barbarian, that he consented to raise the siege. He also *restored* to the Pope such cities as he had seized on, in the Roman

* Vid. Muratori, Ann. 759. p. 80. Ann. 762. p. 87.

Duchy.* Nay, more, with such a contempt for the former objects of his ambition, and with such profound remorse for his past career of blood and rapacity, did the words of the venerable Pontiff inspire him, that he abdicated the throne shortly after, came to Rome, and having received the monastic habit at the hands of Zachary, retired to the monastery of Mount Casino; while Thæsia, his queen, and her royal daughters, became nuns, and founded the convent of Piombaruola.† Astolfus, who obtained the throne thus vacated, happening to die without issue, in the year, 766, a violent contest for the succession arose amongst many pretenders. The scale seemed to incline in favour of Desiderius, Duke of either Istria or Tuscany, until, to *his* great alarm, and the general surprise, the royal Benedictine of Monte Casino, with that inconstancy so characteristic of the barbarian nature, declared his wish to abdicate the tonsure, and again resume the "iron crown." "Then it was," continues Muratori, "that no other resource was left to Desiderius, but to throw himself upon the successor of St. Zachary, Pope Stephen III: making at the same time unbounded profession of his willingness and anxiety to see regarded as inviolate the donation of King Pepin, and all the cities and territories belonging to it still detained by the Lombards restored. Through

* Anast. Bib. in Vit. Zach.

† In the Storia di Monte Casino, Napoli, 1843, is given an inscription set up by one of the abbots, An. 1550, to keep in memory the fact that King Rachis had cultivated his little vineyard as a monk.

the influence of the Pontiff, the royal monk was dissuaded from violating his solemn vows; but as for Desiderius, no sooner had he got the power to perform them, than he set at naught all his promises. He was ever ready, however, with his tribute of fair words and plausible excuses, until the death of Pepin seemed to leave the patrimony of St. Peter without any protection. But no sooner had he become thoroughly assured of that event, than, in the year 772, he broke in upon the states of the Church; giving up to sack, slaughter, and conflagration, the whole country, towns and cities, castles, and farm-houses, from Sinigaglia on the Adriatic, on by Montefeltro, Urbino, Gubbio, through Umbria, where the ravager possessed himself of Otricoli, and so into what was at that period called Lombard Tuscany, where the ashes of Bieda were extinguished in the blood of its people."* "All' udir questo," observes Muratori, "chi cercasse *delicatezza di conscienza*, e prudenza nel re Desiderio, non le trovarebbe." "Delicacy of conscience," indeed! The irony is exquisite, that places "delicatezza di conscienza," in the bosom intimacy of this most perfidious, even of Lombard kings. But his perfidy, as so often happens, overreached itself. While with implacable rapacity, he grasped at the diadem of the Pope, he lost his own, and the Lombard dynasty soon after descended unhonoured into the

* See Introduction for the position of Bieda, and the other places here mentioned.

grave, which it had dug for itself by its incessant aggressions on the rights of St. Peter.

Having secured the plundered provinces by strong garrisons, he withdrew to Pavia, there to prepare for a renewal of the invasion ; and, on the opening of the following year, Pope Hadrian I and his people were filled with alarm at the tidings that he was moving down upon Rome, at the head of his armies. The courageous Pontiff hastened to provide against the impending storm, and was soon surrounded by the warlike and faithful populations, who flocked from the lands of the ancient Latins, Umbrians, and Etruscans, full of enthusiasm for his defence. The provinces on the other side of the Apennines proved no less faithful in this trying emergency. The rebuilding of the walls, and fortifying of the city in every way were pressed forward with the greatest enthusiasm and energy. All were ready to fly to arms, and, " with the help of God and St. Peter," to defend the city against the assaults of the invader to the utmost extremity.*

The basilicas of St. Peter and St. Paul, being outside the city walls, were divested of whatsoever might tempt too strongly the " delicacy" of the Lombard conscience : the Vatican was strongly barricaded from within with bars of iron. When these

* Omnes armati erant et parati ; ut si ipse rex adveniret ei fortiter cum Dei auxilio et beati Petri, fulti orationibus prædicti sanctissimi præsulis (Hadriani) illi resisterent. Anast. in vit. Hadriani, p. 104.

preparations were complete, Eustratius, Andreas, and Theodosius, Bishops of Albano, Palestrina, and Tivoli, were sent forward to meet the invader. They were to intimate that the sentence of excommunication would be launched against him, in case he persisted in the projected invasion. He had already advanced with his forces as far as Viterbo, when the legates met him, with what Muratori calls their "disgustosa ambasciata." That embassage had the desired effect, however. The barbarian ferocity of the invader was cowed before the unarmed majesty of the Pontiff; the wonder which occurred in the days of Attila and St. Leo, is renewed; and "with great reverence, and in confusion," says the historian, "he struck his tents and retired."*

At this critical juncture, the ambassadors of King Charlemagne, who had recently succeeded his father, Pepin-le-bref, arrived in Rome. They were Gregory a holy bishop, Gulfard an abbot, and Albinus a nobleman, who was singularly honoured by the youthful monarch's favour and confidence. We are told that he was "deliciosus ipsius regis." Their commands were to ascertain the truth of what had been solemnly stated by the envoys of King Didier, who, while he was laying waste the states

* Suscepto eodem obligationis verbo per autefatos episcopos, ipse Longobardorum Rex illico cum magna reverentia a civitate Viterbiense CONFUSUS *ad propria reversus est*. It would seem from this last line, as if the threat of the legates had the effect, not so much of bringing the tyrant to his senses as of disbanding his army. See Anast. ubi supra.

of St. Peter with fire and sword, and making most desperate efforts for the capture of the Apostolic city itself, had sent to Charlemagne the most solemn assurances, that restitution of all the states and cities had, according to his treaties with Pepin, been fully and honourably carried into effect. It required but little time and but few words to unmask this disgraceful attempt at deception. With their own eyes, the ambassadors saw the true state of affairs, and after hearing from the Pontiff the dark tragedies, the murders, the incarcerations, the secret plots, and open invasions, by which this perfidious prince had ceased not to pursue his ambitious designs, they returned accompanied by Legates, from Pope Hadrian, who were to urge the necessity for prompt interference on the part of the Frank King, in his character of Patrician of Rome. In the letters of which they were the bearers, the king was adjured not to leave unfulfilled what his sire, the royal Pepin of blessed memory, had vowed to St. Peter, but to rescue the Church from the peril in which it was placed. And in order that nothing might be left undone, by which an amicable adjustment could be secured, the legate and the ambassadors were ordered to pass through Pavia, on their way beyond the Alps, and to endeavour by another appeal to obtain justice, and thus avoid a resort to more violent means of redress. The joint entreaties and representations of the ambassadors and legates were of no avail whatever. After so many oaths and pledges, formerly and most solemnly given to the contrary, the ultimatum of the Lombard was, that "he would restore nothing."*

The conduct of Charlemagne on this occasion, as observed by an ancient biographer, is every way worthy of his title of the "most Christian King." A second time, he sends his ambassadors, if possible, to recall King Didier to the paths of honour and justice. Nay, to such lengths of forbearance did he proceed, that in order to entice him to do what was right, even at the suggestion of his cupidity, they had it in command to offer him an immense amount of treasure—"fourteen thousand *solidi* in gold," provided he would peaceably consent to redeem the pledges to which he had sworn. "But neither by gifts or by entreaties," continues the ancient biographer, "could his most ferocious heart be won from injustice."†

"Then it was, and not till then, that the heaven-protected King of the Franks, Carolus Magnus, collecting his forces, despatched beforehand a division of the grand army to seize the passes of the Alps.‡ These had not only been already occupied by King Didier, surrounded by the flower of the entire Lombard nation, but, steep and difficult as they were

* Sed minime quicquam horum apud eum obtinere valuerunt, asserens se minime quicquam redditurum. Anast. ubi supra.

† Sed neque deprecationibus, neque muneribus ejus ferocissimum cor flectere valuit. Ib.

‡ We quote from the same ancient writer, who, it is most probable, was himself living at the time of these events.

by nature, they had been fortified by enormous barricades, walls, and entrenchments, constructed with consummate art.*

The first proceeding of Charlemagne, on finding himself in presence of the hostile army thus strongly posted, was to resort once more, and for the third time, to an embassage. Besides the advantageous offers already made, his envoys were to express the willingness of the most Christian King to immediately retire with his forces, provided King Didier, would only promise to restore what he had unjustly usurped, and to give three sons of Lombard judges as hostages, until the treaty should have been carried into effect. But this approach to conciliation was met by the Lombard in the same spirit as the former ones. All these reiterated offers were vain. Blinded by the worst passions, without any thing of the foresight, or firmness, or even bravery of a hero, he seemed to rush forward with mere brutish fury upon the doom which was to put an end for ever to the dynasty of his nation.†

"Whereupon," continues the ancient authority,

* Desiderius et universa Longobardorum exercitum multitudo ad resistendum fortiter in ipsis clausis assistebant, *quas fabricis* et diversis maceriis curiose munire nisi sunt. Anast. Bib. ubi supra.

† Sed neque sic valuit ejus malignam mentem flectere. Unde omnipotens Deus conspiciens ipsius maligni Desiderii iniquam perfidiam, &c. Anast. Bib. ubi supra. Both the continuator of Paul Warnefrid, and Sigonius, fully adopt the view of these transactions which is put forward here.

"the Almighty, in punishment of this implacable obstinacy in injustice, permitted such a panic of trepidation and terror, to seize on the minds of the king, of his son Adalgisus, and of the universal Lombard army, that under cover of the night, and at the very hour in which the Franks were taking measures for a retrograde movement, back again across the mountains, they fled, abandoning their tents, their baggage, and covered the whole country of Piedmont with their rout, though not pursued by any visible enemy."*

Between the conquering career of Charlemagne on this occasion, and that of Constantine, when the standard of the cross, called the *Labarum*, was seen for the first time at the head of the Roman legions, there are several striking traits of resemblance. Both crossed the Alps by Mount Cenis; both, as if by miracle, succeeded in clearing the passes of Susa, and in scattering armies, at the first onset, that, in appointment, position, and numbers, were far superior to their own. The cause, for which their lives were so magnanimously risked on the field, was the same; the rapidity with which Charlemagne succeeded in traversing the Lombard dominion from the Alps to

* "Dum vellent Franci alio die ad propria reverti, misit (Deus) terrorem et validam trepidationem in cor ejus, vel (et) filii ipsius, Adalgisi, scilicet, et universorum Longobardorum, et, eadem nocte, dimissis propriis tentoriis, atque omni supellectile, fugam omnes generaliter, nemine eos persequente, arripuerunt." Anast. ubi supra, p. 185.

Verona, and in capturing that city deemed impregnable, is still more surprising, if possible, than Constantine's career of victory, over precisely the same ground. In both these heroes, the effulgence of a valour and a success the most brilliant is enhanced by clemency, and the most enthusiastic devotedness in the cause of the Christian religion; and to crown the comparison, both were received at Rome with the most magnificent triumph. That of Constantine we have attempted to depict in a former work, the manner in which the greatest Christian hero of the "dark ages," as they are called, is thus narrated by a writer who was probably an actor in the pageant which he describes.

"While encamped under the walls of Pavia," he says, "the king of the Franks, considering that the Paschal solemnity was approaching, resolved to carry into execution the ardent longing by which his breast was inflamed, to accomplish his pilgrimage as he had vowed, and to pour out his soul at the venerated tombs of the Apostles. With this intent, taking with him divers bishops, abbots, and judges, with dukes, graffions, and nobility of all ranks, he proceeded, at the head of a numerous force detached from the besieging army, by marches so rapid through Tuscany towards Rome,* that he succeeded in arriving there on the eve of the most glorious and triumphant festival of

* By the Siena route, that is over the heights of Rodicofani, and on by Aquapendente, Bolsena, Orvieto, &c., it must have been, for he passed by where Florence is seated at present.

the Resurrection. Wonder and extacy contended in the breast of the Pontiff on receiving such tidings; on the instant, the chief nobility and magistrates of Rome were despatched by him with various banners, in order to receive the most Christian king at a station, called *ad Novas*, a distance of thirty miles from the city. At a mile outside the gates, the militia of the regions, under their chiefs, and with colours flying, were drawn up in military array to receive him. There, also, stood marshalled, the youth of the various nations, attracted by the love of letters and the divine sciences, to the colleges of Rome. They carried branches of the peaceful olive in their hands, and their voices were joined melodiously in the songs of welcome, and the loud acclamations in appropriate words which hailed the Christian champion and escorted him on his way. He dismounted from his war-horse, when he saw the clergy approaching in procession, each region with its cross and other sacred standards; and, surrounded by the chief prelates and paladins of the Franks, proceeded onward on foot, traversing the very same route by which Constantine had marched to his triumph—the approach which leads from the Milvian bridge between the ridge of the Monte Mario and the Tiber, to Saint Peter's. Having arrived before the vestibule, where the Pontiff with the College of Cardinals, the Apostolic attendants, and a vast assemblage of the Romans expected his arrival, he knelt, and ascending the steps which lead to the threshold of the Apostles, on bended knees, devoutly impressed a kiss on each step as he ascended.* With open arms, and with the Christian salute of peace, the successor of St. Peter received the hero-king · the choirs joined by all the clergy, the Roman military, and the multitude entoned the canticle—"Blessed is he that cometh in the name of the Lord"—; and thus, hand in hand, amidst those holy and rapturous acclamations, Pope Hadrian and Charlemagne advanced to the shrine of Saint Peter; where, prostrate before the altar of the Most High, their effusions of thanksgiving and gratitude were poured out to the God of armies and to his holy Apostle, for the victory, signal as it was bloodless and providential, by which not the See of St. Peter alone, but the Italians had been rescued from Lombard aggression—a scourge the most cruel which even they had ever experienced."

The same writer to whom we are indebted for these particulars, and who was himself most probably an eye-witness of the scenes which he describes, informs us, that an humble and earnest request was next made by Charlemagne, that, for the fulfilment of his pilgrim's vow, he might have the Pontiff's permission to enter the city, and pay the prescribed visits to the several churches. He adds that, before

* Omnes gradus, sigillatim, ejusdem sacratissimæ beati Petri ecclesiæ diosculatus est, et ita usque ad prænominatum pervenit pontificem. Anast. Biblioth. in vit. Hadr. p. 107.

this permission was granted, a solemn compact was entered into over the body of the Apostle, by which Charlemagne was bound not to take any unfair advantage of the city gates being opened to receive him, and by which it was guaranteed, on the part of the Pontiff, that the king's person and liberty should be sacred from every attempt, while within the city. This treaty is not less demonstrative of the fact that the Pope held the supreme power in Rome, and that his sovereignty over the city was entirely independent of the Frank kings, than it is of the perpetual apprehension of violence and stratagem, which, in those ages of barbarism and constantly recurring invasion, kept men's minds on the alert, as in time of war, and incessantly filled with alarms.*

After these formalities, the gates of the Eternal City were thrown open to receive the victorious

* The passage in Anastasius is so important and curious that we do not hesitate to quote it in extenso.—Expleta vero eadem oratione, *obnixe deprecatus est* isdem Francorum Rex antedictum almificum Pontificem, *illi licentiam tribui Romam ingrediendi* ad sua orationum vota, per diversas Dei Ecclesias persolvenda. Et descendentes pariter ad corpus Beati Petri, tam ipse sanctissimus Papa quamque autefatus excellentissimus Franconum Rex, cum judicibus Romanorum et Francorum, *seseque mutuo per sacramentum munientes,* ingressus est Romam, continuo, cum eodem Pontifice, ipse Francorum Rex, cum suis judicibus et populo. The sese *mutuo,* &c., is thus rendered by Sigonius, "accepto datoque super sacrosancto Apostoli corpore sacramento, neutrum neutri insidias paraturum." Any other meaning would involve the absurdity that Charlemagne was a priest, and gave communion to the Pope, *seseque mutuo* per sacramentum, &c.

monarch of the Franks. Surrounded, preceded, and followed by prelates, paladins, magnates, and princes, Frank and Roman, of every order, and in grand military array, the hero and the Pope rode side by side across the Tiber. Never had the city of triumphs witnessed such a sight before; and thus along the Campus Martius, the Great Circus, the Forum, by the Palatine, and the Coliseum—the chief glories of paganism, then in ruin,—the representative and chief vicar of the meek Redeemer and the warrior King of the most chivalrous nations in the world arrived at the Lateran, amidst incessant songs of triumph, outbursts of acclamation, and unbounded demonstrations of rejoicing, as well from the multitudes who thronged the way, as from those who beheld the glorious pageant from the windows, the house tops, and from the various vantage positions among the Seven hills, and the ruins of the pagan city.

All these transactions occurred on the morning of Saturday in Holy Week—a day, on which it was customary for the Pontiff to officiate in person in the solemn baptism of catechumens, administered in the great font and baptistery erected by Constantine, soon after his conversion to Christianity. Charlemagne, after assisting at these holy rites, returned to where his forces lay encamped around the Vatican. The next day, which was the most glorious and joyful festival of the Resurrection, after assisting at the solemn mass celebrated by the Pontiff, in the basilica of Santa Maria, *ad præsepe*, he was feasted at the Apostolic table in the Lateran Palace.* The two days following were kept as festivals with great solemnity; the Pontiff celebrating, on Monday in St. Peter's, and, on Tuesday, in the basilica of St. Paul; and the King assisting on both occasions. At length, on Wednesday, they began to apply themselves to secular affairs, and, coming with great state to St. Peter's, where the magnates of the Franks and Romans were assembled, the Pope, after adverting to what had passed in the Great Assembly of the Franks at Carisiac, A. D. 754, when the most solemn pledges had been given to Pope Stephen, both by Charlemagne himself, and by his royal father King Pepin, with respect to the states and cities, usurped by the Lombards, besought of Charlemagne again to renew those acts, and to confirm them by a public and solemn sanction. Accordingly, the tablets on which they had been inscribed having been brought forth, by the King's desire, and read, and compared with the copies of the same in the hands of his own ministers, their authenticity and exactness were at once acknowledged by all; and Charlemagne, amidst the applause of his prelates and the great feudatories of his kingdoms, proceeded to ratify and confirm the donation of Pepin, in its fullest extent.

* Et missarum solemnia celebrata, perrexit cum prænotato pontifice in Lateranense Patriarchium, illicque ad mensam Apostolicam pariter epulati sunt. Anast. Biblioth. in vit. Hadrian, p. 107.

It is on this occasion that the writer in Anastasius and the chroniclers of after times proceed to describe the extent of the provinces, thus definitively placed under the sovereign sway of the Pontiffs; before following their example, however, it will be satisfactory to collect such facts, widely dispersed as they are, which relate to this subject, and to group them so as to give a connected idea, not only of the boundaries of the Papal States at this epoch, but also, so far as it is feasible, to sketch their internal condition.

CHAPTER IV.

In pausing to reflect on this singular power, the rise and progressive development of which we have traced thus far, the first feature to arrest our attention, is, that, as it had its origin in the devotion with which Christians regarded St. Peter, as being the prince of the Apostles, and entrusted with the sceptre of Christ's kingdom on earth, so did it continue to grow and increase, through the force of the same Christian conviction. Upon no other ground but this, does it receive any accession whatever, whether from princes or people. Thus, when from the various countries in the environs of Rome, from Latium, Tuscany, and Spoleti—that is, from the countries of the ancient Latins, Etruscans, Sabines, and Umbrians—the populations, worn out with disasters of every species, and utterly destitute of defence, protection, or hope, are seen to crowd round the Pontiffs as their only refuge; it is to St. Peter they deliver their lives, and their liberties, with the right to govern and rule over them, as his subjects. For example, of some of them it is said—"Flying to St. Peter for refuge, they yielded themselves up to the aforementioned Pope (Hadrian I.) swearing allegiance to the Prince of the Apostles, and to the said Pope, as his vicar :"* of other populations who were anxious to follow the same course, it is said: "all the other inhabitants of the duchy of Spoleti, longed most intensely to yield themselves subjects of St. Peter, and of the holy Roman Church."†

The reclamations of the various Pontiffs, made on occasion of the invasions and ferocious outrages perpetrated on the States, by the Lombard kings, are invariably made in the name of St. Peter. They called these States, at one time, the *justitias Beati Petri*, at another time, the *plenarias Beati Pietri justitias*—St. Peter's rights: the plenary rights of St. Peter. It is to St. Peter, they demand to have them restored.‡ When such restitution is actually made, the title deeds are made out, not in favour alone of the then reigning Pontiff, but also, and in the chief place, of St. Peter. Thus, when the cities and their territories usurped by Luitprand, in Spoleti and the Duchy of Rome, are restored to Pope Zachary, it is said to be "by title of donation to

* Illi ad Beatum Petrum confugium facientes, prædicto papæ se tradiderunt et in fide ipsius Principis Apostolorum, atque prædicti Sanctissimi Pontificis jurantes, more Romanorum tonsurati sunt. Anast. Bib. in vit. Hadr.

† Et reliqui omnes ex eodem ducatu Spoletano inhiauter desiderabant se tradendum in Servitio Beati Petri, sanctæque Romanæ Ecclesiæ. Ib.

‡ Anast. ubi supra.

St. Peter himself, the prince of the Apostles."* The letters of Pope Stephen to Pepin, abound in passages to the same effect.† And all such acts of restitution or gift, as we have already seen, were wont to be carried with great formality, by envoys commissioned for that purpose, to Rome, and there deposited on the tomb of St. Peter. This was done in the case of the deed, inscribed in letters of gold, by which we have seen King Aripert restoring the patrimony of the Cottian Alps. This diploma was laid on the tomb of the Apostle.‡

When Pepin was urged by the envoys of the Byzantine emperor not to persevere in befriending the Apostolic see, as he had vowed and promised, and which their master Constantine *Copronymos*, so odious in history, when repeatedly called upon and entreated, was unable or unwilling to do, what was his answer? he protested with the solemnity of an oath, that the risks, the sacrifice of treasure, and the warlike toils entailed by his expedition across the Alps in the face of a hostile nation, he had been induced to encounter, not by any human considera-

* Per donationis titulum ipsi Beato Petro Apostolorum Principi, &c. Anast. in vit. Zachar.

† Vid. Baronii, Ann. an. 755. n. 2. et n. 17, 18.

‡ This custom of depositing grants and charters on the altar, or on the tombs of the saints, was not restricted to Rome. The great charter of King Ethelwulf to the Church, he deposited on the altar of St. Peter, at Winchester. See a Catholic Hist. of England, by W. B. MacCabe, Vol. ii. p. 59.

tion, or merely to favour the Pope, but solely for his love of St. Peter; and that as for revoking an offering which he had once made to St. Peter, all the treasures of the world, not to speak of what their imperial master offered him as a bribe, should never induce him to do it.* The writer in Anastasius adds, that, after the states and cities had been delivered up to him by the Lombard, king Pepin sent to Rome the act of donation of all the said cities and states to St. Peter, to be possessed by the Roman Church, and by all the Pontiffs in the Apostolic see, for ever—"Which deeds of donation," he says, "are preserved, being deposited in the archives of our holy church, to the present day."†

That the devotion of the father to St. Peter had

* Asserens isdem Dei cultor, mitissimus rex, nulla penitus ratione easdem civitates a potestate beati Petri, et jure ecclesiæ Romanæ, vel (et) pontificis Apostolicæ sedis quoquo modo alienari (se pati);—Affirmans etiam sub juramento quod per nullius hominis favorem sese certamini sæpius dedisset, nisi pro amore beati Petri et venia delictorum—asserens et hoc, quod nulla eum thesauri copia suadere valeret, ut quod semel beato Petro obtulit, auferret." Anast. Bibl. in vit. Stephani iii (p. 87.) It appears from the letter of Pope Stephen, in Baronius an. 755. n. 3. that Pepin was encountered by the Lombards full of confidence in their overwhelming numbers—"ut illi qui *innumerabiles* existebant, a paucis hominibus fuissent interempti," &c.

† De quibus omnibus receptis civitatibus donationem in scriptis a beato Petro, atque a Sancta Romana Ecclesia, vel (et) omnibus in perpetuum Pontificibus Apostolicæ sedis misit possidendam, quæ et usque hactenus in archivio sanctæ ecclesiæ recondita tenetur. Anast. Bibl. ibid.

not degenerated or waxed cold in the son is sufficiently manifested in the very attitude in which the mighty Charlemagne, the most magnanimous character, perhaps, and certainly the grandest figure in history, approaches the threshold of the Apostles. But we are not left trusting to mere deduction as to this fact: it is attested in express terms by the historian, who was a looker-on at the scenes which he describes. "The aforesaid most Christian king of the Franks," he says, "gave command to Etherius, his chaplain and notary, to prepare the new diploma of donation by which he granted and confirmed the cession of the said cities and territories to SAINT PETER."*

Hence at every stage of its growth, from the state of germ in which we first discovered it, up to the fulness of maturity at which we now behold it arrived, we find this principle of devotion to that great, that capital institution of Christianity, and main stay of religion, as represented in the princeship of Saint Peter over the Chnrch, to be to the temporal realm of the Popes what the sap of vitality and development is to the tree. If the first Christians carry the price of all they possess to cast it at the feet of Saint Peter, it is because to him have been confided the keys of the kingdom of heaven; because it is he who is instituted the head and prince over all—both pastors

* Christianissimus Carolus Francorum rex ascribi jussit per Etherium religiosum, ac prudentissimum capellanum et notarium suum, ubi concessit easdem civitates, et territoria BEATO PETRO. Anast. p. 108.

and people; it is because PETER is the corner-stone of the Church, placed immediately on the Eternal Rock, the Lord and Redeemer himself. And if resources and power, provinces and cities, with the rights and the majesty of sovereignty continue to accumulate round the Pontiffs of Rome, (as we have seen them to do, from the love, the devotion, and the trust of both people and princes,) on what other ground is it but the belief of Christendom that they are the rightful, apostolic successors, vicars, and representatives of the Apostle, to whom this supreme office was given?

From this primary fact, therefore, it follows, that so far as the devout intentions of Christendom, both princes and people, together with the solemn acceptance of those intentions and wishes on the part of the Church, can impart a sacredness and a character of exclusive dedication to the Almighty, and to His immediate service, to any description of property or possessions—as of altars, temples, sacred vessels, or lands for charitable and religious purposes—it follows, we say, that that species of dedication attaches in an eminent degree to the States of the Church,—devoted, as we have seen them to have been, by kings and by people, to the advancement of the self-same objects for which the princeship of the Apostles, and the keys of the kingdom of heaven, the sceptre of the Church, were conferred on St. Peter. These regions of the earth are, therefore, to be regarded, in some sort, like the precincts of the sanctuary itself: a spot reserved and set apart from all the rest of the world, for His own immediate and special service—being placed for that purpose, and by his own hand, under the jurisdiction of His vicar, to whom the whole "earth and its fulness" belong. They are His as peculiarly, and by a reserved jurisdiction, as were the cities which of old were assigned to the Levites. The first lien on these regions, once the cradle and stronghold of Pagan dominion—the head-quarters of Satan—is, that they shall for all time to come sustain the princeship of Christ's chief vicar on earth, and thus contribute to secure the stability, and promote the extension of the Christian religion; as formerly, by their resources, they so long and so furiously contributed to persecute it, and resist its diffusion. These are no fanciful reveries; they are deductions inevitably and obviously resulting from the FACTS, as these are indelibly engraved on the tablets of history.

The next peculiarity which strikes us, as characteristic of the Papal dominion, is, that the Popes were compelled, by the sheer force of events, to act the part of kings for centuries before they were invested with any formal designation as sovereigns, or had come into possession, as such, of one single rubbio of their present dominions. More than one hundred and thirty years before the sovereignty of Rome, and of the territory known since then as the Patrimony of St. Peter was, we may say, forced on Pope Gregory the Second, by the entreaties, and the enthusiastic admiration and attachment of the people, his predecessor, St. Gregory the Great, stands out before us not alone as the king of Rome, its only hope and defender, but also as the saviour of Italy. He is hailed, and recognised fully in this capacity, by the most embittered opponents of those Papal pretensions of which we are treating. Such writers as Gibbon, Giannone, Muratori, Lebeau, admit that, for full two hundred years before the imperial diadem of the West was placed on the brow of Charlemagne by the *ex proprio motu* act, and by the hand of a Pope, the successors of St. Peter had been, to all intents and purposes, the only *de facto* sovereigns of Rome, and its dependencies--the only champions and safeguards of the rights and interests of the Italians. Thus, by the confession of enemies, it is proclaimed that the Popes were not eager, were in no hurry, to grasp at the sceptre of temporal kingship. On the contrary, the whole tenour of history, as it is hived up in the genuine and mostly contemporaneous records from which we have quoted—but not in that sort of history, we admit, which is spun out by passion from the perverted and feverish fancy—that sceptre seems to be forced into their hand by the same omnipotent authority which entrusted the keys to St. Peter *

* Thus, to confine ourselves to Gibbon; he says, c. 49, "the weakness or neglect of the Greek emperors COMPELLED them (the Popes) to consult, both in peace and war, the temporal safety of the city." Again, "Gregory awakened the Emperor, exposed the guilt and incapacity of the exarch and his inferior ministers; complained that the veterans were withdrawn from Rome for the

The third characteristic of this temporal sovereignty, which strikes us as being peculiarly its own, consists in the species of arms which the Pontiffs make use of to vindicate and defend it. It is the sword of the "word of God," which they unsheath in every instance, when the rights of that sovereignty are assaulted, and, for the most part, the effect of its celestial effulgence alone is sufficient to secure their success. Thus, when King Luitprand has beleaguered Rome, and seems determined to capture it, it is by no other power than the words of St. Gregory II, the foe is compelled, not only to raise the siege and sound a retreat, but to despoil himself of his military belt, his sword, his mantle, his crown, in short, and all his other *regalia*, that, deposited on the tomb of the Apostles, they may serve as the testimonials and the trophies of the victory which the successor of St. Peter has won from him, by no other force than that of Christian persuasion. Exciting the invader to compunction for

defence of Spoleto; encouraged the Italians to defend their cities and altars, and condescended, in the crisis of danger, to name the tribunes, and to direct the operations of the provincial troops." Further on, still speaking of the same Pope: "He presumed to save his country without the consent of the emperor or the exarch." Again: "The merits of Gregory were treated by the Byzantine Court with reproach and insult; but IN THE ATTACHMENT OF A GRATEFUL PEOPLE, HE FOUND THE PUREST REWARD OF A CITIZEN, AND THE BEST RIGHT OF A SOVEREIGN." And all this was nearly two centuries previous to the period of which we are treating!

the wrongs and cruelties his army had inflicted already, or were preparing to perpetrate on an afflicted and unoffending people, by his words only, and the apostolic majesty of his office, the Pontiff preserves the Roman state from ruin; and by the victory thus achieved, the sovereignty of the Popes over the patrimony was for ever secured.*

Again, when, twenty years later, four of the cities of the Roman duchy are once more usurped by the Lombards, how are they recovered from the grasp of the invader? In two discourses pronounced in his presence, and that of his "dukes and satraps," such is the effect produced by Pope Zachary's exhortations (admonishing him, by authorities from the divine writings, "to desist from his forays, from the spilling of blood, and rather to cultivate and to cherish the arts of peace"), that the fierce Lombard, being subdued by such pious effusions, and so moved to admiration and reverence, that, not only did he restore the four cities, confirming them anew by formal act and diploma to St. Peter, but furthermore, surrendered the territory of Sabinia, which

* Ad quem (regem Longobardorum) egressus pontifex, eique presentatus studuit ut potuit regis mollire animum commotione pia, ita ut se prosterneret ejus pedibus, et promitteret se nulli inferre læsionem; atque sic ad tantam compunctionem piis monitis flexus est, ut quæ fuerat indutus, exueret, et ante corpus Apostoli poneret, mantum ream (regalem), balteum, spatam, atque ensem deauratum, necnon coronam auream, et crucem argenteam."—Anast. Bib. in vit. S. Greg. II. p. 70.

had been usurped for thirty years previously by the dukes of Spoleti. Nay, more, he adds to all this, the patrimonies of Narni, of Osimo, Ancona, Polimartium, together with other estates in the neighbourhood of Sutri, called Magna Vallis.* Well may the historian of these events wind up the narration of them with this remark: "And thus, through the favour of Heaven, Pope Zachary, with the palm of victory, returned to Rome;" for certainly, no emperor, consul, or king, of former ages, ever passed under its gates, with claims to be hailed as a victor so sublime and so untarnished as his! This conqueror immediately assembled his people, and instead of imbruing his hands in the blood of the vanquished, as was the custom with the conquerors of old, in order to propitiate the idol-god of the Capitol, he called on all to unite with him in thanksgiving to the King of kings, who "holdeth in his hand the

* "Sextæ feriæ die—ante fores Basilicæ Beati Valentini Episcopi et Martyris, isdem rex cum reliquis optimatibus, et exercitu suo sanctum virum suscepit. Factaque oratione mutua, et salutatione (sic) sibi persolventes dum (Pontifex) eum fuisset commonitus colloquiis, impensaque charitate, ab eadem egressus ecclesia in ejus obsequium rex dimidium fere miliarum perrexet (leading the horse on which the Pope rode), et sic in suis tentoriis uterque eadem die sunt morati. Sabbatho vero iterum convenientes divina perfusus gratia Deo placitis admonitionibus eum est allocutus, prædicans ei ab hostili motione, et sanguinis effusione quiescere, et ea quæ pacis sunt semper sectari. Cujus piis eloquiis flexus et constantiam sancti viri et admonitionem admiratus, omnia quæcunque ab eo petit per gratiam Spiritus Sancti obtinuit."—Anast. in vit. Zachariæ.

wills of men." Whereupon, having assembled together in the Pantheon, which is the basilica of Santa Maria *ad Martyres*, the Romans and their sovereign Pontiff issued forth entoning the litanies, as they proceeded thence to the blessed Prince of the Apostles' Church, there to return thanks.*

Another occurrence of a similar kind, narrated by the same writer, is, in its circumstances, so curious and so highly calculated to throw light on the period of which we are speaking, that we shall leave him to tell it in his own words.

"The affairs just related having been brought to a close in the tenth indiction, in the eleventh, the province of Ravenna being oppressed and harassed to an intolerable excess, by the aforesaid King of the Lombards, who was preparing to move against the city of Ravenna itself with all his forces, and to besiege it, the most excellent Eutychius, Patrician and exarch, together with John, Archbishop of the church of Ravenna, and all the people, not alone of that city, but of the Pentapolis and of Æmilia, having drawn up their petition in writing, most urgently implored of the Pope to try and deliver them from the jaws of destruction. On the instant, Bishop Benedict, the vice-dominus, and Ambrose, the primicerius of the notaries, were dispatched by the Pontiff as his legates, to entreat of

* "Et sic regressus est, Deo propitio, *cum victoriæ palma* in hanc urbem Romam. Qui etiam omnem populum aggregans," &c.—Anast. ubi supr.

King Luitprand to stay the invasion, and to restore to the Ravignani (not to the Greek or his exarch, observe), the castra (city) of Cesena. The legates however were not so much as allowed to come near the Lombard camp. Perceiving the invader to be obstinately bent on his purpose, the holy Pontiff already named, appointed one Stephen, who bore the title of duke and patrician, to govern Rome in his absence; and, armed with the trophy of the faith, like the good shepherd who abandons for a while those of his flock which are in safety to succour the others which are in danger of perishing, he prepared to hasten in person to the scene of distress. But before departing on his long and perilous journey, surrounded by the priesthood, the clergy, and all who were to attend him on the march, he recommended himself and his enterprise to St. Peter, the prince of the Apostles; and such was the effect of his supplications, that, though it was midsummer at the time, the clouds which overcast the heavens seemed to protect them as they proceeded, from the oppressive heat; but, in the mild evening time, when they were about to pitch their tents, the clouds cleared away, leaving the heavens placidly smiling, and beautiful to behold. Thus, they came to the basilica of St. Christopher, at a place called *ad Aquilam*, near the fiftieth stone from Ravenna. Thither, the most excellent, the exarch had come to receive the Pontiff, and from thence they proceeded, still overshadowed by the cloud, to the city of

Ravenna, and there arrived, the Holy Father entered at once into the basilica of St. Apolinaris, to pour out his fervent prayers, in thanksgiving for the favours he had experienced thus far in his journey, and to draw down the continuance of the divine aid and protection. As he issued forth from the city gates, once more to pursue his perilous march to Pavia, he was saluted with the blessings and the acclamations of the whole city, of every sex and age: old and young, men and women, uniting their voices in thanksgiving to the Almighty, for bestowing on them a supreme pastor, so ready to risk every thing for the sake of his people.

"From Ravenna, the Pontiff had sent forward as his legates, to inform the Lombard of his intention to visit him in his capital, the Cardinal presbyter Stephen, and Ambrose, the primicerius, by whom a messenger was sent back with letters, in all speed by night, to implore of the Pontiff not to venture amongst the Lombards; for that, after their arrival at the city of the Lombards, called Imola, they had ascertained that all sorts of plots were on foot to surprise him on his journey to Pavia, and even to deprive him of life.

"Nothing daunted by these menacing dangers, but full of reliance on the assistance of his heavenly Master, Pope Zachary pressed forward on the steps of his legates, who on reaching Pavia were refused an audience—so enraged was the king that the pope should attempt to interpose between him and his prey. By no fear of danger or of repulse, however, could the Pontiff be checked or turned aside in his march, and on the twenty-eighth day of June, he was approaching Pavia. King Luitprand could not help sending forward the optimates to meet him. Escorted by them, he drew near to the Lombard capital, but did not enter the city, until after he had paused for some hours at a basilica outside the walls, called *ad cœlum aureum,* in order to solemnize the office and divine mysteries in honour of the vigil of the blessed prince of the Apostles, St. Peter."

From the sequel, it would appear that the Pontiff might have adopted with justice on this occasion the famous despatch of Cæsar,—veni, vidi, vici,—so sudden and so complete was his triumph over the aggressive schemes and ferocious passions of the barbarian. Received with every demonstration of honour in the Lombard capital, he was on the next day conducted by the princes and nobles of the nation to the same basilica, where he celebrated the solemn mass, and was afterwards, with every mark of cordiality and veneration, entertained at the royal banquet, by King Luitprand himself. On the day following, when the Pontiff had come to the palace, whither he was conducted in great state by the princes and the multitudes of the city, such an impression did he make by his salutary admonitions on the obdurate breast of the king, that he agreed to deliver up to him the entire of the Ravennate—both territory and cities—as also the two-thirds of Cesena and its district, the other third being retained by him in pledge, until the conditions of the treaty—the exact terms of which are not stated—should have been complied with by the other contracting parties. Moreover, the king himself issued forth in person, to pay the greater honour to Pope Zachary on his departure; conducted him to a great distance, and thence sent with him those who were commissioned to surrender the cities and provinces, which, without violence or the shedding of one drop of blood, but solely relying on the divine intervention, secured by prayer and sacrifice, and on that word, more penetrating than any two-edged falchion, this aged and unarmed priest of the Most High had succeeded in rescuing from the iron grasp of the conqueror. "Thus did the Almighty deal wonderfully in his mercies," concludes the biographer, so frequently quoted. "Not alone the Ravignani, but all the populations of the Pentapolis, he liberated from the fetters of oppression and misery. They speedily saw themselves surrounded by the blessings of corn, and oil, and wine, in the greatest abundance."*

Nor was this the last or the most signal victory achieved with these divine arms, which were so irresistibly wielded by the hands of Pope Zachary. By the good use he made of them, he not only forced

* "Operatus est autem Deus mirabiliter, et Ravennatium et Pentapolensium populos ab oppressione, et calamitate qua detinebantur, liberavit, et saturati sunt frumento, oleo, et vino."—Anast. Bib. in vit. Zachariæ.

the successor of Luitprand, King Rachis, to relinquish his career of invasion, after he had spread his conquests not alone over the Pentapolis, but made his ravages felt on the Roman side of the Apennines; he, moreover, so wrought upon him by the terrors which an angry judge has in reserve for those who fill whole countries with wailing and havoc through the delirium of an insane and wicked ambition, that he resigned all the conquests so cruelly and unjustly made into the hands of the Pope; and, coming the next year to Rome in pilgrimage, with his queen Thæsia, and the princess Ratruda, his daughter, deposited his regal crown, as has been already narrated, at the feet of the Pontiff, received at his hands the clerical tonsure, and then retired to Monte Casino, as a Benedictine monk; while queen Thæsia and her daughter became recluses in a convent which they had richly endowed in the same country.*

Fourthly, nothing can be more manifest than that the holy see must have been subjected to a tyranny not less impious and brutal than that, from which we shall see it so repeatedly and so ignominiously suffering during the tenth age, and so miraculously escaping in the eleventh, so early even as the

* See the entire history, as it is told by the, we may say, cotemporary writer, Paulus Diaconus, otherwise called Warnefrid, a Lombard himself, in his work de Gestis Longobardorum, &c.—"Devoté, cum uxore et filiis, ad Beati Petri principis apostolorum limina venit, acceptâque," &c.—l. 6. cap. 59.

period of which we are treating, had not its sovereign independence been brought about in the manner we have already stated—that is to say, by means so extraordinary, and out of the common order of events, that it is impossible not to recognise in them the finger of Providence. There is a proof, the clearest that can be, of this assertion. We take it from Sigonius, who has digested and condensed the original narrative, as we read it in the acts of Pope Stephen III.*

For some time after he ascended the throne, for which he was indebted to the influence of the Roman Pontiff, at whose instance the opposition of the ex-king Rachis and his party was got rid of, the comportment of King Didier was marked by moderation; it was, indeed, exemplary in the most eminent degree. But being seized by that mania for conquest, which would seem to have been inbred and hereditary in the Lombard dynasty, he set himself to contrive the means for involving the Roman Church and all Italy in disorder. With this intent, he instigated duke Todo of Nepi to invade the see of St. Peter, promising, underhand, to give him support. Whereupon, while Pope Paul was at the point of death, the duke, with his three brothers, made a descent on the city—gaining admission by the Porta San Pancrazio on the Janicular Mount—and sustained in this sacrilegious invasion by a tumultuary force of his retainers, assembled at his call from Nepi and

* Ap. Anast. Biblioth.

the surrounding cantons, he succeeded, in defiance of the most sacred ordinances of the canons, in forcing one of his own brothers, Constantine, a mere layman, into the cathedra of the Apostle. The usurpation of this antipope—the first, it may be said, to profane the see of St. Peter—was a source of the saddest disorders, of bloodshed and scandal, to a deplorable amount, as any one may see by referring either to the original records of the transaction already alluded to, or to the narrative of Sigonius.* There was a regular battle fought on the Janiculum between the brothers of the antipope, at the head of their faction, and Christophones and Sergius, the leaders of the Catholic party. The latter, after the conflict had long remained doubtful, were triumphant, chiefly through the valour of the Lombards of Rieti, who fought bravely for the liberty of the Church. But the disasters, arising out of these wicked intrigues of King Didier, did not end with the two years of usurped authority on the part of his minion: they were followed by a tragedy, one of the darkest to be met with even in the annals of Italy. For, under pretence of making a pilgrimage to the tombs of the Apostles, shortly after the above-mentioned occurrences, this truly wicked prince took possession of St. Peter's, and so played his part, as to procure the death, in a manner the most cruel and murderous, of the two Roman princes, the primicerius Christopher and his son; because their zeal and

* Historiar. de Reg. Ital. l. 3. An. 767—769.

courage had been chiefly instrumental in the overthrow of the antipope whom his machinations had intruded on the chair of St. Peter. Not satisfied even with this measure of vengeance on the two who had been foremost in frustrating his wicked designs, having won over the duke of the city, who was called Paulus Affiarta, he succeeded in getting all the rest of the princes and chiefs of the Romans, either thrown into prisons or forced into banishment.* However, that Providence which gave such a sovereign to Rome as Pope Hadrian I, once more confounded his projects. It was either during the mortal illness of Pope Stephen, or perhaps after his demise, that the opportunity was seized on by the wicked instrument of Desiderius, for disposing of those whom he wished, for the furtherance of his plans, to have out of the way; and no sooner has Hadrian ascended the throne, than we find him, on the very day and hour of his election, recalling the exiles, and loosening the bonds of those who had been cast into dungeons.†

* "Paulo Affiarti duci Urbis, quem sibi consultò amicum, fidumque muneribus magnis effecerat, mandavit, ut comperto crimine, Christophero primicerio, et filio ejus secundicerio manus injiceret, ac vita spoliaret; et ut potentissimo quoque cive aut in custodiam dato, aut in exilium pulso, spiritus, animosque Romanorum contunderet," &c.—Sigonius, ubi supra. An. 769

† "Hic namque in ipsâ electionis suæ die, confestim eadem horâ quâ electus est, reverti fecit judices illos hujus Romanæ Urbis, tam de clero quam de militiâ, qui in exilium ad transitum Domini Stephani papæ missi fuerant a Paulo cubiculario cognomento

Fifthly, the fate not alone of religion, but of the learning and civilization of Europe, was involved in the establishment of this Papal dominion. That without this sovereign independence, the Papacy must have become a mere tool or a spoil in the hands of the barbarians, as was the patriarchate of Constantinople in those of the Greek despots, has just been established; while, on the other hand, it is not questioned by any historical scholar, not utterly perverted by prejudice, that it is in a pre-eminent degree to the influence of the Papacy, we are to attribute the rise and progress of the mediæval nations from a barbarism the most profound, to what is regarded as at least the starting point of modern civilization.* In fine, it is a deduction not less evident, that, upon the establishment of this power, depended the safety and the well-being of the various nations of Italy.

We have seen that nowhere but round the chair of the Pontiffs was succour or safety to be found by the Romans, after the total overthrow of the power of the Cæsars had left them, like sheep without a shepherd, to the cruel havoc and incessantly recurring invasions of the bloodthirsty and ruthless barbarians. Repeatedly, we see them rescuing their country from the jaws of destruction. The proofs

Afiarta, et aliis consentaneis impiis satellitibus. Sed et relictos qui in arcta custodia mancipati ac retrusi erant, absolvi fecit, et ita omnibus pariter cum eo exultantibus, pontificalem, Deo auspice, suscepit consecrationem."—Anast. in Vit. Hadriani.

* See Macaulay's History of England, Introductory Chapter.

of this we have already seen in abundance; and, indeed, it was by the gratitude and confidence arising from a sense of these benefits that they were gradually exalted to the independent sovereignty of the States.*

As for the miseries entailed on the ancient inhabitants of countries, the scenes of such incessant and hideous invasions, as seem to have formed part of the system with the Lombards, the following picture

* "Concluons de ces témoignages, et de tous les faits exposés dans cette premiere partie, que la souveraineté temporelle du Saint-siége a été fondû, dès son origine, sur les titres les plus justes et les plus honorables, c'est-à-dire, sur le vœu legitime des peuples obandonnés de leur anciens maitres; sur la juste conquête des Français, que l'Italie, par l'organe des papes avait apelés a son secours; et sur les services inappreciables qui lui avaient rendus, pendant plus de deux siècles, et dans les circonstances les plus difficiles, la prudence et la générosité d'une longue suite de pontifes."

In the work so frequently alluded to—Pouvoir du Pape, &c.—p. 320, every word in the foregoing quotation will be found supported by a host of authorities, for the most part from writers who are not friendly to the Popes as temporal princes; thus, Daunou, Essai Histor. t. 1. p. 29 et 30, after shewing how fully justified was the resumption of independence by the Italians, after two centuries of abandonment had proved that they had nothing to hope from the Greeks, concludes in the following terms:—"Délaissés par leurs maîtres, les Romains durent s'attacher à leurs pontifes, alors presque tous Romains, alors aussi presque tous recommandables. *Pères et défenseurs du peuples,* mediateurs entre les grands, chefs de la religion et de l'empire, les papes reunissaient les divers moyens de credits et d'enfluence que donnent les richesses, les bienfaits, les vertus, et le sacerdoce supreme."

of them is stamped with the impress of the original sources, from which it has been evidently carefully studied :—

"While avaricious violence perpetually wandered over the country, reducing the poor to slavery, the rich to poverty; to-day destroying the greatness which it created yesterday; delivering every thing to the chances of a struggle, always imminent and unexpected,—during these scenes it was, that in some famous cities, near the tombs of the saints, in the sanctuary of the churches, the unhappy of every condition, whatever their origin, were seen to take refuge;—the Roman despoiled of his lands; the barbarian pursued by the wrath of a king, or the revenge of an enemy; companies of labourers pursued by bands of robbers; often whole populations, who had no longer laws or magistrates to invoke, who could nowhere meet with safety or protection. Under the egis of the Church was their only chance; and for the defence of this only asylum of the faithful, the bishops had nothing beyond the authority of their characters, expostulations, or censures. To repress ferocious rioters, to inspire the vanquished with energy, they had no weapon but faith. Daily experience demonstrated the inadequacy of their means; their riches excited envy; their resistance, wrath; frequently assaults, gross outrages, followed them even into the sanctuary while celebrating the offices of religion; blood, often that of the clergy, even their own, was seen to flow in the churches.

Finally, they exercised the only moral magistracy that survived amidst the wrecks of civilization,—an office the most perilous, beyond all doubt, that ever existed."*

As for the boundaries of the States, after narrating the events which led to the formal establishment of the Papal dominion over the Duchy of Rome, Sigonius, who follows the most ancient authorities, proceeds to mention the cities and towns which it contained. They were, "Rome with its castles, towns, and villages, on the Tuscan side of the Tiber; that is, Porto (corresponding with the present Fumicino, at the mouth of the Tiber), Centumcellæ (near the modern Civita Vecchia), Ceræ (now Cer-Vetri), Bleda, Maturanum (both on the Maremma between Civita Vecchia, Viterbo, and the frontier of Tuscany), Sutri, Nepi, Castel-Gallesio, Orta (close to the Tiber and the site of lake Vadimon, long since dried up), Polimartium (Bomarzo, near Mugnano, on the plain between the Cimino mountains and the Tiber); Ameria (now Amelia), Tuder (Todi), Perusia (Perugia), Narnia (Narni), and Ocricoli; and in the regions of Latium, or on the Roman side of the Tiber—Signia, Anagnia, Ferentinum, Alatrium, Patricum, Frusino, and Tibur."†

Such was the extent of the territory over which the Popes began to wield the sceptre of temporal kingship from the year 727.

* Guizot. Hist. Eccl. Franc. See also Michelet Hist. de France, t. 1. p. 252-261.

† Hist. de Regn. Italiæ, l 3. An. 727. p. 119.

In the year 742, the territory of the ancient Sabines, together with the patrimonies of Narni, Ancona, Osimo and Numano were added to this, their primitive realm, when Pope Zachary obtained the restitution from King Luitprand, of the four cities, as has been already related.* In the year following, the provinces of Ravenna and of the Pentapolis were in some sort brought under, either the direct dominion or the protectorate of the see of St. Peter, in consequence of that intervention by Pope Zachary, when he went to Pavia. The idea is far from being groundless, that previous even to the first expedition of Pepin, the Adriatic provinces were, in one form or other, under the temporal suzerainté of the Pontiffs; and in almost every instance, where allusion is made to the act of Pepin in the ancient documents, he is said, not to have given, but restored the exarchate and Pentapolis to the see of St. Peter. Pope Stephen, also, both in his letters, and in his conference with the Lombard usurper, demands them as his right, and the emissaries sent by Astolfus to deter the Pope from persisting in his demand seem to consider the matter in a similar light.†

* Hist. de Regn. Italiæ, An. 742. p. 129.

† "Avant l'expedition de Pepin en Italie, le Saint-siége y possédait déjà une veritable souveraineté, fondée sur *le vœu légitime des peuples,* qui dans l'extrémité où ils etaient réduits, avaient librement confié au Pape tous leurs intérêts temporels ; d'où l'on doit conclure que Pepin et Charlemagne ne furent pas, à proprement parler, les fondateurs, mais seulement les protecteurs et les soutiens de la souveraineté temporelle du Saint-Siége ; et

As for the boundaries of the provinces comprised in what is usually termed the donation of Pepin, the exarchate of Ravenna of that day coincided pretty nearly with the territory now known as Romagna—a name which it seems to have borne occasionally, from the time Justinian recovered it from the Goths; for the subjects of the Byzantine emperors, whether inhabiting the east or the west, were commonly called Romans. It extended along the Adriatic from Rimini to the Po. Comacchio is specially mentioned as included in the donation. Towards Modena the donation would appear to have been commensurate with the ancient province of Æmilia, which would carry it much farther westward than the modern frontiers of the States. Thus, when narrating the proceedings of the envoys, commissioned on the part of King Pepin to receive from Astolfus the surrender of the territories and cities, the ancient writer in Anastasius says: "Accompanied by the messengers of King Astolfus, the venerable abbot Fulrad, making his public entry into each city both of Æmilia and the Pentapolis, and receiving formal surrender of the same, took with him hostages of the chief (Lombard) nobility in each city, and, with the keys of the cities, brought them to Rome. Also the keys of Ravenna and of the other cities of the exarchate, he carried with him, and placed them on

que le résultat de leurs expeditions en Italie, ne fut pas précisément d'y établir cette souveraineté, mais de la protéger, de la consolider, et de la rendre *definitivement independante des empereurs de Constantinople.*"—Pouvoir du Pape, &c. 1ere par. ch. 2. p. 318.

the confession of St. Peter, together with the written deed of donation already mentioned, by which the king had bestowed the aforesaid cities and territories on the Apostle and his most holy vicar the Pope."*

These boundaries were greatly dilated in that instrument which was drawn up by direction of Charlemagne, on the Wednesday in Easter week, A.D. 774, after he had ratified the act of donation, to which he, with the other Princes and nobility of the Franks, had been a party. Amongst other additions of vast extent, are mentioned the duchies of Spoleti and Beneventum; also the island of Corsica. "And when the diploma was prepared," says the ancient writer, so often quoted, "the most Christian King of the Franks confirmed it with his sign manual, and caused all the bishops, abbots, judges, and princes of the Franks to sign it. Then placing the deed, first upon the altar of St. Peter, and finally inside in his holy confession, both the King of the Franks and his judges bound themselves by oath the most awful, to observe faithfully all its

* "Prænominatus autem Fulradus, venerabilis abbas et presbyter, Ravennatium partes cum missis jam fati Aistulfi regis conjungens, et per singulas ingrediens civitates tam Pentapoleos quam et Æmiliæ easdem recipiens et obsides per unamquamque auferens, atque primates secum una cum clavibus portarum civitatum deferens, Romam conjunxit. Et ipsas claves tam Ravennatium urbis, quamque diversarum civitatum ipsius Ravennatium exarchatus unâ cum supra scripta donatione de eis a *suo* rege emissa in confessione beati Petri ponens, eidem Apostolo, et ejus vicario sanctissimo papæ," &c.—Anast. Bibl. in Vit. Steph. III.

conditions; in ratification of which, the book of the Gospels usually resting on the body of St. Peter was lifted by Charlemagne to his lips. Then, with his own hands, he placed the diploma so signed and ratified, which his notary and chaplain, the venerable Etherius, had written, beneath the said book of the Gospels, on the body of the Apostle, and took with him a copy of it, which was made by a notary of the holy Roman Church."*

With the knowledge of the genuine facts of the case which he now possesses, it will be scarcely expected or required by the reader, that we should enter into the disputes to which allusion was made in our opening chapter. After following that power through the successive stages of its rise and development; after considering the forms by which it was sanctioned on so many solemn occasions, and

* " —— necnon cunctum ducatum Spoletinum et Beneventanum; factâque eadem donatione, eam propria sua manu ipse christianissimus rex corroborans, universos episcopos, Abbates, judices, etiam et *Graphiones* (Lan*grafs*, mar*grafs*, &c.) in ea subscribere fecit. Quam prius super altare B. Petri, et postmodum intus in sancta ejus confessione ponentes, tam ipse Francorum rex, quam ejus judices, beato Petro et ejus vicario sanctissimo Hadriano Papæ, sub terribili sacramento se omnia conservaturos, quæ in eadem donatione continerentur, promittentes tradidere, apparem (*i.e.* exemplar) ipsius donationis per eundem Etherium describi faciens, ipse christianissimus rex Francorum, intus super corpus B. Petri subtus Evangelia, quæ ibidem sunt, est osculatus, pro firmissima cautela, et æterni nominis sui et Froncorum regni memoria, propriis suis manibus posuit, aliaque ejusdem donationis exempla, per scriniarium hujus sanctæ nostræ memoratæ Ecclesiæ descripta, ejus excellentia secum deportavit."—Anastas. Bib. in Vita Hadriani.

the jealousy with which its prerogatives were vindicated from the slightest infraction, even when there was question of complimenting such a benefactor as Charlemagne, he will have but little difficulty in forming his own conclusions, as to whether the sway of the Pontiffs, at this period, over Rome and the States of St. Peter, was a sovereign power or not.* But with the jurists and partizan writers who championed the cause of the German Kaisars during their wars with the see of St. Peter, and with many also amongst the French, from the reign of Philippe le Bel to the reign of Louis XIV, the case was different. Urged to the inquiry, not from a love of truth, but with a determination to make out such a verdict as would be agreeable to the taste of such censors as Frederic Barbarossa; as the murderer, by proxy, of Boniface VIII, or as the dastardly tyrant, who, while parading the high-sounding titles of "great" and "most Christian," threw down the glove of defiance to the venerable successor of the

* Thus, in Epist. of the Codex Carolinus, 55, 57, 63, 97, (alias) 40, 59, 65, 84, 85,—Pope Adrian I, in writing to Charlemagne, speaks of "this our Roman city"—"our Romans"—"our city of Castel Felice" (in Tuscany)—"our city of Centum Cellae"—"our territories"—"our men." Again, Ep. 84, 95 (alias 85, 91), he speaks of "our confines," and "your confines"—"your states," "our states"—"your subjects," "our subjects." His predecessor, Paul I, is spoken of by the Romans, as we have already seen, as their sovereign, Ep. 15. (alias 36)—also Stephen II, in several of his letters to Pepin, subsequent to Anno 754, makes use of the language of a sovereign with regard to the Romans, Ep. 7, 10.

Apostle, Pope Gregory XI,—for presuming to order that cut-throats and banditti should not spill the blood of their victims in the streets and piazzas of Rome, with impunity—it will be easily conjectured that the productions of these courtier-historians and jurists are not to be despised, either as to number, or as to the ability and zeal which they display. All living interest, however, in the controversy which they carried on against the Pontiffs, having sunk along with the two dynasties by which it was originated and upheld into the tomb of oblivion, we shall dispense ourselves from exhuming it, and merely add a few other facts to those already bearing on the same conclusion, to place the nature of the power exercised by the Popes in its genuine historical light.*

It is obvious that when the request of the Byzantine ambassador was refused, in the manner which we have seen, by King Pepin, that every shadow of the Greek sway over the States had vanished; it is equally obvious that the transfer, then and there, made of the States to St. Peter and his vicars, the Popes, was without any reserve whatever. It is to Rome the Lombard hostages are brought; the keys of the cities are placed on the tomb of St. Peter, to indicate that, in him and his successors resides the right to govern and rule over them. The narrative in Anastasius expressly intimates that the

* Whoever wishes to see these questions ably and thoroughly sifted has only to consult the following work—Pouvoir du Pape au Moyen Age, &c. p. 261, et seq. Paris, 1845.

Romans were in no wise the subjects of Pepin. Abbot Fulrad, who carries the diploma of donation, the hostages, and the keys to Rome, is said to have done so by command of "*his* king." We have seen how humbly permission is asked by Charlemagne to enter the city of Rome, and what formalities were required at his hands before he obtained his request. At the gates of Lyons or of Cologne, would he have petitioned the respective archbishops of those cities for permission to enter their gates, or have submitted, at their dictation, to such conditions as he unhesitatingly binds himself to by oaths the most solemn, and that too, at a moment when he has arrived from the field of victory, and is prepared to confer favours the most unparalleled on the Pontiffs? This incident is decisive; it leaves no room to doubt in what light the authority of the Popes over Rome and its dependencies was regarded by Charlemagne.

As for the co-ordinate sovereignty which a certain class of writers would set up for the Senate and people, it may exist, as no doubt it does, in the heated imagination of the revolutionist who would substitute the dagger of Brutus for the keys of St. Peter; but nowhere is it to be traced in the muniments and transactions by which the independence of the States of the Church was established. "It is true," says a learned writer already referred to, "that the ancient municipal government had not expired in Rome, at the juncture when the yoke of the Greek emperors was got rid of; on the contrary, there is every reason to believe that the municipal régime continued long after to subsist not only there, but also in several other cities of Italy ;* but then, this régime, common to the cities of the exarchate, and also of the duchies, implied, in the Romans, no sovereign right that could cope or clash with that of the Pope, but only the privilege of superintending such interests as are usually assigned to civic corporations, in the government of the city."†

Unfortunately for the theory that the Pope, when he exalted Charlemagne to the dignity of an Emperor, sunk down himself into the rank of a subject, the last will and testament of Charlemagne has been handed down to us. From that document, it is clear that the Papal States were not looked upon by Charlemagne as constituting any part of his realm. In his will, he sets out with this preamble: "We make known to all," he says, "that it is our will, if so it please the Almighty, to leave our three sons the inheritors of our kingdom and empire; and unwilling to transmit to them this possession, confusedly and in such a manner as to give rise to disputes, we partition the whole body of our realm into three divisions, assigning one to each of our sons, to rule over and protect it."‡

* Muratori, Antiquit. Medii Ævi. Dissert. 18 et 45, t. 1 et 3.

† Pouvoir du Pape, &c.—p. 279-280.

‡ "Non ut confusè atque inordinatè, aut sub totius regni dominatione, jurgii controversiam eis relinquamus ; sed trinâ partitione

After this preamble, the Emperor assigns to each of his three sons a portion of his dominions, of which he enters into a detailed description. In the enumeration of provinces, those forming the Lombard kingdom are not forgotten: but of the duchy of Rome or of the exarchate, we find not a word. And be it remembered that this partition is expressly stated to embrace the "totum regni corpus"—the whole realm of Charlemagne, in its entirety. A proof more decisive than this cannot be imagined, that the sovereignty of the States of the Church resided in the Popes, exclusively. In his last will and testament we have the word and voucher of Charlemagne himself that it was so. Had the territories within the Papal States' boundaries been looked on as a part of the "totum regni corpus"—a part of that realm, every province of which the aged emperor, to prevent disputes, was anxious to describe and allot with precision, could they have been possibly passed over in silence? But Charlemagne knew that they were not his to bestow; and when he does allude to them, it is to admonish the princes, that to defend and uphold the rights and prerogatives of St. Peter, is the charge and function of royalty which they are to regard as most sacred, and as paramount to every other. He does not bequeath to these future rulers of Christendom, the inheritors of

totum regni corpus dividentes, quam quisque illorum tueri vel regere debeat portionem distribuere et designare volumus."—Baluz. Capitular. &c. t. 1. p. 439.

all his own rights in their plenitude, any control or jurisdiction over the Popes as sovereigns; but with a solemn and stringent command, he informs them that it is first and paramount amongst the duties and privileges of their position, to keep vigilant ward over the rights, which, inasmuch as they are the legitimate successors of Saint Peter, belong to the Pontiffs. "But above all things," he says, "we order and command that the three brothers do conjointly undertake to guard and defend the church of St. Peter, in the same manner as, in former times, was done by our grandsire Karl, and by king Pepin, our father of blessed memory, and afterwards by ourselves." With evidence thus conclusive to show that the supreme uncontrolled sovereignty of Rome and its dependent states resided in the successors of St. Peter, and in them exclusively, whether there be question of the Roman Senate (at that time but a mere municipal body), or of the Frank Emperors, it may well be a subject of surprise to candid-minded persons, how a fact so manifestly historical could have been the theme of so many conflicting opinions; but this surprise will be moderated in proportion to the clearness of the conceptions that are formed—in the first place, regarding the complexity of the system of government, in which the protectorate of the Emperor, as champion of the see of St. Peter, and the municipal body, or senate, had each its separate functions; and, in the next place, regarding that fluctuation and uncertainty which caused states in those ages to be as different from what they are in times of civilisation, so far as there is question of the observance of law and the stability of rights and institutions, as day is from night.* With two such sources of instability and contradiction, the jurist could have kept up the controversy for ever.

* "Super omnia autem jubemus atque præcipimus, ut ipsi tres fratres curam et defensionem ecclesiæ Sancti Petri simul suscipiant, sicut quondam ab avo nostro Carolo, et beatæ memoria genitore nostro Pepino rege, et a nobis postea, suscepta est."—Ap. Baluze, Capitular. ubi supra.

CHAPTER V.

Having thus traced the temporal dominion attached to the see of St. Peter, from the act which deposited at his feet the charities of the first Christians, to this clause in his last will and testament, by which Charlemagne declares the vindication of its rights and prerogatives to be a charge and a duty paramount to all others for the Christian commonwealth, and for its sceptered rulers; we could wish the materials were less scanty than unfortunately they are, which would enable us to pass, from tracing this power in the abstract, to depict it in action—to depict it as shaping the destinies of the countries which have been brought under its sway by a progression of events so unlike any other in history. These materials have never as yet been collected together; no attempt has been ever made to work them into anything like a picture of the period; a general understanding apparently having been come to, to let it rest in the shade. The era of the Italian republics, and the conflict between the Empire and the Papacy have so completely absorbed the attention of the modern writers who have cultivated the mediæval history of Italy, that the epoch which we are at present considering has been either overlooked altogether, or dismissed in some paragraph, consisting, generally speaking, of as many errors and misstatements as words. It is only to the original sources, as they have been collected by Muratori, Sigonius, the father of the Ecclesiastical Annals, and others; and more particularly to the collection of the original—we may add, the contemporary lives of the Popes—we are to look for the notices, such as they are, which throw light on the state of the country—its aspect, at this period, and the condition, political and social, of those who inhabit it.

Whole territories handed over to solitude, which had once been the scenes of civilization, and improved and adorned in the highest degree — the destruction of cities, of the temples devoted to Christian worship, and of the abodes of learning,—forests, marshes, and deserts, spreading widely and rapidly over the once cultivated lands, in all directions—such were the monuments that registered the achievements of the Lombards, and the progress of their dominion in Italy. The sufferings of the Italians in former invasions, and the ruin—awful and widespread as it was—which befel under the Herulian, the Ostrogoth, the Hun, and the Greek, were but dust in the balance, compared with the woes and devastations of which the Lombards were the agents. It is admitted by Muratori—his researches, as we find them treasured up in his Antiquities of Mediæval Italy, and in his Annals, bear testimony to the fact at every turn—that during the Lombard era, whatever of the ancient civilization as yet survived was doomed to destruction—that the desert and the morass recover the ground of which industry and intelligence had so long and so happily robbed them—that history becomes obscured almost to darkness; and, that, as for the populations either actually under their scourge, or exposed to their eternally recurring invasions, they became plunged in an ignorance, which he strongly, but appropriately terms "ferocious."

The atrocities of Alaric were tempered by some tincture of Roman civilization, and of a chivalrous nature; the same may be said, though to a minor degree, of Genzeric, of the King of the Herulians, Odoacer, and even of Attila. In all these instances, too, the disasters, though enormous, were transient; and from such, no matter how desolating for a time, it is astonishing how rapidly and completely a country recovers. If the reign of Theodoric, and the duration of his kingdom, were more protracted, though full of insult and of suffering for the Italians, the period was one of recovery and improvement, in many respects. But the barbarity of the hordes who followed the standard of Alboin was atrocious and profound to excess, and the rage of the Byzantine eunuch, (whose thirst for revenge had let them loose on the unfortunate people for daring to groan and cry out under his unbearable tyranny),* would seem

* Narses observed, on learning this, "Si male feci cum Romanis, male inveniam." Longinus was sent to supersede him. To the

to have burned fiercely in their veins, to the last. It was a leaven in their nature, which could hardly be mitigated by the humanizing influences of faith, and by which the very best of the Lombard princes are seen to be seized, at but too frequently recurring periods. They are hurried away by it, as if they were goaded on by some species of frenzy. Without provocation, and through a sort of intermittent fever of cruelty and rapacity, they commit the fiercest ravages with fire and sword—burning the habitations, plundering the crops, dragging away the tillers of the earth into captivity, or slaying themselves, their wives, and their children with the edge of the sword, in the fields where they are peacefully reaping and gathering in the fruits of their toil.

Even Totila, at the time he was destroying the cities, bridges, strongholds, and edifices of all sorts, with a view to rob his great antagonist Belisarius of a military advantage, not only abstained from molesting the husbandman, but took him under his special protection. In the misrule of the Greeks, also—nefarious though it was to excess—there was

insulting threat of Sophia Augusta, that as he was a eunuch, she would have him to prepare wool for the spindles, in the apartments of her female attendants, he replied: "Talem se eidem telam orditurum, qualem ipsa dum viveret deponere non posset. Itaque odio metuque exagitatus, in Neapolitanam civitatem secedens," &c. He sent to the Lombards the tempting fruits of Italy, the better to entice them to forsake the *paupertina Ponnoniæ rura* for Italy, *cunctis refertam divitiis*."—Warnefrid, de Gestis Longob. l. ii c. 5.

this mitigation—it was an additional bond between the Italians and such wrecks of the ancient civilization as had retreated within the city of Constantine, before the everywhere-triumphant irruptions of the barbarians. It would not be impossible to prove even from the data, scanty as it is, which we possess for this period, that the advantages in arts and letters derived by Italy during the fifteenth century from Constantinople, were not greater than those which reach her from the same quarter, during the eighth. But, in considering the Lombard tyranny, we can discover no drawback on its horrors. None even of that effulgence of valour and military success, (which, by dazzling the imagination, but too often leaves us blind to the guilt and the mischiefs of conquest,) is to be discerned as distinguishing any one epoch of their career. As for the conquest of Italy, or rather such portions of it as they succeeded in seizing, it was effected not so much by any prowess on their part, as by the long and murderous struggles between the Ostrogoths and the Greeks (accompanied by famine and pestilence, which had fearfully thinned the ranks, and paralysed the energies of the people), together with the treason of Narses, who, instead of offering them any resistance, threw open all the portals of the land to receive them.* We have seen how St.

* During the protracted war between the Greeks and the Ostrogoths for the possession of Italy, by the sword, famine, and plague, fifteen millions of the inhabitants are said to have perished.

Gregory the Great, without aid either from Frank or Greek, succeeded in defeating their repeated attacks on the immediate territories of Rome, and on the city itself: at a time, too, when its walls were nothing better than deeply gapped and tottering ruins. Over the Adriatic provinces they were never able to establish their power. With enormous odds as to numbers, position, and all sorts of military resources, they were scattered by comparatively insignificant forces, in the various encounters with Pepin and Charlemagne, with the most disgraceful facility.* Even in their degeneracy the Goths defended their conquests with a brilliancy that runs away with our applause, as the glittering and skilfully armed, and well drilled battalions of Justinian are repeatedly crushed and scattered by their irresistible onslaught. This feeling is still more strongly excited, when we behold such generals as Belisarius cooped up by their successes, in some miserable sea-port like the Ostia of that epoch, after expending every resource of an exhaustless treasury, and of his immense superiority in the science of war; or when we see him repulsed in his attempts to save the capital, pressed by siege, and unable even to maintain these conquests, from which the rustic bands of Totila had swept him. But the dominion which the Lombards had held

* All this is sustained by the testimony of the continuator of Warnefrid, in the sixth book, *De Gestis Longobardorum*. Sigonius and the more modern authorities are unanimous in the same view.

for more than a century, they lost without even the ceremony of fighting a pitched battle. They seem to have invariably disbanded at the first charge of the Franks: on some occasions without waiting for any attack. By the concurrent accounts of writers of their own nation and times. they appear not to have waited on that occasion when the very fate of their nation depended on the event, to carry away with them any baggage but that of their own obesity in the rout. They seem to have fled from the field, if not with the fleetness, most manifestly with the trepidation of stags or hares to their cities—even there, prepared to surrender without once sallying forth, it would seem, or attacking the enemy.*

It is no wonder, therefore, that Charlemagne in coming to rescue them from the thraldom of oppressors at once so bloodthirsty, so worthless, and so vile, should have been hailed by the ancient Italian populations as a deliverer: for the destruction of the Lombard dominion was a revolution, altogether in favour of the ancient Italians. They had invariably kept aloof, as a rapacious and cruel ascendancy, from the conquered people. Hence, this was an intervention which struck down the oppressor and lifted up the enslaved; and from it, we date a revival of arts, of letters, and of the other blessings of peace. That

* Verona, one of the strongest cities of Italy, seems to have surrendered as soon as Charlemagne made his appearance before it, with only a division of his army. See Warnefrid, L. 6. ver. fin. and Sigonius, an. 774.

disastrous order of things is followed by a century of comparative security, felicity and progress, which inaugurates the perfect establishment of the Papal sovereignty, as we shall have occasion to shew in a subsequent chapter.

This deliverance from the Lombards was everywhere hailed by the Romanze population; but, nowhere else throughout the peninsula, was the reaction so complete and so striking, as within the boundaries of the Papal States. There, as we have seen, was the aboriginal hive,—there, the primitive possessors had taken deepest root in the soil—there, the admixture of alien elements in the populations was less perceptible than any where else. There, it would seem as if the aboriginal nations, the Latins, Sabines, Umbri, Hernicans, and Etruscans, were emerging once more into existence and freedom. They lift up their heads, once more, when the tempests of ages have passed.

Of the ancient stock of the Romans, properly and strictly so called, hardly a vestige was left after so many invasions which broke with tenfold fury on the once haughty mistress of empire. Besides, the impassioned monomania of the barbaric nations, whether Goths, Huns, Vandals, Herulians, Turkolingi, or Lombards, to imbrue their hands in the blood of, for them at least, the universally detested people of tyrants—such was the enormous opulence of the patricians, the equites, and, indeed, of the nobility and chief citizens of every class, that their very eminence above the victims of their oppression, the *coloni,* (mostly the aboriginal natives), and the slaves, marked them out for the most speedy destruction. Such was the ferocity of their enemies, and, though barbarians, such their thirst for gold, that it was customary with them to carry their researches for concealed treasures, even into the palpitating vitals of their more distinguished and wealthier victims "The Roman patricians," says Mariotti, "who survived the invasions, mostly emigrated to Constantinople, or settled in the Adriatic and Greek cities of the south."* If any of that order still clung to their estates on the open country, it is not easy to conceive how they could have escaped or been spared, when the entire soil of Italy on which they were able to make good their invasion, was partitioned out by the Lombard kings, between only thirty chief families of dukes and counts, who subdivided their estates amongst their retainers—reducing all, without exception, who were found on them, to the condition of serfs.† Again, in no one single instance can any Roman family trace its descent to a higher antiquity than the tenth century. Even the Massimi, confessedly the oldest of the Roman princely houses, have no secure footing beyond it. De Tournon could find no signs of a peculiarly Roman type in the populace of the Eternal City : the middle class, or *bourgoisie* of the city are notoriously a mere medley of *forestieri,* as they are called : and as for the Colonna and Orsini, like the overwhelming majority of the Italian princes and noblesse through-

* Italy Past and Present, vol. ii. p. 245. † Ib. p. 257.

out the peninsula, it is not disputed by any one that they are not of ancient Roman, but of barbarian extraction. Never, perhaps, was the extinction of a race more perfect—we mean outside the precincts of Rome itself, than in the case of the haughty and long dominant people.*

Thus do we behold the ancient stock whom we saw crushed by the Romans, when these are made, in their turn, to taste the cup of the vanquished, again reappear, and stand erect on the soil, and possess, and enjoy it. This is a position far from being merely conjectural; it admits of the most satisfactory proof.

When such investigators as Niebuhr and Micali, have collated the documentary records of the past with those of the present—as they are to be read in the language, in the customs of the people at present possessing the Roman soil—they have been startled, at every turn, by the exact agreement between them —shewing that still the original race has remained rooted to the soil, despite of two, yea, three thousand years of revolutions—of revolutions which swept away factions, changed all forms of government; supplanted kings by consuls; for these substituted emperors: crushed the old Italian nationalities under the iron power of Rome, and levelled the colossus of Rome itself in fragments, afterwards,

* "A Rome," says de Tournon, "toute distinction de race est impossibile â faire; et c'est en vain que jai cherché dans les Transtévérins ces types antiques que les voyageurs admirent traditionnellement." Vol. i. l. i c. 10. p. 249.

by the fury of the barbarians. Like the underwood, when the lords of the forest, struck down by the tornado, have rotted, the Volscian, the Umbri, the Sabines: the old Etruscan and Latin populations re-appear again, and are reinstated by an admirable re-tribution of Providence, in their pristine possessions. They are confederated under a regime of such unex-ampled benignity, that the blood of the slaughtered and of the oppressed of long by-gone generations would appear to be abundantly recompensed in the blessings descending on those who inherit it.

According to Niebuhr the boundaries on the Campagna, the very names even of farms, are in hundreds of instances, altogether unchanged from what they were in ancient Roman times, five and twenty centuries since.* Only consider what was the character of the 1000 years by which the two epochs are sundered—that of which we are speaking and that in which Niebuhr made

* From the Pandects, and from inscriptions and ancient docu-ments, says Niebuhr, it is known that a *fundus* usually bore a peculiar name, which did not change with the possessor for the time being, but was so permanent that even at the present day, if any one were to institute a search for the purpose, especially in the Roman Campagna, he would undoubtedly find many hundred clearly distinguishable instances of Roman names of estates. Of the four *fundi* mentioned in the donation of A. Quinctilius, at Ferentinum, two have retained their name almost unchanged, nor is this mentioned as in any way remarkable. St. Jerome tells us that the *fundus*, which the poet Atticus received for his share of the assignment of lands to the colony at Pisaurum bore his name. Niebuhr, Rome, v. 1. p. 632. Hart's Tr.

his researches—and say if it be a violent conclusion which holds, that, at the former epoch, the features of resemblance must have been incomparably more numerous and more impressive than they are now.

In the towns, also, of the Papal or Roman States, more decidedly than any where else, the municipal forms held men to the past. The system with which the agricultural classes had become thoroughly indoctrinated. by a usage which was immemorial, was another bond. In every Benedictine convent, we find a school of agriculture, for which Cato, Varro, Columella—all the Scriptores Rei Rusticæ, in short —were the class books. Again, when the Norman dialect is swallowed up by the English, no one hesitates to conclude that the race formerly vanquished on the field of Hastings has grown up and overpowered the handful of victors—that in the language alone, the proof is decisive that the Anglo-Saxon, and not the Norman race, is now, and has been for centuries, lord of the soil. Well then, this analogy demonstrates with equal force that the aboriginal Pelasgi and the Oscans form still the mass of the people in Latium ; for the Latin was formed from the dialects of these two nations, blended together.

Every thing in the age, and with the populations we speak of invited to retrospect,—to revive aboriginal customs and restore or refresh the memory of the past. Piety, by which the mind resorted to times and scenes that were hallowed by the conflicts and sufferings of the Apostles, and of martyrs, not for

Christianity alone, but for country also. Pilgrimage shews with what enthusiasm such retrospects were cherished. Worldly wisdom, even the very yearning after, and appetite for progress excited the same disposition. For the barbarian, for all, no matter of what race; but above all for the natives of Middle Italy in those times—especially from the fifth to the tenth age—there was no such short road to improvement as to study the past. Such retrospects are not now more judicious, are not more an expedient of matter of fact necessity, for the sculptor, or the painter, than they were, for the farmer, for the breeder of stock, the horticulturist, the architect, the soldier, the artizan, the scholar, the legist, the student of the medical art of the times in question; nay, it was the same for the very juggler or buffoon, who aspired to astonish the crowd.*

The very process of subjugation introduced by the Ostrogoths, and not meddled with, so far as it went, by the Lombards, was another most infallible means of fastening the ancient coloni or primitive populations, as *adstricti glebæ*, upon the soil. They became immoveable property; they became more strictly a part of the firm-set earth, of the estate which they

* The *Pulcinella* of the present day beholds, with a grimace and a caper of wonder, his own veritable portraiture in the ancient Oscan buffoon or pantomime, on the frescoed walls of Pompeii. See Spalding. Italy and the Italian Islands, quoting from Gell. The bifolco, as represented in the frescoes of Tarquinii, is in the same costume as the herdsman of the Campagna and Maremma of the present day.

tilled and inhabited, than the tree which could be cut down and sold, or burnt; than the crops of legumes and of corn which were, season after season, carted away to the market. Even their owner could not remove *them.* He could enumerate the descendants of the Volscian, the Etruscan, the Sabine, and Oscan, in the schedule by which he demonstrated the value of his property in the estate. As he did with the trees or the buildings, the vineyards, the woods, the mills, the fisheries, so far as the inventory went, he was entitled to do the same with his serfs. He sold them as part of the estate, but he could not drive them off the soil as he did the other stock, to sell them in the market of Rome, or Ravenna. This held them in permanence, and by a just retribution of Providence, in a sort of obscure enjoyment and security on the soil. A law made to prevent a serf from leaving the estate, *or becoming a* PRIEST, shews that such frequently were ordained—a law is not made for exceptions. It follows, therefore, that the serfs were of the old Italian blood, for from such only, for ages, was the militia of the church recruited.*

* De Tournon shews that the Etruscan, Volscian, and other ancient races—Hernicans, Marsi, Sabines, can still be traced.

"Il semble qu'on puisse reconnaître quatre races bien distinctes: la première, qui habite les monts Albanes et leurs contreforts, a pour caractères principaux une taille élevée, des membres souples et vigoureux, des traits réguliers, le nez tantôt droit, tantôt légèrement aquilin, les yeux grands et noirs, et un air de tête singulièrement fier et doux: on dirait le type des Apollons et de Bacchus.

Another proof that the soil is still inhabited by the aboriginal race, after the Roman Empire has disappeared, is found in the names of the various kinds of agricultural produce, as of corn, legumes, fruits, and in the terms of rustic economy—all so little altered that the stout husbandman, the farmer, or the shepherd who fought, a thousand years before, in the ranks of the Latin League, had they returned to life again, would have found themselves at home in the dialect of the market-place, of the forest, the pasture and the ploughland. The plough itself,

Cette race, qui semble représenter les Latins et les Volsques, disparaît dès qu'on a quitté les hauteurs. Les rudes montangnes d'Alatri et de Veroli sont l'habitation d'une autre race dont la taille est moins élevée mais dont les membres sont plus forts ; ses traits reguliers lui donneraient un grand caractère de beauté si le rapprochement des sourcils ne donnait aux plus belles têtes une expression extrêmement rude et s'il n'y avoit dans tontes les habitudes de ces hommes quelque chose de sauvage qui s'harmonise parfaitement avec les peaux de chèvres ou de moutons dont ils se vêtissent ; on croit voir le sang des terribles Herniques couler dans leurs veines. Les environs de Corneto et le versant septentrional du Cimino offrent aussi une race remarkable par la hauteur de la stature, l'élégance des formes, la regularité des traits et la douce expression de la physionomie ; c'est là que se trouvent, mais en petit nombre, les plus beaux hommes de la province, et on se plaît à les considérer comme les représentans de la noble Etrurie. Enfin, une quatrième race semble s'être conservée dans les montagnes de la Sabine ; sa taille est peu élevée, mais ses membres sont nerveux, et la regularité des traits, la beauté d'un profil droit, la grandeur des yeux, l'abondance l'une chevalure bouclée, la caractérisent : ne serainent—ils pas les fils des compagnons de Tatius et de Numa." Vol. 1. pp. 248-249.

the wine-press, the aspect of the flocks, the herds, the pulse-garden, the orchard, the harvest fields, the threshing-floors and the vineyards would look so like, so little altered, that it would have been easy for them to fancy that every thing had remained almost unchanged during the ten centuries, since the day, when they had turned their backs on their homesteads, to march to battle.*

In the movement which has thus displaced the throne of Nero to make room for the chair of St. Peter, the startling and highly significant effects produced are diversified and innumerable. A more pointed and finished antithesis than the two orders of things cannot be imagined ; but in nothing is it more striking, than in this resurrection of the primitive nations. By nothing can what then took place be fully illustrated, we are persuaded, by what has taken place in any other revolution in history. When one dynasty or race overpowers another, the sway, the privileges of ascendancy are usually transferred from one set of individuals to another ; that is the case, no doubt, but the force by which that sway and ascendancy is upheld, the fashion in which they are wielded, we may say invariably remain unaltered. In the outward costume of the time, as in dress, manners, language—

* See Muratori, Dissertazioni sopra le antichitá Italiana, Dis. 24, t. 1. p. 317. Abbiamo le specie di varij grani conservanti l'antico lor nome, &c.

some partial change may appear, but the minds of men, the principles of thought and action—their notions of right and wrong, of honour and disgrace, are not altogether subverted. Or again, if, as in the conquests of the Anglo-Saxon, the Tartar, or the Arab, all these things are changed, it is by the process of destruction—as wave drives wave before it—they swept their predecessors from the face of the land, and there were no materials left for a contrast. But in the instance of which we are speaking, the transfiguration is perfect,—extending to principles of belief, of morality, of action—but at the same time that the contrast, as to the essentials of things is thus astonishing, the two orders of things—that which has been prostrated, and that which is standing erect, the sway of the Pope and the sway of the Cæsars, are held together and bonded in juxta-position so provoking to the fancy, that it is impossible to look on the one and not to be put in mind of the other; or not be led to institute comparisons between them. It looks as if on the field of conflict, where the poor despised, illiterate fisherman of Bethsaida, on the one side, and Nero, the head and then sovereign Pontiff of the world, arrayed in the purple, in the height of its pride and passion, on the other, had met as the champions and representatives of two irreconcileably hostile systems—systems in which vice and virtue, truth and imposture, charity and ferocity, liberty and tyranny, Christianity and

Paganism were, hand to hand, engaged in a war which was to end only in the destruction of the one or the other of the belligerents, but in which no quarter or truce could ever be given. It looks, we say, as if the victory being decisive on the side of St. Peter, all who had been the victims in a pre-eminent degree, of the principles of aggressive force—of iron-handed oppression, of a selfish arrogance, so intense as to scorch up everything that had ever presumed to withstand it, were now lifting up their heads and exulting that the day of their redemption had after long ages arrived. The old Latin league—the Sabines, the Etruscans, the Marsi, the Volscian, the Hernican, the Umbri, and all the other ancient nations who were seated on the present realm of St. Peter, when the Rome of Romulus and of Nero unsheathed the falchion for their destruction, have started anew on the scene. We behold them in those harassed and confiding crowds of fugitives, who, from Latium, from Tuscany, from Campania and Umbria, from Rieti, and Perugia, the Pentapolis and Ravenna come fleeing from the Greek and Lombard tyrant and ravager — imploring help first, and after receiving that, to be adopted as the serfs of St. Peter.

This sovereignty, then, they have won not by inflicting outrage and misery on the people, as was the case with those who preceded them ; it is by the mercies, the benefits of every description which their dynasty has under heaven been the means of dispensing, that they have won their dominions.

By foes and friends it is agreed that, long before they were possessed of one rubbio of the territory within the boundaries of the States, the Popes had become invested with, and had admirably discharged the highest and most onerous functions of kings. Rome was saved by them, on many occasions, for centuries before they could call it their own. They garrisoned the towns, they rebuilt the walls, they either repulsed the invaders by their spiritual arms, or, failing in preventing them, they left nothing undone that, by the most princely charities, could alleviate the miseries their ravages had entailed on the people. Their legates went forth surrounded by all the majesty the Church could arm them with, and bearing her treasures in heaps, to seek the Lombard freebooter in his camp, and there ransom the captives. They resisted the invasions of famine when the earth closed up her bosom, or when the ravages of the Lombard had transformed its fields already whitening for the sickle, into scenes of waste and ruin. Like Joseph in the crisis of Egypt's distress, they threw open their granaries. They merited incessantly to have the eulogium of the holy Liturgy applied to them, "Hic est ille fidelis servus et prudens quem constituit dominus super familiam suam, ut det illis in tempore tritici mensuram."*

* Missale Romanum. in Misâ Pont. Conf.

They established colleges, repaired and beautified the churches, opened asylums for orphanage, the aged, the sick, and the broken-hearted They stood as a wall of brass against the assaults of barbarism, and under their steering hand, the Church like another ark, freighted with the hopes of a new society and a new history, bore up gallantly amidst tempests the most tremendous, of trials, lawless crime, ignorance, persecution, and infuriated brutality. Their works shine out gloriously in an age of disaster and gloom—at a time when every other governing authority lay prostrate or had disappeared altogether, their power rose amidst the weltering scene of wreck and confusion, serene and terrible even to the most ruthless tyrants and infuriated barbarians. It rose like a rock, immoveable amidst the chaos of society. It was the egis of order, the protection of the weak from the mighty. Charity, light, were with it, and the peace of God, which, diffused in the heart, cured every pain, and healed even the wounds and bruises of memory. Such were the doings of this newly inaugurated dynasty of the Popes. By such arts as these, it was, and not by intrigue, or arms, or ambition, the Pontiffs at length became kings *de jure*, as they had been the kings, *de facto*, of Rome and its immediately dependant province, for centuries.

So utterly is the power, and the people of Romulus and the Cæsars uprooted, that the ancient populations and the newly risen power of the Pontiffs, are left as it were in immediate historical and social contact. The empire by which both were persecuted, the one for their attachment to freedom, the other for their attachment to the Faith, being now destroyed utterly, and having disappeared like a phantom, the Pontiff and the people—the afflicted and the Father of the afflicted, the *servus* and "SERVUS SERVORUM DEI" are found united, not so much in the same realm as in one family consisting of myriads, of which the supreme Vicar of the Redeemer is the Guide, the Father, the Priest, and the King. It is, in short, as if the Etruscan, Sabine, Latin peoples had risen up from the graves into which they had fallen under the swords of the Roman invaders, to be comforted, and to be crowned.

Here was a resurrection for the long-buried Latium! Struck down, after many a struggle, by the elder consuls, dictators, and kings: ravaged and lacerated in the diabolical conflicts of the republican factions—lost in the blaze of imperial splendour, or discovered by the eye of the oppressor only when taxes were to be dragged from their vitals, or conscriptions made, that at the expense of their blood demented ambition might riot in carnage—here on the old homes of the Sabines and the rest—the Volscian, the Etruscan, the Hernican, can at last rejoice to himself under the sceptre, not of a conqueror like Camillus—the destroyer of cities—not under a tiger like Sylla, or a matricide monster like Nero, but under His vicar who came to save and to solace " that which was lost"—the victims of the mad and merciless passions of pride, sensuality, avarice, and ambition.

That form of existence reappears in which we for the first time beheld them emerging from the twilight of antiquity—that form in which they grew into prosperity and power, each within its own restricted domain. The Marsi, the Hernicans, the Etrusci, the Latin towns with their little territories are discernible once more: again their municipal independence, revives; their agricultural economy is the same, under the mild and parental tutelage, rather than the sway of the Pontiffs, as it was before their ancestors had lost their freedom, under the Romans.*

These nations had not, as of old, been dragged in fetters to the feet of their conquerors; they crowded thither as fugitives for protection and aid. In "bonds of love" alone were they fettered to the throne of the Popes. They said " it is good for us to be here"—they felt themselves so grateful and so happy—and thus the vicar of the Saviour became a king. He did not rob those nations—he enriched them—he fed them in famine time: ransomed them when they were captives—consoled them when they were afflicted.

"To the Popes alone," says the Count de Maistre, "is reserved the honour of not holding any terri-

* Niebuhr, Rome. 1. p. 632.—Guizot is of opinion that little or no change in the lot of the Coloni, or farming population, took place from the fall of the Empire, up to the fourteenth century.

tory to-day, which a thousand years ago, he was not possessed of."

To what ends do they turn their conquests? Like the Cæsars, perhaps, to exhibit a butchery of their fellowmen for the public amusement—to buy up in the market, and train a host of gladiators "to make a Roman holiday:" to build villas on every pleasant spot—in the valleys, on the hills, the isles of the sea, along the shore, there to waste their days and the plunder of the nations in every species of sensuality? The Popes also have villas, but they are what are called "*domus cultas*," in the old biographies, immense agricultural establishments for the support of the poor. True they distribute donatives, but it is not to the pretorian cut-throats—ever rejoiced to sell their country to the highest bidder—but it is to the distressed—to "our brethren the POOR OF CHRIST." They use their power fearlessly, but it is to exalt the humble, to ransom that which was captive, to diffuse redeeming knowledge, to turn the weapon of the destroyer from the bosoms of his unoffending victims, against his own.

Marcus Aurelius, whimpers or declaims some sentimentality—and Voltaire's world is filled with high sounding glorifications of philosophy in the purple! In the times of this Emperor, the humanizing influence of Christianity had commenced to make itself felt; nevertheless, he treated the Romans to a butchery of captives, on the arena. Can it be gainsaid, except by passion, that one pope has done more for oppressed, afflicted humanity, than all the kings, dictators, consuls, and emperors of pagan Rome put together did for it, from first to last? We should not fear to take up the cartel for Saint Gregory the Great, or Hadrian I, not to speak of a hundred others, against the whole of them.

Neither Cæsar or Trajan achieved such wonders for social advancement, as did several of the Pontiffs of those early times, not to speak at all of what they effected for the Gospel. They interpreted the Christian law in every instance in favour of the slave—in favour of the afflicted—in the same spirit of mercy, in short, in which its Divine Author delivered it. It was mercy in action, administered by them. On the Sabbath all *servile* work was declared by them to be unlawful and sinful; that is, they secured one day, at least, of rest and freedom, out of every seven, for the millions of slaves with whose groans and sufferings all Europe was full in those ages. Punishment of the cross, that is the ancient Roman mode of putting SLAVES to death, was through their influence abolished; manumission was encouraged by every means—merciful and kind treatment of the people was preached—the poor were exalted—mendicants covered with rags and sores were invited as guests by Saint Gregory. He waited on them in person at table; and this was a practice of routine with the Popes who succeeded him. Christian clergy were ordained and anointed to be the humble, devoted, respectful servants of the afflicted of every class.*

* See Macaulay's History of England, vol. i. p. 33. "The su-

The Popes saved the works of the ancients, hoarded them up, cultivated the field of the intellect, multiplied manuscripts. Whoever preserved the life of a citizen was entitled by the laws of the Roman Commonwealth, to an honorary crown—whoever added a province was honoured with a triumph—for the Popes who ransomed captives, saved myriads in famine, in plague, fire, war, and inundation—who not only added provinces to Rome, but saved and founded Rome itself—according to the tariff of guerdons in ancient Rome, how find wreaths enough for them?

They were the first sovereigns to labour for the diffusion of knowledge. For 800 years of its existence, no public encouragement was given by the pagan government of Rome to learning. Schools were encouraged, certainly, both by the ancient patricians of Rome, by its most renowned worthies, and by all the emperors; but they were schools of murder, in which the unfortunate gladiators were made perfect, by lecture and exercise, in their revolting profession. Vespasian was the first to found a college for the study of letters, and this at a period, after the policy introduced by the Popes had begun to make itself felt, in the diffusion of the Christian religion. But all the arts—music, paint-

periority of Popery in its humanizing influence is admitted, it is the shield and comfort of the oppressed. To this day, in some countries where negro slavery exists, Popery appears in advantageous contrast to other forms of Christianity." Becket, *a man of the people*, p. 24. "Catholicity had emancipated all the bondmen of England, before the Reformation came in."

ing, architecture and literature, and the sciences, (astronomy in particular), such of them as then, flourished—were not less indebted to the Popes at this remote epoch, the eighth century, than they are on all hands allowed to have been in after ages. But of this we shall have a more appropriate opportunity to speak, when, in our next chapter, we are describing the city.

The Popes were the first who ever reigned by opinion. Opinion was the force which carried them to the throne. Never did Cæsar, or Sylla, or Trajan, achieve by the sword such victories as the Popes won by opinion. By opinion, the eternal city was saved in the time of St. Gregory the Great, when all the rest of Italy lay prostrate, and was on all sides forsaken and ruined.

The Popes were the first who ever reigned for the people. They were the *humanitarians* without pretension, and properly so called, making common cause with the oppressed, the refuge of the outcast, the shield of the weak, the solace of the afflicted, fathers to the orphan, friends to the broken-hearted, the stewards good and faithful, who in the season of distress meted out relief to the needy. In return, they found on the part of those whom they had thus subsidized by the benefits of every description which they conferred upon society, a surer support and defence than was ever found by the Cæsars in their Prætorian cohorts.*

* After making their acknowledgments to Pepin, patrician of the Romans, for having espoused the defence of the true faith,

Proofs not a few—in addition to those to be found in the foregoing pages—of what is here advanced will be brought to light in the investigation as to the origin, progress, the material aspect, and social condition of the primitive Rome of the Popes.

Such is the pre-eminent interest attaching to the capital of the realm with whose history we are engaged, that too great a prominency can hardly be given to the investigation as to how it was founded, how it increased amidst trials and disasters of every kind, until at length it is raised to a magnificence which comes on us by surprise, in an age in which it has been usual with writers to tell us that its history was involved in the greatest obscurity.

"It is difficult to form a distinct image of the doomed city during the increasing misery of those five ages, from A. D. 500 to A. D. 1000."† Such is the avowal of one of the latest and most laborious investigators of the history of the city! We shall find the reverse to be the fact, in the following book.

then threatened by the Greeks, the senate and people, A. D. 763, take occasion to expatiate on the firmness and unalterable affection of their loyalty towards their sovereign, most blessed father, and most excellent pastor, Pope Paul:—"E protestano d'essere fermi, e fedeli servi della santa chiesa di Dio, e de beatissimo padre, e Signor' nostro Paulo papa, *perchè egli e nostro padre, ed ottimo pastore, e non cessa di operare per la nostra salute, siccome ancor fece papa Stefano suo fratello, con governar' noi come peccorelle ragionevoli a lui consegnate da Dio, mostrandosi sempre misericordioso, e imitatore di san' Pietro, di cui e vicario.*"

This letter is the 36th of the Caroline code. It is given entire by both Cenni and Pagi, [ann. 757,] with critical annotations.

* Spalding, Italy and the Italian Islands, v. 3. p. 144.

BOOK II.

CHAPTER I.

Far as the ken could range, there extended, on every side along their march, a scene of desolation strewed with the ruins of Vitruvian villas, temples, pleasure gardens, tombs and aqueducts. The waste waters of the latter had filled all the valleys, and over flowed the low grounds of the Campagna, converting into marshes and mantling pools those regions that. erewhile, had been blooming with all the delights and charms which fiction assigned to the Hesperides. But it was as they approached nearer and nearer to the walls that the catastrophe, by which the once proud and glorious Queen of Cities and of universal empire had been reduced to the condition in which they now beheld it—so forced itself upon their minds and senses, that light-hearted guardsmen as they were, (fierce by nature, and inured to scenes of horror and of desolation), in their ranks the laugh and the rough jest subsided as they advanced. Grave, thoughtful, and even touched with sorrow, they moved along through the marble wilderness, lone and terrible, from which there issued no sound or sign of life.

Before them, the thoroughfares of the nations extended as silent and forlorn as the double line of majestic tombs and mausoleums through which they passed. The watch-towers and the inscriptions above the city gates had been dismantled and torn down, encumbering the entrance with their massive fragments. The bronze gates themselves had been carried off as trophies in the plunder train of the barbarian. The rock-built walls of Rome lay low; and the tramp of their war-horses was muffled by the grass, as Belisarius and his guards rode slowly and in silence under a succession of triumphal arches, defaced and ruined, down towards the Forum and the Capitol, along the "sacred way."

The fox looked out from the casements of the Palatine, and barked sharply at the intruders as they rode on. Wolves prowled through the vacant streets, or littered or fed their cubs in the halls of the Golden House. Wild dogs were hunting in packs through the great circus, through the baths, along the Campus Martius, and on to the gardens of Sallust and Macænas, or round the purlieus of the great theatres and the promenades of the Suburra. Outlandish beasts of various kinds, as if escaped from the menageries and keeps of the amphitheatres, (where they used to be preserved and fed for the fights and the hunting exhibitions of the arena,) were to be seen sleeping and enjoying themselves in the sunshine of the porticos; or they were occupied in tearing one another to pieces, as of old the factions were wont to do, around the rostrum and in the assembly place of the people. Others growled, and snarled, and gloated over the unburied carcases, and gnawed or mumbled the bones of the already whitening skeletons of the dead. Ravens and vultures desisted from feeding their sanguinary nestlings, or from battening on their rancid prey, to hoot and scream at the warriors as they wound slowly among prostrate columns, entablatures of temples, and trophies shattered to fragments, from having been hurled down by the Gothic engines, where they now lay cumbering the way of triumphs by which they were ascending to the Capitol; or starting on the wing, from their perching places on trophy or triumphal arch, these birds of evil-boding croaked hoarsely and hovered, flapping their sable wings above the plumage of their helmets.

After the departure of Totila had allowed him the opportunity, Belisarius with some squadrons of his guards had sallied forth from Ostia, resolved to visit the scene of such an unexampled tragedy, and to test with his own eyes what awe-struck rumour had proclaimed, that the conqueror had destroyed the walls and chief monuments of the Queen of Cities, and reduced it to a perfect desert. With his squadrons disposed on the alert at different points among the ruins, the Greek general is now upon the "Hill of Triumphs—the place where Rome embraced her heroes." Once more the Roman eagle soars upon his standard above the

Tarpeian tower, that eyrie from which for a thousand years it had flown forth to conquest, and the martial clarion makes the field of Mars resound once more; but instead of the warlike response of legions and wings of cavalry, clamouring to be led against the Samnite or the Parthian, there broke out at the sound, from every quarter of this grand theatre of ruin, a hideous medley of yells and howling, yelp, bark, and roar, out-topped by the shrill cries of ill-omened birds, of owls and bats, startled from their roosts in the sanctuary recesses, and from the niches and cornices of the curiæ and the senate-house. The warriors listened for some human response to their summons, but in vain they listened, and listened again. There was the Palatine, there the Forum, the Capitol, the Campus Martius, yonder were the Janiculum and the Aventine, with the yellow Tiber between them, its waters glittering as if with gold, beneath the beauteous summer sky of Italy—but the Emperors, the legions, the haughty senate, the dictators, and the Roman people, where were they?

When that savage uproar had at last subsided—except ever and anon the outbreak of a distant howl or bark, reverberating dismally among the empty palaces, and along the valleys and the river banks, there settled down a lugubrious stillness over the entire scene, and all within the boundaries of the Seven-hilled city was again as silent as the grave.

Never had mortal eye beheld a catastrophe more

startling and impressive than that which was now before the eyes of Belisarius. Fortune had turned back upon her steps, in the scene before him, and made it her sport to reverse and upturn everything upon that very place, where, beyond all others, men had become elated with imagining that she had at length descended from her slippery globe, and fixed her perpetual sojourn—for once and for ever weaned from her inconstancy. It would seem as if the fickle goddess had lured the Romans to the highest pinnacle of grandeur and felicity, only to render their downfall the more tremendous; had helped them to build up testimonials of their works, merely that the vouchers of her own instability, which she was bent on registering in their ruins, might endure for ever.

After having been deified, and having temples and priests, and altars, consecrated for their worship by the nations they had vanquished and degraded, the emperors of Rome were led about as harlequins to grace the triumphs, and to afford mirth in the brutal carousals of the Goths. The iron legions, which had trodden down the independence of nations, had been trodden down in their turn, and slaughtered to the last man in this revolution, far and away the most terrible the world has ever witnessed. During its throes, the slave had seen his tyrant lord a suppliant at his feet for life—a beggar at his gate for a vile pittance of bread or broken meat. To escape from dignities for which the

Gracchi, the Scipios, and the Cæsars, had contended, men of patrician lineage had themselves branded and ranked as slaves. To be a Roman, once a distinction prouder than that of royalty, had become the vilest badge of infamy.* The lords of palaces, that resembled magnificent cities, rather than private dwellings, and of estates which included kingdoms within their limits, beheld themselves without a rood of land, or a roof to shelter them.

"In this revolution," says a writer who belonged to the staff of Belisarius, "the sons and daughters of Roman consuls, tasted the misery which they so often had spurned or relieved, wandered in tattered garments through the streets of the city, and begged for the most sordid pittance, perhaps without success, before the gates of their hereditary mansions."† Others expired of famine upon silken couches, amid halls of more than regal extent and splendour, or were led away (a lot still more insupportable) to minister to the rude conquerors amidst those devastated villas and pleasure-grardens, which reminded them of many a bright summer-time

* "When we would brand an enemy," says Luitprandus, "with the most disgraceful and contumelious appellation we call him a Roman." Hoc Solo, id est, Romani nomine quicquid ignobilitatis, quicquid timiditatis, quicquid avaritiæ, quicquid luxuriæ, quicquid mendacii, immo quicquid vitiorum omnium est comprehendentis, &c. Luitprand. Legatio, ap. Muratori, Scrip. Italic. vol. ii. par. 1. p. 481.

† Procopius, quoted by Gibbon.

passed in dalliance and enjoyment. To the very weft itself, the fates had unravelled their own most gorgeous tissue, and, from the ruins of the Palatine and the Capitol, had abandoned to the scoffing winds the fame of kings, and consuls, and emperors, with which they had interwoven and adorned it. Even the memorials of her ancient glories only served, and that not slightly, to multiply and increase the calamities of Rome. The sight of these, and of the scenes of invasion and conquest which they so vividly recalled to memory, exasperated and goaded the barbarians into fury. They regarded it as a sacred and patriotic duty to slaughter the craven multitudes they found loitering around, and boastful of their alliance with monuments, intended to perpetuate the memory of the injuries and insults inflicted by their sires upon humanity in general, but more especially on the ancestors of the very warriors to whom victory had now afforded the most unrestricted opportunity of revenge. And indeed, it would seem as if so many millions had been gathered together by allurements of largesses, by shows, by every species of sensual indulgence, in short, and even by the disasters which had driven from the provinces such multitudes to seek for defence and shelter in the capital, that, being crowded together within one narrow precinct, the scythe of the destroyer, to use the language of Alaric to the Roman envoys, might mow them down with the greater facility and despatch. "The metropolis of the nations," as St.

Jerome observes, "had become their sepulchre, and the rotting of their pampered bodies had fattened the soil, and almost filled up the valleys of the Seven Hills."

The description of this scene, by one who beheld it, has come down to us: it is depicted by the Greek writer Procopius, who was secretary to Belisarius, and the words he uses, emphatically expressive as they are of desolation and ruin the most complete, must satisfy the reader that in the attempt to fill up, in the foregoing fancy sketch, the details of the picture, there is nothing even approaching to exaggeration of colouring. "The Goth," he tells us, "had threatened to reduce the place where Rome had stood to the condition of a sheep walk, or of a pasture for cattle;" and when he comes to speak of the state in which the city was actually found, at an interval of forty days after Totila had retired into Campania, with his plunder train and the wretched remnant of the senate and the Roman people, whom he at the same time dragged away into captivity, he describes it as a howling desert without one single inhabitant in human form. "In Rome," he says, "not a human being was permitted to remain, but he (Totila the Goth) left it altogether desert."* Not less precise

* De Bel. Gothic. l. iii. cap. 22.

is the account of the same event which we read in the chronicle of Marcellinus: "Every thing which had belonged to the Romans, Totila seized as spoil, and the Romans themselves, he led away as captives. After this devastation, Rome was so desolate, that, for forty days and upwards, there was not to be seen in it one single inhabitant, but only herds of cattle and wild beasts."*

Allusion to this total overthrow and destruction of the city of the Seven Hills could not be avoided in a history of the Papal States. That history has for its chief feature the origin and vicissitudes of the city of the Popes, as contrasted with the city of the Cæsars, from amongst the ruins of which it has arisen: and in tracing the former to the point from which it takes its rise, we find ourselves carried back to the memorable epoch in which the latter—the Rome of paganism and of the Cæsars had literally become a desert; and when, but for the intervention of the successors of Saint Peter, it must have shared the fate, it had in instances beyond number inflicted, and been utterly blotted out from the list of cities. "Like Thebes, or Babylon, or Carthage," says Gibbon, "the name of Rome might have been erased from the earth, if the city had not been animated by a vital principle, which again restored her to honour and dominion."

The object of the present chapter is to trace the events, the risks, the sufferings, and various other

* In Chron. p. 54. quoted by Gibbon.

vicissitudes through which this vital principle was developed, and struggled to expand, until in the reign of Pope Hadrian I, and Leo III, it exhibits itself before us in the form of a city, singularly majestic, and altogether different, not alone from the Rome which has passed away, but also from Rome such as the nine last centuries have beheld it; for Christian, like Pagan Rome has experienced its reverses—has been, not once, but oftentimes, ruined and rebuilt again. During the tenth century, for instance, the Rome which we are about to describe was entirely changed as to its external aspect by the erection of the war-towers and fortresses of the Roman nobles, and by the conflagration and sack which ensued, on its being taken by Robert the Norman, the primitive city thus transfigured was in a great measure destroyed. The new city which sprung up from that state of ruin, and which attained the highest degree of splendour from the times of Innocent III to the death of Boniface VIII, (A. D. 1198 to A. D. 1303), was found by Martin V, (A. D. 1420) in a state of sad and irretrievable decay, the effect of nearly a century's absence of the Popes. It may be said of the city as we at present behold it, that it cannot be carried to a higher date than the epoch just mentioned; and, certainly, it bears as little resemblance to the Rome of which we have now to speak, as did the city of the Antonines to that of the earlier commonwealth and of the kings. Indeed this primitive Rome of the

Pontiffs has hitherto been as little known, or at least as little spoken of, as were Herculaneum and Pompeii, while the ashes and the lava still lay undisturbed above them, though perhaps not less worthy of being studied, or less filled with wonders, than they.

The Catacombs were the first city of the Popes. A history of greater extent than our plan permits us to embrace, and of the highest interest belongs to this "subterranean Rome," but our present purpose being with the city above ground, let us endeavour to collect, from what has been left on record by a contemporary writer, some idea of what may be called the glorious resurrection of Christian Rome, from those regions of death and darkness which were its abode, during the three centuries of persecution.

The lonely tombs of the Apostles, the catacombs, the places where the martyrs had been tortured, or where their blood had been poured out like water, and their members scattered to dogs and beasts of prey; in short, whatever bore the slightest relationship to Christianity became on a sudden, that is, when the persecutions were over, the objects of the most enthusiastic interest and respect. Even the most bigoted gave way to emotions of wonder and gratitude in the general fervour of excitement. They were not a little astounded at these things, wondering at so great and unexpected an alteration of affairs; and crying out that the God of the

Christians was the great and only God. They thronged round the champions of Christ wherever they appeared, and gazed upon them as beings more than human; insomuch, that they who before breathed nothing but threats and vengeance against the Christians, now hailed them with plaudits and cheers of welcome, as they issued from the innumerable crypts and tombs around the city, seeming almost to realize and display beforehand to the unbelievers, and even in this life, the joy and the glories of the resurrection. Moreover, those who had been banished, or who had abandoned all, and taken to the forest and the caves of the mountains for the sake of Christ, or who had been long buried in the mines, were now beheld returning to their own habitations; and being glad and overflowing with delight, they came along in companies, lauding the Almighty with hymns and psalms, not only through villages and country places, but along the great highways, and even through the streets and forums of the city. "And you might have seen those who had been but lately in bonds, groaning under the most severe punishments, and driven from house and home, now reinstated, with joyful and pleasant countenances, and with many and signal honours, in their own dwellings, being held in high repute and veneration by their former enemies."*

That stately palace which had been appropriated

* See Euseb. Eccl. Hist. book ix. ch. 1.

to their own use by the emperors, from the attainder and execution of Plautius Lateranus, in the reign of Nero, was now made over in perpetuity by Constantine to the successor of St. Peter, for whom, during so many centuries, there was no security or respite from imperial vengeance, even in the subterranean crypts and sepulchres of the dead.*

The power and solicitude so long exerted to deprive the martyrs even of an obscure grave were now busied in adorning the scenes of their sufferings, and in erecting magnificent and costly mausoleums above the places of their burial. For the most part, these primitive churches, usually styled basilicas, were erected, outside the walls, near the entrances of the principal catacombs, where the princes of the Apostles, and most renowned martyrs

* How this palace became forfeit is fully stated in Rome under Paganism and the Popes, vol. i. p. 247, et seq. See also Juvenal, lib. iv. sat. 10. The fact of its having been transferred to Pope Melchiades by Constantine is borne out, not only by the pieces (probably authentic) given in the decretals of Isidor Mercator, but by an uninterrupted series of witnesses of the most undoubted integrity, who attest that the Lateran became from that time the chief seat and dwelling places of the Popes. Thus, in speaking of the Council concerning the Donatists held the year following, (A. D. 313), St. Optatus of Milevi says it was held in the Lateran (lib. i. Contr. Parm.) St. Jerome, ep xxx, says of Fabiola, "Totâ urbe spectante Romanâ, ante diem Paschæ in Basilica quondam Laterani, qui Cæsariano truncatus est gladio, staret in ordine pænitentûm." And Prudentius, ad. Symmach. says, "Cœtibus qui Magnas Laterani currit ad ædes."

had their tombs. Thus it was the Rome of Christianity and the Pontiffs took its rise.

From the night after the Prince of the Apostles had suffered martyrdom, being crucified on the ridge of the Janiculan mount, the crypt hard by the circus of Nero where his dead body had been reposed, after his disciples had stolen it by night from the cross, became a most hallowed spot, and a place of prayer and pilgrimage for the Christians. It formed one of the greatest privileges of his successors to be laid in death beside the great founder and first viceroy of Christ's kingdom. A little oratory or tomb called sometimes a *Platonia*, in reference to the resurrection, had been erected there, so early as the year A.D. 106, by one of his own faithful priests, who afterwards succeeded him in the pontificate. It had however shared the fate of all the places consecrated to Christian worship, or rather it was in the very first instance the mark of the persecutor's destructive fury. It was still a heap of ruins, when, on a certain day, the legions, the senate, and the Roman people being there assembled, the Emperor came to the place where his predecessors had so inhumanly tormented and massacred the Christians, and Saint Peter their chief most cruelly of all—having doomed him like his Divine Master to the ignominious death of the cross. Then, having dismounted from his chariot, and laid aside his diadem, he prostrated himself before the shrine of the Apostle—called by the Latins *confessio*, and *martyrion* by the Greeks—

that is to say, the place where he sealed the *testimony* of his faith with his blood. The Emperor is said to have poured out floods of tears, so that they streamed down the ornaments of his imperial robes. Then taking a spade, he dug with his own hands the first traces of the foundation of the basilica of the Prince of the Apostles, and carried away from the foundation on his shoulders a basket of earth in honour of each of the Apostles.*

* The dimensions of the temple erected at that time were these: the nave, from the great entrance to the chancel, beyond which stood the altar, measured 390 palms, and from beyond the altar to the absis, or semicircular termination where stood the Pontiff's chair, 36 palms; the tribune was 44 palms, making 430 palms the entire length, not including the width of the transept, which was 406 palms, or 270 feet long. The nave was in height 170 palms, and the distance between the two massive pillars from which sprung the arch connecting it with the transept, was 48 palms; but between the colonnades on either side, that is to say, the width of the nave measured 106 palms. On each side of this nave were two aisles, making four aisles in all, besides the centre one, or the nave itself.

The two interior aisles, or those next the nave were each 38 palms wide and 82 in height; each of the exterior ones was 62 palms high and 39 palms wide, and the colonnades of the Corinthian order that separated the nave from the aisles, and the aisles from each other, consisted each of 22 pillars; those next the nave being 40 palms high, those between the aisles only 26.

The basilica founded under the circumstances described in the text, remained until the construction of Saint Peter's of the present day rendered its removal indispensable. For the authorities, and for a description of the Constantine Basilica, consult Erasmo Pistolesi. Il Vatican. Descr. Ed. Illustr. vol. 1. p. 39-40.

In front of the basilica, was an atrium—called the paradisus—of quadrangular shape and enclosed by four porticos: that one next the basilica, consisting of 46 columns, was long as the basilica was wide—that is, it was 285 palms in length, in width 50 palms, and in height 59. It served as a vestibule to the basilica, into which you entered by three lofty portals, one on the right, one on the left, and one in the centre, which last mentioned portal was the greatest of the three. But as for the two lateral porticos of the rectangular atrium, each of them was 250 palms long and 40 broad; the fourth side, in the centre of which were the gates of ingress to the atrium or court, was necessarily equal in length to the corresponding side forming the vestibule of the temple, but it was only 40 palms wide, and 55 palms in height. In the very middle of this atrium —called the paradise—there was a great fountain embellished with symbolical ornaments, such as the Agnus Dei, the cross, palm branches, winged cherubims, and flowers in marble and in mosaic. The tazza or basin of this fountain was surrounded by a colonnade of porphyry; out of its centre there seemed to grow a stately pine of bronze which had formerly served to embower the idol-image of Cybele, in a recess of the Pantheon. Under the umbrage of its spreading arms, the limpid waters poured out by gilded dolphins now served to cool and refresh the Christian pilgrim—reminding him, withal, of the purity and calmness of spirit required in the worshippers of Him, before whom "nothing that is impure can enter, and at the threshold of whose great sanctuary he was at length arrived."*

From this fountain smaller ones, placed all round the atrium in the porticos for the purification of those who entered the temple, were kept perennially supplied; and besides the great fountain for the pilgrims, there was another called by the people Sabatina. This fountain was nearer than the other to the seventy-five steps of marble, each two hundred palms long, which formed the ascent to the platform before the vestibule—which platform, also of marble, was two hundred palms by seventy-six in depth, towards the vestibule of the basilica. This vestibule itself was covered with gilded tiles, and the façade, or front elevation of the basilica, rising above it had the apex of its pediment surmounted by a cross, from which golden rays, as it were of glory, darted out on every side; and under the architecture and between the windows, of which there were two tiers of an arched shape, all the spaces were decorated with figures and groups in fresco or mosaic, representing the Apostles in various attitudes

* St. Paulinus, who saw this atrium, while one may say it was still new, speaks of it as follows: "Vel quâ sub eadem mole tectorum geminis utrinque porticibus latera diffundit: quâve protento nitens atrio, fusa vestibulo est, ubi cantharum ministra manibus et oribus nostris fluenta ructantem fastigiatus solido ære tholus ornat et inumbrat, *non sine mystica specie*."—Ad Alethium, Ep. xxxi.

of adoration—our Lord being depicted on high—Saint Paul on his left hand with the sword of the word of God, and, on his right hand, Saint Peter with the keys of the kingdom of Heaven.*

The rapidity with which this sacred edifice sprung up from among the ruins of the Neronian circus and of the temple of Apollo, from the materials of which it was almost entirely constructed, is scarcely credible: for the genius of Constantine, as impetuous and impatient of delay, as it was brilliant and decisive in action, could not brook the ordinary routine of art; but in his architectural enterprises, as in his campaigns, bringing the immense resources at his command to bear upon the point of interest, caused not only temples but cities to rise, as if by magic. Hence there was about the basilicas of the Apostles and martyrs of his erection, all the air of trophies thrown up on a field of battle, suddenly, and under the impulse of an enthusiasm, too tumultuous to be heedful of precision, and only eager to signalize and

* See "Il Vaticano Descritto ed Illustrato da Erasmo Pistolesi," ubi supra.

The great fountain described above was either added altogether, or newly ornamented by Pope Symmachus, about the year 500, according to an ancient MS. cited by Pistolesi. The pine which stands at present in the Vatican garden of the Belvedere is thus alluded to by Dante, in describing a giant—

"La faccia sua mi parea lunga e grossa
Come la pine di san Pietro a Roma."

Canto xxxi. del. Infer.

So that it was still overshading the fountain when Dante was at the Jubilee of the year 1300.

commemorate the triumph. They were on this account the more appropriate; and what they wanted in artistic correctness and elaboration of detail was eclipsed in one universal blaze of splendour; was forgotten in delight and wonder at the gorgeous effect produced by the brilliant colouring and barbaric gold, with which every object shone resplendent, from the mosaic pavement to the capitals of the columns and burnished ceilings.*

Objects of the most divine and touching import saluted the gaze to whatever side the spectator turned. Here was the scene of the Nativity, with the Virgin Mother, the divine Infant reposing on her bosom, and the angelic choirs proclaiming in hymns of celestial melody "the peace of good-will to men:" there the baptism in the Jordan or the eucharistic supper: then the Saviour restoring sight to the blind, curing the paralytic, calling Lazarus from the tomb, or feeding the five thousand in the wilderness—the multitude seated around upon the grass—with every minute detail of the Gospel narrative depicted to the life. In another part, the transfiguration on Mount Tabor, the crucifixion of Christ, his burial, his resurrection, his ascension into heaven,

* That such was its effect on Saint Paulinus, who beheld it not very many years after its erection, we may conjecture, from what he says in his letter to Alethius—"Quanto ipsum apostolum attolebas gaudio, cum totam ejus basilicam densis inopûm cœtibus stipatus es, vel quâ sub alto sui culminis, mediis ampla laquearibus longum patet, et Apostolico eminus solio coruscans ingredientium lumina stringit, et corda lætificat."—Ep. xxxi.

the descent of the Holy Ghost in tongues of fire on the day of Pentecost were represented.

But what most of all arrested the eyes, and caused them to overflow with tears, welling up from a contrite heart, were the stages of the Saviour's passion; for with such vividness and pathos had the painter represented the "Man of Sorrows," from his bitter agony in the garden, until his expiring upon the cross, that the most obdurate beholder could not but be moved to sympathy and repentance.*

But though all parts of the temple shone with resplendent beauty, it was the sanctuary—called the *presbyterium*—that attracted the eye in a pre-eminent degree, not only by its elevation above the other parts of the temple, but by the admirable light which illumined it, and by the sacred emblems and decorations of gold, and silver, and precious stones, that glittered on the lamps, coronas, candalabrums, shields, and various other ornaments round the altar, as well as upon the sacred vessels, the books of the gospels and liturgy and upon every thing in a word connected with the divine mysteries which were celebrated there.

The Emperor caused a shrine for the relics of Saint Peter to be fabricated of Cyprian bronze. This was overshadowed by a baldachino or canopy of silver supported by pillars, some of porphyry, others of a costly marble, called tresthynian by the Greeks. The cross placed on the sarcophagus or shrine,

* See Ep. of St Greg. II to Leo the Isaurian, ap. Baron. An. 725.

which served for the great altar, was of the purest gold and of one hundred and fifty pounds' weight. At foot, this cross bore an inscription, in diminutive characters of a brilliant jet black, stating that Constantine Augustus and the Empress Helena, his mother, had caused that basilica to be made refulgent, and had embellished it with regal splendour. The absis or tribune—the presbytery where the apostolic throne was placed—being entirely burnished with vermilion and gold, most strictly verified the inscription. The four candelabrums, two on each side of the altar, were of bronze, ornamented with medallions and relievi in silver, representing the Acts of the Apostles. Each candelabrum weighed three hundred pounds, and was supported upon ten claws. They also made an offering to the altar of three golden chalices, each weighing ten pounds, and set with fifty emeralds each, besides two silver vases (for wine of sacrifice), each of two hundred pounds weight; twenty chalices of silver, each of ten pounds weight, with other sacred vessels and patenas, some of silver, others of the purest massive gold—one in particular being adorned with emeralds and various precious stones, to the number of two hundred and fifteen. The golden lamp which they hung before the shrine weighed thirty-five pounds: it had fifty lights, each light issuing as it were from a dolphin's mouth. The lustre or pharos of the chancel was of the same form, but of silver, and to the right and left of the basilica were sixty other silver lamps, each with its dolphin lights, but of only eight pounds weight. The censer or thurible weighed fifteen pounds, and was all over gold and diamonds. In the altar itself was nothing but silver and gold, to the weight of three hundred and fifty pounds It was inlaid and thickly studded with precious pearls and emeralds. After enumerating these and many other offerings, the writer in Anastasius proceeds to mention the various estates situated chiefly in Egypt and the east, the gifts of the emperor and empress-mother for the support of the divine worship, in this basilica of Saint Peter. Let it suffice to say, that, on a moderate calculation, the gross amount of their gifts may be set down as £78,227, per annum.

Besides the Lateran and Saint Peter's, the basilicas of Saint Paul and of Saint Lawrence, both outside the walls, were built by Constantine: also the basilica of the Holy Cross in Jerusalem, so entitled because it was "built to receive a portion of the cross of our Lord Jesus Christ." Like the Lateran, it was connected with an ancient palace: it is called by Anastasius, "basilica in palatio Sessoriano." At the prayer of his daughter Constantia, the emperor also erected the basilica of the holy martyr Saint Agnes, beyond the walls, on the road to Nomentum. There is mention of two other churches of this same epoch, one a title, that is, a parochial church, called *titulus Equitii*, from the name of the priest who gave the ground on which it was built; the other was outside the walls, at the third stone on the Via Lavicana, the basilica of the holy martyrs Marcellinus and Peter, called *inter duas lauros.* There, was the mausoleum where Helena, the saintly mother of Constantine the Great, was interred. It exists to the present day.

These, with many others, no doubt, not mentioned in Anastasius, were all built during the pontificate of Sylvester I, from the year 314 to 336. Here we have the first nucleus of the Rome of the Popes.

The next Pope, Marcus,* built two basilicas, one of S. Balbina, on the *Via Ardeatina,* where he was himself interred; the other in Rome, at the foot of the Palatine hill.

Two basilicas and three cemeteries are set down to Pope Julius I.† Of the former, one was near the Forum, the other on the *Via Flaminia*—probably the church of the holy martyr Valentine, which was not far from the Milvian bridge. The cemeteries, churches and oratories built in, or over the ancient catacombs, were on three of the greatest highways, the *Via Flaminia,* the *Via Aurelia,* and the *Via Portuensi.*

No mention of any building under Liberius.‡ The Arian persecution was, at that time, at its height. "Persecutio magna, ita ut clerici et sacerdotes neque in ecclesias, neque in balnea haberent introitum."§

A basilica was built by Pope Felix I,‖ on the *Via Aurelia,* a mile from the gate of San Pancrazio.

* An. 336.

† An. 336 to 352.

‡ An. 352 to 355.

§ Anastasius Biblioth. in vit. Liberii.

‖ An. 355 to 367.

Two basilicas are assigned to Pope Damasus,* one to Saint Laurence, *juxta theatrum*, hence called San Lorenzo *in Damaso;* the other on the *Via Ardeatina,* where this holy Pontiff's body was interred. He also erected a species of mausoleum called a *Platonia,* over the place where the bodies of the Apostles Peter and Paul had been deposited for some time.

No mention of building under Pope Siricius.† His immediate successor, Pope Anastasius,‡ erected a basilica in the second region of the city, in *Via Mamertina,* not far from the Capitol—perhaps San Pietro in carcere. At the time Anastasius wrote, this church was called the *basilica Crescentiana.*

Under Pope Innocent I,§ the church of Saints Gervasus and Protasius was built. It was during this pontificate the taking of the imperial city for the first time occurred, when it was totally sacked and partially destroyed by Alaric, and his Arian Goths. Before we follow the Pontiffs in the labour of constructing the Christian city, let us pause to observe the fate of what they had already erected during this visitation, the most terrific, perhaps, as it was the first in that tremendous series of calamities which ended as we have endeavoured to describe in the opening of the present chapter—that is, in the utter overthrow and depopulation of the Pagan city.

* An. 367 to 385.
† An. 385 to 398.
‡ An. 398 to 402.
§ An. 402 to 417.

CHAPTER II.

"SEEK not, servant of heaven," cried Alaric to the hermit, by whom he was met when on his march through the narrow passes of the Apennines, the *saxa incisa*, "seek not to turn me from my mission. It is not from choice I lead my army against that devoted place. Some invisible power, that will not suffer me to halt a single day, urges me on with violence, crying out to me without ceasing: Forward! March against that city, against Rome, and make it desolate!"* Such was the spirit in which Alaric marched to the assault which ended as we next proceed to describe, passing over the various incidents of the siege.

"At the hour of midnight," says Gibbon, "the Salarian gate was silently opened, and the Romans were suddenly awakened by the tremendous sound of the Gothic trumpet." Thus was the mystical Babylon, like its prophetic type the city of Belshazzar, surprised in the midst of its security. "It was by night," says St. Jerome, "that Moab fell: its wall was laid prostrate by night."† For although be-

* Socrat. His. Eccl. lib. VII. c. 10.

† "Nocte Moab capta est, nocte cecidit murus ejus." S. Hieron. ad Princip. op. tom. 1. p. 121.

leaguered by the barbarians, (with whose presence they had become familiarised by the two preceding sieges, which were raised by the payment of enormous subsidies) the Romans had such confidence in their lofty, rock-built walls, and in the legionaries by whom they were defended, that, like the Babylonians, when *their* city was on the point of falling into the hands of their enemies the Persians, the denizens of the Eternal City continued to revel, and then retired to their beds, apparently without the shadow of apprehension of the terrible fate impending over them. Procopius says the senators were fast asleep as the Goths were entering the gate.*

"The cruelties which were exercised on this occasion," says the Italian annalist, "one cannot relate without shedding tears." The city, constructed as it were from the spoils, and overflowing with the tributes of so many vanquished nations, was now at the mercy of the barbarians, infuriated as they were by the wildest passions. They were lighted on their way of slaughter by flaming palaces and temples, from the villa of Sallust—a perfect sanctuary and garden of Epicurus—on to the Suburra, the Forum, the Capitol, and above all to the golden house of Nero, which crowned the imperial mount. In the pursuit of plunder, and of the most obnoxious blood, they were guided by the forty thousand fugitive slaves, who laboured during that night of horrors with more assiduity than ever they had exerted

* De Bel. Vandal. lib. ii. c. 2.

under their taskmasters' stripes, to requite the offices they had received at Roman hands, and to wash out the hateful vestiges of their chains and slavery in the gore of their former taskmasters and tyrants. The things not to be uttered which Rome had so often perpetrated during the sieges, and massacres, and burnings of a thousand years were now retaliated rigorously and with usury upon herself. Her nobles were submitted to tortures the most cruel and ignominious, in order to wring from them the confession of where lay their hidden treasures.* The plebeian masses were mowed down in such multitudes, that the survivors, it was said, did not suffice to inter the slain. The Forum, the Circus Maximus and the Coliseum, the Capitol and the Palatine, with all the other seven hills: the streets, the theatres, the baths, the temples ran foaming with Roman gore: the palace halls and chambers were the scenes of every unutterable outrage. The seven-hilled city was in flames. The trophies and monuments, in which the lords of the earth most prided themselves, were the chief objects of Gothic fury:† and it was said by eye-witnesses of these terror-scenes that the trophies, temples, and other public edifices, which defied by their solidity the brands of the barbarians, were struck, and levelled to the earth, by thunderbolts from heaven.‡

* Socrat. ubi supra.

† Multa insignia monumenta spectatu dignissima, &c. ib.

‡ Orosius. lib. ii c. 19.

But the Almighty, in punishing with chastisement so terrible the obstinate remains of paganism in Rome, caused his mercy to shine forth at the same time with his justice. It was proclaimed by the King of the Goths that he warred not against Saint Peter; he ordered the churches, and places consecrated to Christian purposes, to be respected; appointed the two great basilicas of the Apostles Saint Peter and Saint Paul as inviolable sanctuaries of refuge: and, so strictly was this order observed, that the barbarians not only halted in the career of slaughter, on arriving at their hallowed precincts, but many of them conducted thither such as had moved them to pity, in order that under the protection of the Apostles, they might be saved from the rage of others, who might not be found equally inclined to compassion.*

"It happened," says Orosius, "as the barbarians were rushing in every direction through the city in quest of plunder, that a sacred virgin, who had grown old in the divine service to which she had consecrated her entire being, was discovered in her convent by a Gothic chieftain, who demanded all the gold and silver in her possession. She replied with Christian composure that the treasures in her keeping were, indeed, immense; but while the Goth stood in admiration and astonishment, gazing at the splendid hoard of massy gold and silver vessels

* S. August. de Civit. Dei, l. ii. c. 1—7.

which she revealed to his view, the virgin of Christ observed:—'Before you are the sacred vessels used in the divine mysteries at the altar of St. Peter the Apostle; presume to touch them if you be so minded; but, upon your own head, be the consequences of your sacrilege. As for me, too feeble to defend them, I shall not vainly attempt resistance.'

"Struck with reverence and religious awe, and not a little moved by the holy enthusiasm of the nun, the Gothic chieftain, without attempting to lay hands upon the sacred treasure, sent intelligence of what had happened to King Alaric. An instant and peremptory order was returned to have all the vessels promptly conveyed, just as they were, to the basilicas of the Apostle, and to guard and protect the nun and all other Christians joining in the procession for carrying them thither.

"The convent was situated on the Cœlian Mount (probably near the Lateran), so that the entire city was to be traversed in order to reach St. Peter's. It was then that an astounding spectacle presented itself to all. Through the greatest thoroughfares of the city, and amidst all the horrors of that night, a solemn train is seen advancing, with the same order and measured step as if it moved not through the scenes of slaughter, violence, and conflagration, but through hallowed aisles, and on some joyous festival of the Church. A martial retinue of the Goths marched as a guard of honour, to adorn the triumph with their glittering arms, and to defend their devout companions who bore the sacred vessels of massy gold and silver, aloft upon their heads. The voices of the barbarians are united with those of the Romans, to swell the hymns of Christian praise; and these sounds are heard like the trumpet of salvation, re-echoing far and wide amidst the sack and destruction of the city. The Christians start in their hiding places, as they recognize the celestial canticles, and crowd from every direction to follow the sacred vessels of St. Peter. Even multitudes of Pagans, (for as yet nearly all the higher classes were Pagans) joining loudly in the hymn of Christ, take part in the procession, and thus escape under the shadow of the sacred name, that they may live to assail it after the danger has passed, with greater violence than ever.* Joined by the fugitives from every side, the pageant seems interminable; and in proportion as it is lengthened by new accessions, the barbarians vie with each other for the privilege of marching as guards on either side of it, armed with their battle-axes and naked swords."

Thus it was that heaven displayed its power to conduct the objects of its solicitude, through the very midst of despair and death to a harbour of safety:

* This is in allusion to the vehement outcry against Christianity by the Pagans, after the departure of the Goths. They upbraided the Christian religion as the origin of all the calamities of the Roman world, and it was in refutation of this insane fanaticism that St. Augustine wrote his great work, De Civitate Dei, and Orosius, his history.

the city was, as it were, sifted of the Christians, that still remained in it by means of this procession. In the very crisis of ruin, they were separated and saved from common havoc, as if by the intervention of angels. But the most astounding feature of the miracle was the suddenness with which the Goths were soothed and won to such effusion of zeal and religious enthusiasm, in the very crisis of their fury. They abandoned the pursuit of plunder, and wielded their blood-stained weapons to protect the lives and treasures of their vanquished enemies. This may appear to be a thing incredible, but attested as it is in the most circumstantial manner, and in the face of the Pagans, by such authorities as St. Augustine and Orosius, it cannot be, and is not doubted; nor will any one, indeed, who is well versed in the history of the middle ages be in the least degree startled at a transition so incongruous, from paroxysms of blood-thirsty rage to outpourings of piety. Such is one of the characteristics of the barbarian nature, which it required many centuries, and all the skill and constancy of the Christian religion, to steady and reclaim.

This single scene from the great tragedy of Rome's destruction, we have been chiefly induced to lay before the reader, in order to make that intelligible which might otherwise appear a mystery, *viz.* —how it could have happened that the Christian community in Rome, and their sacred structures were not involved in one common ruin with the city of which they formed a part. Here we have the detailed account of how it fared with both in the first attack—the Vandal Genzeric conceded to St. Leo the Great a similar exemption, when he took and plundered the city—the first act of Totila, after he became master of Rome was to hasten as a suppliant to the shrine of St. Peter. A portion of the walls, which Belisarius was assured by the Romans that St. Peter had taken under his special protection, remains from that day to this in precisely the same state—that is, in an apparently tottering condition, so that it goes by the name of the "muro-torto." The same writer, Procopius, who tells us this singular anecdote, mentions also with regard to St. Paul's and other Christian buildings beyond the walls, that they were most religiously respected by the Goths, in the various sieges under Vitiges and Totila, at the very time that they tore down the suburban villas, and broke up the ancient aqueducts which supplied the doomed city with water.* Thus it was that the strokes by which the pagan city was reduced to ruin, only served to disencumber the em-

* "Templum est Pauli apostoli, quod a mœnibus Romæ stadiis xiv. distat. Alluitur fluvio Tiberi, nullis septum operibus; quanquam, ab urbe pertinens ad templum hoc porticus, et vicina utrinque ædificia, faciles negant ad locum aditus. Porro, Gothi sacram hanc Pauli ædem apostoli, itemque alteram Apostoli Petri sic reverentur ut neutram toto belli tempore, ne minimum quidem, violarint; at sacerdotibus de more sacra illic omnia procurare licuerit."—*Procop. de Bel. Goth.* l. ii. c. 5.

bryo Rome of the Popes, and bring it out into the most impressive and significant light. We return to shew how its erection continued to progress.

Again returning to the Lives in Anastasius, we find the Pontiffs urging on the erection of the Christian city. Nine or ten years after the events we have been describing, Pope Zosimus* is constructing "many churches,"† also an oratory in the cemetery of St. Felicitas. Only one, the basilica *Juliæ* or *Juliani*, is set down to Pope Celestine.‡ The basilica of St. Mary, called the *Liberian* basilica, because founded in the time of Pope Liberius, was completed by Sixtus III.§ This Pontiff built, Saint Laurence, probably on the spot where the holy martyr suffered. This basilica was sometimes called San Lorenzo *in Formoso*, and sometimes *in Pane perna*. In the cemeteries of Calixtus, (San Sebastian's) he built a platonia, "wherein he inscribed the names of the Popes and martyrs."

It was in the reign of his successor, Pope Leo the Great,‖ by whom the city was saved from the rage

* A.D. 417—423.

† This is the first time the word *Ecclesia* is used in Anastasius to signify the material structure. Basilica was the usual designation used at this period; St. Patric, who flourished at this time introduced it into Ireland, Baslic and Domnough, *i. e.* Domnica, are the most ancient names for a church in Irish.

‡ A. D. 423—432.

§ A. D. 432—440.

‖ A. D. 440—461.

of Attila, that Rome was fallen upon by the Vandals and Moors, who were conducted by Genzeric to complete the work of plunder and destruction, in which the Goths had led the way. The Pope at the head of his clergy went forth to meet the barbarian, and succeeded in greatly mitigating his wrath—dissuading him from his resolve to utterly destroy the city, and exterminate the inhabitants. The destruction fell almost exclusively upon the pagan monuments; for besides carrying away all the idols of the Capitol, and the ornaments of the shrines and temples, the roofs of the latter were stripped of the gilded bronze with which they were covered. Genzeric also had promised to respect the Christian churches, but the Vandal was not so observant of his promise as Alaric had been, or his commands were not so faithfully obeyed. This however, is mere conjecture, collected from the following entry in the life of Saint Leo:—"He renewed all the silver vessels used in the divine ministrations throughout all the parishes, after the city was destroyed and sacked by the Vandals: he repaired Saint Peter's, adding to it an absis which he adorned: also Saint Paul's and the basilica of Constantine, another name for the Lateran. Two new churches were built by this Pontiff. Saint Stephen's, on the *Via Latina*, a mile outside the gate, and the church of Saint Cornelius, near the catacombs, on the Appian way. He appointed certain members of the clergy, with the title of

Cubicularii, "to keep constant watch and ward over the tombs of the Apostles."

"The decay of the city," says Gibbon, (speaking of the Rome of the Cæsars at this period),* "had gradually impaired the value of the public works. The Circus and theatres might still excite, but they seldom gratified the desires of the people: the temples were no longer inhabited by gods or men; the diminished crowds of the Romans were lost in the immense space of their baths and porticos, and the stately libraries and halls of justice became useless to an indolent generation. The monuments of consular or imperial greatness were no longer revered as the immortal glory of the Capitol; they were only esteemed as an inexhaustible mine of materials, cheaper and more convenient than the distant quarry. The fairest forms of architecture were rudely defaced for the sake of some paltry or pretended repairs."

The works of Pope Hilary,† were three oratories in the Baptistary of Constantine, of Saint John the Baptist, of Saint John the Evangelist, and of the Holy Cross, "all of silver and precious stones." A monastery, beside Saint Laurence beyond the walls: a bath and prætorium hard by Saint Stephen's: an oratory of Saint Stephen in the Lateran basilica, and two libraries, in the same place. He appointed officers to make the rounds of the churches appointed for the stations.

* A. D. 450. † A. D. 467.

Saint Stephen's in Monte Celio, Saint Andrew's, near the Liberian basilica, Saint Stephen's, near Saint Laurence, and the basilica of Saint Bibiana, beside the Licinian palace, are the works of Pope Simplicius.* Felix III erected the basilica of Saint Agapitus, near Saint Laurence. For Pope Gelasius, and Pope Anastasius, nothing is set down in the way of building, but there is this to the purpose, said of the former: "a lover of the clergy and of the poor, he endowed the churches. He liberated from danger and from famine, the Roman city."

Works of Pope Symmachus†—several oratories; a portico of four sides, round the great fountain of Saint Peter's, which he adorned with lambs, and crosses, and palm branches, in mosaic; vestries (called Episcopia) on the south and north sides of Saint Peter's: Saint Agatha's, on the *Via Aurelia;* San Pancratius; Saint Silvester and Martin, in Trojan's baths: the basilica of Saint Michael the Archangel; the oratory of Saints Cosmas and Damian; at Saint Laurence, an hospital for the poor.

In the times of Hormisdas,‡ there came a crown (regnum) set with gems from the King of the Franks, Clovis the Christian, a gift to the blessed Peter the Apostle, also many vessels in gold and silver came from Greece, besides books of the Gospels and other sacred objects, all of gold, and set with precious stones; also two candelabrums of

* A. D. 467. † A. D. 498—514. ‡ A. D 461—467.

silver, the offering of King Theodoric (the Goth) to Saint Peter. The cemetery of Saints Nereius and Achileius, *in Via Ardeatina*; the cemetery of Saint Felix, and the cemetery of Saint Priscilla, *in Via Salaria*, in which was the church of Saint Marcellus, were repaired and adorned by Pope John I. The basilica of Saints Cosmas and Damian, *in Via Sacra*, was built by Felix IV;* and that of Saint Saturninus, on the *Via Salara* by Pope Theodosius I. Under Bonifacius II, no building mentioned, but he is said to have provided better for the support of presbyters, deacons, subdeacons and *notaries*, from the inheritance of the Church which he recovered (de adeptis hereditatibus). He also saved his people from famine.

John II.† No building—only rich gifts and ornaments.

Agapitus.‡ No building. Under Pope Silverius the following was the state of the city. At that time all possessions (beyond the walls), whether private or public, or belonging to the churches were ravaged and laid waste by fire: the sword destroyed the people. War, famine, and pestilence came at once; nor were the churches or the bodies of the holy martyrs spared by the Goths. What is here set down to the account of the Goths, must be checked, however, by the statement of Procopius to the contrary, which we have already quoted. Within

* A. D. 523—526. † A. D. 531—535.

‡ A. D. 535—536.

the city (held against Vitiges by Belisarius) great was the famine; and only that wells were opened, water should have had its price (as in Jerusalem): for the besieging army had broken up the aqueducts that used to supply the city.

Under Pope Vigilius rich offerings were made by Belisarius from the spoils of the Vandals, from whom he wrested their African conquests. Thus the plunder carried off from the pagan temples by Genzeric came back to adorn and enrich the Christian city. He offered to Saint Peter, by the hands of Vigilius the Pope, a cross of gold one hundred pounds weight, inlaid with precious jewels. Upon it were represented his victories. He also founded, in the *Via Lata*, an hospital for the poor and the afflicted—victims of so many and such terrible wars. Also in the *Via Flaminia*, near the city gardens, a monastery of Saint Juvenalis, which he enriched with many gifts and possessions.

As for the general aspect of the ancient or pagan city, amongst the ruins of which we see the Christian city slowly but steadily springing up, we learn from Procopius that the aqueducts had been broken, the thermæ, the amphitheatres, the theatres, had all been abandoned, and the admiration of the historian is confined to the tomb of Hadrian, to the infinite number of statues, the works of Phidias, Lysippus, and Miron, that adorned it, and to the solicitude with which the Romans preserved as much as possible the stable edifices of their city, and amongst other objects, the galley, in which, it was said, their Trojan ancestor Æneas had first explored the Tiber.

But even these few detached ornaments must have been much diminished, especially during the successive Gothic sieges. In defending the Mole of Hadrian—the modern and mediæval Castel Sant' Angelo—against the assaults of Vitiges, the Greek soldiers broke the Phidian statues that stood in close and beautiful array round its terraces, and hurled them down upon the heads of their assailants; and it may well be imagined that whatever came first to hand, or was most contiguous to the breach to be filled up, was seized and made use of without scruple, when the walls were hastily repaired by Belisarius, at the time that Vitiges was pouring down his forces to beleaguer the almost defenceless city. The same process must have been gone through, when he had in a great measure to rebuild them, before Totila came to besiege it, for the second time.

From an order sent by the Empress Theodora, commanding the Greek governor of the city to seize the person of the Pope (Vigilius)* and to have him dragged in chains to Constantinople, it appears that Saint Peter's was to be respected as an inviolable sanctuary, even when all reverence was cast aside with regard to the other churches. "*Except it be in* SAINT PETER'S, spare him not," wrote the Empress; for if in the Lateran, or in any other church,

* A.D. 540—555.

you can lay hands on Vigilius, place him on shipboard, and bring him hither before us; or, by Him who liveth for ever, I will have thee (Belisarius) excoriated alive!" "Nam si non feceris, per Viventem in sæcula, excoriari te faciam."*

Pope Pelagius†—we still quote from Anastasius:—"Amongst the clergy none could be found to take part in his promotion to the chair of Saint Peter, because the monasteries and the multitude of religious, and of the sapient nobles withdrew themselves from communion with him (thinking that he was a party to the barbarous outrages offered to Pope Vigilius, who died a martyr in exile.) But Pelagius, taking counsel with Narses (who had succeeded Belisarius in Italy, and resided in Rome), it was agreed that he should join the procession of the Litanies from San Pancratio to Saint Peter's, and when all were assembled there, Pelagius ascended the ambon, (the pulpit from which the Gospel used to be chanted and expounded to the faithful,) and lifting the cross of our Lord, and the Gospels, on high above his head, he gave satisfaction to all that he was innocent of the wrongs inflicted on the martyred Pontiff. This same Pelagius it was, at that time the Cardinal Archdeacon of Rome, who had

* Anast. Bibl. in. Vit. Vigilii. There are traits of resemblance, not a few, between this imperial lady, and another whose name was notoriously associated, in the year 1847, with certain attempts at Church reformation, in Munich.

† A.D. 555—559.

prevailed with Totila to put a stop to the slaughter, and to spare at least the lives of the sad remnant of the Roman people, who had taken refuge round the tomb of Saint Peter, before which, the Gothic conqueror, though an Arian, had come, as has been already mentioned, to offer up his vows.

This Pontiff* caused the gold and silver vessels and the vestments to be replaced through all the churches, and commenced the basilica of the Apostles Philip and James, which was finished by his successor, John III.

Of this latter Pope† it is said : "He loved the cemeteries of the martyrs, and caused them to be restored." We have seen how they were ravaged by the Goths during the almost incessant sieges, which, at length, left Rome a desert. We find the Romans urging him to assume the temporal dominion of the city, threatening rather to submit their necks to the yoke of the barbarians, than any longer endure the cruel tyranny and exactions of Narses. The eunuch, in his fury at finding himself so detested, and exasperated by the insulting terms in which Theodora wrote to rebuke him, withdrew from Rome, and invited the savage Lombards to invade and devastate the beautiful but devoted country, which he was bound in honour and duty to defend with his life. On his return from Naples, whither he followed Narses in order to appease his

* A.D. 555—559. † A.D. 559—573.

rage, and to dissuade him from his nefarious purpose, Pope John took up his abode in the catacombs of the holy martyrs Tiburtius and Valerian. There he dwelt for a long time, and there also he consecrated many bishops. This was during the first most terrible onslaught of the Lombards.

Pope Benedictus.* No building—the terror of the Lombard everywhere—direful famine—"fames *nimia*"—the fortresses everywhere given up by the Greeks to the invaders; yet such is the love for the churches, above all for that of Saint Peter, that, though in his times we find, superadded to those of invasion and famine, the scourge of inundations so awful, as to excite apprehensions of a second deluge, still the succeeding Pontiff, Pelagius II,† causes the "tomb of the blessed Peter the Apostle to be covered with lamina or slabs of silver richly gilt. In his days was such havoc as had never been in any former age. He converted his own house into a refuge for the aged and the poor. The cemetery of Saint Hermes, and the basilica of Saint Laurence (both ruined, no doubt, by the Lombards), he rebuilt from their foundations, and round where the body of Saint Laurence was reposed, he adorned with silver tablets." Here we find the working of that "vital spark" by which, as Gibbon says, the city, which must have otherwise been erased from the earth, was again restored to honour and dominion. It was

* A.D. 573—577. † A.D. 577—590.

such a flame of purest love of the divine glory, as that many waters of adversity could never extinguish it.

So much has been already said in a preceding chapter of the fortunes of the city under Saint Gregory the Great, and the Popes his immediate successors, that, in order not too much to fatigue the reader, we shall hurry forward to the times, in which the Rome of the Pontiffs is beheld emerging in all its splendours from the clouds of unparalleled dangers and disasters through which, as we have seen, it had to struggle from its origin. We feel the less scruple about this omission, because all the churches erected in the interval between Gregory the Great and Hadrian I, will come under notice in that half century,* during which, the latter and Pope Leo III continued to labour in carrying the city to the highest pitch of perfection, and in exhausting in its adornment the resources of art and opulence to such an astonishing extent, as to more than place them on a par with those among the Cæsars, who did most for the defence and beautifying of the pagan city.

The first care of Pope Hadrian† was to complete the city walls and gates, in order to protect the inhabitants and the churches against the Lombards, whose fury had become exasperated to the last degree by the failure of those assaults to which they

* A.D. 604—774. † A.D. 772—795.

had continually returned, with invasion after invasion, and siege after siege, during a lapse of more than two hundred years.

How, except by miracle, Saint Gregory the Great and other Popes were able to prevent them from seizing a prey for which they yearned more than for any other, it seems difficult to conceive, while the walls remained in the condition to which so many sieges and efforts for their overthrow had reduced them. As for the Byzantine emperors, and their minions the exarchs of Ravenna, they had no solicitude about Rome, except to strip it of as much plunder as they could;* hence we find the care of rebuilding its defences, as well as the government and maintenance of the city, devolved on the Popes.

A short breathing-time from the attacks of the Lombards had been seized on by Pope Sisinius, in the year 708, to prepare materials for the mighty undertaking—"he being actuated," says the writer in Anastasius, "with solicitude for the preservation of the inhabitants of this city." The foundation of the new walls was laid by Pope Gregory II, the work was urged forward by the succeeding Popes, chiefly by Gregory III, up to the accession of Hadrian, who, bringing together a vast number of masons and people of all sorts, from the cities and towns on both sides of the Apennines, introduced such a spirit of order and emulation amongst the

* Constantine Copronymos is said to have done more in twelve days to ruin and plunder Rome, than all the barbarians together. See Hobhouse, Illustrations of the Fourth Canto, &c.

builders, all of whom he amply paid and provided for, that he had the consolation to see this immense ring-wall completed, in such fashion as is thus described by some Christian pilgrim, probably Count Eginhard, who visited Rome in the retinue of Charlemagne, in the year of our Lord 800.

"From Saint Peter's gate," he says, "that gate itself included, there are to the Flaminian gate (near the present *Porto dèl Popolo*), towers 16, bastions 782, posterns 2, loopholes—large, 107, small 66. From the Flaminian gate, the gate itself included, there are to the Pincian gate, closed up, towers 28, bastions 644, greater loop-holes 75, lesser 117. From the Pincian, closed up, the gate itself included, there are to the Salarian gate, towers 22, bastions 246, greater loops 200, lesser 160. From the Salarian, counting the gate itself, there are to the Numentan gate, towers 10, bastions 118, loops, greater 200, lesser 65. From the Numentana, the gate itself being counted, there are to the Tibur gate, towers 57, bastions 806, greater loop-holes, 214, lesser 200. From the gate of Tibur, the gate towers included, there are to the Porta Prænestina, towers 18, bastions 302, greater loop-holes 80, lesser 108. From the Prænestina to the Porta Asinaria (now the Lateran) there are towers, that of the Prænestina gate included, 26, bastions 504, greater loops 180, lesser 150. From the Asinarian to the Metrovian gate, towers 20, bastions 342, loops, greater 130, lesser 180. From the Metrovian to the Latin gate, towers 20, bastions 293, loops, larger 100, lesser 183. From the Latin to the Appian, towers 12, bastions 174, larger loops 80, lesser 85. From the Appian to the Ostian, towers 49, bastions 615, larger loops 330, lesser 284. From the Ostian gate to the Tiber, towers 35, bastions 733, loops, larger 138, lesser 211. From the Tiber (right bank) to the Portuensan gate, (now Porta Portese), towers 4, bastions 60, larger loops, 10, lesser 15. From the Porta Portese to the Porta Aurelia (now San Pancrazio on the ridge of the Janiculum) back again to the Tiber, towers 24, bastions 327, loops, larger 160, lesser 131. From the Tiber (right bank, that is in *Trastevere*) to the Porta Sancti Patri (the point of departure), towers 8, bastions 488, loopholes, larger 21, lesser 7, postern gates 2. Gate of Saint Peter, *in Hadriano,* towers 6, bastions 164, loops, larger 14, lesser 19. The sum of all the towers, 383, of the bastions, 7020, posterns, 6, loopholes of larger size, 2066."

Which of the Cæsars could boast of a work greater than this—the walls of Rome, rebuilt on the foundations of a circuit to which they never attained in Pagan times? If you begin at the Flaminian gate, and accompany the pilgrim round by the Pincian, Salarian, Nomentan, and so on by the Ostian gate to the left bank of the Tiber; and then, from beyond the Tiber, ascend by the wall as he describes it, up to the old Acropolis on the Janiculum, the present San Pietro in Montorio—and thence descend the steep declivity to the Tiber again, you will have made the round of the walls of Aurelian, who gave to the Pagan circuit its greatest extent.* He, however, only pushed forward the pomerium, according to ancient usage, in certain

* The gates of the Aurelian wall, were:—

1. P. Aurelia, mentioned by Procopius, corresponded with the modern Porta San Pancrazio.
2. P. Triumphalis.
3. P. Flaminia (Porta del Popolo).
4. P. Pinciana (shut up).
5. P. Salaia (Porta Salara).
6. P. Nomentana (Porta Pia).
7. P. Viminalis (at one angle of the camp of the Pretorians).
8. P. Gabiusa (at the other end of the camp).
9. P. Inter Ageres (near the same place).
10. P. Æsquilina (P. Maggiore).
11. P. Prænestina (P. San Lorenzo).
12. P. Cælimontana (closed up).
13. P. Asinaria (P. di San Giovanni).
14. P. Nevia (closed up).
15. P. Latina (closed up).
16. P. Capena (P. San di Sebastiano).
17. P. Ostiensis (P. di San Paulo).
18. P. Portuensis (P. Portese).
19. P. Janiculensis (near San Pietro in Montorio).
20. P. Septimania (in the Longara).

From the bridge close by this gate (within), the wall ran along the left of the Tiber, to the P. Flaminia. The right bank was unprotected by a wall, until the wall, to enclose St. Peter's, commenced by Leo III, was finally completed, according very nearly to the present circuit, by Leo IV. Nardini, Roma Antica, l. i. c. 10.

localities, but he did not rebuild the walls throughout their entire extent, like the Popes. Moreover, all that region beyond Tiber, from where the wall of Aurelian, running down the side of the Janiculum, touched the river brink, round to the gate of Saint Peter, and the mausoleum of Hadrian, was an addition to the ancient circuit. This part was defended by fifteen great towers, and 652 bastions—a proof of its being of considerable extent.

Before we enter the memorable scene encompassed by this majestic rampart, with its bastions, gates, loop-holes, and towers, there are outside (especially along the chief approaches), some objects to excite not only attention but wonder. They must have imparted an air of grandeur and solemnity to this primitive city of the Pontiffs, which belonged not to the city of the emperors itself, even in its palmiest days. These were the basilicas, churches, and oratories of the martyrs, replacing the tombs and mausoleums which formerly studded the highways on either side as they approached the gates; and still more striking and characteristic of the Papal city, the lofty and apparently interminable porticos by which Pope Hadrian had connected the three great basilicas and places of pilgrimage, *viz.* Saint Laurence, Saint Paul's, and Saint Peter's, with the gates of the city—from which, the two former were considerably more than a mile distant.

This he did in order that the pious multitudes, in resorting thither in fulfilment of their vows, might not suffer from the rains of the winter, or, in summer-time, from the scorching sun. The biographer has recorded the motive: "considering how he could best consult for the safety of the multitudes of people who came that way, and were liable to be crushed and injured by reason of the straightness of the colonnade through which they had to pass to Saint Peter's, this far-sighted sage," (Pope Hadrian) "determined to construct a colonnade, lofty, and so large, as to admit the throng of worshippers, with ease and safety." Some idea may be formed of this gigantic undertaking, from the fact recorded by the same contemporary biographer, that for the substructures on the river side for supporting the first arches of the colonnade, no less than 12,000 huge blocks of travertine stone were required. From what is said of that one which led to Saint Paul's, which, as well as the basilica of Saint Laurence, was more than a mile from the gates, it would appear that these colonnades were consecrated and adorned with chapels and oratories, at different stations. As beheld amidst the cypress-crowned heights, the monuments and ruins of past ages, the groves, vineyards, gardens, and all that splendid gala of the most florid bloom and verdure, with which the environs, under a protracted peace, must have become invested, these three greatest sanctuaries of the Christian nations—connected as they were by these immense colonnades of marble pillars, with the tower-crowned walls of the city—the mausoleums of the saints and martyrs springing up along all the highways, but in greatest number along the Appian, Aurelian, Nomentan, and Salarian roads—together with the concourse in which the Roman, the barbarian, and the Greek were mingled: in which the humbled Frank, the penitent Lombard, the Vandal and the Goth were hastening, no longer to fill the city with sack and slaughter, but to weep and supplicate there for forgiveness, or to lose themselves in heavenly reveries beside its shrines and sepulchres—all this was fraught with such fascination for the eye and the imagination, and was so suggestive to memory of contrasts so sublime and stirring, that the like never could have arisen from beholding the approaches to the Pagan city, even in its days of greatest magnificence.

It is not one but two cities, though harmonizing, still singularly contrasting with one another, we are to look for, within the ring-wall itself. In proportion as the city of the seven hills and of the Cæsars is disappearing under the strokes of time and violence, reverting in fact to the wilderness once more, the city of the Popes is seen arising from among the ruins, in Christian majesty, and arraying itself with a barbaric profusion of embellishment, of variegated marbles, mosaics, silver, gold, and the most brilliant jewelry.

At the second siege of Rome by Totila, there

was so much cultivated land within the walls that Diogenes the Greek governor thought the corn he had sown would be sufficient to supply the garrison and citizens in a protracted defence.* "The contiguity of the immense ancient fabrics, when once in decay," continues the same writer, "must have been dangerous during earthquakes, which might shake them down. (Here was one reason why the ancient site was abandoned.) The water might be confined in inundations, and prevented from retiring by the walls of buildings as large as provinces. Within little more than a century no less than five of these floods of the most destructive character are recorded. (Another cogent reason for forsaking the ancient site.) Such open spots as were decorated by single monuments were likely to be overwhelmed by the deposit left by the water and collected round those monuments. On this account the Forums, and even the Palatine, although an eminence, being crowded with structures appears to have been buried deeper than the other quarters under the deposit of the river, and the materials of the crumbling edifices." The consequence was that the ancient site became to a great extent abandoned. The city in a great measure shifted its ground: but, withal, throughout the entire extent of the enclosure, the basilicas and shrines of the saints, the cloistral

* Procop. de bello Gothico. l. 3. c. 36, quoted by Hobhouse, Hist. Illustrations, &c. p. 105.

abodes of those who entoned, by night and by day, the divine praises, and ministered at the altars, were interspersed with the trophies, temples, palaces, and other proud vestiges of the past, fast lapsing into decay, overgrown with rank grass and weeds, or garlanded with shrubs and wild flowers. Monasteries have sprung up among the baths and theatres, the basilicas of the Apostles and martyrs stand erect upon the arenas where those heroes of the cross were subjected to so many torments; the palace halls of the patricians and of the Cæsars are converted into places of refuge and of solace for the orphan, the helpless, and the afflicted; and instead of the cruel fasces and the axe, or the rapacious eagle, it is the standard of redemption and peace which is seen at the head of the processions, which move so frequently across the *Campus Martius* and the *Forum*, or along the *Via Sacra*, under the triumphal arches, and which as they wind onwards, make the valleys and the seven hills re-echo with the praises of the soldiers and martyrs of the cross.*

Instead of attempting any systematic description of the interior of Rome, we submit one to the reader which was drawn up about the period of which we are treating, it is thought, most pro-

* Charlemagne and Alcuin on the grandeur of Rome. The latter writes to Charlemagne: "sed de hoc quidem mihi improperare voluistis, me fumo sordentis Turonorum tecta, auratis Romanorum arcibus preponere." Ap. Baron. an. 800. n. i. p. 596.

bably, by Count Eginhard, the favourite secretary of Charlemagne, who, as we shall have occasion to see in the next book, not only visited Rome, but continued to sojourn there during the greater part of the year of our Lord 800.

CHAPTER III.

In the Vetera Analecta of Mabillon, who was the first to bring to light this most curious relic of the Carlovingian era, the account which is given of it is as follows. It was met with in the library of Einsidlen by the learned monk during one of those exploring expeditions which the Benedictines of Saint Maur were accustomed to make through ancient libraries, whether belonging to cities or monasteries, during the seventeenth century. He judged it to be of about the year 800. The first pages of the old MS. Codex, in which it was found, were taken up with certain notes or abbreviated remarks, attributed to Julius Cæsar, with an interpretation of the same appended: next followed a collection of eighty Roman inscriptions, and then the Descriptio Regionum Urbis, as it is called; though it does not at all adhere to the ancient division of the regions.

The fourteen regions of the ancient city of the Cæsars, were, according to Nardini, distributed thus:

1st Region, beyond the Porta San Sabastiano, for the most part, but a small portion of it was within the gate, called by Rufus and by Publius Victor, *Regio Prima, Porta Capena.*

2nd. Cœlimontana, perche stà quasi tutta sul

celio. Rufus. *Regio Cœlimontium*, on the Cœlian Mount.

3rd. South division of the Esquiline.

4th. Detta *Via Sacra*, overo *Templum Pacis*. It began where the third ended, presso il Giardino de' Pii.

5th. Detta Esquilina. It included the Viminal as well as the Equiline, is called by Rufus *Exquilina cum colle Viminali.* Joined the fourth at the Suburra.

6th. Detta *Alta Semita*, on the Quirinal.

7th. *Via Lata*, the modern Corso to the Piazza Colonna.

8th. *Forum Romanum*, la più illustre di tutti.

9th. *Circus Flaminius*, from the Pantheon towards the Isle of the Tiber.

10th. *Palatium*, included the Palatine mount.

11th. *Circus Maximus.*

12th. *Piscina Publica.* Il piano tra il circo massimo, e le terme Antoniane (Caracalla), between the Aventine, the Tiber, and the walls.

13th. *Aventinus*, included the Aventine mount.

14th. *Transtyberina.* Trastevere and the Vatican.*

It will be manifest to the reader that no such order as the foregoing is adhered to by our anonymous pilgrim, whom we now propose to accompany, step by step, in his excursions through the city, such as Pope Hadrian left it. There are several breaks and

* Roma Antica, l. 3. 27.

abbreviations in the jottings of the pilgrim, which we shall notice or fill up, wherever it is possible to do so, as we proceed.

A portâ Sci. Petri usque ad . . . . In D . . . . thus the MS. begins. Then, it is from the gate of Saint Peter we start, in this first excursion; but to what point our steps are directed we cannot determine—there is a break instead of the name in the MS. *usque ad . . . .* We move along however from St. Peter's towards the Tiber—that is certain—passing under the new colonnade all the way to the bridge; whether the ancient triumphal bridge, long since destroyed, or one opposite the mausoleum of Hadrian, the present Ponte Sant Angelo, we can only conjecture. *Circus Flaminius*—we have crossed the Tiber and the greater part of the Campus Martius, somewhat in the direction of the modern Strada Giulia; for here we are, the Circus Flaminius on our right, on our left the Pantheon, pointed to by our pilgrim as the—*Rotunda.* We come next to towering and extensive ruins; he calls them the *thermæ Commodianæ*, but the baths of Commodus are put down by Rufus in the first region, mostly outside, and, altogether, in the neighbourhood of the Capenian gate; whereas, we are still somewhere between the isle of the Tiber and the Capitol; for the next place we come to is—*Forum Trajani et Columna ejus.* The next word which drops from our guide is—*Tiberis;* but it is not easy to say whether it refers to the river itself, which is not likely, we were so far from it only this moment in "the Forum of Trajan and beside his column"—or to some statue, probably of a fountain adorned with an effigy of the river-god. *Arcus*—we next pass, either close to, or under an ancient triumphal arch, and find ourselves at the church of Saint Hadrian, which stood close to that of Saints Sergius and Bacchus—*ubi umbilicum Romæ*, which was the central point of Rome. Next we come to Saint Cyriacus. This ancient church which has for ages ceased to exist, is said by Cardinal Baronius to have been in the Via Lata—whether in the street, or only in the region of that name, he does not say. The Cardinal adds that it was the fifth station. It was called S. Cyrici *in thermis*. It was one of the ancient titular churches, and had close beside it a convent of nuns. There is mention made of it in the second Roman Synod under Pope Symmachus, and in the register of Saint Gregory the Great, l. 9. ep. 22. The title was transferred from Saint Cyriacus, to the church of Saints Quiricusand Julitta, San Cyriaco having fallen into ruin.* *Forum* is the next entry; but in what forum we are, it is not easy to decide. There were eighteen of them, in the ancient city. It is probably not the Forum Romanum, but the forum of Nerva, perhaps; for we find ourselves, soon after passing it, at *Sca. Agatha.* "There are the images," observes our guide, "of Paul and Saint Mary." This must

* Vid. Baron. Martyrol. Rom. Martii. 16.

be Sant' Agatha dei Gothi (now belonging to the Irish); because we find ourselves in the *subura*, just after passing it. The Suburra lay between the Carinæ and the Quirinal, on which stands Sant' Agatha, as did the *thermæ Constantini*, the next entry. The baths stood where the Palazzo Ruspoli stands at present. We next arrive at Saint Vitalis' *in vico longo*; and in this long street the pilgrim points our attention to *Caval-Ope*—an equestrian statue, but of whom, we are left to conjecture. We have arrived at the shrine of a martyr—*Scæ Euphemiæ in vico Patritii*—who suffered at Calcedon in the great persecution under Diocletian. There was another church of Saint Euphemia on the *Via Appia*, in ancient times. The church, in which we are now with our pilgrim-guide, is in the street of Patricians, which ran in the hollow between the Esquiline and Viminal hills; and here we end our first excursion, for, in the next line, we find our guide once more at Saint Peter's gate.

In porta sci. Petri usque ad Por. in Sinistra. Per Ar. Sci. Apollinaris. This church of Saint Apollinaris, who was a disciple of Saint Peter's, we know from Anastasius, was hard by the great basilica of the Apostle. Again we have crossed the Tiber from the Vatican, and left behind the great portico, and the burgh of the Anglo-Saxons, for we are arrived at the church *sci. Laurentii in Lucina*, about midway up the modern Corso, and in the very midst of the ancient Campus Martius. Near it, the guide points out—*obeliscum*—probably that one which was erected by Augustus as gnomon of a sun-dial, on the Monte Citorio; for we next find ourselves at—*Forma Virgi*—and we know that this aqueduct crossed the *Via Lata*, somewhere about the modern piazza Sciara. *Sci. Sylvestri*—which of the three Saint Sylvesters the pilgrim has brought us to, whether to San Sylvestro *in capite*, or San' Sylvestro *in Monte* or San' Sylvestro on the Quirinal, it is difficult to determine; but probably, it is San' Sylvestro *in Monte*, because that one stood near ruins of ancient baths, and the guide says in the next breath—*Ibi Balneum.* Passing by Saint Felix *in Pineis*, a vestige of one of the ancient consecrated groves, we come *ad scam. Luciam in Orthea.* Santa Lucia had more churches than one in Rome. There were Santa Lucia *della chavica* or *del Gonfalon*, Santa Lucia *in Selci*, Santa Lucia *della Tinta*, and Santa Lucia *di Ginnasi alle Botteghe Scure.* It is probably at the last mentioned we have arrived; for, in the next step, our guide points to San' Lorenzo *in Damaso*, on our left—*In S . . . Sci. Laurentii in Damaso,** and then to the theatre of Pompey, between the Pantheon and the Tiber. He next speaks of a *Cypressus*, but whether he means a real tree or only the representation of one in bronzé or marble, we know not. We return by the church *Sci Laurentii*, no doubt in Damazo, for we cross the *Capitolium*, pass by Saint

* The court of the palace attached to this basilica was the scene of Count Rossi's assassination, A. D. 1848.

Sergius, *ubi umbilicum Romæ.* The guide says something about *Severus,* alluding no doubt to the triumphal arch of that Emperor, for he goes on to mention *Cavallus Constantini,* and we know that the equestrian statue of Constantine was in the Forum: indeed, the word *Romanum* which follows shews that it is in the Roman Forum we are.

There is the most unequivocal proof that the ancient pavement of the Forum was as yet unencumbered by ruins and earth, which by inundations and other causes accumulated in after times, to from fifteen to thirty feet. The pillar of Phocas would be enough of itself to decide the matter. Following our pilgrim guide, however, we leave it by way of the . . . *ura, i.e. Subura,* pass by *Sca. Pudentiana in vico Patritii,* where stood the palace of the senator Pudens, which afforded hospitality to the Prince of the Apostles on his first arrival in Rome. *Laurentii in Formoso*—is the next church to which the pilgrim brings us. It was on the highest point of the Viminal hill, and is sometimes called *in Paneperna,* since the finding thereabouts of the epitaph of a Roman matron which began thus: "Perpenna Helpidi." Our guide alluding to the manner in which suffered the holy martyr, St. Laurence, on this very spot, observes, as he points it out: "*ubi ille assatus est.*" He retraces his steps through the Subura, pointing in passing to the ruins of Trajan's Baths, close by the basilica of St. Peter *ad Vicula. Iterum per Suburam Thermæ Trajani ad Vincula.* The second excursion closes here.

Viam Salariam. This means that we are about to start for the Via Salara, on which were a great many churches, tombs, cemeteries, oratories, and catacombs of the martyrs. We start as before from St. Peter's, pass under, or close by, the ruined triumphal arch, . . . *cum*, perhaps that one which opened of old on the Pons Triumphalis—we leave the Flaminian Circus to the right—*In D. Circus Flamineus.* The guide says: " there is St. Agnes" —alluding to her church in Piazza Navona, where was the Lupanar, in which the Virgin martyr was exposed. *Thermæ Alexandrinæ*—built by Alexander Severus, near the Pantheon. Hard by, we pass *Sci. Eustachii, Rotonda, et Thermæ Commodianæ*—a misconception of our venerable guide already noticed. *In S* . . . on our left, *Columna Antonini, Sca. Susanna*—near the baths of Dioclesian—*et aqua de Forma Lateranensi*—a fountain somewhere near the Termini, supplied from the Lateran aqueduct. *Thermæ Sallustianæ et pyramidem.*—This brings us to the Salarian gate, by which Alaric entered Rome, and close to which stood that renowned villa of Sallust. This seems to close the third excursion, for our guide next announces his intention to go from the Nomentan gate to the Forum.

A porta Numentana usque For. . . . On the left—*in S.*—he points out the *thermæ Diocletianæ*, passes by *Sci. Syriaci Sci. Vitalis, Scæ. Agatha in Diaconia, Monasterium Scæ. Agathæ. Thermæ Constantini.* All this is on the Quirinal. He next observes, that, beyond the walls, as you pass along the *Via Numentana, Sca. Agnes* is on your left, on your right, the church *Sci. Nicomedis.*

A porta Flaminia usque. Pariturium—we next find ourselves on our way from the Flaminian Gate, corresponding with the modern Porta del Popolo, on our way to the *Pariturium*, whatever that was. That it was somewhere as you go to the Capitol, by the road or street corresponding with the Corso, we know; for we pass, first by a church of Saint Sylvester, then through a portico, on to a column like that of Antoninus, by an arch and the Virgo aqueduct in ruins; then by the church of Saint Marcellus —the same as San Marcello in Corso of the present day—again through the portico, as far as the Apostles—the church of the Santi Apostoli, it is probable. The guide remarks, that outside the walls, on the Via Flaminia, stands the church of Saint Valentine, on the right hand side of the way—*In dextra Sci. Valentini.*

As yet, our guide has kept us chiefly in the 9th region, or that of the *Circus Flaminius;* in the 7th, or that of the *Via Lata;* and in the 6th, called *Alta Semita*, or the Quirinal; touching but slightly on the confines of the 5th, or *Esquiliæ* region; of the 8th, or *Forum Romanum* region; and of the 14th, or *Transtiberina*, which embraced all of the pagan city that was beyond the river. We subjoin the summary description of these regions, as given by Rufus, that the reader may have the opportunity of still further contrasting the pagan with the papal city. They are placed below so as to cover the ground pretty nearly as we have already surveyed it, in company with our pilgrim-guide; that is, the 14th, or last of the regions, for us is the 1st; because, therein was the Vatican, with Saint Peter's, which is plainly head-quarters in our pilgrim's city; next we place the 9th and the 7th, the regions of the *Circus Flaminius* and of the *Via Lata*, embracing the entire plain of the Campus Martius, bounded by the Pincian Hill, the Capitol and the Tiber; and forming the plain upon which the modern city is seated, for the far greater part. To these we add the 6th, or the region of *Alta Semita*, as embracing the Quirinal, the entire of which we have traversed.

The word *vicus—vici* in the plural—means in the regionaries rather a parish than a street, for each vicus had in it an ædicula, or district temple—"come le parochie de' nostri tempi," as Nardini says. Suetonius says there were in ancient Rome 1000 of them in all. In this number are not included the temples of the Dii Majores, as they were called, as of Jove, Minerva, Venus, or such as were erected in consequence of some particular event, or those of the alien deities, such as Isis and Serapis, to whom were dedicated a vast number of temples. Indeed, as the ancient writers tell us, Tertullian and Saint Ambrose among the rest, the ancient city was filled with temples; the streets, at every corner and recess, with altars. In the language and estimation of the augurs, the whole city was a temple; and within its bounds some token of vile and impious idolatry met the eye at every turn. The word insulæ, in the Regionaries, signifies a palace-like block of buildings, vast in extent, and of immense height, in which the lower order dwelt in apartments on the different floors; so that there were no small, mean-looking houses in ancient Rome, at least from Nero's time. Domus is a palace; horrea, a public or state depôt for all kinds of property. Therein, the citizens stored their property for greater security and convenience. They thus far resembled our custom-house stores, and were first suggested as a public convenience by that excellent emperor, Alexander Severus. The balnea of Rufus are public baths; lacus means a reservoir or basin for supplying a particular district with water; they had fountains attached. Pistrina were the public bakeries, from which the populace, who were provided with diet, baths, and public sports in amphitheatre and circus, at the expense of the provinces, had their loaves—panes—served out to them. The Vico-magistri of the regions were street police; perhaps, they may be more correctly compared to our special constables, for they were chosen by the citizens in each neighbourhood; and the curatores were divisional magistrates, in whose courts, during the first three centuries of our era, we often meet with the Christian martyrs under examination and torture. With these few notes, which it would be easy to swell into a chapter, we submit below the summary from Rufus, of the regions already traversed with our pilgrim-guide of the year of our Lord 800.*

* 14ta. Transtyberina continet Gajanum, Vaticanum, Frygianum, Naumachias 5, hortos Domitios, balneum Ampelidis et Prisci, et Dianæ, Molinas, Janiculum, Statuam Valerianam, cohortes 7 Vigilum, Caput Gorgonis, Fortis Fortunæ templ. Aream Septimianam, Herculem cubantem, Campum Brytianum, et Codetanum, hortos Getæ, Castra lecticariorum, vici 78, ædiculæ 78, V. M. 48. C. 3. ins. 4,405, domus 150, horrea 22, balnea 86, lacus 180, pistrina 23, p. 30,488.

9na. Circus Flaminius, cont. Stabula 4 factionum,* ædem Herculis, porticum Philippi, minutias duas veterem et frumentariam, Cryptam Balbi, theatra 4, in primis Balbi, quod capit loca 30,085. Campum Martium, Trigarium, Ciconias Nixas, Pantheum, basilicam Matidii, et Martiani, templ. D. Antonini, et columnan Coclidem altam ps. 275½. Hadrianum, thermas Alexandrinas, et Agrippinas, Porticum Argonautarum, et Meliagri, Isiam et Serapiam, insulam feliculæ. vici 35, ædiculæ 35, V. Mag. 48, curatores 2, insulæ 2,774, domus 140, horrea 22, balnea 43, lacus 63, pistrina 20, pedes 32,500.

7ma. Via Lata cont. Lacum Ganymedis, cohortes 7 Vigilum, Arcum novum, Nympheum Jovis, ædiculam Caprariam, Campum Agrippæ, templ. Solis, et Castra. Porticum Gypsiani et Constantini. templ. duo nova Spei et Fortunæ, Equum Tyridatis regis Armeniorum, Forum Suarium, Hortos Lorgianos, Mansuetas, Lapidem pertusam, vici 15, ædiculæ 15, V. Mag. 68, Curatores 2, insulæ 3,805, domus 130, horrea 25, balnea 75, laci 76, pistrina 15, pedes 15,700.

6ta. Alta Semita con. templ. Salutis, et Serapidis, templ. Floræ,

* Public stables for the factions or charioteer-clubs of the Circus.

When next we join him, our guide says he is on his way from the Tibur gate to the Roman Forum —*a porta Tiburtina usque Forum Romanum;* but as he is traversing the same ground as before, we leave his text without remark to the reader. *In D. Thermæ Sallustianæ*—he has gone round outside the walls from the Tibur gate to the porta Salara; by which, when he enters, he has the villa of Sallust on his right. *Sca. Susanna*—on Quirinal —*et Cavalli Marmorei*—the horses of Phidias?— *Sci. Marcelli*—in Corso—*ad Apostolis*—the Santi Apostoli, close by—*Forum Trajani, Sci. Hadriani.*

Via Laranense. But though he mentions thus indistinctly the Via Lateranensis, he is not near the Lateran, but still on the Campus Martius—*Sci. Laurentii in Lucina. T—nini* alludes to the column of Marcus Aurelius Antoninus. *Obeliscum. Columna Antonini. Via Lateranense.* Perhaps he means the route by which the Pontiff was wont to ride in state from Saint Peter's to the Lateran; as from the Quirinal to the Vatican, there is in the modern city a line of streets called the Strada Pontificia, it being the route of the Papal cortege on

Capitolum Antiquum, Statuam Mamurri plumbeam, ædem Quirini, malum Punicum, hortos Sallustianos, Gentem Flaviam, thermas Diocletianas et Constantinianas, decem tabernas, Gallinas Albas, Aream Candidi, cohortes tres Vigilum, vici 17, ædiculæ 17, V. Mag. 18, curatores 2, insulæ 3,403, domus 146, horrea 17, balnea 85, lacus 72, pristina 16, pedes 15,700.

occasions of state. *Thermæ Alexandrinæ*, so called from Alexander Severus. *Sci. Eustadii et Rotonda. Thermæ Commodianæ Minervium et ad Sanctum Marcum* — still on the Campus Martius, close under the Capitol.

Subura. We are *en route* for the fifth region, Esquiliæ. Passing through the Suburra quarter, we come to the church *Sci. Isidori*, then to Saint Eusebios', traverse the *Via Subtus mon* . . . in the district still called "I monti." *Sci. Vitus, Scæ. Mariæ in præsepio, Iterum Sci. Viti, Scæ. Euphemiæ.* Here we are in the hollow under Santa Maria Maggiore or *in presepe*, between the Viminal and Esquiline, after traversing the latter in great part; for Santa Euphemia was in Via Patricii, a street which ran through this valley. But our guide returns on his steps towards Santa Croce, for he passes by Saint Bibiana's Church, the Claudian aqueduct, an arch, a nympheum or great tank in that quarter, and points to something, one cannot tell what, which was outside the Tibur gate to the left. *Item alia Via Tiburtina, Forma Claudiana, per Ar. Scæ Bivianæ, Nympheum, in Via Tiburtina foris murum, in Sinist.* In an after part he puts *Palatium Pilati*, between *Sca. Euphemia* and *Sca. Maria Major.* Sancta Bibiana's Church, was said to be "ad ursum Piliatum," a place often mentioned in the Acts of the Martyrs. The summary of this fifth region, that of the Esquiline, we give below. It was the region rendered fashionable by the voluptuary Mæcenas, and so often frequented by Horace.*

It is at the Porta San Pancrazio we next rejoin our guide on his way to the portico from Saint Peter's to the Tiber. Then he visits the dungeon where Saint Peter was confined in the Mamertine prison, at the foot of the capital. The same in which Jugurtha was starved to death, and where still gushes up the fountain that sprung forth at the command of the Prince of the Apostles from out the solid rock, as occurred of old, at the word of Moses in the desert. Next we find him at the church of Saints John and Paul, on the Cœldan Mount, and at Saint Gregory's, in the same vicinity, *in Clivo Scauro*; then he turns back towards the Forum, enters Saint Sergius's, crosses a bridge, is on the Capitol—and so, through various other turns, as will appear from his own words, until he arrives once more, at Saint Vitus', on the Viminal hill.

A porta Aureliana usque ad Por. Fons. Sci. Petri, ubi est carcer ejus. Sci. Johannis et Pauli. Sci. Gregorii. Sci. Sergii. Per Pontem. Capitolium. Umbilicum. Per. Ar. Sci. Hadriani. Eques Con. Sci. Cyriaci, et Thermæ Constantini. Forum Rom.

* 5ta. Esquiliæ cont. lacum Orpheis, Macellum Liviani, Nympheum D. Alexandri, cohortes duas Vigilum, Herculem Sylvanum, hortos Pallantinos, amphitheatrum castrense, campum Viminalem sub aggere. Minervam Medicam, Isidam Patritiam, vici 15, ædiculæ 15, v. mag. 48, curatores 2, insulæ 3850, domus 180, horrea 22, balnea 75, locus 74, pistrina 15, pedes 15,600.

Forma Claudiana. Item Thermæ Diocletiani Scæ. Agathæ, Sci. Vitalis—on this Quirinal, near the vale of Quirinus, built in the year 416 by Innocent I, and dedicated to Saints Gervasius and Protas, martyrs, sons of Saint Vitalis. *Scæ. Pudentianæ. Sci. Laurentii in Formoso, ubi assatus est. Monasterium Scæ. Agathæ, usque ad Scum. Vitum. Cum.* for Arcum. *Scæ. Agathæ. Sci. Eusebii, in sinistra. Sci. Hippolyti. in dextra Sci. Laurentii . . . Viam Prænestinam.*

We are now back again in the fourteenth region, or beyond the Tiber; for our guide points to—*Molinæ*—mills for grinding corn, on the declivity of the Janiculum, and driven by water from the *Aqua Sabatina.* Next is the *mica aurea,* then the churches *Scæ. Mariæ* in Trastevere, of *Sci. Chrysogoni* in the Longarina, as ancient as Saint Sylvester—reopened A. D. 731, by Gregory III—a cardinal's title from the time of Pope Symmachus, A. D. 500. He enters the church *Scæ. Cæciliæ,* also in Trastevere, and immediately crosses by the isle of the Tiber; for we next find ourselves on the Palatine Hill, descending to the Church of Saint Theodore, on the ancient site of the temple of Romulus or of Vesta, close to the Roman Forum. We pass to *Sancta Maria Antiqua,* between the temple of Venus and Rome, and the temple of Peace, and, finally, to Saints Cosmas and Damian, erected A. D. 528, on the ruins of a temple of Remus, by Pope Felix IV. It was repaired by Saint Gregory the Great, by Sergius I, A. D. 689, by Hadrian I in 780, and Saint Leo III adorned it, in this same year 800. As we have now traversed the fourth, the tenth, and the eighth regions, or those of the temple of Peace, the Palatine and the Forum, the latter of which was of all the fourteen the most renowned and important, we shall subjoin the summaries of them from Rufus, having first quoted the ipsissima verba of our pilgrim-guide, which have been interpreted in the preceding sentences. *Molinæ. mica aurea. Scæ. Mariæ. Sci. Chrysogoni, et Scæ. Cæciliæ. Palatinus. ad Scum. Theodorum. Sca. Maria Antiqua, Sci. Cosmaæ et Damian.* Further on, he mentions the church *Sci. Georgii*, in the Velabrum, and sometimes said to be *ad Velum Aureum*. It was in the valley between the Capitol and the Palatine. It was the stational church on the day—Saint George's day—the attack was made on Pope Leo III, as we shall see hereafter.*

* 4ta. Templum Pacis cont. porticum Absidatum, arcam Vulcani, aurium buccinum, Appolinem sandaliarium, Telluris templum horrea Carthurea. Tigillum Soronium, Colossum altum 202½: habet in Capite radia numero 7, singula pedum 22½, metam sudantem, templum Romæ et Veneris, Ædem Jovis Statoris, Viam Sacram, Basilicam Constantinianam, templum Faustinæ, basilica Pauli, Forum transitorium, suburram, balneum Daphnidis, vici 8, ædiculæ 8, v. mag. 48, curatores 2, insulæ 2757, domos 88, horrea 18, balnea 75, lacus 83, pistrina 12, pedes 13,000.

10a. Palatium cont. casam Romuli, ædem matris Deûm et Apollinis, Rannusii, Pentapylum, donum Augustanam et Tiberi-

He is starting once more from St. Peter's gate, probably with a procession of other devout pilgrims like himself, when next we meet our guide. *A porta Sci. Petri usque—Per Arc.* Having traversed very nearly the same ground, and enumerated nearly the same objects as in the first excursion, except that in passing the *Minervium* he says "*ibi Sca. Maria,*" he comes to the *Palatium juxta Jerusalem:* then to Jerusalem itself, that is, to the basilica of the Holy Cross built by St. Helena on earth which was carried from the Mount of Calvary. This, he calls *Hierusalem.* On one side of it was a palace, on the other an amphitheatre, both in ruins. The palace was called *in Suxoriano,* corruptly, for Sessoriano: the amphitheatre belonged to a camp, probably that of the foreign mercenaries, which was

anam, ædem Jovis Victoris, domum Dionis, Curiam veterem, Fortunam respicientem, Septizonium D. Severi, victoriam Germanicianam, Lupercal, vici 20, ædiculæ 20, v. mag. 48, curat 2, insul. 2643, domus 88, horrea 48, balnea 14, lacus 89, pistrina 20, pedes 9600.

8va. For. Rom. et Magnum Cont. rostra, genium P. Romani aureum et equum Constantini, senatulum, atrium Minervæ, Forum Cæsaris, Augusti, Nervæ, Trajani. templ. D. Trajani et Columnam coclidem altum p. 128½—cohortes 6, vigilum. Basilicam argentariam, templ. Concordiæ, umbilicum Romæ, templ. Saturni et Vespasiani, Capitolium, miliarium aureum Juliæ, templ. Castorum, Vestæ, horrea Germaniciana et Agrippina, Aqua cementem quatuor Scauros sub æde, atrium Caci, vicum Jugarium, Argentarium, Græcostasim, Porticum Margaritarium, Elephantum herbarium, vici 34, ædiculæ 29, horrea 18, balnea 83, lacus 120, pistina 20, pedes 13,067.

placed in the *Cœlimontana* region. Next he points to the *Forma Lateranense, and the monasterium Honorii;* and from this Lateran quarter, passing through the *Porta Prænestina,* he leads us to *Sca. Helena et Scs. Marcellinus et Petrus.* This was the mausoleum of St. Helena, with the church adjoining of the holy martyrs Marcellinus and Peter. It was some two or three miles on the way to Prænestæ, and is often entitled in the Acts of the Martyrs and other ancient writings, *ad duos lauros.* Like every other strong building, we shall find it metamorphosed into a stronghold, in the tenth century. Hence it is still known as the Torre Pignatara, in allusion to the flower pots which were inserted by the degenerate architect in the dome, in order to lighten the pressure. *Palatium juxta Hierusalem. Hierusalem. Amphitheatrum. Forma Lateranense. Monasterium Honorii. Porta Prænestina. Sca. Helena. Scs. Marcellinus et Petrus.*

He seems to return by the *Porta Asinaria,* the same by which Cicero came home so crest-fallen from his attempt to win, as a conqueror, the honours of a triumph, and corresponding very nearly with the modern Porta San' Giovanni, through which Rienzi led the charge that laid the chivalry of the Colonna in the dust. Again, he is on the Campus Martius among the churches, and amphitheatres, and ruins of arches, and porticos, and aqueducts, on to the Forum. Then in the palace of Nero—*Palatium Neronis*—the next moment at St. Peter's *in chains, Æcclesia Sci. Petri ad Vincula.* We now pass under the arch of Titus and Vespasian, adorned with the tables of the Law, the seven-branched candlestick, with other sacred furniture and emblems of the Jewish temple. We proceed down the *Via Sacra*, pass the *Amphitheatrum*—now the Coliseum —*ad Scum. Clementem*, and so on by the *monasterium Honorii*, and the Claudian aqueduct to the Lateran palace—*ad Scum. Clementem, Monasterium Honorii, Forma Claudiana. Patriarchium Lateranense.*

Now we return again to the hollow where stands the Coliseum, which was in the 3rd region or that of Isis and Serapis.* Starting from a point called the Seven Ways, close to Constantine's triumphal arch, and between the latter and the Septizonium, we ascend the Cœlian mount, with Saints John and Paul to the left, come to the Lateran aqueduct, the same as the Claudian—to Saint Erasmus, the monas-

* 3tia. Isis et Serapis cont. Monetam, Amphitheatrum, quod capit loca octoginta Septem millia,* ludum Matutinum, et Dacicum,† domum Britti, præsentissimum choragium, lacum pastoris, scholam‡ quæstorum, et Capulatorum, thermas Trajanas et Titianas, Porticum Livii, Castra Misenatium, vici 12, ædiculæ 12, v. mag 49, curatores 2, insulæ 2757, domos 60,§ horrea 14, balnea 80, lacus 65, pistrina 16, pedes 12,350.

* Amphitheatre with 87,000 seats—Coliseum.

† School for Dacian Gladiators.

‡ Another Gladiatorial School. § Sixty Palaces.

tery to which we shall see them hurrying Saint Leo III, after the traitorous attack of St. George's Day, A.D. 799, and the attempt to pluck out his tongue and deprive him of sight. Next we go to Sancta Maria Domnica, erected where formerly stood the house of a pious matron Ciriaca, in Greek, Domnica, on the south side of the Cœlian, near the Castra Peregrinorum, or where the foreign troops were quartered ; then to another Saint Mary's—an oratory which stood a little inside the Latin Gate. He then mentions the Church of St. Gorsianus, no doubt near the same place : *De Septem Viis usque Porta Asinaria, in Sinistra. . Johannis et Pauli. Forma Lateranense, ad Scum Erasmum, Sca. Maria Domnica. In Via Latina intus in Civitate, Oratorium sanctæ Mariæ. Sci. Gordiani.*

The movements of our pilgrim become still more discursive as he proceeds in his rounds of the city, or, more properly speaking, of the regions within the walls—interspersed with ruins, and churches, and monasteries, with vast tracts of gardens, vineyards, and even with corn-fields, then, no doubt, as at present.—*De Porta Appia usque Sanct.*—We are, at length, in region number one of the pagan city, starting from the Appian Gate, the same as the ancient Porta Capena, and near the modern Porta San' Sabastiano. We pass the immense baths of Caracalla. *Thermæ Antoninianæ.* The arch of Remembrance. *Arcus Recordationis* — probably some relic of the great Circus. We are come to the

Cochlea fracta—the bridge, we think, which Horatius Cocles so valiantly defended, and then, as now, broken down. Thence through a portico—that of the Four-faced Janus, still standing—to Saint Theodore's, near the Forum, over the Palatine to the *Testamentum*—the *Septizonium*, or monument of Severus. This Emperor was an African, and, hence, the head of a colossal statue which was there went by the name of *Caput Africæ*. This is the point of the Seven Ways, from which we left a while ago. Our guide now draws attention to the *Meta Sudans* and the *Arcus Constantini*, which are close by; and proceeds to the *Quatuor Coronati*, on the Cœlian. This church was built by Pope Melchiadis, repaired by Honorius I, A. D. 630, also by Hadrian I: it was adorned by Leo III, about this very time, when our pilgrim visits it. He is next in Saint John's in Lateran, after visiting *Scum. Stephanum in Cœlio Montem.**

* 2da. Cœlimontium continet templum Claudii, Macellum-Magnum,* Luparios, Antrum Cyclopis, cohortes vigilum,† castra peregrina,‡ Caput Africæ, arborem Sanctam, domum Philippi,§ et Victitianam, ludum Matutinum, et Gallicum,|| Spoliarium,¶ Samarium, Armamentarium, Micam Auream, vici 7, ædiculæ 7, Vicomagistri 48, Curatores 2, insulæ 3,600, domus 124, horrea 14, balnea 32, lacus 42, pistrina 12, pedes 12,200.

* Slaughter-yard. † Cohorts of the night-watch.
‡ Camp of Foreign mercenaries. § *Palace* of Philip.
|| Training school for Gallic gladiators.
¶ For dead bodies of gladiators.

He then leaves the enclosure of the walls by the *Porta Metrovia*, between the Cœlimontana and the Latin gate; leaves to the left the church of St. John (probably where the Evangelist suffered as Tertullian describes), goes on ad *Scum. Syxtum*, at the catacombs—visiting the churches of Saints Euphemia and Theodorus, on the Appian way. In passing, he points to the *Schola Græca*—whether a school of Greek letters, at the time, or the ruins of a barrack of Greek gladiators, one cannot be certain—though it is more probably the latter, as the Greeks had their chief establishment during those ages, at Saint Saba's on the Aventine. . . . . *la Græca in Via Appia.* He next points to the *Forma Jobia*, or aqueduct of Diocletian, who was called Jovius, and enters the church of the holy martyrs Saints Nereius and Achilleius to pray. He seems to recollect that he omitted to mention or to visit the church *Sci. Januarii, via extra Civitatem, ubi Xystus martyrizatus est*, and also that of Saint *Eugenia.* Thus have we traversed the first region, or that of the Porta Capena, and touched, but not extensively, on the 12th, or that of the public fish-pond, *Piscina Publica*, which does not appear to have been at any period entirely occupied with buildings. It is the great plain spreading out from the Cœlian and the Aventine to the walls and the Tiber. There, is the Monte Testacio—excavated for wine vaults; and there, in ancient times, were the bleach grounds, where the college or guild of fullers used to spread out before the Roman sun, the garments of the Gens Togata.*

Once more we start from the Seven Ways to pass through the *Circus Maximus*, the *Mons Aventinus*, on our left, *et sic per porticum usque ad* . . . . . a break in the MS. But from the fragmentary notices, our pilgrim-guide—whether Count Eginhard, who after Charlemagne's demise became a priest, or some other devout and learned Christian,—would appear to have made regular visits to the churches, cemeteries, and catacombs, which lay by the way side of the various great thoroughfares by

* 1st. Porta-Capena continet ædem Honoris, et Virtutis, Camænas et lacum Promethei, balneum Torquati, et Vespasiani, Thermas Severinas, et Commodianas, aream Apollinis, et Galli, Vicum Vitrarium, Aream Panariam, Mutatorium Cæsaris, balneum Bolani, et Mamertini, aream Carsuræ, balneum Abascanti, et Antiochiani, ædem Martis, et Minervæ et tempestatis, flumen Almonis, Arcum D. Veri Parthici et D. Trajani, et Drusi, vici x. vicomagistri 48, curatores 2, insulæ 3,250, horrea 13, balnea 86, lacus 84, pistrina 20, continet pedes 12,219.

12ma Piscina Publica cont. aream radicariam, Viam novam, Fortunam Mammosam, Isidem Athenodoriam, ædem Bonæ Deæ subsaxanæ, signum Delphini thermas Antoninianas (Caracalla) septem domos Parthorum, Campum lanatarium,† Domum Chilonis, cohortes 4 vigilium, Domum Cornificii, privatam Hadriani, vici 14, ædiculæ 17, v. mag. 48, Curat. 2, ins. 2,487, domus 114, horrea 17, balnea 63, laci 81, pistrini 20, p. 12,000.

† Fuller's bleach-field.

which one approached the city.* Thus we have *In via Portuensis extra civitatem* . . . that is along the road to the Port—now Fumichino, outside the Porta Portese ; *in via Aurelia extr. civ.* i.e. along the way outside the Porta San Pancrazio ; again, *in via Salaria*, &c., and in fine,—*in via Pinciana extra civitatem, in Dextra Sci. Proti et Hyacynthi, Sci. Hermetis.* Besides these churches, not heretofore noticed by him, we find *Scam. Anastasiam*—erected by the Roman matron Apollonia, A.D. 300, on the northern brow of the Palatine, recently rebuilt by Saint Leo III, A.D. 795,—*Sca. Petronilla,* near, if not in, St. Peter's. *Marci et Marcellini, ad scum. Soterum sci. Cornelii, Xysti, Faviani* (for Fabiani) *Antheros et Miltiadis, ad Scum. Sabastianum.* Also the churches of *Abdo et Senes, Pancratii, Processi et Martiniani, Saturnini,* of Saint Felicitas and her seven sons,—*scæ. Felicitatis et VII filiis,* of Saint *Basilisca, sci. Pamphili, sci. Johannis caput*—the head

* Regio 11ma. Circus Max, qui capit loca 405,000 cont. 12 portas. templ. Mercurii, ædem Ditis Patris, Cererem, Portam trigeminam, Apollinem Cœlispicem, Herculem Olivarium, Velabrum, Arcum D. Constantini, vici 18, ædiculæ 19, v. magistri 19, curat. 2. insul. 2,600, domus 89, horrea, 16. balnea 15, laci 20, pistrina 15, ps. 11,500.

† Regio 13tia. Aventinus cont. templ. Dianæ, et Minervæ, Nymphea tria, thermas Varianas, et Decianas, doliolum, mappam auream, Platanones, horrea Galbæ, porticum Fabrariam, scholam Cassii, Forum pistorium, vici 17, ædiculæ 17, v. m. 48, C. 2 ins. 2,487, domus 130, horrea 25, balnea 64, cacus 88, pistrina 20, ps. 209,000.

of Saint John the Baptist, cut off at the feast of Herod. It was kept as a relic in the church of San Sylvestro *in capite* or *ad caput* . . . .

Then follows the circuit of the walls completed by Pope Hadrian, as we have already given it.

We have abstained from attempting to reduce the foregoing chaos, in which the ruins of the Pagan, and the basilicas and other monuments of the Christian, city are so strangely confounded together. Such a spectacle must of itself give rise to clearer notions regarding the real aspect of Rome, arising for the first time above the horizon of history, as Rome of the Popes, and cannot fail to be more suggestive of the befitting reflections, than any language of ours could possibly be. How startling, and how instructive, the contrasts which have forced themselves on our notice at every step! Ruins of Nero's golden palace, basilica of St. Peter in chains, Trajan and St. Paul, St. Lawrence and Diocletian, the previous triumphs of the Capitol and the heavenly patience of the Catacombs; oratories of the humble saints resplendent with gold and jewels, and arches of triumph in decay; the fountain of St. Peter overflowing and splendid, the Claudian aqueduct laid low; the shrine and the amphitheatre; the prison of the Apostle a place of pilgrimage, the temples of the Capitol forgotten; the palace of the Cæsars, and the crypt of S. Calixtus—churches, pyramids, obelisks, basilicas, temples, amphitheatres, equestrian statues of conquerors, effigies of the saints, Jerusalem, and the

Circus Maximus are all made to float before us in a kind of kaleidescope splendour and disorder, which, while it dazzles cannot fail to suggest reflections the most solid and cheering to every Christian mind. It tells us that Christ has triumphed in his saints. The humility, the patience, the purity of his Gospel have proved more than a match for all that was strongest, and most vehement in the perverted passions of humanity. In each of these contrasts, we have an additional and overpowering proof, that what the divine Author of Christianity predicted of himself has been accomplished, viz. that being lifted up, he would draw all things to himself, that the cross would become the throne from which he would rule the world, and subdue it.

How mighty, how fiercely, and how long contested was the battle between Paganism and Christianity, the Cæsars and the successors of St. Peter, for the dominion of that enclosure, is attested by the aspect of the field. It also tells at a glance on which side was the victory. The army of the cross is encamped upon the scene of conflict. The mausoleums of the martyrs are crowded with admiring votaries and sparkle with every precious ornament; those of the pro-consuls, and emperors, and patricians, are prostrate in ruins, or abandoned to beasts of prey, and ill-omened birds. The sceptre of the kings, and consuls, and Cæsars, so wrathfully torn from their grasp by the barbarians, has been placed by the devotion of the same barbarian conquerors in the hand, which has no title to it in their eyes, but that it is anointed to wear the ring of the fisherman. The same throne which they hurled to the ground, when it belonged to the Cæsars, they are prepared, as their acts have proved, to maintain and vindicate with their lives, now that it is occupied by the Popes.

The proudest title of those conquerors of the Roman world is to draw the sword in their defence, and for the maintenance of their rights. Among the forlorn halls of the Seven Hills, through their valleys, and along the Tiber, the canticles of victory are heard re-echoing by night and by day—proclaiming, on the part of the Crucified, that he has enabled what is foolish of men to confound the wisdom of the wise, and made infirmity overpower what in the whole world was strongest.

It would seem that Pope Hadrian had no sooner completed the walls, than he turned to repair the aqueducts. These majestic and most useful structures have been justly viewed with wonder and admiration, in the most civilized times, as the greatest, perhaps, amongst the works of the Romans. We have seen how the Goths during the successive sieges of the doomed city left nothing untried to cut off all supplies of water from the besieged, by the destruction of those aqueducts, which carried to the Queen of Empire the treasures of the coolest and most pellucid springs and fountains, even of the distant Apennines, as it were upon a succession of triumphal arches. The Lombards, during the two hundred years in which they may be said to have never permanently suspended the siege of Rome, were not less furious or persistent in the work of destruction; and melancholy to hopelessness was the aspect of dilapidation and ruin they presented, when Pope Hadrian ascended the throne.

The aqueduct with which the Pope commenced was that one which supplied Saint Peter's, the Aqua Sabatina of the ancients. It was originally built by Augustus, and brought a copious stream from Lake Alseatinus, a distance of five-and-thirty miles, to the ridge of the Janicular Mount.* How Pope Hadrian proceeded with its repairs, we leave it to his biographer to tell.

"The aqueduct (*forma*) from which the water used, of old, to be conveyed through the *Centenarium* into the cloister of Saint Peter's basilica, and into the baths close by, where our brethren the poor of Christ were wont to bathe in those refreshing waters, and to receive the alms of Saint Peter, had for the space of twenty years been broken, so that it no longer supplied either the Atrium of Saint Peter (that is either the fountains or *the baths*) or turned the mills for grinding corn on the Janicu-

* See description of the States, p. 75 & 76.

lum, as it used formerly to do. It seemed hopeless to look for its repair; for no less than one hundred arches of the aqueduct, and those of immense altitude, had been destroyed to their very foundations—[an achievement, no doubt, of the Lombards.] However, this blessed and holy Pontiff, having collected a great multitude of people, so ordered and urged forward the work, that the arches being rebuilt, and the leaden ducts which had been either totally carried away as plunder, or irremedially damaged, having been replaced, the waters resumed their course, supplying a copious and refreshing tide, not only to the fountains in front of the basilica, and to the baths, but also through the city; that is, adown the declivity of the Janiculum, where the corn-mills were all set in activity again."

In like manner he repaired the Claudian aqueduct, from which the baths of the Lateran and of the churches and hospitals of that region were supplied: as was also the baptistery of the church of our Saviour Jesus Christ. This must have been of great benefit to the city—a great solace to the poor, and to the way-worn pilgrims, for whom these baths were chiefly designed.

We find him also restoring the aqueduct known in ancient times as the *Virgo*, so that from that time the stream it supplied was so abundant as to suffice for nearly the entire of Rome.

To say that from the aqueducts, Pope Hadrian proceeded to rebuild and beautify the churches would not be to fairly represent his character. One of the earliest titles of praise bestowed upon him was, that he was a "lover of the churches"—*Amator Ecclesiarum.* This was a work which his zeal would not allow to be second to any other.

Nothing could convey a notion at once more afflicting and impressive of all that the Pontiffs and their people had to suffer, not alone from the inroads of the Lombards, but from the persecution and sacrilegious rapacity of the Greeks, than the sad and ruined plight in which the basilicas and churches great and small were found, when the re-establishment of peace and justice once more permitted the Pontiffs to resume what we have seen to have been with them, from the remotest ages, as well a favourite as a sacred task. We find Pope Hadrian commencing, as usual, with Saint Peter's, and here again we shall leave his biographer to tell the story.

"He adorned Saint Peter's.—Amongst his gifts to this basilica was a vestment of surpassing beauty, sparkling with gold and gems, having figured on it the story of Saint Peter's liberation by the angel. In front of the confession, he laid down a pavement of purest silver to the weight of 150lbs. *Item*, for the great doors, immense curtains of cloth of silver, and fifty-five other curtains, embroidered purple, to be used on festival days for festooning the arcades of the aisles. Also a pharos or lustre, typical of the cross, suspended in front of the presbyterion or sanctuary, and made to hold one thousand three hundred and seventy wax candles—ordaining that it should be lighted only on four great festivals every year—that is, on the Nativity, at Easter, on the feast of the Apostles, Saint Peter and Saint Paul, and on the anniversary of each reigning Pontiff."

These were but a few of his gifts to Saint Peter's. To Saint Andrew's, which is hard-by, he presented a cyborium, weight 135lbs. of the purest silver. The shrine where rests the body of the Apostle of the Gentiles (Saint Paul), he had inlaid with lamina of silver to the weight of 30lbs., besides adorning the basilica with curtains for the doors, and festoons of costly tissue for the arcades like those of Saint Peter's. The atrium, also, or cloister—so neglected that oxen and other animals used to come and browze on the grass which grew there, he caused to be paved with marble. To the altar of our Lady *in præsepe*, he gave two vestments of cloth of gold, with the Assumption wrought in precious stones on each. Curtains also, as in the two aforesaid churches. The same he did for the Lateran, and for Saint Laurence beyond the walls. There is also a note of vestments to Saint Valentine's and to Saint Pancratius'. He new-roofed Saint Mark's, and also Saint Laurence *ad Taurellum*. Rich offerings to Saint Felix *in pineis*, which he raised from a ruined state :—put a new roof on Saint

Laurence *in Damaso*, finished the portico round the basilica of the Apostles *in via lata*, left incomplete by Pope Paul who commenced it. The cemetery of Saints Peter and Marcellinus on the *Via Lavicana,* near the basilica of Saint Helen, he repaired ; as likewise the roof of Saint Tiburtius, and made steps down to the crypt where sleep the bodies of those blessed saints. Gifts to Saint Hadrian's—Rebuilds Saint Prisca—Gifts to Saints Cosmas and Damian *in tribus Fatis.* New-roofed Saint Clement's, in the third region ; also the basilica of Saint Silvester *in Orphea.* Repaired the church of Saint Januarius, near the Porta San Lorenzo, and made rich presents to the chapel in the cemetery of Saint Abdon and Sennen, outside the Porta Portese.

Finding the monastery of Pope Honorius in ruins, he restored it, endowed it, and placed there a body of regular clergy under an abbot. They were to celebrate the divine office in the basilica of the Lateran : that is to say, the hours of matins, prime, terce, sext, and also none, and vespers. This he did to add fresh fervour and power of melody to the divine praises to be chanted there, in hymns, and canticles, and psalms, by these double choirs—the monks of Saint Pancratius, already established there, being on one side, and those of the aforementioned monastery of Pope Honorius, *viz.* of Saints Andrew and Bartholomew, on the other.

The parochial church of Saint Susanna martyr,

between two palaces near Saint Quiricus, when in a ruinous and tottering condition, he repaired—also the basilica of Constantine in the Lateran, he all but rebuilt; also Saint Laurence *in Palatinis*, uniting it with the neighbouring monastery of Saint Stephen, called *in Baganda*, and placing monks in it who were to serve the church of Saint Mark confessor and pontiff, which he greatly enriched: raised from its ruined state the deaconry of Santa Maria *in Schola Græca*, or as it is otherwise entitled *in Cosmedin*—from the fashion in which it was decorated—and rebuilt it on an enlarged plan, and richly adorned it: likewise the title of Saint Lorenzo *in Lucina*, and the church of Saint Martin situate near the title of Saint Sylvester: also the title of Saint Sixtus, the basilica of Saint Hadrian, also Saint Pancratius, and the neighbouring monastery of Saint Victor. The basilica of Saint Eusebius he rebuilt; also the temple of the Apostle, called *Eudoxia ad Vincula;* also the church of Saint Stephen, where the body of Saint Leo pontiff and martyr sleeps, with the cemetery attached to it of Saint Cyriaca; also the basilica Jerusalem *in Sessoriano;* also the church of Saint John the Baptist, near the Latin gate,* and at the

* Is this an error? Tertullian says that *near the Latin gate*, Saint John *the Evangelist* was plunged into a cauldron of boiling oil, in the reign of Domitian; and at present there exists a little chapel dedicated to Saint John the Evangelist, in the same place.

third stone on the *Via Appia,* the church of the Apostles called the Catacombs, where rests the body of the martyr Saint Sebastian with many others; also the title of Pudens, that is, the church of Saint Potentiana, and the basilica of Saint Theodore *intra velum* (velabrum ?) near the Sulpitian palace.

He decorated the basilica of St. Petronilla near St. Peter's, and repaired the title or parochial church of St. Praxede, as also the basilica of St. Euphemia, inside and out. That of Sts. Gordianus and Epimachus, the cemetery of SS. Simplicius and Semilianus: of Quartus and Quintus martyrs—of St. Sophia, with the cemetery of Tertulinus outside the Latin gate: also the church of St. Tiburtius and Valerianus, and of Maximus; the basilica of St. Zeno, with the cemetery of the saints Urban pope, Felicissimus, Agapitus, Januarius, and Cyrinus, martyrs, all in a cluster outside the Appian gate—"uno cohorentes loco." Also the title of the ever-blessed Virgin Mary, called of S. Calixtus *in Transtevere;* also St. Marcellus in *Via Lata* (now in *Corso*); also the cemetery of the holy martyrs, Hermes, Prothus, and Hiacinthus, with its church of vast dimensions; also the cemetery of St. Felicitas, on the Via Salara, with the church adjoining of St. Sylvanus, martyr, and S. Boniface, confessor pontiff, and on the same Salarian road, another cemetery and church, the latter of St. Saturninus, the former of the saints Chrysanthus and Darius; also the cemetery of St. Hilaria, the cemetery *Jor-*

danorum, viz. of saints Alexander, Vitalis, and Martialis, martyrs, as also that of the seven virgins. Likewise, on the same *Via Salaria*, the cemetery of St. Silvester, confessor pontiff, and the church of St. Felix outside the *Porta Portese*, that of St. Candida, also the church of the proto-martyr St. Stephen on *Monte Celio*, the basilica of St. Eugenia, and the title of Pamachius, of Saints John and Paul, also the church of St. Laurence *ad formosam*. He made rich offerings to the basilica of St. Martina, to the church of the ever-blessed Virgin, which is called *ad martyres*, (the Pantheon); brought from Perugia two enormous gates of bronze, exquisitely adorned with relievi, and caused them to be placed as portals for the bell tower of St. Peter's.

The environs of the holy city, especially in the vicinity of the ancient crypts, catacombs, and cemeteries, were studded with churches, monasteries, and oratories, which were also frequently met with along the great highways that lead to the city.

Thus we have found Pope Hadrian repairing and beautifying churches along the Salarian, the Appian, and the other ancient roads, not only close to the city, and in the neighbourhood of the great basilicas of the Apostles, and of St. Laurence, and at the catacombs, but at a distance of several miles from the gates. Thus, he rebuilt the basilica of SS. Rufina and Secunda in the diocese of Silva Candida, also the basilica of St. Peter the Apostle, on the *via Appia, in Silice*, near the ancient Bovillae. Beyond it was St. Thomas's. He repaired the church of St. Sabina in the territory of *Ferentello*, the church of St. Secundinus in Prænestæ, the basilica of St. Peter in *Massa Merrulana*, (one of the estates) and the church of St. Euplus, which was connected with the colonnade leading to St. Paul's. So that it was not without good reason the biographer said in his praise: "like a good pastor, all the churches of God, as well without as within this city of Rome, he rebuilt and embellished; the walls also of the city, and their towers which lay in ruins, he raised up and completed."*

All these were noble—nay, it must be said of some of them—the walls, the aqueducts, that they were stupendous works. Any one of them would have sufficed to secure that sort of fame for Pope Hadrian which his namesake, the Roman emperor, sought to acquire by most useless and wanton extravagance in his buildings. That they were most indispensable for, and highly conducive to the safety and well-being of millions cannot be called in question. No work more holy or more worthy of Christianity, than the procuring the beauty of the house of God, and in eternizing his glory by preserving, and multiplying, and rendering impressive by the most costly offerings and ornaments, the shrines and mausoleums of His martyrs and apostles.

* Anas. Bib.

Nor must we, in forming our estimate of these works of the Popes, forget to take into account the civilizing and salutary effects which must have been, and which we know were actually, produced upon pilgrims innumerable, by the sight of these majestic basilicas in which they were wont to gather from every region of the barbarian world, not only to lament and confess their crimes, to supplicate for blessings, but also to be schooled, through their senses of sight and hearing, in those arts, which, of all others, have most power to reclaim, to soften, and, by a sort of enchantment of the faculties, to metamorphose the stolidity of the barbarian into the elevated and refined sentiments of a civilized being. But withal in the presence of such mighty undertakings, and the expenditure of such enormous sums as must have been required for such costly works, the inquiry, not untinctured with anxiety, arises in the Christian mind: amidst all this expenditure and these works so magnificent, were the wants and the woes of the lowly poor of Christ forgotten? It is true, that according to the wisdom of the present age—according to the gospel of political economy, for Pope Hadrian to have expended his treasures not in alms but in affording employment—employment too which was most profitable, if not indispensable to society, by preserving, and improving, and widely disseminating the utilitarian, as well as the fine arts, he established a higher, or at least, a more tangible claim on the gratitude of posterity, than if he had expended them exclusively in dispensing charity; nevertheless, it will be edifying to find that these advantages of a mere terrestrial character have not been purchased at the expense of the virtues, which, little as they may be prized by human philosophy, are ranked in the first class by the Gospel. Here again, we refer the reader to the contemporary writer of this Pontiff's life.

In Anastasius there are notices of several estates, the produce of which was administered, as belonging to the poor of Christ. Thus there was one *domus-culta*, as it is called, in the *territorio Vigentano*, about fifteen miles from Rome. This, called the *fundus capreorum*, was Pope Hadrian's own hereditary estate. He enlarged it greatly by purchasing other lands and tenements in its vicinity, and having done so, he directed, under pain of anathema, that the whole produce of this estate, the corn, wine, olives, vegetables; the sheep and cattle of its pastures, the swine of its chesnut and oak forests, the poultry of its yards, the game of its moors and mountains, the fish of its streams, together with its income from water-mills, and other rights, customs, and holdings, should carefully, and with the best ordered economy, be husbanded for the exclusive "use of our brethren, the poor of Christ for ever." "IN USUM FRATRUM NOSTRORUM, CHRISTI PAUPERUM, PERENNITER PERMANEAT."*

* Anast. Bib. in vita Hadriani.

Then follows the order of distribution, which was to be made in that part of the Lateran patriarchate, "ubi et ipsi pauperes depicti sunt"—the hall or portico wherein are represented, in different pictures and scenes, the poor of Christ. Of the other three domos-cultas, or farm-houses of the poor, one was at Galeria, at the tenth stone on the Via Aurelia, near the church of Saint Rufina; the second was on the Via Portuenis, about the twelfth mile-stone; there was the monastery of Saint Laurence *in insula Portûs Romani*;* and the third, called *Calvisianum*, was situate fifteen miles from Rome, on the road to Ardea.

Three deaconries he established outside the gate of Saint Peter (on account of the pilgrims); one of our Lady, the blessed and ever-glorious mother of God, *in atrio*; another also to our blessed Lady, *in caput Porticus* (at the end of the colonnade); and the third called of Saint Silvester, close by the hospital of Saint George (of the English). These he lifted up from their ruined state, and enabled to minister shelter and solace to the pilgrims, coming to the tombs of the Apostles from the remotest countries. These deaconries he ordained to make a procession, the 5th feria of every week, with psalmody, as far as the baths, and there assist the poor, and distribute alms amongst them.

These deaconries, which he intended for the relief and solace of the distressed, he also richly endowed

* In the Delta of the Tiber.

with farms, vineyards, olive-groves, and all other kinds of property, that by the rents and income therefrom accruing, the deaconries might continually feed and solace the distressed—" ut de reditia eorum, crebris exactionibus Diaconiæ proficientes, pauperes Christi reficerentur."

Not less distinguished by these mighty and truly Christian works and institutions was the pontificate of this great Pope, than was his self-devotedness and paternal solicitude for the safety and welfare of the city and of the Roman people. On one occasion, the basilica of Saint Anastasia Martyr, with the adjoining baptistery and ergumenarchium, taking fire by night, through the negligence of the monks, was, with all the surrounding buildings, burned to the ground. The Pope, on hearing this, was immediately on the spot in person with his attendants, and spared no efforts to extinguish the flames; but nothing could be saved except the shrine or sarcophagus containing the relics of the holy martyrs. All, however, was ere long rebuilt and placed in its former splendour by the Pontiff's zeal.

Another incident mentioned in Anastasius is this:—In the twentieth year of his pontificate, the Tiber, during mid-winter, overflowed its banks, and swept onward with such violence, that entering by the Flaminian gate, the flood not only overthrew the portals, but bore them as far as the arch called *tres faccicelas*. It destroyed the portico called *Palatina*, hard by Saint Mark's, also the bridge of Antoninus.

In the *Via Lata* the water was twelve feet deep. In the country parts much damage was done: the tide overturning the dwellings, sweeping away the stock and other substance of the peasantry, and tearing up the fruit trees and the corn. In the city, great was the tribulation and distress, for the inundation lasted for three days and nights with undiminished fury. With the solicitude of a father, the Pontiff had boats collected, and thus sent bread and other assistance to those who were not able to leave their houses; and when the water had subsided, which was not for several days, he visited the Via Lata, the region which had felt the inundation most, in order to assist and console the sufferers.

CHAPTER IV.

The palace of the Lateran, commenced by Hadrian I, was completed by Leo III. This last-mentioned Pope built a similar palace hard by Saint Peter's. "A triclinium he built in the Lateran," says Anastasius, "greater than all other tricliniums. He embellished it in proportion to its magnitude, with divers columns, as well of porphyry as of statuary marble, with sculptured roses and lilies on the architraves and panels; the absis (still existing) he decorated with mosaic work." Into the details, however, of what this Pontiff added to all already done by his predecessor for the churches, hospitals and colleges, we must not allow ourselves to be enticed; they fill nearly the entire of the one-and-forty enormous folio pages of Anastasius in which his life is recorded. The churches and sanctuaries indebted to his munificence are accurately specified by the contemporary writer of his life. The inventory furnishes proof conclusive, that the Pagan city was not more remarkable for shrines and temples to idols, and the diabolical phantoms of heathenism, than was this primitive Rome of the Popes for the sanctuaries and basilicas of the saints and Apostles of

Christ. As for the treasures so expended, they are not to be counted; but let those who doubt that such mines of wealth could be thus lavished on the service of God, and the shrines of his martyrs and saints, reflect on a domestic example—that of the Anglo-Saxon sanctuaries, which delighted to imitate, in the distant province, the models which their saints and pilgrim-kings had gazed on with awe and wonder at Rome.* Huge golden censers, ciboriums, chalices, and vases of every size, and all thickly studded with precious gems: plateaus of silver to cover the altars, the tombs of the Apostles, and even the surrounding pavement; gates for the sanctuary, and tabernacles of the same metal; coronas, chandeliers, and candelabrums of immense size; curtains of richly embroidered tissues for hanging round the altars and the arcades; vestments, statues, pictures, books of the Gospels, heavy with gold and jewellery, are of frequent recurrence in the catalogue of his gifts. Thus—"the basilica Salvatoris and Saint Paul's, he adorned with images; to the basilica of the blessed Laurence Martyr, outside the walls, he presented three statues—our Lord, Saint Peter, and Saint Laurence, with an antependium (in front of the altar) of the richest materials, representing the scenes of the passion, death, and resurrection of the Redeemer." Amongst his gifts to Saint Andrew are costly vestments, sparkling with diamonds, and embroidered with the history as well of our Lord's

* See Dr. Lingard's Anglo-Saxon Antiquities.

giving to Peter the power of binding and loosing, as of his martyrdom and that of Saint Paul. On a vestment given to Saint Mary Major's, was represented the history of the passion, beginning, *Hoc est corpus meum quod pro vobis trodetur ;* another, with the procession of the greater Litanies represented on it. To Saint Peter, his great patron, he presented a book of the Gospels in gold, studded with emeralds and pearls of surpassing size and brilliancy, weighing upwards of 70 lbs.

But munificent as he was to the sanctuaries of religion, and full of zeal for the glory of God's house and the majesty of his worship, he was not less open-handed in providing for the afflicted and the distressed. In sooth, it was on account of this virtue of charity, which he had been assiduously practising from his tenderest years, according to that dictate of our Lord—to "hide from the left what the right hand doth," and in impressing the same practice upon all within his sphere, Saint Leo had been elected to the Apostolic throne with wonderful enthusiasm and unanimity. Moreover, he had been ever a great admirer of learning, as he was now a great encourager of it, and a patron of learned men.*

For aiding the accomplishment of this gigantic enterprise of building a new Rome, not less wonderful in its way than that which had perished, a variety

* Anast in Vit. Leon. III.

of circumstances conspired. The Comaschi and other townsmen, especially in Lombardy, of the old Roman stock had already attained to celebrity as architects and masons, and had been incorporated or chartered as such, by the Roman Pontiffs; so that they became the founders of that masonic fraternity so celebrated in the middle ages, and whose works, or rather miracles of art and genius, are destined, it would appear, to remain for ever unrivalled.* With these, and with the crowds of artists of every kind, painters, sculptors, mosaicists, and workers in the precious metals, in the loom, and in embroidery, who were driven before the storm of the Iconoclast persecution into Italy, and particularly to Rome, where they were received with paternal welcome and cherished and patronized by the Popes, there is manifestly nothing to deduct, on the score of exaggeration, from what is recorded of Pope Hadrian and of his immediate successor Leo III, whether as to

* So early as the year 661, San Michele at Padua was erected, a perfect model of the so-called Lombard architecture.† Towards the close of the eighth century the Popes conceded a monopoly in Ecclesiastical Architecture to the masons of Como—called "Magistri Comacini." Thus originated the Freemasons of the middle ages. They carried their art to a pitch of perfection, which, now that their secrets are lost, it may be considered hopeless to attempt.‡

† See Lord Lindsay, vol. ii. for its symbolism, &c.

‡ Ib. p. 14.

building or beautifying the churches, or to providing the most exquisite vessels for the altar, and vestments for those who served it. It is manifest that, at this epoch, the city of the Pontiffs must have been not only one vast temple, so filled was it with churches and shrines, but also a vast university, where all the arts both useful and ornamental were revived, and, in not a few instances, cultivated with the highest success.

So early as the pontificate of Gregory II, asylums were opened in Rome for the exiled artists.* The advantages accruing to Italy in the 15th century, from a similar immigration of Greeks, is known to every one. At the period in question, Byzantine art was in its meridian, and from the specimens in every branch which have come down to us, one can decide at a glance that nothing in its kind, so far as lightness and elegance of design, as well as of finish and quaint richness in the details, could be finer than was the Lombard or Byzantine style of the 8th century. An entire city, its walls, towers, and innumerable churches, basilicas, oratories, hospitals, colleges, and palaces, thus constructed must have

* Immense crowds of artists were driven from Constantinople and the east on the breaking out of the Iconoclast persecution. They found refuge mostly in Rome. The Mosaicists alone were so numerous that the Popes had convents established for their exclusive accommodation. See *Elements d'Archeologie, &c. par Dr. Batissier*—Paris, 1843, p. 364. n. 2.

had an indescribable charm for the beholder, on account of the harmony of all the parts, in a style at once so elegant, so rich, and so impressive—a charm, too, which must have been greatly enhanced by the historical and Scriptural paintings with which it was the fashion, at that period, as well as in more modern times, to embellish the exterior, not less than the interior, of palaces and temples. The contrast with the ruins of the pagan and classic ages, in which the new Christian erections thus adorned were placed, gave rise to many instructive as well as impressive effects.

The churches were classed under the four following denominations :—1. Patriarchal.—2. Titular or Parochial.—3. Diaconal.—4. Oratories or cemetery churches. The patriarchal immediately under the Pope himself were not titles, nor had they peculiar parishes, their jurisdiction embracing all. Such were the Lateran, the Vatican, S. Mary Major's, Saint Paul's, and St. Laurence *in agro Verano.* With these were classed certain other great churches which were not titles either, but were called minor basilicas, such as Santa Croce in Jerusalem, Saint Agnes beyond the walls, Saint Mary of Martyrs, that is, the Pantheon, and some others.

The parochial churches, which had attached to them the care of souls, were called titles. Each had care of a peculiar district with fixed boundaries—this was called its parish or diocese. The title of cardinal originally belonged to all the priests attached to these titles. Afterwards this dignity was allowed only to the first amongst them. About the time of Innocent I, or of Pope Zozimus at farthest, these titles had increased to the number of twenty-eight, and so continued during several ages.

In the acts of a Synod under Pope Symmachus in the year 499, there is a list of those titles in which they are set down in the following order:—

1. Saint Praxede.—2. Saint Vestina.—3. Saint Cecilia.—4. Saint Pamachius.—5. Saint Clement.—6. Saint Julius.—7. Saint Sabina.—8. Saint Chrysogonus.—9. Saint Pudens.—10. Saint Æquitius.—11. Saint Damasus.—12. Saint Æmiliana. 13. Saint Crescentiana.—14. Saint Eusebius.—15. Saint Nicomedis.—16. Saint Cyriacus.—17. Saint Matthew.—18. Saint Tigrida.—19. Saint Julius.—20. Saint Romanus.—21. Saint Byzantis.—22. Saint Anastasia.—23. The Holy Apostles.—24. Saint Priscæ. (S. Gaii not numbered, but S. Julius is down twice).—25. S. Praxedis (Bis.)—26. Saint Lucina.—27. Saint Laurence.—28. S. Marci.—29. S. Marcelli.—30. S. Lucinæ (Bis.)

In this list are not found the Patriarchal churches, nor the titles of SS. Silvester, Susanna, Xystus, Balbina, Marcellinus and Peter, the Quatuor Coronati, all of which are set down as titular in a Synod of Saint Gregory the Great, in which Synod the title of Pamachius is named of SS. John and Paul; in a Synod, under Pope Zachary, St. Mary's is set down as a title.

The original object of their institution was two-fold, that in them the sacraments of baptism and penance might be administered to the converts from paganism, and the interment of the martyrs provided for.

As for the society residing within this precinct such as we have been endeavouring to describe it, its organization and general aspect diverged much less than might be imagined from the model of those ancient and warlike ages, when Rome was not so much a city, in the usual sense of the term, as a great military station, or permanent encampment surrounded by enemies, and ever on the alert for war. No longer, it is most true, were the objects of conquest the same; much less so were the modes of achieving it. The symbols of mercy and peace had supplanted the sanguinary ensigns which were lifted at the head of the legions, when Rome was pagan ; but still, there was the discipline, there the organization of the entire community, under a gradation of officers, not less complete than that by which the decurion or leader of ten was linked with the consul in command, under the commonwealth, or with the emperor, during the later periods ; the impressive and distinct array, with all that belongs not only to the pomp and circumstance of a warfare conducted on the grandest scale, as well as on the most enlightened principles, but all its never-lagging vigilance, and activity, and perpetual attitude of preparedness, were, we may assert it with confidence, even more conspicuously characteristic of the city under the Popes, than under either the kings, the consuls, or emperors.

By order of Augustus, the city had been divided into fourteen regions: from the remotest period, as early as the Apostolic age itself, the division into seven regions called deaconries, was adopted by the Pontiffs, for some mystical reason, no doubt, and most probably to correspond with the seven days of the week; for according to the discipline of the Christian encampment, each of the seven divisions of the entire army of Saint Peter—the Christian people—had its day in succession, or its *feria*, for active service. Thus on *feria* 1ma, or Sunday, the 3rd deaconry or regionary division was under arms—responsible for the camp duty—still to keep up the strictly just idea of the Church being an army in campaign, and the life of the Christian a "warfare upon earth." The 2nd *feria*, or Monday, was for the 4th division, the 3rd *feria*, or Tuesday, for the 5th, the 4th *feria*, or Wednesday, for the 6th, the 5th *feria*, Thursday, for the 7th, the 6th *feria*, Friday, for the 1st division or deaconry; and the Sabbath, *Saturday*, for the 2nd.*

* See ordo Rom. I. ap. Mabil. Musæum Ital. l. i. p. 3. item p. xviii. Nardini, by whom the subject is better treated than by any one else, adhering to Anastasius, has placed the Aventine in the first deaconry, in the second the *Via Mamertina:* the basi-

To superintend the orphan houses and hospices of various descriptions, for the sick, the aged, the pilgrims, the "poor of Christ," was the every day occupation of the minor clergy—acolytes of the various orders, and of the subdeacons attached to a central post in each of the seven regions, under the immediate command of a deacon. There, they formed, in this Christian warfare, a permanent corp-de-gard, or garrison. This officer was responsible, not like the deacons attached to the titles, to the cardinal priests, but to the archdeacon, appointed, and immediately charged by the Pontiff with the care and command of these regionary corps. Their primary duty was to turn out, each on its appointed *feria*, at the head of the militia of their region—a body of armed men under appropriate officers—and thus proceed (but not without leaving in the deaconry a force sufficient to attend the hospital and other duty) to the Lateran, or whatever palace the Sovereign Pontiff was resident in at the time, in order to escort his holiness in solemn procession to the basilica, title, or deacon-church, as the case might be, in which it had been ordered to hold the STATION, or general review and exercise of the faithful, or of that division of the army of the cross, which on the occurring *feria*, or festival, was bound

lica of Saint Laurentius, *super Sct. Clementem*, in the third; and the Caput Tauri, he places in the fifth. From an inscription in the Roma Subterranea of Arioghi, it appears that the title of Saint Vestina was in the fourth region.

to special attendance. On the greater festivals, there was a muster of the militia of all the regions, as usual, before the dawn. They formed before the Lateran, and were ready at the first signal to proceed to the stational church, or the *Campus Martius* of the day.

In the ordinals of the period, the processions, and what was done at the stations are minutely described. In this place, it will be sufficient to mention that the regionary bands had their standards, the acolytes had, some their censers, others carried wax lights,—the sacred vessels for the altar, and the furniture of the sanctuary—such as the chalices, patens, scyphons, with other sacred vessels: the snow-white linen receptacles for the eucharist, the book of the Epistles, and the book of the Gopsels, the vases, ewers, and towels for the hands, were carried in great state, each piece separately, and by the appropriate officer. The titles of these functionaries are a proof of how greatly the Rome of the Popes as well as that of the Cæsars had been influenced by commerce and intercourse with the Greeks. Thus, there were the Primicerius, and the Secundicerius of the holy Roman Church. These were the highest dignitaries of the palace—they had the jurisdiction of judges over all the subordinate officers and dependants of the Papal Court,—just as the City-prefect was the judge in causes for the lay community at large, and as the Archdeacon—an office abolished by Saint Gregory VII—had a court, to which, whatever concerned the clergy of the deaconries—whether regionary or otherwise, was reserved. The titular or parochial clergy were under their respective cardinals, and the monasteries under their abbots. But as for the above mentioned dignitaries, the primicerius and secundicerius, they were also entitled counsellors of the Pontiff, because he advised with them in matters of weight. They were, in short, his chief ministers. One of their privileges was to sit above the bishops in choir, and, at matins, to be called to the eighth lesson. Apocrisiarius was, at that period, the title of a nuncio or a legate.* There was also a primicerius scholæ cantorum—the president of the College of Singers; a primicerius of the notaries, an order of functionaries established by Saint Clement I; a primicerius defensorum—the captain of a military order established by Saint Gregory the Great, to have guard of the Lateran and the other Papal establishments: a primicerius of the judges who presided in the different courts. But none of these, except the two first mentioned—the primicerius and secundicerius of the holy Roman Church, were immediately attached to the palace.

The vice-dominus, another high functionary, was governor of the household, or major-domo. The saccellarius was the treasurer and paymaster, so called from the sachel or large purse he used. Then, there was the proto-scriniarius, chief of the secre-

* Apocrisiarius, minister Romanæ Ecclesiæ a secretis, Legatus secretus. Hincmar. Ep. 3.

taries or scriveners. The adnomenclator had an office similar to that of the gentleman-usher of modern times. There was an arcarius, who had charge of the plate and other costly objects. It was his duty, when giving out the various pieces to those acolytes and others, who were to carry them in the procession, or minister with them in the sanctuary, to take an inventory of the pieces, and also of the jewels with which they were in most cases adorned. The modern camerlingo and the ancient camerarius held the same office. The office of the bibliothecarius, a high dignity of the Papal palace, combined the functions of librarian, archivist, and secretary for foreign affairs, in one and the same person.

These moved for the most part immediately in front of, or close after the Pontiff, who was attended by his court, all in proper costume: the clergy wearing their vestments, and the entire march being characterized by military order, but without the display of arms. Thus the *Ordo* says, they, the regionary clergy and the rest, are to move in separate companies or bands, "in diversis turmis"—sections or squadrons, perhaps, we should say: and between the companies, were regular intervals.

It was the duty of the cardinal of the station to turn out at the head of his subaltern clergy, with the cross and thuribles for incense, and, at a certain point of his approach, to be prepared to receive the pontiff. After receiving his blessing, he was to conduct the Pontiff to the scene of the festival. There, the cardinals and their titular clergy ranged according to order and dignity round the *presbyterium*, usually occupying the absis (a slightly elevated stage or dais at the upper or west end of the basilica); the choir in its place, between the head of the nave, that is, according to basilica arrangement, between the back of the altar and the faithful separately arranged,—the males in the south, the females in the north aisle,—are all prepared to receive him. We propose to give, in an Appendix, the minute description of the solemnities.

The reader, whose taste may lead him to examine the subject, cannot fail, we imagine, to be struck with a resemblance between the scene as there set forth, and one which is described by Saint John, as having been revealed to him in Patmos during one of his visions, when he was permitted to behold how the same sacrifice, offered up on those altars of the Apostles and martyrs, is celebrated in that eternal temple, where Deity is visibly revealed to the beatific vision of the angels and the elect. In these glorious old basilicas of Rome, at that period refulgent with newness, how gorgeous and like to a creation of enchantment must have been the effect, when their arcades were adorned with the most brilliant and richest embroidery of the looms of the East—their niches, their altars, tabernacles, oratories, shrines and sanctuaries, massive with barbaric gold, and lighted up for worship by candelabrums and lamps beyond number, were glittering with the donaries of Constantine, of Belisarius, of Clovis, Totila, Theodoric, Offa, Luitprand, Charlemagne—in short, of the greatest of every dynasty, and of every race of conquerors, ambitious to make their exploits and their love of Saint Peter shine forth and dazzle the nations with their priceless jewellery.* When the

* The following is the account of the manner in which Saint Peter's was wont to be illuminated at the period of which we are speaking. By day or by night, no one of the many chapels, oratories, or altars was left without a light; before some of these several lights were always burning. These lights amounted in all to 115—"omnes igitur candelæ, quæ quotidie ardent in ecclesia Beati Petri sunt CXV. *ad minus omne nocte.*" On the station day, the whole number was 250—in stationibus vero sunt CCL. On the festivals of the Dedication, of Ascension, and of Saint Peter, what are called the *retia* were lighted. By these, not only the interior of the basilica and its vestibule, but also the Paradise, or exterior piazza, was brilliantly adorned with lights; from the description, it would appear, in a manner not unlike that adopted in the matchless illuminations of the same basilica and piazza, in modern ages. We give the entire passage *in extenso*—it richly deserves it—that the learned reader may judge for himself: "Quot lampades ardeant quotidie in ecclesia B. Petri. *Ex Ord. Rom. XI. app. p.* 161. Ad luminaria in altare B. Petri VIII lampades, in corpore (ejus) die noctuque; ante pectoralia tres lampades; in unoquoque capitulo una, et in unâquâque coronâ, una candela per totam noctem accendatur, donec missa finiatur. Quæ nimirum capitula sunt ad minus XXXIIII usque ad crucifixos. Omnes igitur lampades ab altari B. Petri usq. ad crucifixos sunt quinquaginta omni nocte.

"In stationibus vero unoquoque capitulo quatuor candela; in rete, quod est in atrio ecclesiæ XII. in virga XVIII. ante veronicam X. die noctuq. ante imaginem B. Mariæ, quæ est de fragrance of Araby the blessed, ascending in wreathed clouds from many a golden thurible like prayers of the saints, perfuming the atmosphere, regaling the ravished senses of every tribe, and tongue, and nation, there represented in the most fervent and noble of their children, gathered as pilgrims round the shrine of Saint Peter; and when the sanctuary itself was arrayed in the glory of the eucharistic sacrifice—the priests and levites in their grades around the altar, the Pontiff on his throne announc-

mosibo (mosivo) post veronicam, I. In S. Processo I. ad Sam. Mariam de Cancellis III. In arca majori, ubi andivinus requiescere corpus B. Mathiæ Ap. I. nocte et die; nocte vero tota VIII. ad Stam. Crucem. In S. Johanne ad Fontis (in the baptistery) I. in S. Lucia I. ad S. Pastorem I. ad S. Greg. I. nocte dieque, in unoquoque eorum in Vaticano I. in Sancta Maria in Oratorio I. ad S. Leon. I. Petro et Paulo I. ad S. Barthol. I. ante crucifixos II. in rete IV. in virga III. ante portes ecclesiæ deforis V. in unoquoque porticalium III. in S. Petronilla II. in S. Andrea I.

"Omnes igitur candela, quæ quotidie ardent in eccl. B Petri sunt CXV. ad minus omni nocte; in stationibus vero sunt CCL. In Dedicatione, in Ascensione, et festo S. Petri et octava ejus retia accendantur; sed rete magnum quod est in atrio ecclæ. scilicet ante portam argenteam, in festo S. Petri et octava tantum.

"Præterea quatuor funes de *antiqua consuetudine* extenduntur in festo B. Petri et oct. ejus, in atrio ejusdem ecclæ. *i. e.* in paradiso, in modum crucis, et ligantur de porticalibus (the porticos?) ad pineam æneam, quæ est in paradiso; et in unoquoque fune VI candelæ suspenduntur. In gradibus vero, scilicet ante ecclam. B. Mariæ *in Turri*, extenditur unus magnus funis a porticali quod est super gradus mortuorum usque ad donum Petri Johannis de Pampano, in qua de jure debet ligari secundum tenorem locationis; et suspenduntur in eo XVIII *candelæ*."

ing the Gospel of salvation, or in adoration before the Victim—the hosannahs, and songs of jubilee and praise borne aloft on the triumphant and surging tide of many voices; were not the scenes, the sounds, above all, the hopes, the emotions, the soaring of heart and mind, which all this excited, immeasurably more august and impressive than anything ever beheld in the capital and sanctuary of the Pagan world? Were they not, of all things on earth, most like to what the solemn public act and expression of homage, to be offered in the name of the human race to heaven's eternal Emperor, ought to be? It was such a scene, in fine, as that to which the Evangelist seems to point, when he exclaims: "The holy city, the new Jerusalem, I saw descending from heaven, adorned as a bride prepared for her spouse; and I said, Behold the tabernacle of God with men, and he will dwell with them."

To sum up, in a few words, the chief features of this primitive Rome of the Popes, what spectacle more wonderful or instructive can be imagined? View it as the field of battle, on which the "powers of darkness" had been overthrown, after a struggle of three hundred years, and forced to recognise the victory of the Cross—then, how appropriate and significant that very air of disorder which has made such a medley, as we have seen, of the ancient and the new, confounding the Christian and the Pagan order of things together—the one laid low and lacerated with ruin, the other glowing with newness, adorned and erect. How vividly is the beholder reminded by all this, that the victors have only bivouacked upon the field, preparing to advance to other triumphs? In this light, the processions are the grand march of a triumphant army to parade. The banners consecrated by victory are uplifted, and the spoils and insignia commemorative of the conflict are displayed with pomp. Outbursts of acclamation break forth, but they are no longer the shouts of insulting triumph over captives whose only crime was their attachment to freedom. They are the litanies, which are lifted up among the valleys of the seven hills, with a power that resembles the "sound of many waters." Upon the field of Mars, through the Forum, on the Capitol, along the Great Circus, and round the blood-soaked arena—those scenes where the air was wont for ages to be rent with vociferations of myriads, as if drunk with human gore—the canticles of mercy and charity, the kyrie-leison, the Halleluia, the "Gloria in excelsis Deo, et in terra pax hominibus," the praises of Christ and of his saints, are made to reconsecrate the echoes, so often and so ferociously profaned. These processions are led round, and cross the field of conflict in every direction, to attest that the Lion of the tribe of Juda has conquered. They build up his trophies: they surround with pomp the tombs where the most heroic of his soldiers, who fell in the arms of victory, lie buried. They make trophies from the spoils of the vanquished. The temple of all the gods is consecrated to the Queen of all the saints and martyrs; the Pantheon is the temple of S. Maria ad Martyres. On the Circus of Nero stands the mausoleum of Saint Peter, the *limina Apostolorum.*

Not only was Rome a field of battle; according to the laws of augury, it was also one vast temple. The Apostle Saint John represents it as the great school of error and debauchery, where the nations, both kings and people, were poisoned with the chalice of spiritual death. We have seen that it was essentially, and from its embryo, a camp—a place of arms, eternally machinating and preparing the means for new conquests. The Rome of the Pontiffs also may with the strictest propriety be regarded as but one vast sanctuary, so crowded was it in all directions, without as well as within the walls, with basilicas, oratories, churches, consecrated cemeteries, and innumerable shrines and altars. From their lives, one would be led to suppose, were no other evidence supplied him, that they considered it the highest function of their Apostolic office to attend with solicitude and the most unbounded liberality to the repairs of this temple; to beautify it with every object most brilliant in nature, most exquisite in art, and most costly in the estimation of mankind; in fine, to fill it with tokens of worship in every part, and to leave nothing undone that, in its majesty, the mystic significance, the heavenly order which distinguished it, in the richness and perfection of every thing, whether addressed to ear or eye, connected with it—that worship should be as worthy as mortals could make it of its divine and only object.

Nor had the new city less pretensions than the old to be regarded as the great model school of the nations; but oh! in a sense, and with an influence, how severely contrasting with the past. We dwell not, however, on this phase of the subject—that is upon the view in which Rome is seen to stand preeminent in the science of the saints, in maintaining the integrity of the Gospel against the innumerable efforts made by heresy to corrupt it, or to give to its teaching a perverted sense; in perpetually exhibiting, by the sublime and diversified religious and charitable institutions within its walls, the entire Gospel in action—illustrated, by example; and in supporting those seminaries of sacred learning which, on attentively surveying it, we shall discover to form one amongst its characteristics, and not, by any means, the least striking one. But we abstain from entering this avenue of the subject, and, turning to our proper sphere, direct our attention to the study of the Papal city, considered in a purely terrestrial light. And in this direction, we start with a testimony from the most brilliant, but, certainly, not the least inconsistent historian of the present day.

"Many noble monuments," he says, "which have since been destroyed or defaced, still retained their pristine magnificence; and travellers, to whom Livy and Sallust were then unintelligible, might gain from the Roman aqueducts and temples some faint notion of Roman history. The dome of Agrippa, still glittering with bronze, the mausoleum of Adrian, not yet deprived of its columns and statues (?), the Flavian amphitheatre, not yet degraded into a quarry, told to the Mercian and Northumbrian pilgrims some part of the story of that great civilized world which had passed away. The islanders returned with awe deeply impressed on their half opened minds, and told the wondering inhabitants of the hovels of London and York, that near the grave of Saint Peter, a mighty race, now extinct, had piled up buildings which would never be dissolved till the judgment day."*

It was less however to the classic, than to the Christian view of Rome that the thoughts and affections of the pilgrim were usually directed. The advantages, so eloquently recited, as arising from the intercourse, by pilgrimage and for religious affairs, of the barbarian nations with Rome, are by no means overrated: they are but trifles, however, when compared with others by which those nations became enriched, through their commerce with the "mother and mistress of all churches."

We do not find that any particular attention was paid to, or any high-flown enthusiasm expressed by Charlemagne, at beholding the memorials of that art in which he stood pre-eminent,—higher far than Trajan or even than the conqueror, who was at once the greatest of the Cæsars and of the Romans. It

* Macaulay's History of England, vol. i. pp. 9, 10.

is not recorded that he offered any peculiar homage to the trophies of Marius, to the tomb of the Scipios, or the colossus of Nero. It may be possible that he did; but we do know that his first act, on entering Rome, was to ascend the threshold of the Apostle, on bended knees, kissing the ground as he advanced. We find him humbly petitioning to be admitted within the gates of Rome, having an army at his back that could carry it by storm, and this, for the purpose of redeeming his pilgrim-vow, and of yielding up his mighty soul to rapture and to prayer before the trophies of the martyrs who had conquered not alone the world, but, what was immeasurably more arduous, themselves; and this for no thirst of blood or of vain-glory, but for the pure and glowing love of Jesus Christ. Next, after the pardon of his sins and the securing of the interests of the Christian commonwealth which had called him thither, this hero (more unrivalled perhaps as an organizer of civilized, that is, of Christian society, and as a lawgiver, than as the conqueror who subdued the most ferocious nations, and conducted to a successful issue the greatest number of campaigns on the grandest scale, of any warrior that ever lived) when he is to select the objects of the greatest interest for him, in the eternal city, we find him asking for professors of sacred music, humble men brought up in the Schola Cantorum. Through the influence of instruments, apparently so worthless, and of others versed in letters and the arts, the intuitive genius of

Charlemagne distinctly felt and knew that more was to be done in soothing the savagery, and elevating the thoughts and feelings, of his subjects, than if he had been able to transport the Seven Hills with all their superincumbent rubbish beyond the Alps, and plant them in the heart of his kingdom.

We have the most distinguished men of those ages writing to borrow books of the Popes—we read of nations petitioning for apostles to initiate them in the faith of the Gospel, and of communities asking for some sage and devoted leader to conduct them in the way of salvation, or for relics of some champion who suffered for, and with, his Redeemer; but, of petitions for a paving stone of the Triumphal Way, a brick from the Flavian amphitheatre, a sprig of the Ruminal tree, a chip, or a rusty nail from the bridge of Horatius, some dust from a circus, or some mud from a cloaca, we can discover no record or vestige whatever. Instead of this we meet with a Saint Bennet Biscop, a Saint Wilfrid, preparing, by the study of the basilicas in all their proportions and details, and by making themselves masters in the various arts and sciences, to re-produce the same architectural miracles in regions, at that time, the most remote and benighted. These pilgrim-students saw the page of instruction open and luminous, to whatever side they turned in Rome.

Can it be possible to exaggerate the advantages to be derived from the perfect model of Christian society, which was, at that period, presented before the eyes of the millions who visited Rome? There, in the person of the Pontiff-king, surrounded by all that could most indelibly impress the imagination, and the senses, of the nations such as they were then, we behold a spectacle of all others the best calculated to create and confirm respect for authority, which was the primary want of those turbulent, and, at best, but semi-barbarous ages. The sight of an entire population regimented as were the Romans of that day, each one knowing his own officer, his proper post, the hour and the standard which regulated his march—how overrate the order which must of necessity have been the result, not alone within the temple, where every class, and sex, and age, had its determined position, but also, in the processions, and in the other movements of society; or how overrate, either, the impressive effect of an example like that, on the future ideas and deportment of those, who, with reverent feelings and for the first time, beheld it? This discipline, and harmonious organization, they saw not alone in the sanctuary and around the altar, where every move, and attitude, and sound, and look, and thought, were as distinctly regulated by rubric, and with discrimination and taste as refined, as the groups in a beautiful picture, or the notes of a composition in music. They met with it, on occasions, when the impressions they had brought with them to Rome would have led them to anticipate nothing but tumult, and uproar, and confusion; witness the reception of Charlemagne, as we have described it, on the first of the several visits he paid to Rome of the Pontiffs.

Nor were the barbarian nations left trusting to these casual lessons. It is true that every pilgrim turned student in Rome, even though remaining but for a few months or weeks, was sure to make such progress as to place him whole centuries in advance of his more plodding compatriots, who had never been there; but, in addition, there were multitudes of every nation of the west, and of other countries also, and more especially from Greece, residing in permanent establishments in the Pontifical city. The proofs of this recur at every page in the lives of the Popes. We see the Saxon, the Frank, the Lombard, the Burgundian colleges forming a constant element of the grant pageants, such as the procession to receive a king, an exarch, an emperor, or a pontiff, on approaching to Rome. The annals of even the most remote of the western nations—the Irish—the lives of their saints, abound in notices of the holy pilgrims who journeyed from that remote corner of the earth, to the tombs of the Apostles. One of the first purposes to which we find a respite from the inroads of the Danes converted in the ninth century is, to send an embassy from the Irish princes, to obtain, from Charles the Bald, a free and secure passage through his dominions for the Irish pilgrims to Rome. In an unpublished Irish MS. called the Leabher Breac—a collection of singular importance and interest in an historical point of view—there are a great many such notices. They abound still more in the Lives of the Irish Saints, as published by Colgan. As we see by what is mentioned in the celebrated Epistle of Saint Cummian published by Usher, these Irish pilgrims, whether going as envoys, or students, or to satisfy their devotion, continued to tarry there for years. In the Annals of the Benedictines, a very curious account is given by Mabillon of what occurred on occasion of a company of Irish pilgrims stopping at Saint Gall's, on their return from Rome. The two chief of them were Marcus, a bishop, and his nephew, called Marcellus—that is, the little or beloved Marcus. The community at Saint Gall's—at that period highly distinguished for the flourishing school of their cloisters—were so taken with the scholarship which these ecclesiastics displayed, that no entreaties were spared to prevail on them to remain—Marcellus at Saint Gall's, and Marcus at Saint Martin's at Rheims—as professors. They at length consented, and such scholars as Walfrid Strabo and others, not less illustrious for learning and the cultivation of letters in the ninth century, were amongst their pupils; but the followers of the Irish Bishop became so excited, when they learned that they were to return to Scotia, (as Ireland was then designated,) without him, that it was from a window, the doors of the convent having been strongly barred, that the bishop was obliged to give them his blessing and the money-purse for the journey, to which they turned in tears, and heart-broken, at leaving their beloved Marcus and Marcellus behind. The Greeks had regular monastic communities at Rome, and we shall see from the life of Pope Hadrian II, by Gulielmus Bibliothecarius, that besides these there were crowds of devout and learned persons sojourning there, not only from Constantinople, but from Alexandria, Antioch, and Jerusalem. So long as there were any Christians in the African province, they also resorted to Rome. As for the Lombard, Frank, Gothic, and other continental nations, it would be superfluous to dwell on the proofs of their uninterrupted commerce with Rome. The English, though more remote (the Romans, of old, regarding their country as the end of the earth) were, notwithstanding, so numerous that their residences swelled into a town; for it was called in their own language a "Burgh,"—a name which attaches to the quarter of Rome situated round the hospital of the Santo Spirito, to the present day.

We can form no adequate notion, at this distance of time, of the vast and varied influence which such a combination of circumstances must have exercised over the nations. For the barbarians, who were little better than wild beasts when they first broke in on the provinces of the tottering empire, the Papal city had been throughout the origin of every blessing and improvement, of every remedy for mollifying their ferocity, and of every help for elevating them in the scale of society. The unsophisticated emotions of gratitude, naturally resulting from such a relation, were fortified and developed in an eminent degree, when the colleges founded in Rome for the ingenuous youth of the new nations had been for some time sending forth scholars, in swarm after swarm, to communicate the erudition, the poetry, the arts, the accomplishments, and the varied experience, with which, having been enriched in the great emporium—placed, as we have seen, between the two great worlds of the Pagan and Christian order of things—they went forth "to renew the face of the earth." For, as we set out with stating, the city of the Pontiffs, as truly and obviously as it was a temple, a field of battle, a college, was also a camp, in which, were incessantly exercised, and hardened, and accomplished for the most arduous service, the forces which were to go forth, not as those of Cæsar had done, to shed oceans of blood, but to effect such conquests as Saint Augustin effected in Britain, Saint Patrick in Hibernia, Saint Boniface in Germany, and so of all the other western nations—every one of which stands indebted for the Gospel to Rome.

It is only when considered in this, their genuine light, that the various movements, exercises, formalities, of processions, stations, regimenting of the clergy and laity, in the temples, and outside of them also, with the other practices, and habits, of the details of which, had our limits permitted, we could have conveyed a far more circumstantial and vivid description, that these leading characteristics of the Rome of the Popes are seen to acquire the significancy that strictly belongs to them. To describe the boasted perfection of discipline in the legions who fought under the eagle, it was said, that, with the exception of bloodshed, there was no perceptible difference between their exercises on the Campus Martius, and the hardships and conflicts of active service. The same was to be said of the legions, who marched forth under the cross. They had been so well prepared by voluntary austerities, and laborious activity, that, for them, the toils and the dangers which heroism alone could encounter or bear were robbed of their terrors.

Nor were the contrasts between Rome as the head-quarters of Paganism and of Christianity confined to what took place within the boundaries of the encampment itself—it was, when those two adverse systems were viewed in their action on the world abroad, that those contrasts affected the imagination with greater force. Rome under the Popes also had her legions, and her generals who carried the boundaries of her empire to an extent, which that of the Cæsars had never reached. But their invasions were a source of joy inexpressible to the vanquished, and of advantages not to be calculated, infinite as they were, and never to have an end. They came not to take away liberty, but to bestow it; not to usurp the dominion and the riches of earthly provinces, but to throw open, to the nations, the rights, and immortal privileges, and enjoyments of the "kingdom of heaven." Their falchion was the word of God; their banner the cross of the Redeemer; the vanquished were proud of, and rejoiced in, their subjugation. They found in it the source of inexhaustible blessings. Thus have we been enabled, by steadily adhering to the facts of history, not only to ascertain with precision the true fountain-head of the Papal sovereignty, and to trace its progressive development, but, in these latter reflections, to lay our hand, palpably, upon another great aim of Providence in so wonderfully founding and maturing this power. At a preceding stage, we established the grand and incontrovertible fact, that, for the effectual and perfect exercise of their functions as the successors of the Prince of the Apostles, it is an ordination of Providence that the Popes should be sovereigns; from what has been stated in the last few pages, it cannot be questioned that the highest and best interests, not of religion alone, but of civilization also, required that the resources of a kingdom should be placed in their hands.

In tracing this astonishing power, the horizon widens and becomes grander with each step as we advance—we are now on the verge of a movement, the most sublime, in the spectacle it opens before us, and, in its consequences, the most enduring and vast, as to mere earthly results. We allude to the act, which, in placing on the brow of Charlemagne the diadem of Christian empire, imparted to that suspension of chaos, and that social and political organization which was contingent, up to that moment, on the life of a man near seventy, the permanency and the susceptibility of improvement and of becoming hourly more consolidated and better defined, that prepared the work of his genius to withstand the most awfully anarchical agencies which are to be unchained in the tenth century, and thus to become the basis of the present civilized system. This founding of Europe, somewhat after the same fashion as that in which Venice was founded among the Lagunes—the entire barbarian world up to the latter years of Charlemagne having presented no other aspect but one of universal instability, turbulence, and disorder—we shall not only discover to have been the work of a Pope; but we shall see what is more singular still, that it is out of an occurrence, in itself the most shocking, and which in ordinary hands must have proved an unmitigated and disgraceful calamity, in its effects, that good so imperishable and so immense was extracted by the wisdom and energy of Pope Leo III.

APPENDIX,

No. I.—Vol. I. p. 451.

The following notes are from two ancient Ordinals of the Roman Church. They prescribe the ceremonies of the Papal High-Mass. Both are given by Mabillon in his Museum Italicum, tom. 2, p. 1—51. The Ordo which is considered the more ancient by Mabillon, and to which he assigns the first place, was regarded by Onufrio Panvinio as not so ancient as that to which Mabillon assigns the second place; but both are on all hands allowed to belong to a most remote antiquity. That first in order, according to the Museum Italicum, we may say with certainty was made use of by St. Gregory the Great, in arranging his Sacramentarium. Very ancient MS. copies of it were found in the Archives of Monte Casino, of St. Gall's, of Einsidlen, and in the Colbertine Collection. Mabillon's edition is printed from the St. Gall's MS. That this copy was not made until after the times of Hadrian I. is manifest from a rubric and prayer inserted in it,—viz. Num. 24—*ut flecteretur pro Carlo rege*, and Num. 28—*oratio pro rege Francorum*. Had it not been made previously to A.D. 800, the title of *Imperator* instead of *Rex* had been applied to Charlemagne, who is the *rex Carolus* and the *rex Francorum* of the text.

The Pontiff after being received by the regionary guard and clergy on his approach to the stational church, in the manner already stated, and having alighted, aided by two deacons, proceeds at once to the sacristy—*secretarium*, supported by the aforementioned deacons, one on either hand. The Pontiff being seated is saluted by the deacons, who immediately proceed to change their vestments in the vestibule of the *secretarium*. There also the deacon who is to chant the Gospel, by direction of the Pope's vicar, registers or marks the place of the Gospel, the book being held for that purpose by an acolyte, and in some cases by two, on account of the great weight of the ornaments with which it was customary to cover the *evangelium*. The acolyte followed by a sub-deacon carries the Gospel to the *presbyterium*, or, as we now call it, the sanctuary. The sub-deacon receives it on his vestment in front of the high altar, on which he reverently places it. The faithful have already taken their allotted places in the Church, the females in one aisle the men in the other, the princes and patricians in the *senatorium*: the clergy are ranged in the sanctuary,—the bishops to the right, the presbyters to the left of the cathedra,—and the *schola cantorum* in the choir, between the nave and the altar, or in the chancel.

In the meantime, the Pontiff is being vested in the secretarium, the regionary sub-deacons officiating—one bearing the alb—*lineam,* from the plane of the altar where it was handed to him, folded, by a tonsured *cubicularius;* another bearing the cincture—*cingulum;* a third the amict—*analogium;* a fourth the linen dalmatic—*lineam dalmaticam;* a fifth, the chasuble—*planetam. Et sic per ordinem induunt Pontificem.* The pallium, held by a sub-deacon of the Palace, is taken by whichever of the regionary deacons or sub-deacons the Pontiff may please to assign the honour to, and adjusted with three jewelled pins, one on the back of the chasuble, another on the front, and another on the right shoulder. Having so adjusted the pallium, the deacon salutes the Pontiff saying: "My Lord, we crave a blessing"—*jube Domine benedicere.* "May the Lord have us all in his keeping," is the Pontiff's answer: to which the deacon responds, *Amen.* All the time the Pope is being vested the primicerius and secundicerius assist in adjusting the vestments—*ut bene sedeant.*

Then the regionary sub-deacon who holds the Pope's maniple—*mappulam*—folded on his left arm, goes to the portals and chants the word "Schola," that the choir-leader may come to receive the Pope's commands. The leader or *archiparaphonista,* who is also called the *quartus scholæ,* responds "adsum," and presenting himself before the Pontiff, the section of the Schola by whom the mass is to be chanted is designated. The name of the sub-deacon who chants the Epistle—*Apostolum,* is also announced to the Pope; the sub-deacon of the maniple, saying, while adjusting that vestment:—"*Servi domini mei, talis subdiaconus regionarius leget Apostolum, et talis de Schola cantabit.*" This order being sanctioned by the Pontiff, is to be rigorously adhered to, under the severest penalties,—*Et postea non licet alterum mutare in loco lectoris, vel cautoris. Quod si factum fuerit, archiparaphonista a Pontifice excommunicabitur—i.e. is liable to be suspended from his office.*

All this, though long to describe, being accomplished in a few minutes, the archiparaphonista—on instruction from the Pontiff—standing at the sacristy door chants the word "accendite," then, while those ministers whose office it is, are lighting the altar and the sanctuary lamps, he comes to the presbyterium and saluting those of the Schola who have been designated, saying "Domnii jubete," martials them in two cohorts—*acies,* to the right and left in front of the altar, the children being divided between the two cohorts in equal numbers—*infantes ab utroque latere infra per ordinem.* While the choir is being thus arranged and the altar lighted, the thurible is prepared with incense from the golden *thymiaterium* by one of the assistant sub-deacons; and when the first notes of the antiphon of the *introitum* are heard, the deacons enter the secretarium from the vestibule; the Pontiff rises, and giving to his archdeacon his right hand and his left to the second deacon to kiss, proceeds towards the sanctuary supported on either side by his deacons. He is preceded by a palatine sub-deacon and two others with the thurible of incense, and by seven regionary acolytes with tall wax tapers in their hands.

While the procession is thus proceeding, from south to north, it is met by another in which two deacons, in alb and stole, are seen bearing that portion of the blessed eucharist which was set apart in the mass of the preceding day; for the more vividly to shew forth how the Divine mysteries, though celebrated every day, are still but one and the same sacrifice, it was the discipline to reserve at the solemn mass, a part of the consecrated host to be mingled in the chalice with the sacrifice of the following day. It was also the custom for the Pope to send to each of the titles or parishes a part of the host which he offered at his own mass, that the particles thus sent being mingled in the chalice by the several cardinal priests, their communion with their head might be thus rendered perfect, and preserved. Bishops were wont to retain a part of the host offered at the mass in which they received consecration, and to mingle it, in like manner, in the chalice on certain commemorative days, thus to consecrate their communion with the prelate from whom they had received the holy order.

Before coming to the Schola, the seven acolytes with the wax torches divide, four entering the sanctuary by the gate to the right hand, and three by the gate to the left of the altar. The Pontiff kneels before the altar, bowing down before it, and as the second ordo says, *adorat sancta,*—alluding to the blessed eucharist deposited thereon—*Et pertransit Pontifex in caput scholæ, et in gradu superiore, inclinato capite ad altare, primo adorat Sancta, &c.* Then rising, he prays, signing his forehead with the cross, and having given first to the hebdominary bishop, next to the arch-priest, and lastly to the senior deacon, the kiss of peace, he signs to the prior of the Schola to sing the *Gloria*, that is, the doxology by which the *Introitum*, or act of entering into the sanctuary, is concluded. At the *Sicut erat in principio, &c.* the deacons rise, and two by two kiss the altar and return. Then the Pontiff, after kissing the altar and the Gospels laid upon it, proceeds to his throne, and stands facing the east. When the *Kyrie eleison* has been sung, the Pontiff, turning towards the people, entones the *Gloria in excelsis Deo*, and then looking again towards the east, continues to pray till the canticle is ended. Then turning again towards the people, he sings *Pax vobis—Peace be with you;* and after the prayer by which this is followed, the bishops, all ranged on the right of the throne, the presbyters on the left, round the sanctuary, are seated, while the officiating sub-deacon, assisted by the sub-deacons of the region, marshalled to the right and left of the altar ascends the tribune—*in ambonem*—and recites—*legit*—the Epistle. The Epistle ended, a cantor—*cum cantatorio;* that is, a book usually called a Gradual, or Antiphonary—mounts the steps of the tribune, and announces the *Responsum*,—certain verses of a Psalm chanted alternately by the cantor from the steps of the tribune and by the faithful; the *Alleluia*, or the tract, according to the time, was sung from the same place.

Before proceeding to chant the Gospel, the deacon knelt, kissed the Pontiff's feet—*osculans pedes Pontificis;* the latter repeating over him the prayer, "The Lord be in thy heart and on thy lips, &c.—*Dominus sit in corde tuo et in labiis tuis*," *&c.* The deacon kisses the book of the Gospels before lifting it from the altar. He is preceded by two regionary sub-deacons, to minister the incense and hold the book for the deacon, and by two acolytes bearing torches. When all the assistants have kissed the book, it is deposited in a rich case, which is sealed and kept by an acolyte, whose duty it is to bear it back to the Lateran.

Preparations for the offertory have been made in the mean time, and the Pontiff, supported on his right by the primicerius of the notaries, on his left by the primicerius of the *defensores*, and followed by the suite of assistants, comes from his throne to the *senatorium*, outside the sanctuary gate at the head of the nave—*descendit ad senatorium*—and receives the offerings of the princes—*oblationes principum*—the archdeacon pouring the *amulas* of wine as they are received, into the large chalice carried by a sub-deacon. This sub-deacon is followed by an acolyte—*cum cypho super planetam, in quo calix impletus refunditur*. The oblations of bread given to the Pontiff are deposited by the assistant sub-deacons in the white linen cloth held by two acolytes—*in sindonem, quem tenent duo acolythi.* Before passing to the aisle set apart for the female portion of the congregation, the Pontiff descends to the station of the defensores between the nave and the altar—*descendit ante confessionem*—to receive the oblations of their officers.

After the oblations have been received, the Pontiff washes his hands at the throne, and then advances to the altar, where the oblations, both bread and wine, have been prepared by the officiating deacons. The water for the chalice is ministered by the *archiparaphonista;* the archdeacon pours it in, making the sign of the cross—*infundit faciens crucem in calice.* The breads—*oblatas*—prepared on the patena, are presented by the archdeacon to the Pontiff, who offers them; the same he does with the chalice, and bowing down continues in silent prayer.

In the mean time, the various companies of guards, with their officers at their head, the defensores of the palace, of the churches, and of the regions, stand arrayed on the plain of the sanctuary; the cardinals, bishops and presbyters, are in their appointed places; the sub-deacons range themselves behind the altar, looking towards the Pontiff, to make the responses; the faithful, each order, sex and age in its allotted station, are absorbed in prayer, and nothing is heard but the solemn melody of the choirs. At a sign from the celebrant on ending his prayer over the *oblata*, their voices are hushed, and the preface, beginning, *Per omnia sæcula seculorum*, is entoned. The sub-deacons join in the responses to the *Dominus Vobiscum*, the *Sursum corda*, and *Gratias agamus;* they also join in the *Sanctus*, which is called the "Angelic hymn." With its expiring notes all remained bowing down, absorbed in silent prayer; the Pontiff, also bowing down, alone entered on the canon, in which are accomplished the sacred mysteries—*Surgit Pontifex solus et intrat in canonem. Episcopi vero, diaconi, subdiaconi, et presbyteri, in presbyterio permanent inclinati* The elevation takes place at the close of the canon, immediately before the *Paternoster.—Cum dixerit "Per quem hæc omnia Domine," sugit archidiaconus solus. Cum dixerit, "Per ipsum, et cum ipso," levat cum offertorio calicem per ansas, et tenens, exaltat illum juxta Pontificem: Pontifex autem tangit a latere calicem cum oblatis, dicens, "Per ipsum et cum ipso," usque, "per omnia sæcula sæculorum, Amen." Et ponit Pontifex oblationes in loco suo, &c.*

An acolyte, with a veil on his shoulders, holds the patena up to the middle of the canon, when it is taken by a regionary sub-deacon, from whom the archdeacon receives it at the words, *Et ab omni perturbanione securi*, kisses it, and gives it to hold to the second deacon. At the words *Pax Domini sit semper vobiscum*, the Pontiff makes the sign of the cross, thrice, over the chalice, and then mingles in it, the SANCTA, the part of the consecrated host of the previous day's mass—*faciens crucem tribus vicibus manu sua super calicem mittit* SANCTA *in eum.* Then the kiss of peace is given—*Archidiaconus pacem dat episcopo priori, deinde ceteris per ordinem et populis.*

The host is then broken—*ex latere dextro*, and the preparations made for the communion of the faithful, the bishops and presbyters in their places in the presbyterium breaking the particles on the patenas, each patena being held by two regionary subdeacons, and the linen receptacles, the *succula*, with the consecrated hosts, by the acolytes. The Pontiff receives, not at the altar, but at the cathedra,—the removal of the host from the altar having a mystic meaning, usually interpreted as shewing forth the resurrection—*qui dum communicaverit, de ipsa* SANCTA, *quam momorderat, ponit inter manus archidiaconi in calicem,* *faciens crucem ter, dicendo : "Fiat commixtio et consecratio corporis et sanguinis Domini nostri Jesu-Christi accipientibus nobis in vitam æternam. R. Amen."* From the hands of the archdeacon he receives the chalice.* The bishops receive the communion at the cathedra, the presbyters and the other orders of the clergy, at the altar. The Pontiff begins the communion of the people in the *Senatorio,* the bishops and presbyters assisting, and the deacons ministering the chalice, with which they are said to "confirm"—*Pontifex descendit—ut communicet eos qui in senatorio sunt: post quem archidiaconus confirmat. Postea episcopi communicant populum innuente Pontifice, et post eos diaconi confirmant, presbyteri autem jussu Pontificis communicant populum, &c.* During the communion the choir ceases not; but continues to sing the canticle called *antiphonam ad communionem,* until a sign is made, after the assistants have all received from the hands of the Pontiff, on his return from the communion of the people to the cathedra. They then sing the "*Gloria Patri,*" &c.

The antiphon concluded, the Pontiff again approaches the altar, sings the last prayer, or post communion—*dat orationem ad complendum;* the appointed deacon, on a sign from the Pontiff makes the announcement to the people : "*Ite missa est*" *R.* "*Deo Gratias.*" The seven acolytes with the lighted torches form in procession to move to the sacristy before the Pontiff, to whom, as he is about to descend from the altar, the bishops in the presbyterium, bowing down, ask his blessing, which is given : and all return, processionally, to the sacristy in the following order : the Pontiff, with his assistant deacons, preceded by the seven acolytes; the bishops, the presbyters, the monks ; the *schola cantorum;* the military standard-bearers, acolytes, mansionaries; the guards of the sanctuary gates and the cross bearers stationed outside the presbyterium, and the junior mansionarii—*Descendente autem Pontifice in presbyterium, episcopi primum dicant, "Jube domine benedice." R. "Benedicat nos dominus." R. "Amen." Post episcopos presbyteri; deinde monachi; deinde schola; deinde milites draconarii, id est qui signa portant; post eos bajuli, post eos cereostarii, post quos acolythi, qui rugam observant; post eos extra presbyterium cruces postantes, deinde mansionarii juniores; et intrat in secretarium.—Museum Italicum, &c* pp. 3—16, et pp. 41—51.

* From the reign of St. Gregory VII, the title of Archdeacon was discontinued in the Roman Church.

No. II.—Vol. II. p. 96.

The story of Pope Joan, so long made to serve the worst purposes, is now repudiated as a baseless fable by learned Protestant writers, in all countries. See "The Life and Times of Hincmar, Archbishop of Rheims, by the Rev. J. Prichard," pp. 220, 221, and "Gfrorer Geschichte der Ost-und-Westfrankischen Carolinger," Vol. 1, pp. 288, 289.

Onuphrio Panvinio has traced the stupid imposture to its origin, and refuted it with that mastery of erudition for which he was unrivalled in his time. See his Annotations on Platina de Vitis Rom. Pontif. The summary is this. After a thorough investigation of the Roman archives, he arrived at a knowledge clear and manifest of the entire fable—*Vetustissimis tam bibliothecæ Vaticanæ quam aliarum libris diligenter inspectis, cæterisque vetustis ecclesiasticis monumentis accuratè perlustratis, tandem in apertam et manifestam totius fabulæ cognitionem deveni.* He traces it to the author of that most absurd farrago, entitled "De Mirabilius Romæ," which may be seen in the Museum Italicum of Mabillon. He was a Cistercian of the thirteenth century, named Martinus, but different from the celebrated Martinus Cromerus Polonus, as Onuphrius proves. Higher than this date, it cannot be traced. From Anastasius Bibliothecarius, who was living at Rome, and engaged in writing or editing the lives of the Popes for many years before the time assigned as that of Pope Joan's existence, and for long after its supposed termination, down to Pandulphus Pisanus, there is a long list of famous writers, by each of whom the succession of the Roman Pontiffs is carefully noted, and in not one of them is any allusion to this fabulous Pope to be found. We need not again revert to the argument given in the text, which is of itself decisive. In the eleventh century, we find St. Leo IX. writing to Michael Cerularius, the schismatical patriarch of Constantinople, in terms which must convince any candid person that the fable had never been heard of at that time—*Absit autem vt velimus credere, quod publica fama non dubitat asserere, Constantinopolitanæ ecclesiæ contigisse, ut eunuchos contra primum S Concilii Niceni capitulum passim promovendo, fœminam et in sede Pontificum suorum sublimasset aliquando, hoc tam abominabile scelus, et detestabile facinus, etsi enormitas ipsius, vel horror, fraternaque benevolentia non permittit nos credere; consideratâ tamen incuriâ vestrâ erga sanctorum censuram canonum, quod eunuchos non solum ad clericatum sed et ad pontificatum indifferenter ac solemniter adhuc promovetis, fieri potuisse pensamus. &c.*

Add to this the inherent absurdities of the tale itself, which places Mayence in England, and makes Athens a famous seat of learning in the ninth century, and more than enough has been said about it.

No. I.—Vol. III. p. 269.

The following is only the second part of a very learned review of what is said regarding Boniface VIII in Sismondi's so-called History of the Italian Republics. In the first part his misrepresentations as to the abdication of Pope St Celestine V., and the consequent election of Boniface, are disposed of. The entire paper was originally written in Italian, and read before the Academia della Religione Catolica, at Rome: it afterwards appeared in an English dress, in the pages of the Dublin Review, Nov. 1841, vol. xi. p. 505. This very interesting historical essay is generally known to be from the able and eloquent pen of the Right Rev. Dr. Wiseman. Indeed, it is quoted as his Lordship's work, in Rohrbacher's Ecclesiastical History.

"Hitherto we have been engaged with the commencement of Boniface's pontificate. Gladly would we transcribe for our readers the magnificent declaration of doctrine which he laid upon the high altar of St. Peter's basilica, on the day of his coronation. But we must pass it by only referring such as wish to see it to the learned continuator of Baronius. To him likewise we send such as wish to be fully instructed in the great public transactions of Boniface's pontificate. In the documents so carefully given by him, they will find ample materials for correcting the erroneous views too commonly given of the Pope's treatment of other nations. They will find, for instance, that the whole of his negociations, and the exercise of his influence and power were directed, not to the sowing of dissensions, the excitement of feuds, or the kindling of war; but to the pacification of Europe, the succour of oppressed princes and prelates, and the adjustment of differences between contending states. He had not been many days upon the throne before he at once turned his attention to the wants of every part, from Sweden to Sicily, and from Spain to Tartary. The vigour displayed by him in all his measures, his efforts to gain by mild persuasions, and when this failed, by energetic steps, appear in every page of his *Registers*, and may be traced in the documents extracted from thence by the diligence of Raynaldus. We could hope to add but little to what he has collected, though we would willingly go into some of the principal occurrences of the pontificate, especially the transactions of Sicily. However, we have undertaken to treat principally of the personal character and conduct of Boniface; and we therefore hasten on to a part of his life which has been more especially misrepresented. We mean the contest between the Pope and the noble family of Colonna, his supposed persecution of it, the destruction of their fortress and city of Palestrina, the ancient Præneste, and his consequent suffering and death.

"We will introduce the subject by a concise but candid analysis of Sismondi's narrative of the contest, and then proceed to examine it by documentary evidence. He tells us therefore, that the occasion on which Pope Boniface most betrayed the violence of his character, was in this affair, the events of which he enumerates as follows:—

"'1. There were in the Sacred College two Cardinals of the illustrious house of Colonna (Peter and James), who had been opposed to the election of Boniface, and only tricked into approving of it. He cites the authority of Ferretti and Pipino. They were sufficiently powerful to be able to manifest their discontent.

"'2. The enmity of Boniface probably drove them to espouse the part of the Kings of Sicily (Arragon); at least, this was the pretext seized by him for issuing a violent decree against them, in which he deposed them from their cardinalitial dignity.

"'3. The Colonnas answered this violent bull by a manifesto, in which they declared that they did not recognize Boniface for Pope or head of the Church; that Celestine had no right or will to abdicate, and that the election of a successor during his lifetime was necessarily null and illegitimate.

"'4. This manifesto increased the Pope's rage, and he confirmed his former sentence, and issued a declaration of war against the Colonnas, in form of a crusade. An army was sent out, under the direction of two legates, and many cities belonging to the family were taken; Palestrina, however, defied their efforts.

"'Upon this, Boniface sent ("we are assured") for the celebrated general, Guido of Montefeltro, now become a Franciscan friar, to come to the siege. "He ordered him by virtue of his vow of obedience to examine how the town might be reduced, promising him at the same time a plenary absolution for whatever he might do or advise contrary to his conscience. Guido yielded to the solicitations of Boniface; he examined the fortifications of Palestrina, and, discovering no way of getting possession of these by force, returned to the Pope, and begged of him to absolve him still more expressly of every crime he had committed, or that he might commit in giving his advice; and when he had secured that absolution, he said: 'I see only one course; it is, to promise much and to perform little.' After having thus advised perfidious conduct, he returned to his convent."

"'6. Boniface, in consequence, offered to the besieged most advantageous terms; promised favour to the Colonnas, if in three days they appeared before him. The city was delivered up, but the perfidious counsel followed.

"'The Colonnas received secret warning, that, if they appeared before Boniface, their lives would be taken; and they fled to distant countries.'

"We really doubt whether history could match this narrative in partial and unwarranted statements. We will examine it part by part.

"First, then, the whole recital of the origin of the differences between Boniface and the *Colonnesi* (as they are usually called) is quite erroneous. The two Cardinals did not oppose his election; neither were they tricked into giving him their votes. Our grounds for these assertions are the following:—1. The narrative of Ferretus is a mere fable, the fiction of some enemy, unsupported, or rather denied by sound testimony; in fact, Sismondi has done no more than here allude to it in general terms. 2. On the other hand, in the instrument drawn up by the Cardinals Colonna, and forwarded to every part of Europe, containing their reasons for disallowing Boniface's election and right to the pontificate; though they vaguely hint at unfair practices in procuring Celestine's abdication, they never once allude to any irregularity in Boniface's election. Now had such a disgraceful trick been played upon the Colonnas, as Ferretus's narrative supposes, it would have cast serious doubts, at least in an enemy's eye, upon the validity of the nomination. This silence is surely of great weight. 3. Boniface himself, on the other hand, in his reply to the Colonna libel, declares that those very Cardinals gave him their votes in the usual form, by scrutiny. 'Nec possent supradicta' (acts acknowledging him for the true pope) 'metu proponere se fecisse, qui nos in scrutinio, more memoratæ Ecclesiæ cardinalium elegerant, et nominaverant eligendum in Papam, quando de nobis timendum non erat.' Would Boniface have ventured to assert this (which, moreover, they never contradicted, either then or afterwards, in his process) to their faces, if his election had been grossly irregular, and he had not been chosen by suffrage, but had named himself Pope? 4. Cardinal Stephanensius informs us that Celestine was chosen Pope by *scrutiny* and *accession*—the usual modes—the Cardinals being wonderfully unanimous in their election. 5. St. Antoninus expressly tells us that the two Cardinals Colonna were among the first to give Boniface their votes.

"2. Did the enmity of Boniface drive them to take part with the King of Arragon? We answer that Boniface shewed no such enmity. Soon after his election, he became the guest of the family, trusting himself confidently into their castle of Zagarolo, and being treated, as he himself acknowledges, with marked kindness. We find also in the *Regesta* of Boniface, in the Vatican Archives, favours granted to them in the second year of his pontificate. What, then, was the origin of the feud, and on whose side did the fault lie? We answer, that its origin was twofold, and the blame entirely with the Cardinals. According to Sismondi, the contest was between the Pope and that noble family, whereas, the commencement was a family quarrel, in which appeal was made to the Pope. Cardinal James Colonna had three brothers, Matthew, Otho, and Landulf, who were co-heirs with him in the vast possessions of the family. By an instrument dated April 23, 1292, preserved in the Barberini Archives, and published in an interesting and important work, for this portion of history, these three gave up the administration and possession of all the estates to the Cardinal; with an understanding, of course, that he was to administer for their joint benefit, though without any obligation of rendering them an account of his administration. The Cardinal kept entire possession, so as to leave his brothers in absolute indigence. Thereupon they appealed to the Pope, who justly enough took their part and called in vain upon their brother to do them justice. This is mentioned in the bull of deposition against the Cardinal, but Sismondi never alludes to it. To read him one would imagine the Colonnas were every way innocent, and the most wronged men on earth, and Boniface exclusively the tyrant. So far was Boniface's quarrel from being against the entire Colonna family, that one of the brothers, Landulf, was named by him a captain in the expedition against Palestrina. The second source of strife was the one mentioned, with some doubt, by Sismondi—the decided partizanship shewn by the Colonnas for the house of Arragon, then at war with the Pope. Our historian would naturally lead us to suppose that Boniface's bull against them was the first step taken towards them. Now, *audi alteram partem;* let us hear the Pope's own statement. He tells us that Frederic of Arragon had sent emissaries into his dominions to stir up enmity to him, and that they had met countenance and favour from the family of Colonna, and had been aided and assisted by it; that he, according to the principles of the Holy See, ever more prone to kindness and forgiveness than to severity, now strove to gain them by addressing them with fatherly kindness, now to persuade them by words of charitable correction; and, these failing, held out to them severe threats; shewing them the shaft pointed, before it was released from the bow. But nothing availed, and the Pope therefore proceeded to demand, as a pledge of their fidelity, the custody of their castles, a right constantly claimed by liege lords, when having reason to doubt their vassal's faith. This they refused, and the Pope had recourse to further steps, but not at once.

"The document from which we extract these public declarations of Boniface's, is the one which Sismondi calls a violent bull, and which he tells us they answered by a manifesto, denying the Pope's title to the Papacy. He is as accurate as usual: the Colonna manifesto was issued, within a few hours, at the same time as the bull; it probably had the advantage of being the first out. But we must fill up one or two important omissions of M. Sismondi. One would naturally conclude from his narrative, that the denial of the Pope's rights was imagined by the Colonnas in revenge or retort for the bull. Now let us look a little at the chronology of events. Let the reader bear in mind that this document, abridged by Sismondi, bears date the tenth of May, 1297. So open were the declarations of the two Cardinals, uncle and nephew, against the validity of Boniface's election, before this period, that on Saturday, the fourth of that month, the latter had sent John of Palestrina, one of his clerks of the chamber, to Cardinal Peter Colonna, summoning him to appear that very evening before him; because it was his wish to put the question to him, in the presence of the other cardinals, whether or no he held him to be true Pope. The prelate conveyed the message; but the two Cardinals instead of obeying, fled with many of their family that night from Rome. This message the Colonnas themselves, admit to have been sent to them, in their libel or manifesto.

"Where they concealed themselves at first is not known; but this is certain, that at daybreak on the tenth, they were at Lunghezza, a house belonging to the Conti family, in company with the apostolic writer Giovanni da Gallicano, two friars minor, Deodato Rocci of Monte Prenestino, and the singular, and afterwards most holy, Jacopone da Todi, and a notary of Palestrina, Domenico Leonardi, who, by their order, wrote the manifesto, denying Boniface to be Pope, which Sismondi speaks of as answer to a bull published at Rome, twelve miles off, the same day, and probably later in the day! This libel, as contemporaries justly call it, they sent in every direction, and even had affixed to the doors, and placed on the high altar of St. Peter's church. Is it a wonder that after this bold act of defiance, against Boniface's power both spiritual and temporal, he took up both swords, and proclaimed war against his contumacious clergy and rebellious vassals? His invitations to his friends were obeyed; the neighbouring states sent him troops, or seized, like the people of Forli, the castles belonging to his enemies; and soon Palestrina alone remained in their possession.

"4. This city had been all along the stronghold of the Colonnas the nest in which all their treasons had been hatched, the refuge to which they could flee in security ;—Boniface therefore turned all his forces against it. On this point we have no comment to make.

"5. But now comes the sad history of Guido of Montefeltro. First, let us ask what historical authority there is for the tale of perfidy, which Sismondi with great "assurance" relates of Guido's being at all present at the siege, or giving any such advice? He quotes, indeed, three—Dante, Ferretus, and Pipino; virulent enemies of the Pope. Between the narratives of the two latter there are glaring contradictions, one at least of which we shall have occasion to see ; and Ferretus, as Muratori well observes, had no better voucher or guide for this tale than the poet, whose very words he quotes. Moreover, throughout the whole of his narrative about Boniface, he evidently writes from hearsay and calumnious reports, using such expressions as, 'they say—it is reported,' as the learned Italian critic observes. Nay, it is in truth, rather startling to find Sismondi referring for his authorities to the pages of Muratori, and never even hinting that their sagacious publisher, in both places repels, as mere fictions and calumnies, the very passage for which he refers. Thus he writes on Ferretus :—"Quæ hic habet Ferretus de Bonifacio VIII. et Guidone antea Montis Feretri comite pervulgata jam sunt; eadem enim paucis ante Ferretum annis literis consignarat Dantes Aligherius . . . . *Sed probrosi hujus facinoris narrationi fidem adjungere nemo probus velit* . . . . Ferretus hæc a satyrico poeta ambabus manibus excepit, quippe et is ad maledicendum pronus. A quo autem fonte hauserit hic auctor universam ejusdem pontificis historiam, *contumeliis ubique ac poene maledictis contextam* conjicere poteris, Lector,"—(might he not be speaking in anticipation of a more modern work ?)—"ab illis verbis quæ aliquando intermiscet, *dijudicant, ferunt ;* ea siquidem procul dubio indicant *iniquos vulgi rumores corrupti a famosis,* ut aiunt, *libellis* Columnensium Urbe depulsorum. Ceterum illustres ipsius virtutes, et præclare gesta enarrant coævi scriptores apud Rainaldum quem vide." Yet this author, so characterised by Muratori, is the one whom Sismondi implicitly follows, without even intimating to his readers that there exists any other account! But did Guido of Montefeltro, come to the siege, or give the perfidious advice attributed to him by Dante? We see many very strong reasons for doubting,—indeed for totally denying it. Guido, of Montefeltro, whose posterity long ruled in Italy with honour, as Dukes of Urbino, was renowned as a general during his life, and in the early part of his career, was a powerful enemy of the Church. In 1286, he was reconciled to the Holy See, and continued faithful to it ; till at length, weary of the world and its vanities, he applied for permission to exchange his helmet for the cowl, and his belt for the cord of the humble St. Francis.

"Father Wadding has given us the letter addressed by Boniface to the Franciscan provincial of La Marca, in which he gives his consent to the pious desire, which he considers manifestly coming from God. The instrument is dated Anagni, July 23rd, 1296. In the month of November following, he took the habit at Ancona. This remarkable change of life could not but powerfully strike those who witnessed it; and accordingly we find it entered into almost every contemporary chronicle. But suppose that, after a time, the friar had again been transformed into a soldier, had he once more returned to the camp, and superintended the siege of Palestrina, is it not as probable that so strange an event would have been equally noticed? And yet no one alludes to it. Wadding justly observes, that the simple statement, by grave and competent witnesses, that he persevered to his death in saintly humility, and unceasing prayer, is surely to be preferred to the fictions of poets. No one, we imagine, will be inclined to doubt the truth of this assertion, which refers to the statement of Marianus, and James of Perugia, a contemporary writer. We will content ourselves with giving a few extracts more from such authors to strengthen his argument.

"The Annals of Cesena thus speak of Guido:—'Millmo, CCLXXXXVI die xvii Novembris, Guido Comes Montis Ferretri, Dux bellorum, Fratrum minorum est religionem ingressus. Currente, MCCXCVIII die Dedicationis B. Michaelis in Civitate Anconæ est viam universæ carnis ingressus, et ibi sepultus.'

"Ricobaldus of Ferrara, simply writes:—'Guido Comes de Monteferetro quondam bellorum dux strenuus abdicato sæculo Ordinem Minorem ingreditur, in quo moritur.' And in another work, he writes of him as then living:—'Hoc tempore Guido Comes de Monteferetro, Dux bellorum strenuus, depositis honoribus sæculi, Minorem Ordinem ingressus est, ubi hodie militat in castris B. Francisci.'

"The Bolognese Chronicles thus speak of him:—'1296. Il Conto Guido di Montefeltro, nobile e strenuo in fatti d'arme.... abandonato il mondo, entro nell' Ordine dei Frati Minori, dove finì sua vita.'

"This silence of all chronicles on so extraordinary an event, is certainly a powerful argument against the assertions of sworn adversaries at a considerable distance from the scene. Several other considerations concur to make us still further disbelieve the latter. First, their disagreement about important circumstances. Ferretus, for instance, makes him actually come to the siege of Palestrina, and examine the fortifications, and pronounce them impregnable, and then, as Sismondi follows him, ask, before giving his perfidious counsel, for absolution, 'perpetrandi criminis.' On the other hand, Pipino tells us that he positively refused to come, on account of his age and religious vow, and therefore must have only sent to Boniface his base suggestion. Now surely this discrepancy between the only two historians who relate the story, upon so palpable and important a fact, as whether Guido was or was not at the siege, and acted the part of a general, is fatal to the whole narrative. Secondly, the total absence of any document on the subject in Boniface's Regesta. By this name is understood the original transcript of all documents issued in a Pope's reign, the collection of which compilations forms the bulk of the Papal Archives. Those of Boniface consist of immense volumes, (one, we believe, to each year), in which are beautifully written on vellum every letter, rescript, or decree issued day by day, divided into two classes, the second of which is formed of what are called the Curial Letters. When we read the history of Boniface's active life, and find that, notwithstanding his constant changes of residence, every document is entered in a fair hand, without an erasure, or sign of hurry, we are led to form an advantageous idea of the order and regularity of his civil and ecclesiastical administration. But then the total absence of any document relating to a supposed transaction of his reign, must be equivalent to a contradiction of its having taken place.

"To come to our present case: we have found in the second volume of his Regesta, Ep. 63, a letter by which Conrad of Montefeltro, *citatar ad Curiam*, is summoned to Rome on business; and another in the Curial Epistles (No. 2), in which Guido himself is summoned to come to Rome by a certain day, that the Pope might consult with him on important affairs relative to the pacification of Italy. Again we have seen that the document exists, (and it is in the Regesta) naming Landulf Colonna, captain in the expedition, and a similar one is there relative to Matthew Colonna, who took a like part against his family. Now is it credible that not a trace should exist, in this collection, or in any other part of the Papal Archives, of any second summons to Guido, either directly or through his religious superiors, to come to the camp, nor any appointment of him to hold command or act as counsellor in the war? Yet it is even so. Not content with our own opportunities of research, we ventured to apply to the obliging and experienced prefect of the Papal Archives, to have a more minute examination made. The result the learned prelate has not only kindly communicated to us in person, but given to the world in an essay just published. We extract the following, sufficient for our purpose:—'What shall I say of the advice supposed to have been given by Guido, of Montefeltro, to Boniface, on the siege of Palestrina, which he refused to undertake, because, to succeed, it was necessary to commit a sin, from which, however, Boniface shewed himself most ready to absolve him? This account is Dante's, a notorious Ghibelline. Requested several times by the same person to search in th Vatican Archives, if any document could be there found, bear ng upon the circumstance; I can pledge upon my honour that I have not found any such;—a certain proof that none exists. The letter, at least, by which Boniface summoned Guido to come, ought to have come under my eye; but not even of this is there any trace in the Vatican Regesta.' This absence of any document in such a place is, we think, conclusive evidence against the supposed occurrence. Lastly, we consider the whole a fable, because we are satisfied that no such perfidious course as the narrative supposes, was pursued.

"6. For, to come to the last part of Sismondi's account of the Colonna contest, we deny that Boniface offered such terms as are described, or that the city was delivered to him under conditions which he violated, or that the Colonnas warned that their lives were in danger, refused to come to him, but fled. Before we proceed to the confutation of this account, we must go a little back. After the publication of the Colonna manifesto, the heads of the family remained entrenched in Palestrina; and, on the fourth of September, it was understood that hostilities would commence. Upon this, the municipal authorities of Rome held solemn Parliament in the Capitol, and sent a deputation to Palestrina, to induce the Colonnesi to humble themselves before the Pope, and make full submission. They promised every thing that was required, and the deputies then proceeded to Boniface, at Orvieto, and interceded for them. He yielded, and promised to admit them to mercy, on condition of their yielding up their castles, and persons. Instead of this, they openly received into their walls, Francesco Crescenzi, and Nicola Pazzi, his avowed enemies; and, in addition, some emissaries of the King of Arragon with whom he was at war. Then, and not till then, first on the 18th of November, and again on the 14th of December, he passed his final measures for war. This treaty or covenant cannot, of course, be the one of which Sismondi speaks; but we have thought it right to relate its history, to shew the character of those with whom Boniface had to deal, and the nature of the contest.

"The city of Palestrina was vigorously besieged, and as vigorously defended; the question is, was it at length delivered up, under promises which were not kept? We answer, certainly not; and here our proofs are, to our minds, conclusive. In 1311, Clement V., at Avignon, consented to a process being instituted against the memory of Boniface, by Philip of France, Nogaret, the Colonnas, and all his other enemies. The preliminaries indicated anything but a wish to favour his predecessor.

In the bull upon the subject, he is full of commendation of the King, and fully acquits him of any improper motives, while he ordered all the letters and decrees against France to be expunged from the Regesta. This was done, as appears from their volumes: though fortunately the friends of Boniface had copies of many preserved. Full liberty was likewise granted to any one to bring forward accusations against him. The Colonnas charged him with the very crime imputed to him by Sismondi, of having received surrender of their city and castles under express compact, 'per bullas et solemnes personas' (Roman ambassadors or deputies), that he should only plant his banner upon the walls, leaving their custody in the hands of the family We have two answers to this charge: one a compendious one, which we would gladly give at length; the other more detailed, put in by Cardinal Francesco Gaetani, existing in a parchment in the Vatican Archives. We will give you the substance of the replies, corroborating them with collateral evidence.

"First, then, it is clear that no such compact was made with the Colonnas, because they cast themselves at the Pope's feet and sued for mercy. Sismondi tells us that, admonished of the danger of their lives if they came before the Pope, after they had agreed to surrender the town, they fled, and did not venture near him. Cardinal Cajetan states, that the Colonnas coming from Palestrina to Rieti, went dressed in black, with cords round their necks, from the gates to the Pope's presence, and prostrated themselves at his feet, one of them exclaiming: 'Peccavi pater in cœlum et coram te, jam non sum dignus vocari filius tuus;' and the other adding, 'Afflixisti nos propter scelera nostra.' Now for this account, which is in flat contradiction to the one preferred by our historian, the cardinal appeals to the cardinals and prelates there present, and to the Prince of Taranto, who was on the spot and willing to bear witness. This narrative is confirmed by abundant testimony: Pipino gives it in his own way. He tells us that they came to him as above described, and that the Pope, 'spretis lacrymosis eorum confessionibus atque precibus, velit aspis surda, non est misertus eorum.' But the latter statement is contradicted by others, as well as Cardinal Francis. A chronicle of Orvieto says that they were received, 'A Romana curia cum letitia multa.' Villani, who asserts the town to have been treacherously taken possession of and destroyed, tells us, that, "the Colonnesi, clerks and lay, came to Rieti, and threw themselves at the Pope's feet *for mercy, who pardoned them, and absolved them from their excommunication.*' Paolino de Piero, no friend of Boniface's, says, that they came *for mercy,* 'whom the Pope graciously, and in a kind manner (*gracios a mente e di buôn aria*) pardoned, and absolved from excommunication: *then Palestrina was destroyed according to compact.*'

"Secondly; when they came to Rieti, the city was already in the Pope's hands, his general having possession of it. Is it likely that he would, after this, have contented himself with only having his standard there, or enter into terms with his subdued rebels?

"Thirdly; the Cardinal denies that any such bulls, as those asserted, existed or could be produced, as none were

"Fourthly; he contradicts the assertion that any ambassadors or mediators were present, but only such intercessors as the Colonnas had themselves brought.

"Fifthly, he asserts, that there was no truth in the assertion that the Pope, after forgiving them, and imposing a penance on Stephen Colonna, sent knights after him to slay him.

"Such is the evidence in favour of Boniface, of which it is useless again to complain, that not the slightest notice is taken, or hint given, by the historian of the Italian Republics. But the cause of Boniface, from whose "process," as it is called in the Vatican Archives, these documents are extracted, was solemnly examined and judged by the General Council of Vienne, convoked and held in 1312, in great measure for that purpose. The decision was entirely in his favour; his memory was discharged from the slightest imputations in the face of every hostile influence, ecclesiastical and civil. He was charged with heresy, witchcraft, idolatry, and disbelief. The proof of his idolatry was, that he had his portrait engraven on some of his gifts to churches; therefore he wished it to be worshipped. Of his disbelief in the real presence, that he turned his back on an altar whilst mass was celebrating. The answer was, the abundance of tears with which he celebrated the divine mysteries, and his splendid presents to many altars!

"We must now hasten to his closing scene, a subject, no less than his opening one, of gross misrepresentation. On one point indeed, all do him justice, in his noble bearing and intrepidity, when taken by his enemies. William of Nogaret, with a French force, and Sciarra Colonna, who, with his family, had long forgotten the pardon of Rieti, with a band of retainers, made their way through treachery into Anagni, the city so cherished and favoured by Boniface. They ran through the streets shouting "Long live the King of France, and death to Boniface!" The people, panic-struck, offered no resistance, and the two bands having forced their way into the palace, entered at different moments and by different ways the papal presence chamber. In the meantime Boniface had arrayed himself in full pontifical vestments; and seated on his throne (or, as Sismondi writes, kneeling before the altar) with a crucifix in his hands, over which he hung, the venerable old man calmly awaited the approach of his enemies. The impetuous Sciarra, at the head of his band, with his drawn sword outstretched for vengeance, rushed into the room, but stood on the threshold, overawed and irresolute before his lord, William of Nogaret followed, with his party, and less abashed, insultingly threatened to carry him off to Lyons, to be deposed by a General Council. Boniface replied with a calm dignity, which abashed and humbled the daring Frenchman: "Here is my head, here is my neck; I will patiently bear that I, a Catholic, and lawful pontiff and vicar of Christ, be condemned and deposed by the Patareni. I desire to die for Christ's faith and his Church." This scene, which we only wonder has never been chosen as the subject of the artist's pencil, exhibits almost beyond any other in history, the triumph of moral over brute force, the power of mind arrayed in true dignity of outward bearing over passion and justice. Even Dante relented at its contemplation, and indignantly sang of his enemy—

"Veggio in Alagna entrar lo fiordaliso
E nel Vicario suo Cristo esser catto.
Veggiolo un altra volta esser deriso;
Veggio rinnovellai l'aceto e 'l fele
E tra vivi ladroni essere anciso."

"After three days' captivity, the people, aroused from their lethargy, liberated him; and in a few days he was conducted to Rome, where on the thirtieth day he died. That his death may have been accelerated by the shock and sufferings of his captivity is not wonderful, considering that he was in his eighty-seventh year, and that his high and sensitive mind would be powerfully affected by the ingratitude of his subjects, and the insults inflicted on him. But such a view would have aroused only our commiseration; and it was deemed expedient that the sympathies excited by the scene of his capture, should be effaced by a spectacle of another character. Sismondi, therefore, again takes Ferretus as his guide, and tells us that Boniface, imprisoned in his apartments by the Cardinals, fell into a violent passion, turned out his faithful servant, John Campano, bolted the door, and, after gnawing his staff, dashed his head against the wall, so as to embrue his grey hairs with blood, and then strangled himself with the bed-clothes.

"We suppose Sismondi was ashamed to follow Ferretus to the extreme, and therefore omitted that he had gnawed his entire stick, a good long one, to bits ('baculum satis procerum dentibus conterit,' and again, 'baculo *minutatim* trito'), that he invoked Beelzebub, though nobody was in the room to hear him, and that he was possessed by the devil. These things would have rather been questioned in France of 1809; they are therefore prudently omitted, and just as much taken of the narrative as makes a good romance. For romance it is from beginning to end. At the foot of the page which M. Sismondi was quoting, he had Muratori's point-blank declaration that the whole story is an *unworthy lie* ('indignum mendacium'), and reference is made to where a full confutation was to be found. But to have made Boniface die in his bed, with the sacraments of the Church, and like a good Christian, would have been very tame indeed, and spoilt all the point of the melodrama which M. Sismondi had made of his history. Yet I fear we must be content with this less tragical but more consoling view of Boniface's end. In his process it was proved that, lying on his bed through illness, "he, according to the usage of the Roman Pontiffs, recited and made profession of all the articles of faith in the presence of eight cardinals, concerning which the letters are extant of our brother, Cardinal Gentili;" and again, he is said, "to have professed in the presence of many cardinals, and other honourable persons, that he had ever held the Catholic faith, and wished to die in it." Again, Cardinal Stephanesius, an eye-witness, gives us the same account, and assures us that his death was most placid:—

'Christo dum redditur almus
Spiritus, et divi nescit jam judicis iram,
Sed mitem placidamque patris, ceu credere fas est.'

"Surely, for the very honour of humanity, these authentic accounts ought to have been alluded to. But what are we to say to his dashing his head against the wall, and his haggard and frightful looks when dead, mentioned by Ferretus, who, moreover, adds, that his corpse was buried in the earth, with a marble placed over it? or of his hands and fingers gnawed, as some write? It pleased Divine Providence to give a striking confutation of these calumnies in 1605, exactly a hundred years after his death. The chapel in the Vatican, which he had built for his tomb, had to be taken down, and his body removed. The tomb (a sarcophagus, not the earth) being opened, his body was found almost completely incorrupt, with a most placid expression; so perfect, that the smallest veins could be traced. It was carefully examined by medical men, and a minute *procès verbal* was drawn up by a notary of its condition, and of the gorgeous pontifical robes in which it was attired. This may be seen at full length in Rubæus. Now, it is certain that nature does not cicatrise wounds after death; and yet not a trace could be found of any on the head; the skin was entire: and as to the gnawed hands, they were so beautiful, 'as to fill with admiration all who saw them.'

"We may now draw to a close. We trust what we have written may suffice to put readers on their guard against the bold assertions of historians on subjects like these. We must not, however, omit one or two remarks. Although the character of Boniface was certainly stern and inflexible, there is not a sign of its having been cruel or revengeful. Through the whole of his history, not an instance can be found of his having punished a single enemy with death. When he sent John of Palestrina to Cardinal Colonna, he might as easily have sent a body of his guards, and brought him by force into his presence. When the Colonnas all came before him at Rieti, he had them completely at his mercy; yet he hurt them not. How, then, can Sismondi's insinuations stand, that he intended to put them to death? Again, he forgave Guido of Montefeltro his many offences, as he did Ruggieri dell' Oria, another capital enemy of the Church. When he was returning to Rome, after his liberation, in a triumph never before witnessed, Cardinal Stephanesius tells us that his principal enemy was seized by the people (Muratori supposes it to have been either Sciarra Colonna, or Nogaret), and brought before him, that he might deal with him; he freely pardoned him, and let him go. So, likewise, when Fra Jacopone fell into his hands, he dealt leniently with him, and confined him, when others would have treated the offence as capital. These examples of forgiveness and gentleness, to which we might add others, ought surely to have due weight in estimating the Pope'a character.

"Moreover, we do not find, in any writer, however hostile to him, the slightest insinuation against his moral conduct or character, and this is not a little with regard to one who has been more bitterly assailed than almost any other Pontiff.* The charge of avarice, which has been often repeated, may well be met by the liberality displayed in his ecclesiastical endowments and presents, especially in favour of St. Peter's church. His justice seems universally to have been acknowledged, Hallam attests the equity of his award between England and France; he reconciled the republics of Genoa and Venice; and all his negociations between powers were to bring about peace. Even his most energetic transactions had this in view Nearer home, Florence, as Dino Compagni assures us, called him in to decide in its own differences, about compensation to Giano della Bella; and the Bolognese, as we learn from Matthew de Griffonibus, sent three ambassadors to him, and he was chosen arbitrator between them, Ferrara and Modena. Velletri named him its

* Those who attach any importance to the slanderous Bill of Impeachment brought before the Council of Vienne, if possible to cast infamy on the grave of the Pontiff, or to the poetic effusions of Fra Jacopone da Todi, will take exception to the wording of this position.

Podesta, or chief governor; Pisa voluntarily appointed him ruler of the state, with an annual tribute; and when he sent a governor there, it was with orders to swear to observe the laws of the place, and to spend all his income upon it. In fine, Florence, Orvieto and Bologna erected statues to him at a great expense, in token of their obligations and admiration. Of his literary acquirements we need not speak; no one has disputed them; and the Sixth Book of Decretals will attest them so long as Christ's undying Church shall last."

No. II.—Vol. III. p. 500.

We are indebted to the great courtesy of one of the Benedictine Fathers of Monte Casino—Dom. Bernardo—for the subjoined documents, neither of which has been ever before published. The first is a memoir by some personage who played a high part in the transactions connected with the resumption of Ferrara, when that branch of the D'Este family which had held it as feudatories of the Apostolic See became extinct, on the death of Alfonzo II. October 17, A.D. 1597. It enables us to fill up some deficiencies, and to correct some of the misstatements, in Ranke's narrative of the same event. The second is the report of Ridolfo Bonfiolo, on the exact boundaries of the famous province of Romagna, made by order of Cardinal Aldobrandino, who was charged by Clement VIII. with the resumption of the lapsed fief of the D'Este, and the regulation of the Adriatic provinces at large.

EX ARCH. CASS. No. 602.*

Relazione dell' Impresa della Città, e stato di Ferrara fatta dal Card^le^. Pietro Aldobrandino.

Non è mia professione di scrivere historie, ne io pretendo per questa via di acquistare lode amando meglio di oprare fatti degni di esser scritti, che di scrivere gli altrui, come più sicura e . . . . strada a ciascuno, e più nobile da far chiaro il suo nome; ma le forze mie non mi concedono per l'una o per l'altra di queste strade di caminare; onde a tal fine io non mi muovo a scrivere la presente storia, mo ho deliberato con semplice stile di narrare la recuperazione, che ha fatta la Chiesa Romana della Città e stato di Ferrara l'anno del Sig^e^. 1598. . . . . Ne credo che si lascierà

* History is silent with regard to the author's name—and this seems to be his own desire:—"Non curandomi io," thus he writes in his preface, "di fare palese il mio nome."

di darmi fede non solamente da coloro chi sapranno chi io mi sia, poiche supranno insieme conoscendomi, che io mi son ritrovato in quell' impiesa con carica ed afficio, che mi faceva noti i più intimi consigli . . . . E perciò che la memoria di questi fatto è ancora fresca, scrivendo io il secondo anno dopo la morte di Clemente VIII. ; il che anche mi rende più libero d'ogni interesse, e men sospetto . . . .

Ferrara dunque Citta Nobile di Lombardia e tra le principali d' Italia, essendo posta sopra il Pò appresso l' antica Padusa verso i confini della Romagna, non ha dubio che come compresa nell' Esarcato di Ravenna è stata gia molti secoli sono del Dominio temporale della Chiesa Romana, ma havendola i Pontifici, forse più dalle calamità de' tempi costretti che di loro voluntà, conceduta insieme con un ampio stato, primo in Vicariato, e poi in feudo, ai Prencipi di Casa d'Este, questi l'avevano con diverse investiture e patti posseduta, finche per successione alle mani di Alfonso Secondo da Este, che fu quinto Duca, pervenne. Egli congiontosi tre volte in matrimonio senza potere havene figlioli e vedendosi estinguersi in se medessimo la linea di quelli di Casa sua che per l' investitura ottenute erano dalla Sede Apostolica alla successione di quello stato chiamati, aveva più volte mostrato desiderio che i Pontofici gli concedessero nuova investitura per altri della stessa famiglia da nominarsi da lui ; ma opponevasi al suo desiderio, che avendo veduto Pio V. i Papi, o per troppa voglia di fare i parenti grandi o per acquistare la volontà de principi, a lasciatisi senza porvi rimedio costringere dalla necessità, essere stati facili ad infeudare i beni Ecclesiastici, di maniera che in poco tempo correva pericolo la Sede Apostolica cosi seguitandosi di rimanere senza dominio temporali, aveva fatto una legge o Costituzione che chiamano Bolla, per la quale giurando esso, aveva fatto giurare e far voto ai Cardinali, che ascendendo al Pontificato non concederebbore più luogo alcuno della Chiesa Romana in feudo . . . . ne darebbero voto, o consentirebbono che ciò da alti sommi Pontifici si facesse. . . . .

Essendo pero pervenuto al Pontificato Nicolo Cardinale Sfondrato chiamato poi Greg. XIII. col quale il Duca aveva qual che parentela, si risolse a tentare . . . . questo negozio. Et andato a Roma supplico il Papa . . . .—[But in vain: the Cardinals in council of state, having declared the petition contrary to the Constitution of Pius V. and a violation of their oaths.]

Il Papa (Clementi VIII.) si era lasciato intendere . . . . di non volere che si fosse trattato d' investitura non volendola in nessuna maniera concedere ed essendosi anche mostrato desideratissimo di accressere per quanto convenisse il Dominio Ecclesiastico, e di ricuperare alla Chiesa le cose alienate da altri, aveva comprato dai Calonmesi Nettuno, e dalla famiglia di Avolas il Monte S. Giovanni . . . . non avendo mai voluto dare orcchie a coloro che l' essortavano *a darli in feudo ai ripoti* . . . . Aveva pare ricuperato dai Sfondrati Montemariano nella Marca e riunitolo al medessimo Dominio—Morì il Duca il di 27. di Ottobre (1597) . . . l' anno 64. dell' eta sua . . . . Ma morendo dichiarò sul suo testamento herede universale e successore in tutti i suoi beni e feudi . . . . D. Cesare da Este figliuolo di D. Alfonso che nacque di figlio naturale di Alfonso primo Duca di Ferrara ed avo di Alfonso secondo; il qual D. Cesare non hà dubbio, che oltre non esser egli ed il suo ramo compreso espressamente nell' inuestiture di Ferrara, per discendare da linea infetta e non legittima, veniva escluso dalla successione di ogni feudo della Chiesa Romana . . . .

Fù preso per espedienti . . . di publicare D. Cesare subito e per erede e per Duca di Ferrara, e cosi fu fatto . . . . Spedì (D. Cesare) a tutti i principi di Italia, Spagna, Francia, e Germania, dandoli conto come nuovo principe, che essendo morto il Duca Alfonso, egli, e per ragione di sangue e per valontà del medessimo, era restato suo erede e successore . . . e Duca di Ferrara.

Ma il Papa vedendo il parere del Collegio unito e conforme alla sua opinione . . . dichiarando deuoluta Ferrara e lo stato alla sede Apostolica con molta devozione e lagrime lo dedico alla Madonna SS[a]. ed ai gloriosi Apostoli S. Pietro e S. Paulo. . . . .

Che egli procederrebbe contro D. Cesare come usurpatore delli beni Ecclesiastici con le monizioni e censure, e poi con le armi. . . . .

Che per questo effetto si potessero levare e spendere i denari lasciati in Castel S. Angelo da Papa Sisto V. . . . .*

Nell' istesso tempo fu comminciata la causa giuridicamente contro D. Cesare. . . . .

Risoluto e dichirato per capo dell' essercito il Cardin[le]. Aldobrandino . . . . venne a Perrugia il giorno dei' 4. di Novembre. . . . . Sene parti il 19. per andare in Ancona. . . . Dichiarò Pietro Caetano, Duca di Sermoneta, che essercitasse l' officio di Maestro di Campo, Mauro Colonna Duca di Zagarola quello di Generale dell' infanteria, Pirro Malvezzi attendesse alla cura del Generalato delle lancèe ed il Marchese della Corgnia a quello dell' archibusieri a cavallo. . . . .

Cominciarono intanto a sapersi . . . per vie di nunzi mandati . . . . gli animi de' prencipi verso questa impresa. . . . . Cominciando dal Gran Duca . . . non ha dubbio che egli inclinava a D. Cesare e l'aiutava dove poteva. . . . .

* In this congregation or consistory we find three of the cardinals opposed to the measure—namely, Lancelotto, Sfondrato, and Tarugi. "Aggiungendo che il Papa come Principe Spirituale doveva fugire l'occasione della guerra." The Pope knew—as the event proved—that it would be settled without any actual appeal to arms. Moreover, not to suffer the Patrimony to be alienated was his paramount duty.

Il Duca di Urbino essagerà ì pericoli della guerra, e del conturbare la pace d'Italia. . . . . .

Mantova . . . si mantenne affatto neutrale.

Parma disse sempre di voler servire il Papa come feudatorio. . .

Più generosomente di tutti adoprò il Duca di Savoia . . . il quali s'offerse . . . di venire a servire il Papa e la Sede Apostolica. . . . . .

I Venetiani tennero un pezzo . . . la parte di D. Cesare. . . . .

Il Rè di Francia . . . . fece anche esso una bell' offerta esposta al Pontifice dal Duca di Luxembourg suo ambasciatore.*

Della persona del Rè di Spagna . . . prima fù concluso il negozio che sene avesse risposta. . . . . .

Il Vice Rè di Napoli e Governatore di Milano . . . . nocquero non poco la Chiesa. . . . . .

L'Arciduca Ferdinando di Gratz . . aiutò il Papa. . . . . .

Ma non fece così l'Imperatore. . . . Mostrandosi non solo favorevole a D. Cesare, ma scrivendo al Papa una lettera poco decente. . . . . .

Degli altri Prencipi e' inutile il trattarne . . . . .

Fù in questo mezzo publicata in Ferrara la scommunica contro D. Cesare con interdetto di tutto lo stato, che possedeva, con l'assoluzione dei popoli dal guiramento . . .

After many days negociation the following articles of peace were signed by the Cardinals Aldobr°, Bandini, and Mattencci on the part of the Pope ; by the Duchess of Urbino, Gualengo and Leandro, in the name of D. Cesare :—

Che rilassando D. Cesare, come rilasserebbe in effetto e prometteva di fare, Ferrara con tutte le sue pertinenze . . . . sarebbe assoluto dalla scommunica, e censure, etc. . . .

Che si permatteva a D. Cesare di ritenere tutti i beni allodiali . . . . ed insieme tutti i mobili . . .

Rimanessero a D. Cesare . . . il juspatronato della prepositura di Pomposa, e quello della Pieve di Bondeno . . . .

Che . . . . D. Cesare ritinesse tutte le fabriche dentro Ferrara . . .

Che la Camera desse ogni anno a lui . . . dieci mila sacca di sale dalle saline di Cervia . . .

* Articolo d'una lettera del Rè di Francia al Duca di Lucembourgh delli 31 di Novemre. 1597. If I mistake not, this letter was published by Salvandez in his magnificent and useful collection of documents for French history.

—" Io laudo grandemente la bella e generosa risoluzione che Nro. Sto. Pre'. ha presa di fare tutto il suo possibile per ricuperare alla S. Sede La Ducea di Ferrara che è sua, et voglio che voi confortiate S. Santità in essa, et continuate a fargli proferta, et alli signori suoi nipoti miei cugini, di tutto quanto dipende da me. . . .

" Io intendo dire già da molte bande, che il Rè di Spagna, et altri principi non desiderano, che la Sede Aposta. s'accresca di questo stato, come quelli che preferiscono il loro intercesse alla ragione et alla giustizia.

Che D. Cesare ritenesse . . . . tutti i gradi, luoghi, sessimi, prerogative, e preeminenze, per grazia speciale di S. S. che avevano i Principi d'Este . . .

Cosi ebbe fine il negozio di Ferrara, e la Chiesa Romana non solo ricuperò uno stato . . . ma con esso acquisto . . . . *una fortezza della qualità di Ferrara*, che cuopre tutto il resto dello stato . . . Accrebbe il suo dominio sino al Veronese, e si può dire, sino alle porte d'Italia, e le sue entrate quasi di ducento mila scudi, l'anno, e trecento mila anime di vassallaggio.

Perche V. S. Illma. e Rma. mi disse che vorria una nota delli confini della Romagna ho fatto un poco di nota che mando . . .

Al Sig^{e}. Card^{e}. Aldobranino. RIDOLFO BONFIOLO.

Romagna.

Descrizione delli confini, e circuito di Romagna, comminciando dalla Torre di Primaro posta nel mare Adriatico e fatta da Greg^{o}. XIII. La detta Torre dunque di Primaro è posta nel mare Adriatico nell' aspetto di tramontano ; seguitando la spiaggia di mare verso Greco Levante, si trova a 12. miglia, Ravenna, dopo altrè 15. Cervia, poi cinque miglia, Ceseratico, poi altri cinque, Belarese, poi altri 8. miglia Rimini, et altri 15. la Catholica, la quale confina con Pesaro, stato del Sig^{e}. Duca d'Urbino.

Voltandosi poi per Sirocco, si sale alla Montagna e si arriva a S. Gio. di Marignan . . . . lasciando certi castelletti si va per la linea di mezzo giorno a Monte Fiore et Mondiano, di poi à Monte Acutolo confinando col territorio di S. Marino . . . et con il stato di Montefeltro, dove è la fortezza di S. Leo lontana non più di tre miglia da Tornano—feudo del Sig^{o} Malatesta, che fu al tempo di Greg^{o}. XIII. applicato alla Camera ; e continuandosi il prospetto di mezzo giorno, si va per i confini del Conte da Bagno feudatario della Chiesa, comminciandosi anco per il stato delli Sig^{i}. Malatesta pur feudatarii, et particularmente per il stato di Abaldola dell' Ill^{o}. e Ecc^{o}. Sig. Gio. Fran^{o}. Aldobrandino verso Bertinoro ; e poi si giuge nei confini della Romagna tenuta dal Gran Duca di Toscana . . . alla città del Sale lontana non piu di tre miglia da Forlì, e continerando il medessimo confine di Fiorenza—pigliando verso Garbino—si giunge a Modiana eguali á Brisighella, il qual confine intra nello stato di Fiorenza come una lingua per lungezza di 11. miglia e giunge a Moradi con un traverso di miglia 12, il quale continuando verso Imola e Fossignano, e Fapano, luoghi e feudi del Sign^{e}. Duca Altemps, confina poco da Forenzuola. Et de indi caminando à pigliare il Dorso et il Declivio del Monte verso la linea di ponente si trova il confine di Bologna col Castello di Casale . . . . e del Castello de Gati, loco delli Pepoli e di Trozza—feudo di Campeggi—e confina col Castello Bolognese, loco della città di Bologna, quale entra nella Romagna con confini stravaganti. Et continuando la linea di Ponente confina con Castel Guelfo, feudo e Marchesato, del Sige. Pirro Malvezzi, et qui comnincia Lugo, Catignola, luoghi del Ducato di Ferrara, trovandosi la Massa, Bagnacavallo, e poi Fusignano del Calcagnini, finche si arriva e torna sul' Pò, per 6. miglia per la linea di Maestro ; e di li si giunge a S. Alberto, loco di Ravenna, quale e Contano dalla Torre di Primaro . . . . 12 miglia. Questi luoghi, cioè Massa, Bagnacavallo, Lugo Sant' Agata, Bachioni . . . sono sotto castel Guelfo, feudo del Sig. Perro Malvezzi . . . A Lugo, Massa, Codigo . . . . vi confina Imola, Castel Guelfo, Castel Bolognese, Faenza, ed il Contado di Bologna. Li luoghi che ha il Signe. Duca nella Romagna di qua dal Pò, sono Motta, Massa, Castello Zagognara, Lugo . . . Questi sono in confina d'Imola, Castel Guelfo . . . . Faenza, Dorsa, e confini di Bologna.

END OF VOL. I.

G. NORMAN, PRINTER, MAIDEN LANE, COVENT GARDEN.

Printed in Great Britain
by Amazon

62573477R10322